D0871748

The Founding Fathers, Education, and "The Great Contest"

HISTORICAL STUDIES IN EDUCATION

Edited by William J. Reese and John L. Rury

William J. Reese, Carl F. Kaestle WARF Professor of Educational Policy Studies and History, the University of Wisconsin-Madison

John L. Rury, Professor of Education and (by courtesy) History, the University of Kansas

This series features new scholarship on the historical development of education, defined broadly, in the United States and elsewhere. Interdisciplinary in orientation and comprehensive in scope, it spans methodological boundaries and interpretive traditions. Imaginative and thoughtful history can contribute to the global conversation about educational change. Inspired history lends itself to continued hope for reform, and to realizing the potential for progress in all educational experiences.

Published by Palgrave Macmillan:

Democracy and Schooling in California: The Legacy of Helen Heffernan and Corinne Seeds
By Kathleen Weiler

The Global University: Past, Present, and Future Perspectives
Edited by Adam R. Nelson and Ian P. Wei

Catholic Teaching Brothers: Their Life in the English-Speaking World, 1891–1965
By Tom O'Donoghue

Science Education and Citizenship: Fairs, Clubs, and Talent Searches for American Youth, 1918–1958
By Sevan G. Terzian

The Founding Fathers, Education, and "The Great Contest": The American Philosophical Society Prize of 1797
Edited by Benjamin Justice

The Founding Fathers, Education, and "The Great Contest"

The American Philosophical Society Prize of 1797

Edited by
Benjamin Justice

WITHDRAWN
UTSA LIBRARIES

palgrave
macmillan

University of Texas
at San Antonio

THE FOUNDING FATHERS, EDUCATION, AND "THE GREAT CONTEST"
Copyright © Benjamin Justice, 2013.

All rights reserved.

First published in 2013 by
PALGRAVE MACMILLAN®
in the United States—a division of St. Martin's Press LLC,
175 Fifth Avenue, New York, NY 10010.

Where this book is distributed in the UK, Europe and the rest of the world,
this is by Palgrave Macmillan, a division of Macmillan Publishers Limited,
registered in England, company number 785998, of Houndmills,
Basingstoke, Hampshire RG21 6XS.

Palgrave Macmillan is the global academic imprint of the above companies
and has companies and representatives throughout the world.

Palgrave® and Macmillan® are registered trademarks in the United States,
the United Kingdom, Europe and other countries.

ISBN: 978–1–137–27101–3

Library of Congress Cataloging-in-Publication Data

    The Founding Fathers, Education, and "The Great Contest" :
The American Philosophical Society prize of 1797 / edited by
Benjamin Justice.
        pages cm.—(Historical studies in education)
    Includes index.
    ISBN 978–1–137–27101–3 (hardback)
    1. Public schools—United States—History—18th century.
2. Education—Awards—United States—History—18th century. 3.
Contests—United States—History—18th century. 4. American
Philosophical Society—Awards—History—18th century.
I. Justice, Benjamin, 1971– editor of compilation.
LA215.F68 2013
370.97309033—dc23   2013004446

A catalogue record of the book is available from the British Library.

Design by Newgen Imaging Systems (P) Ltd., Chennai, India.

First edition: July 2013

10 9 8 7 6 5 4 3 2 1

Library
University of Texas
at San Antonio

CONTENTS

FIGURES AND TABLES

FIGURES

TABLES

FOREWORD

Carl F. Kaestle

When I began graduate work in the history of education in 1966, the interpretive battles and methodological discussions going on energized me. Some historians saw education as the whole process by which knowledge was transmitted across generations; other historians saw public education not as an engine of democracy but as a mainstay of class relations. It was a time of great debates and new developments.

But I was also fascinated by the narratives, facts, and stories that I was learning for the first time. I had always been interested in education, but I was new to the study of its history. What were the nine colonial colleges and their denominational affiliations? What effects did those affiliations have for their students? What did our founding leaders say about the role of education in a republic? What effects did they have? In the 1840s, who were the leading school reformers in Indiana, in Ohio, in New York? Did they all say the same things as Horace Mann of Massachusetts? One job of graduate students and young scholars is to ascertain whether the interesting questions about each story have been adequately researched and interpreted.

One episode that we all learned about was the contest sponsored by the American Philosophical Society (APS). Competitors were asked to propose a system of education for a republic, specifying its rationale, its organization, and its purposes. I still have my copy of Frederick Rudolph's *Essays on Education in the Early Republic*, which appeared just as I entered graduate school. It includes the two cowinners of the APS contest. Over the years I have quoted one of them, Samuel Harrison Smith, to illustrate republican education theory. Smith said, for example, that in a republic "it is not in the interest of such a society to perpetuate error, as it undoubtedly is the interest of many societies differently organized." And again, "Under a republic, duly constructed, man feels as strong a bias to improvement as under a despotism he feels an impulse to ignorance and depression."[1]

Yet I barely scratched the surface of these essays. When I later wrote about the early national period, I focused on existing educational practices, contrasting urban and rural settings. This had its merits but did not deal adequately with the contending philosophies and ideas about the political economy that influenced educational debates in the early national period.[2] The subsequent years did not bring a great deal of research and interpretation to this interesting episode. *Et voila*, now we have this gem of a book.

Why is it a "gem"? First, it arose from a research mentoring program at a professional meeting, a worthy enterprise. Six graduate students met with two experienced historians to develop an agenda and dig into the materials at the American Philosophical Society. Research training is of course ubiquitous in academia, so in that sense, this venture was hardly unique. Many of us recall large research projects that engaged graduate students in researching and writing of books on the history of education.[3] But the circumstances of this collaboration were interesting. It was begun at a meeting of the History of Education Society. I applaud this initiative, because I have long believed that our small subfield has been characterized by productive and supportive relationships across the generations of scholars, both through the History of Education Society and Division F of the American Educational Research Association. So what could be a better idea than to actually *do* some collaborative research when getting together at a meeting?

Second, the setting of that training session was Philadelphia, where the 1795 contest also took place. This volume recreates a vivid sense of the importance of Philadelphia, and the American Philosophical Society, in the heady days of the early republic, when that city was not only the national capital but also the largest city in the country, and the APS was the hub of intellectual life in the capital.

Third, some great sleuthing went on in this project. I don't want to give away secrets, but these researchers actually established—either certainly or with great probability—the identity of three of the seven authors. The two winners were identified at the time, and the other two remain unknown. Two of the chapters of this book describe the methodologies used to make these identifications. I got excited just reading about these discoveries.

Fourth, this volume is good intellectual history. The "founding fathers" are too often quoted on education as if there was wide consensus about the role of education in a republic, which turns them into a sort of Mt. Rushmore pantheon. The discussions in this book place the APS contest in the longer context of Enlightenment discussions of education, and they carefully address the issues of consensus and diversity of views. On the positive connection between education and republican government, editor Benjamin Justice remarks that three important ideological frameworks in the early republic—Enlightenment, Radical Whig, and Calvinist—agreed on the positive relationship of widespread education to the creation of virtue and stability among citizens. Almost missing in the new United States was the Tory view, influential in England, which stressed limits on popular education lest it breed discontent and instability. In the United States those who extended the Tory view to restrict poor white students were a wistful conservative minority.[4] Despite this vague general consensus about the value of education in a republic, the promoters of education in the early American republic differed on important details: on the education of women, on the role of religion, about how much opportunity would be offered for education at the higher levels, and about who would pay for mass and higher education.

Fifth, the editors have included the text of the essays, an added attraction of this book. The rather long essays by Smith and Knox, the winners, are abridged here because they are available elsewhere. But four of the other five survived in manuscript at the American Philosophical Society, and the fifth (which was returned to its author at his request) is represented by the review panel's assessment. These are presented in full, for the first time in print.

Sixth, this book focuses attention on the early national period (traditionally dated as 1780–1830), which has been understudied in the history of education. Too often people rush from the American Revolution to the "antebellum" period (1830–1860), but the decades from the signing of the Constitution on into the early decades of the nineteenth century have their own history—not only political, but also social and cultural—and it has not been contemplated enough in the history of education. Now a new generation of young professional historians, several of them represented here, are remedying that deficiency.

After the initial mentoring session at the 2009 meeting, as this project progressed, three of the six participating graduate students produced chapters for this book, and the two senior scholars associated with the mentoring session were joined by five other "seasoned" historians of education to produce the chapters you will read in this volume. Benjamin Justice has done an excellent job of previewing these chapters in his introduction, so I shall not detain you. Beyond the chapters on methodologies used to identify the authors, there is a substantial section with seven chapters on interpretative issues, such as education and gender, education and race, education and religion, two chapters on practical education for a republic, and a chapter on the allure and suspicion of study abroad in a nonrepublican Europe. Rich fare.

NOTES

1. Samuel Harrison Smith, *Remarks on Education*, in *Essays on Education in the Early Republic* (Cambridge, MA: Harvard University Press, 1965), 188–189.
2. Carl F. Kaestle, *Pillars of the Republic: Common Schools and American Society, 1780–1860* (New York: Hill & Wang, 1983), 3–12.
3. For example, David Tyack, Thomas James, and Aaron Benavot, *Law and the Shaping of Public Education, 1785–1954* (Madison: University of Wisconsin Press, 1987); David Tyack, Robert Lowe, and Elisabeth Hansot, *Public Schools in Hard Times: The Great Depression and Recent Years* (Cambridge, MA: Harvard University Press, 1984); Michael B. Katz, Michael J. Doucet, and Mark J. Stern, *The Social Organization of Early Industrial Capitalism* (Cambridge: Harvard University Press, 1982); and Kristen Nawrotzki, Anna Mills Smith, and Maris Vinovskis, "Social Science Research and Early Childhood Education: A Historical Analysis in Head Start, Kindergartens, and Day Care," in Hamilton Cravens (ed.), *The Social Sciences Go to Washington: The Politics of Knowledge in the Postmodern Age* (Piscataway: Rutgers University

Press, 2004), 155–180. I had a similar experience in Carl F. Kaestle, Helen Damon-Moore, Lawrence C. Stedman, Katherine Tinsley, and William Vance Trollinger, Jr., *Literacy in the United States: Readers and Reading since 1880* (New Haven, CT: Yale University Press, 1991), written with four graduate assistants.

4. See Carl F. Kaestle, "'The Scylla of Brutal Ignorance and the Charybdis of a Literary Education': Elite Attitudes toward Mass Education in Early Industrial England and the United States," in *Schooling and Society* ed. Lawrence Stone (Baltimore, MD: The Johns Hopkins Press, 1976), 177–191.

ACKNOWLEDGMENTS

This book was born over a glass of wine at a reception at the Annual Meeting of the History of Education Society in 2008, during a conversation I was having with Kim Tolley. We had only just begun speaking when, abruptly (and politely), she excused herself to "go find some graduate students to talk to."

It was nothing personal, she explained. She always made a point of introducing herself to students at the reception to make them feel welcome. I was bemused.

Later that evening, I attended a planning session for the 2009 meeting in Philadelphia, where we discussed possible collaborations with city entities. I suggested to society vice president Jon Zimmerman that we do something with the American Philosophical Society, where I had done research on the education essay contest of 1795. Quickly the two ideas came together for me: organizing a research mentoring session for graduate students where they actually did history at a history conference. I approached Kim and, with Jon's blessing, we put together a session at the APS archives, where a group of six promising graduate students worked with us to revisit the essay contest. Of those, three have written chapters for this volume. They are joined by seven seasoned historians who represent the range, creativity, and cutting edge of the study of education during the early American republic. And we are all grateful that Carl Kaestle graciously agreed to write the foreword.

Many other people helped make this book possible, including, but not limited to: each of the graduate students who participated in the original program, Christina Davis, Lisa Green, Michael Hevel, Campbell Scribner, Nia Soumakis, and Eric Strome; the administration and staff of the American Philosophical Society, especially Charles B. Greifenstein, Earle Spamer, and Roy Goodman; Tal Nadan of the New York Public Library Manuscripts and Archives Division; the staff of the College of Physicians of Philadelphia, The Pennsylvania Historical Society, Ant Howe and Nina Caddick of the Kingswood Unitarian Congregation (UK), Carley Turner, the sage Bob Hampel, series editors Bill Reese and John Rury; Burke Gerstenschlager and Sarah Nathan at Palgrave Macmillan, and Tracey Meares.

CHAPTER 1

Introduction

Benjamin Justice

Ready?

> [Write] an essay on a system of liberal education, and literary instruction, adapted to the genius of the government, and best calculated to promote the general welfare of the United States; comprehending, also, a plan for instituting and conducting public schools in this country on principles of the most extensive utility.

This was the question posed by the America's premier scholarly association, American Philosophical Society (APS), in 1795. In a list of seven contest questions on various subjects, the education question came first, and had the largest prize, including $100 (in 1795 dollars) and publication by the APS.[1] The winners were chosen two years later, in 1797.

In today's English, the question would mean:

> Design the best system of education for the United States, appropriate for the wealthy as well as the poor, including secondary and higher education as well as elementary schools, reaching people in remote areas as well as cities, promoting the common good and strengthening our republican form of government.

No easy task in any era.

But these were no ordinary times. The nation's political leaders were among its finest intellectuals. That group of men had just completed their political revolution, with the states ratifying their Constitution and Bill of Rights. Other revolutions in France and Saint-Domingue (Haiti) upended old regimes and appeared to forge fundamentally new relationships between people and government (inspiring both optimism and fear). Despite their considerable failures to end chattel slavery, honor the land rights of indigenous people, or abolish the subordination of women, the men we refer to as the founding fathers had nevertheless achieved a rare moment in history—applying ancient and modern theories of government to the creation of a new country.

The APS education prize contest captured the excitement and apprehension that the founding fathers felt about that creation. With no king and no state church, writers on both sides of the Atlantic argued that only through the virtue and intelligence of its citizens could the American republic survive; and in federal and state law, governments took measures to encourage the spread of useful knowledge and virtue. They ensured the delivery of mail, protected free speech, encouraged learned societies like the APS and voluntary ones like the Freemasons, formed or reformed colleges and academies, and created funds to subsidize local schooling efforts. In New England, state governments reaffirmed colonial laws that required towns to maintain free elementary schools or pay fines for noncompliance.

How to spread learning across the populace was indeed a problem, if one viewed education as being formal, functional knowledge of reading, writing, and arithmetic. The very aspects of American society that intellectuals celebrated about America's republican character made it difficult to educate the masses. America was diverse—culturally, regionally, and religiously. Settlement patterns varied by region, placing many families at significant distance from each other, and from seats of government. Deeply held cultural traditions varied as well, leaving people in different parts of the United States more or less inclined to value formal education. Moreover, distrust of government and hatred of taxes made government-based solutions to public policy challenging, where they were even possible. The rebellion of whiskey distillers that boiled in Western Pennsylvania from 1791 to 1794 reminded citizens and leaders alike that the authority of the new national government was not as well loved as the latter might hope.

There were other problems as well, more serious and intractable, that the florid language of the American Revolution simply ignored, or, in the case of slavery, actually reinforced. Nearly one-fifth of all the people in the United States were enslaved, forming a racial caste whose marking as a separate people followed them even into freedom. (The Constitution considered a slave to be three-fifths of a person when it came to representation in Congress.) Half of Americans were women, covered by patriarchal traditions and laws that made it challenging for them to claim an equal right to education unless they were the fortunate daughters or wives of the middle or upper classes.

Educating the mass of citizens, whether in the positive sense of enhancing the interest of liberty or in the negative sense of social control, or some of both, became a central preoccupation of intellectuals in the 1780s and 1790s. Interest ran across the political spectrum. Even before the war with Great Britain ended, Thomas Jefferson joined John Adams and other leaders in the effort to write grand educational provisions into state law.[2] Over the course of the 1780s, as America slouched toward a replacement for the Articles of Confederation, the question of education in the republic gained popularity in magazines and newspapers.[3] Among these were fully formed, almost utopian plans for systems of mass education through public school-ing. Benjamin Rush published essays recommending a statewide system of public education for Pennsylvania, from universal elementary school through college, for girls as well as boys; Noah Webster traveled across the country delivering lectures and selling his new American textbooks, before using his federalist newspaper, *American Minerva*, as a mouthpiece for educational reform; George Washington urged Congress to found a national university. Alongside a similar university proposal at the Constitutional Convention of 1787, James Madison proposed that the federal government be empowered to "encourage, by proper premiums and provisions, the advancement of use-ful knowledge and discoveries."[4]

Madison's educational proposals failed, but the APS picked up the slack, serving as the nation's leading intellectual institution and even, for a time, the informal library of Congress. Centered in the heart of America's largest and capital city, Philadelphia, the American Philosophical Society was uniquely situated to take a crack at the problem of education. Founded by Benjamin Franklin in 1743, the APS sought to encourage and disseminate useful sci-entific and philosophical information. It was the Age of Associations, when Enlightenment intellectuals across Europe and, to a lesser extent, America, formed clubs and academies to share ideas and discoveries. By the 1790s the APS had become a significant institution in the transatlantic intellectual world, maintaining correspondence with similar institutions all over Europe. For a time, APS facilities were home to portions of the University of Pennsylvania. The membership list boasted the names of leading men of the day, founding fathers and European Enlightenment thinkers from Franklin, Washington, Adams, Jefferson, Madison, and Rush to Linnaeus, Lafayette, Talleyrand, Priestley, Condorcet, and Crevecoeur. In their regular meetings, the Society read and discussed contemporary issues in science, government, economics, and philosophy. A core of seven appointed members from various fields met at least once a month, usually joined by others who dropped in.[5]

The APS began awarding its first prize, the Magellanic Premium for dis-coveries "relating to navigation, astronomy, or natural philosophy," in 1786. But the idea of sponsoring prize contests was much older, of medieval ori-gins, and had become a staple of various European learned societies, which routinely sponsored essay and scientific contests on a variety of subjects. The most famous precursor to the APS education prize came from an Academy of Lyon essay contest, sponsored by the Abbe Raynal, in 1780. History teachers will appreciate its enduring appeal: "Was the Discovery of America a blessing or a curse to mankind?"[6]

The role of formal education in a republic, as a specific subject, had been a part of Enlightenment conversations in Europe and the United States throughout the eighteenth century as well. In France, the Chalons Academy sponsored a prize essay contest from 1779 to 1781 on the "best plan of education for the people." Later, from 1797 to 1803, the Class of Moral and Political Sciences of the French National Institute held prize contests on the questions, "What are the most suitable institutions to establish morality in the people?" and "Is emulation a good means of education?" And on the Western side of the Atlantic—in fact, just around the corner from APS headquarters—Mr. Poor's [Female] Academy in Philadelphia held a contest in 1789 for a premium on the best essay on education.[7]

According to the APS minutes, members hit upon the idea for a major prize contest in 1795, probably as part of an effort to collect and publish their papers, and, as historian Nancy Beadie argues, in possible anticipation of converting the University of Pennsylvania into a national university. That the APS should be interested in education in particular should be no surprise—several of its regular members served as trustees at local schools, taught at the university, or had themselves authored essays on education. Indeed, as the members of the society contemplated a prize question, they sat in a brand new building resting on land granted to them by the state government of Pennsylvania, in recognition of their great contribution of useful knowledge. The prime location of the land—directly across the street from Independence Hall—testified to the importance of learning to the revolutionary generation.

While the education prize of 1797 came first and had the highest cash award, the APS contest also contained other prizes for the best improvement to ship pumps, the most economical method of heating rooms, the easiest way to calculate longitude from lunar observations, the best essay on American vegetable dyes, the best way to prevent peach tree rot, and the best improvement to lamps, especially for lighting streets.[8] Set in this context, the education prize suggests an understanding of education as being systematic, scientific, simple, and above all, useful. Europeans may have tended to imagine America as a pastoral wonderland, but Americans imagined it as a place where they could conquer nature and bend it to the will of the plow, the spade, the wonders of science, and the principles of good government.[9] The American Philosophical Society possessed the right blend of resources, motivation, training, naïve optimism, and arrogance to imagine they could create a one best system of education for the United States.

What they were really after, however, was a far bigger prize; and their essay contest was but a small moment in the great contest of Western political thought, conceived in Plato's *Republic*, Christianized by Augustin in *City of God*, and thrust into America by Thomas More's *Utopia*: How to perfect the human experience through the creation of ideal social institutions. One of the most influential writers on the subject, Montesquieu, wrote in the *Spirit of the Laws* (1748) that "the laws of education ought to be in relation to the principles of government." Having founded their republic as a *novo ordu seclorum*, a new order for the ages, the founding fathers of the APS hoped to design the best system of education to match it.[10]

As with all utopian projects, the dreams implicit in the APS education prize exceeded the reality. The education question did not frame an open competition of new ideas, but instead reflected the pet educational reform agendas of APS members. It had two very distinct parts. The first half of the question dealt with what should be taught: curriculum and possibly pedagogy (as implied by the word "system"). "[Write] an essay on a system of liberal education, and literary instruction, adapted to the genius of the government, and best calculated to promote the general welfare of the United States;[.]" Rather than make their question general, the APS asked for specific types of education, from two very different traditions. The first, "liberal education," referred to elite education, and required a discussion of college curriculum that, at the time, aroused passionate debate over the role of ancient languages. On the other hand, the phrase "literary instruction" could refer to mass education in basic literacy (reading and writing), or to academy- or college-level curriculum in vernacular literature. Both of these, the question challenged, should reflect and promote the "genius" of the newly minted government and the interest of the nation as a whole.

As a problem, liberal education did not rank with mass education, nor with the challenge of institution-building embedded in the second part of the question. It did reflect a war of words, however, in which Rush and other leading members of the APS were prime protagonists. In postrevolutionary America, a liberal education centered the "dead" languages of Greek and Latin. A liberal education was, to a large degree, synonymous with an academy diploma or college degree, but it was both more and less. It was an education afforded by free time for contemplation—quite literally, it was "liberal" in the sense that in Ancient Athens, it was the education of a free man of means and not a slave (although some women had one too).[11] Invoking a "liberal education" entitled a man to be heard on matters of politics and government, as John Dickenson had done famously in the introduction to his popular prerevolutionary tract, *Letters from a Farmer in Pennsylvania*.[12] For many, a liberal education also implied a certain moral stature—even in the case of a woman.[13] A few periodicals even aimed to provide a "liberal education" to those who lacked one, by giving readers a monthly dose of high intellectual culture.[14]

The dominant ideologies of the day—Enlightment, Radical Whig, and even Calvinist—argued that the American republic could survive only if its people were virtuous and well informed, and their rulers even more so.[15] But while there was widespread consensus among writers that a liberal education was necessary for creating future leaders (especially among those who *had* a liberal education), writers generally split into two camps with regard to the future of liberal education. Traditionalists championed the continued study of the oratorical and moral traditions of classics and classical languages, developing increasingly sophisticated rationales for existing practice. Reformers of a more "Philosophical" mindset—outspoken APS men such as Franklin and Rush—argued that a liberal education should be more useful, inquiry-based, and scientific.[16] Pennsylvania smoldered as a hotbed of the reform movement.[17]

The second part of the APS essay question was really a separate one: to develop a practical plan to build and operate public schools across the nation. It read, "comprehending, also, a plan for instituting and conducting public schools in this country on principles of the most extensive utility."

The "public" portion of the question reflected a preoccupation of prominent leaders with a well-informed and virtuous citizenry on the one hand, and a homogeneous citizenry on the other. While the word "public" was not meant in the modern sense of the word, neither did it reflect any one specific definition or consistent usage. It could merely indicate education taking place "in public," as opposed to in the home. But it was more than that too. The "public" schools described by the Northwest Ordinance of 1787, for example, were to be funded in part with rent from public land, and overseen democratically by local voters. New Englanders funded their "public" schools partially through local tax, and defined them legally as having democratic, lay control by citizens, while also encouraging local clergy to oversee them (or ignored public school laws altogether).[18] Southern states almost universally rejected the notion of public support for common education. At the collegiate level, "public education" had yet other meanings. Graduates of Dartmouth referred to themselves in 1786 as having a "publick liberal education."[19]

What the APS probably meant by public schools in their contest question was that the schools should exist in the public sphere, for the use and benefit of the general public, at some form of common expense. Presumably, though it was not stated explicitly, these schools needed to embrace the curricular concerns of the first part of the question, that is, liberal education and literary instruction. Finally, these schools needed to be described in a single plan that would cover the whole nation, or "country," from the rural South, which had no tradition of public support of education, to New England, which boasted one of the most literate, best-educated populations in the world.[20]

Thus the APS education contest did not ask for the best or most original essay on education, but rather for an essay on specific reforms. Beginning with "liberal education," it moved outwardly to increasingly general issues, with the unifying themes of utility and national character. Despite their eagerness to emphasize the unique aspects of American society and government, however, the APS addressed the very same issues that concerned the French learned societies. The men of the APS could have emulated the young women at Mr. Poor's Academy by simply asking for the "best essay on education." Instead they asked for a single plan that would cover the entire United States, encompassing primary and secondary education, taking a stand on the issue of liberal education, and doing so in a way that was practical and uniquely American.

Still ready?

Would-be contestants were not. The advertisements appeared in May of 1795, setting separate due dates for each contest; the education deadline was January 1, 1797. A year passed with no mention of an entry. By October 1796 still with no mention of an entry, the Society tried more advertising, and recorded in the minutes that "[t]he Corresponding Secretaries are desired to take measures for distributing throughout the United States and Europe the papers containing the premiums offered by the Society on certain subjects proposed by them." Finally, on December 30, the secretary reported having three essays. By a new April 1 deadline, the APS would have a total of seven.[21]

The peer-reviewers followed a strict review methodology. Each entry had to be anonymous, accompanied by a separate envelope with the name and address of the author, which would be opened only in the case of winning essays. The secretary numbered and/or titled each essay and someone read it aloud to the members of the society. The APS then assigned each to a review committee, which was to write an impartial précis for the benefit of the whole body. Not all entries were created equal, however, and not all reviews were quite as impartial as they may have claimed. From the point of view of the APS, the entries fell into two general categories—contenders and pretenders. Contenders received careful, complimentary reviews. Pretenders received a cattle-call approach accompanied by a liberal dose of scorn. Seven entries arrived in all—only three were contenders.

The four pretenders varied in length and intellectual rigor. Both in form and style, these essays fit the genre of the popular magazine essay, complete with *noms de plume*, including "Hiram," Academicus," a drawing of a hand, referred to as "Hand," and "Freedom." Reflecting the magazine genre, none was especially long: 700, 2,900, 2,900, and 6,000 words, respectively. Moreover, not every pretender considered himself or herself a serious contestant from the outset. Academicus, for example, wrote that his essay was not to be considered for the premium. Hiram promised a series of installments, but gave up after two.

As historian Campbell Scribner argues in this volume, the pretenders' essays engaged a variety of specific reforms that deviated from the APS's grand vision. Hiram focused on classroom concerns—the school schedule, rewards and punishments, schoolhouse architecture, and teachers. He paid especial attention to making teaching a desirable profession by allotting a plot of land directly to the schoolmaster to use for rent or for producing his own food, and for attaching a teacher's apartment to each schoolhouse. Should a teacher improve his plot or his apartment, Hiram argued, he should receive compensation from the district.

Academicus divided his essay in three parts. The first wrestled with curriculum theory, toeing the conservative line on dead languages. "While the pupil [is learning Latin]," he wrote, "he is at the same time acquiring also habits of industry and application, which may be of the greatest use to him through life." In the second part of the essay, Academicus discussed teaching literacy to children, emphasizing (and anticipating) a Pestalozzian emphasis on stages of learning based on observation, including the use of phonetics.[22] Finally, Academicus offered a description of a system of building, funding, and maintaining public schools through a statewide property tax, with free tuition for poor children through the academy level.[23]

Hand offered the most socially conservative essay. A national university should oversee all education by setting national standards. In addition, higher education should take a more direct role in managing common schools, training and overseeing of teachers, and providing professional development in the form of periodic lectures on special topics. For Hand, a common school education should be explicitly political, focusing on politics, political philosophy, rhetoric, and morality (including a generic form of religious instruction). In an unusual vein, Hand proposed making mass education more like a form of apprenticeship, where students, with teacher input, identified a chosen profession or trade early on and then tailored their studies to it. Ultimately, however, Hand was more concerned with elite education than mass education, writing that Americans' prosperity depended on "the knowledge, private virtue and unconstrained public good morals of their citizens—especially the ruling part of them from their conspicuous high example."[24]

Freedom had almost no interest in children. He argued that the acquisition of literacy was a mechanical art, virtually devoid of thought or personal expression. He then spent most of his essay weighing every aspect of the academic curriculum against the idea of "utility." With the exception of preparation for the professions, dead languages were out. Basic medical training, on the other hand, was in—no doubt a response to the deadly epidemics that had begun to sweep through Philadelphia in the 1790s.

The three contending essays were entirely different. Each was long and carefully crafted. None had a pen name. All three arrived by the original deadline. The APS assigned each essay to its own review committee and numbered them: No. 1 (by Smith), No. 2 (by Knox), and No. 3 Anonymous (hereafter referred to as No. 3). Knox's essay was 200 pages long; Smith's was 79; and the review of the third indicated that it was 47. The author of No. 3 hoped to collect the essay in the event it lost the competition, asking the committee to return it care of a nearby tavern keeper. When No. 3 did lose, the essay was duly delivered—and thus does not survive in the archives of the APS. What does survive, however, is the review committee's report. The committee reports for the contenders differed markedly from those of the pretenders—both longer and effusive.[25]

The author of essay No. 1, Samuel Harrison Smith, wrote a highly theoretical argument built upon the prevailing discussion in Scottish philosophy about the nature of virtue: were men born inherently good or evil, blank slates, or somewhere in between? From a lengthy discussion of what he saw as the connection between "virtue and wisdom," he proceeded to outline a three-tiered system of free, compulsory public education for the boys and men of the United States funded through property tax. He argued that the first tier schools should be of two types—primary schools for boys ages five–ten, and secondary schools for boys ages ten–eighteen. These should focus primarily on reading, writing, and arithmetic (the three Rs), but at the secondary level should also include history, geography, mechanics, memorizing portions of the Constitution, and other "useful" studies. The second tier, state colleges, and the third, a national university, would be available at public expense to a select group of students promoted from lower schools, as well as to those who could afford tuition. Smith rejected the dichotomy between elite liberal education and mass education—sound educational principles were universal. Smith's radical plan eliminated dead languages for all but university students. He made no argument for religious instruction.[26]

Author No. 2, Samuel Knox, wrote the most thorough and detailed plan. Knox was a veteran teacher of over 15 years and his plan reflected an intimate knowledge of the classroom. Knox imagined a state-run, secular, four-tiered system of mass education for males, including primary or "parish" schools, "county schools" or academies, state colleges, and a national university. Like Smith, Knox argued that each system should select a small percentage of students to move to the next level, but unlike Smith, Knox saw clearer distinctions between education for the masses and education for the elite. Primary schools would teach the three Rs, but academies should emphasize Ancient Greek and Latin first, followed by French and arithmetic. The plans for colleges and a national university did not imagine anything unusual, except that Knox punctuated his plans with obsessive detail, from the size and relative position of professors' residences to the design of the iron gates. Although Knox was a clergyman, he placed relatively little importance on religious education, urging schools at all levels to avoid sectarian instruction or bias. He also urged a uniform collection of national textbooks, and state boards of education to oversee local schools. He conceded the possibility that local families may want to send their girls to primary school, in which case he argued that all schoolmasters should be married, so that their wives may teach separate classes for girls. As with all the essayists, he did not discuss race.[27]

Author No. 3's essay has gone unnoticed by historians, though significant artifacts of it survive either as quotations or in summary. The language is provocative, as the committee noted, and the proposal differs from its peers on key points. First, the author put nonsectarian religious instruction front and center in his proposal, writing, "Morality was ever constructed as inseparable from the principles of Religion." At higher levels of education, the author saw no conflict between science and giving "due homage to the Supreme Creator who established its Laws." As did most of the others, Author No. 3 proposed a three-tiered system of schools, comprising free primary schools for poor children—presumably girls and boys, since they were to be taught by "masters and mistresses," and offering instruction in "national language, Arithmetic, morality, and a general description of the terrestrial globe." These schools would be run by justices of the peace or "corporations." At the next level, central schools or academies would provide two separate courses—a short course for future teachers and a longer academic course that would be the equivalent of college. At the highest level, a national university would set the standard for all levels of education, provide the highest levels of education available, and provide inspectors for lower schools. Existing colleges and universities could become "central schools" in this plan. At the end of the essay, Author No. 3 listed an unusual provision. Schoolmistresses would be ranked equally with professors at the central schools, potentially creating a professional teaching career for educated women.[28]

The seven entries reveal a decided lack of consensus about American education—even in a context as selective as the American Philosophical Society's contest. Written as questions, these uncertainties sound hauntingly familiar to educationists of any generation: Should girls be educated the same as boys? How can (or should) religion be taught in public schools? Is higher education an entitlement or a privilege? Should schools prepare students to be better workers, better thinkers, or better human beings? What role should the federal government have in dictating local school policy?

Given their high aspirations, it should be no surprise that the members of the APS, and we, should be frustrated with the results: four pretenders and only three contenders. Finally, in December of 1797, the APS decided that two of the contenders, Samuel Knox and Samuel Smith, should share the prize. But the body resolved that neither essay was exactly what it was looking for, and immediately explored the possibility of a second contest. It never happened. Over the ensuing century, the winning essays made their way into the canon of early republican writing on education, while the contest became an iconic moment for historians of American education.

In 2009 a team of eight researchers descended on the American Philosophical Society archives to take a new look at the essay contest. Two were seasoned historians. Six were graduate students participating in a research mentoring program. Our challenge was this: How could we reconstruct the events of 1795–1797 using a combination of detective work and historical research, fresh perspectives and new technologies, as well as old-fashioned elbow grease?[29]

First, we wanted to solve a two-hundred-year-old mystery. Because of the blind review process, only the winners' names were revealed at the time. The five losing essays have remained anonymous ever since.[30] Did a famous founding father (or mother) contribute a lost work on education? Knowing authorship could allow us to better understand meaning and politics of educational writing at the time. We had other questions as well: Why were the winners picked? What hidden agendas might have shaped the review process? And how representative were these essays of the broader landscape of American educational thought? For better or for worse, Americans continue to look back to the early republican period, both for its enormous historical significance, and as a kind of wellspring of ideas and wisdom about the meaning of our political system. The APS essay contest offers us a clear link between the political ideals that shaped America and their application to educational thought.

This book represents the culmination of that original foray into the APS archives. Three of the original graduate students are now joined by seven seasoned historians of education to revisit, and reevaluate, the multiple and complex meanings of formal education during the founding decades of the American Republic. Together the essays of this volume reflect the current state of early republican history, from questions of authorship, to inquiries into old and new research methods, to essays that explore the political, legal, economic, religious, social, and cultural history of education in the final decade of the eighteenth century.

Above all else, the American Philosophical Society saw its mission as the promotion of useful knowledge. That project, they believed, was characterized more by the process of inquiry than its products. To that end, this book approaches the APS education prize of 1797 as an open-ended project, in which readers can follow the process of historical inquiry. After this introduction, the remaining parts of the book follow the path of the researcher. Part I, "Methods," includes two very different essays recounting the methods used to identify our anonymous authors. Part II, "Meanings," contains seven thematic essays that provide different themes for understanding the significance and meaning of the APS contest: educational reform, useful knowledge, race, religion, women's education, gender, and higher education. The final section of this book, "Materials" includes transcriptions of all seven of the original essays and descriptions of their authors.

Who wrote the losing essays?[31] The initial question that animated this project proved to be the most exciting. Hiram was without question Francis Hoskins, a fact apparently known to those familiar with the APS archives, and one discovered by Eric Strome when comparing Hiram's essay to another submitted by the same author, which included his actual name. Hoskins was a Philadelphia accountant and author of a math textbook and a book on Freemasonry.[32]

Academicus was very probably John Hobson, a Unitarian minister from Birmingham, England. Nia Soumakis and I first noticed the similarity between the Academicus piece and an essay published by Hobson in 1799. I located political and educational writings by Hobson in Birmingham that strongly resembled the Academicus essay in their content and writing style, while circumstantial evidence points to Hobson as well.[33] Although we have not been able to locate any handwriting by Hobson in England or America, the computer analysis conducted by Strome (chapter 3) points to the very high likelihood of his authorship.

Our most exciting finding, however, is the strong likelihood that Rev. William Smith, provost of the University of Pennsylvania, was the author of essay No. 3. The evidence is both circumstantial and substantive, argues Lisa Green in chapter 2, using the quoted and paraphrased portions of the peer-review of his essay as well as his and the Society's bizarre behavior during the review process. Essay No. 3 appears to have been Smith's last serious bid for the helm of the University of Pennsylvania, or, perhaps, for the presidency of a new, widely discussed national university. Unfortunately, Smith was inadvertently placed on the peer review committee for his own essay. With no dignified way out, he delayed his committee indefinitely until, finally, they were forced to replace him. At some point Smith's authorship seems to have become an open secret. A year later, when the APS convened a special committee to consider the propriety of a second essay contest, the group proposed new, unusually specific set of rules: that one single committee be elected to review all essay entries, "that no Member who intends to write upon the judgment, as a candidate for the premium, accept…a seat in the Committee," and that "any member of the Committee who wishes to decline serving, must resign within two months after the election."[34]

Hand and Freedom remain anonymous despite extensive examination of handwriting samples from likely candidates in the manuscripts and archives collections of the APS, the Pennsylvania State Historical Society and the library of the College of Physicians of Philadelphia. Both writers appear to have been connected to the study of medicine, as students, graduates, or possibly faculty of the University of Pennsylvania who were familiar with the writings or lectures of Benjamin Rush. Freedom wrote as if he had experience as a practicing physician.

METHODS

How do you solve a two-hundred-year-old mystery? Chapter 2, by Lisa Green, recounts the process of identifying William Smith as the author of essay No. 3. Smith's was by far the most significant of the losing essays, and also the most interesting, given that he insisted on having the original returned to a local tavern keeper in the event of his losing. Analyzing the author's positions on several specific educational reforms, as well as the circumstances surrounding the essay, Green asserts William Smith's authorship beyond a reasonable doubt. While such a claim can never be absolute without the original essay in hand, Green's essay focuses on process, not product, and while doing so opens up a rich history of the landscape of educational thought in the United States and France during the 1790s.

Eric Strome's methodological exploration in chapter 3 could not be more different. Strome dexterously explicates the advent and applicability of computer-based content analysis in historical research, including recent developments in the field of stylistics. Strome then applies these methods to the APS education essay contest. Although he finds that the quoted fragments of essay No. 3 are too short for meaningful analysis, he identifies John Hobson as the author of the Academicus essay, confirming the more traditional analysis done by Soumakis and me. More importantly, he demonstrates the power and promise of computing technology for content analysis—a union of scientific method and historical inquiry. The men of the APS would be pleased.

MEANINGS

What can a two-hundred-year-old essay contest tell us about the past? What does the education prize of 1797 mean? The second part of this book, "Meanings," contains seven thematic essays using the APS contest of 1795 as an entry point. The authors traverse much of the landscape of educational history. Some focus on the relationship between private markets and associations and the creation of a "public" sphere where ideas could be promulgated and regulated. Others note the loud silence of APS essayists on questions of race and gender, reinforcing whiteness and patriarchy without explicitly contradicting the supposed egalitarian impulse of the American Revolution. One collides gender and class in an exploration of private French girls' schools. Still others examine the problems posed by religious pluralism and federalism for nation-building through mass civic education and elite higher education.

Campbell Scribner leads with a look at the marketplace of late-eighteenth-century educational ideas. In chapter 4, Scribner asks why the men of the APS could overlook clever and important innovations of their day (seen in the losing essays), while favoring the unworkable and out-of-touch proposals by Smith and Knox. Their blindness, he argues, was due to their obsession with centralization, and their inability to appreciate the importance of localism for ordinary Americans. Scribner notes that historians, too, have tended to share the founders' preoccupation with national plans, only recently appreciating the ways in which proponents of state or national education had to "continually refine its definition," to be locally relevant. In that process, he suggests, school reformers of the early republic began shaping the complex meaning of "public" education as something neither local nor central, but negotiated between the two.

That negotiated space, Nancy Beadie argues in chapter 5, was filled by government and translocal voluntary associations, working cooperatively. Examining the Enlightenment project of "encouraging useful knowledge," Beadie shows us how Freemasonry provided "a kind of ghost system underlying apparently independent local educational initiatives." Government at various levels, she demonstrates, created legal frameworks that enabled local action on the problem of educating the masses. Freemasonry promulgated the message and mobilized citizens locally. It should come as no surprise that many of the men of the APS were themselves Freemasons, engaged in the same process of encouraging useful knowledge that was at once local (and Philadelphia-specific) in nature and international in scope and ambition. Indeed, a very local concern in 1795 with Philadelphia's future as the national seat of government and possible home of a national university may explain the genesis of the education prize itself. Thus the APS education essay contest did not only produce artifacts that testify to the negotiated relationship between the local and the national; it is one.

Forging the kind of translocal identity afforded by the Freemasons—one akin to the federated nationalism that emerged slowly until ignited by the war of 1812—depended on Americans' ability to sort themselves into broad hierarchies of civic identity. In a European-dominated settler society dependent upon the chattel enslavement of African people, race functioned as an vital marker of citizenship. As historian Edmund Morgan has famously argued, race-based slavery developed alongside American notions of freedom during the long colonial period, so that by the American Revolution, most European Americans could imagine they lived in a republic where all men were created equal and born with inalienable rights, even though they did not. Their vision of civic identity was white, propped up either by willful ignorance of (or blindness to) the contradictions of slavery, or by ideas of racial superiority rooted in biblical interpretation, historical anthropology, or pseudoscience.[35]

In a classic instance of the dog that did not bark, Hilary Moss uses chapter 6 to explore the significant absence of any mention of race or slavery in the seven essays of the APS contest. The oversight, she argues, could not be for lack of experience. In a street-level social history of Philadelphia, Moss imagines the daily sights and sounds of APS author Samuel Smith as he traveled to and from the American Philosophical Society meetings. Free African Americans were everywhere in his world—except in his conception of who a citizen was. Whether or not he subscribed to the scientific racism that was beginning to emerge in his day (and which may be found lurking in Knox's more extensive essay), Smith shared a common assumption with most educational reformers: mass education for citizen building was a white endeavor. That assumption, Moss demonstrates, would continue far into the future nineteenth-century America, both at the local level, and as the intellectual heirs to the APS contest began building comprehensive statewide systems of education. Despite the efforts of African Americans and their allies, the maintenance of racial caste remained a core function of common schooling, a dark pillar of the American republic.

Sex provided another crucial marker of civic identity among whites in the late eighteenth century. As with race, the essays of the APS contest made few comments on the education of girls and women in their school plans. In chapter 7, Margaret Nash seeks to understand how this was possible, when both the authors and their reviewers were advocates for girls education and women's rights. To answer the question, she makes a crucial observation: in any gendered analysis of the APS contest essays, we must begin by recognizing that the authors, and readers who judged them, were men. Moreover, they were men in a period when manhood and its relationship to the state and to learning was in flux. The absence any serious discussion of the education of girls and women—even among men who were otherwise committed to both—tells us less about women than about the anxieties of men about themselves. In their effort to define academic study as an expression of manly citizenship, the essayists overlooked or downplayed the place of girls and women in their imagined educational utopias.

Whatever they tell us about the men who wrote them, unrealized plans for public systems of education are not the best place to learn about the world of women's education in the early republic. In chapter 8, Kim Tolley examines the marketplace for private French schools, which thrived in coastal towns and metropolitan centers throughout the United States, including Philadelphia. These schools offered women an ornamental education, focusing on domesticity and motherhood as a way to maintain (or advance) social status and, for the small number of American Catholics, a chance to strengthen religious beliefs. But Tolley's social history of these schools also demonstrates their responsiveness to the changing marketplace. As demand for "useful knowledge" for girls increased in the early nineteenth century, French schools offered more academic courses, while female academies of the more utilitarian or academic mode offered some of the French school curriculum. Thus while APS essayists minimized the significance of girls and women in their plans for a universal education rooted in useful knowledge, the middle and upper classes of Philadelphia and other American cities and towns supported a thriving market for ornamental girls' education that was much slower to respond to the revolutionary impulse. "The spirit of social egalitarianism in the new republic may have been strong," concludes Tolley, "but so was the desire to retain personal choice, privilege, and social status."

Tolley finds that in the private marketplace for elite education, the Catholic orientation of French schools did not appear to be problematic for Protestant patrons until later in the nineteenth century. For would-be architects of universal systems of public schools, however, religion posed a special and enduring problem. In chapter 9, I survey the nature of this problem and the range of solutions that public school planners devised. The trouble with religion in America was that it was diverse, divisive, and in some cases, hostile to a republican form of government. Overcoming these challenges spurred the development of two innovations in particular: the impulse to remove religious bodies from oversight of public schools, and the creation of nonsectarian religious exercises that could offend no one, or in a few proposals, the removal of religion from the curriculum altogether. Generally, such solutions followed state-level politics of disestablishment. Recently, some historians and federal judges who favor vouchers for Catholic schools have claimed that the principles of nonsectarian instruction and public oversight of mass education originated in mid- to late-nineteenth-century anti-Catholicism. School plans from the early republic, including the essays of the APS contest, suggest otherwise.[36]

Concern over the wisdom and virtue of the mass of citizens, however, accounts for only half of the republican model of government. In a republic, the people must select leaders, and those leaders must be the wisest and most virtuous among them. Many founding fathers argued that the future leaders of the United States needed a new kind of higher education—one that recognized and rewarded merit rather than privilege, and that, as Adam Nelson argues, emphasized distinctly American ideas. In chapter 10, Nelson analyzes the connection between nation-building and public higher education through the case of failed attempts to create a national university. Such a plan figured prominently in the most serious of the APS essays, and reflected a broad hope among APS philosophes. What concerns Nelson is the notion that knowledge be produced domestically—both through the education of students and the selection of faculty. Even in an age where learned societies constituted a transatlantic "republic of letters," American intellectual leaders still hoped to instill uniquely American ideas in higher education. As with their broader school plans, however, the American philosophes overreached, and the national university did not come to pass.

MATERIALS

At a June 1797 meeting, society president Thomas Jefferson ordered a special meeting to judge the seven entries for the education prize. For one month, the seven essays lay together on a table, inside Philosophical Hall, which the society kept open every day (except on Sundays), so that members had "ample opportunity of estimating the comparative merits of the Essays on this important Subject." The general public was not invited.[37]

The third and final part of the book, "Materials," brings all the essays together again, on display to the public for the first time. Because of their length, the two winning essays appear here in reduced form. (They are available in full online.) Essay No. 3, last seen in the hands of inn keeper Alex Moore, may be glimpsed in small part, quoted and summarized in the review committee's report. The others are the first complete transcriptions of the original, handwritten versions.

Taken together, the essays provide us with a window into the ideas and beliefs of educational reformers at the birth of the United States of America. While the educational writings of more prominent leaders are well known—Jefferson's plans for Virginia, Benjamin Rush's for Pennsylvania, and Noah Webster's textbooks for the whole nation, for example—the APS contest introduces us to a second tier of educational reformers: a newspaper publisher, an accountant, the principal of an academy, a political refugee, a former university head, and two writers who remain anonymous. The winning essays by Samuel Harrison Smith and Samuel Knox provide us with substantial, well-crafted arguments drawing together the best educational literature in their time. Yet the losing essays, too (even the really bad ones), give us an indication of the problems and solutions of American education through the eyes of more ordinary men.

Why should their vision matter? It's fair to say that all the essays favored the same general late-eighteenth-century Enlightenment orientation as the APS, and were thus not indicative of the full range of views on education at the time; but we must also recognize that it was that view, and those men of the APS, who led the revolution, wrote the Declaration of Independence, federal and state constitutions, and served in the highest political offices in the land. The essays of the APS contest offer us a link between the political vision of the United States of America and its educational significance. What did the founding fathers think about public education in America? It's not an easy question to answer, but the APS contest is a great place to start.

The award of the premium in 1797 to Samuel Smith and Samuel Knox did not signal the end of the conversation about education in the republic, but instead marked its beginning. In the intervening centuries, state-sponsored public education has become a universal public good, found in nearly every nook of the globe, sponsored to some degree by every stable national government. And whether one is in the United States, United Kingdom, or United Arab Emirates, the provision of free, universal, and state-regulated education has become one of the standard measures of the health and well-being of any society. If the APS contest is, for the historian of the early republic, a rich source for understanding the 1790s, it is also, for the scholar of the modernity, a useful starting point for understanding the relationship between public schools and state building that has laid the foundation of global liberalism.

The authors in this book invite you to continue the inquiry process begun by the American Philosophical Society in 1795. Our methods are not bombproof and our "meanings" are not only diverse, but contingent on our understandings at our historical moment. Yet whether we view the great contest narrowly or generally, as a source for political theory or historical understanding (or both), the problem of finding the ideal system of education for the United States remains as relevant and fruitful today as when it was identified by the APS as being worthy of a contest. The knowledge they produced is still useful.

Ready?

NOTES

Portions of this essay appeared in Benjamin Justice, "The Great Contest: The American Philosophical Society and the Education Prize of 1797." *American Journal of Education.* 114:2 (February 2008), 191–213, and are reprinted here with permission.

1. "Premiums," *The American Monthly Review, or, Literary Journal,* May 1795, 2:1 American Periodicals Series Online (hereafter APSO); American Philosophical Society (hereafter APS). Minute Book. Entry for May 1, 1795. APS Archives.
2. Thomas Jefferson, "A Bill for the More General Diffusion of Knowledge," reprinted in Merrill D. Peterson (ed.), *Jefferson Writings* (New York: Library of America, 184), 365–373; John Adams was the primary author of the Massachusetts State Constitution of 1780.
3. Readers may refer to the APSO, which allows for keyword searches online. The number of articles containing the word "education" jumps dramatically over the course of the 1780s.
4. Max Farrand (ed.), *Records of the Federal Convention of 1787*, vol. II (New Haven: Yale University Press, 1966), 321–322.
5. Merle Odgers, "Education and the American Philosophical Society," *Proceedings of the American Philosophical Society* 87:1 (July 14, 1943): 20–23. The website of the APS also contains useful information on its founding and prominent members. See www.amphilsoc.org; John L. Brooke, "Ancient Lodges and Self-Created Societies: Voluntary Association and the Public Sphere in the Early Republic," in Ronald Hoffman and Peter J. Albert (eds.), *Launching the "Extended Republic," The Federalist Era* (Charlottesville: University Press of Virginia, 1996), 273–359; Bernard Fay, "Learned Societies in Europe and America in the 18th Century," *The American Historical Review* 37:2 (January 1932): 255–266; Verner W. Crane ,"The Club of Honest Whigs: Friends of Science and Liberty," *The William and Mary Quarterly*, 3rd ser. 23:2 (April 1966): 210–233. On the presence of

the university, see chapter 5 in this volume; Allen Oscar Hansen, *Liberalism and American Education in the Eighteenth Century* (New York: MacMillan, 1926), 106.

6. Fay, "Learned Societies," 261; Gerald A. Danzer, "Has the Discovery of America Been Useful or Hurtful to Mankind? Yesterday's Questions and Today's Students," *The History Teacher* 7:2 (February 1974): 192–206.

7. Martin S. Staum, "The Enlightenment Transformed: The Institute Prize Contests," *Eighteenth-Century Studies* 19:2 (Winter 1986): 153–179; A Promoter of Female Education, "Essay on Education," *Massachusetts Monthly Magazine*, January 1789, APSO.

8. APS Minute Book, Entries for February 6 and April 23, 1795, APS Archives.

9. Peter S. Onuf, "Liberty, Development, and Union: Visions of the West in the 1780s," *The William and Mary Quarterly*, 3rd ser. 43:2 (April 1986): 179–213, 6–10.

10. Charles de Montesquieu, The Spirit of the Laws, book IV (T. Evans and W. Davis, trans., 1777, London), downloaded from the Online Library of Liberty on December 8, 2012, http://oll.libertyfund.org/?option=com_staticxt&staticfile=show.php%3Ftitle=837.

11. Andrew Ahlgren and Carol M. Boyer, "Visceral Priorities: Roots of Confusion in Liberal Education," *The Journal of Higher Education* 52:2 (March–April 1981): 173–181.

12. Scans of the original are available on the Dickinson College Website at deila.dickinson.edu/theirownwords/title/0004.htm. See also, HONESTUS, Article 3—No Title; "Ne, . . . ultra crepidam.—Cobler, stick to your last." *The American Museum; or, Repository of Ancient and Modern Fugitive Pieces & c. Prose and Poetical* (1787–1788). Philadelphia: June 1788. 3:6; p. 528, APSO.

13. *The New—Haven Gazette, and the Connecticut Magazine*, New Haven: August 24, 1786. 1:28, p. 219, APSO.

14. "INTRODUCTION: Addressed to the YOUTH of these States," *The Christian's, Scholar's, and Farmer's Magazine : Calculated in an Eminent Degree, to Promote Religion; to Disseminate Useful Knowledge; to Afford Literary Pleasures and Amusement, and to Advance the Interest of Agriculture*, Elizabeth-town: April/May 1789. 1: 1; p. 51, APSO; Philosophical Queries. The Pennsylvania Magazine; or, American Monthly Museum (1775–1776). Philadelphia: August 1775, p. 353, APSO; Saul Sack, "Liberal Education: What Was It? What Is It?" *History of Education Quarterly* 2:4 (December 1962): 210–224; Ahlgren and Boyer, "Visceral Priorities."

15. Richard D. Brown, *The Strength of a People: The Idea of an Educated Citizenry in America 1650–1870* (Chapel Hill: University of North Carolina Press, 1996); and Richard D. Brown, "Bulwark of Revolutionary Liberty: Thomas Jefferson's and John Adams's Programs for an Informed Citizenry," in James Gilreath (ed.), *Thomas Jefferson and the Education of a Citizen* (Honolulu: University Press of the Pacific, 2002).

16. Bruce Kimball, *Orators and Philosophers: A History of the Idea of Liberal Education* (New York: Teachers College Press, 1986).

17. Jurgen Herbst, "The Yale Report of 1828," *International Journal of the Classical Tradition* 11 (Fall 2004): 213–231; Sheldon Rothblatt, *Tradition*

and Change in English Liberal Education: An Essay in History and Culture (London: Faber & Faber, 1976).

18. David Tyack, Thomas James, and Aaron Benavot, *Law and the Shaping of American Education, 1785–1954* (Madison: University of Wisconsin Press, 1987), 20–42; Carl Kaestle, *Pillars of the Republic: Common Schools and American Society, 1780–1860* (New York: Hill & Wang, 1983), 182–190. On Massachusetts and Connecticut, see chapter 9 in this volume.

19. "Commencement at Dartmouth College," *Worchester Magazine . . . Containing Politicks, Miscellanies, Poetry, and News*, 2: 29, October 1786, p. 344, APSO.

20. E. Jennifer Monaghan, *Learning to Read and Write in Colonial America* (Boston: University of Massachusetts Press, 2005), 384–385.

21. APS Minute Book.

22. Will S. Monroe, *History of the Pestalozzian Movement in the United States* (Syracuse, NY: C. W. Bardeen, 1907); Academicus, "A Plan for the Education of Youth," p. 245 of this volume.

23. See pp. 243–249 of this volume.

24. See p. 256 of this volume.

25. The card catalogue lists the Committee Report for Essay No. 1 as McGaw, "Remarks on Education." McGaw was the chair of the review committee on Samuel Harrison Smith's Essay No. 1, "Remarks on Education."

26. See pp. 205–217 of this volume.

27. See pp. 219–232 of this volume.

28. See pp. 233–238 of this volume.

29. For a complete description, see Benjamin Justice, "Making History at the History Conference: Bringing Research Mentoring to the Annual Meeting," *Perspectives on History: The Magazine of the American Historical Association* 50:7 (October 2012).

30. The identity of Hiram was known to the compilers of the electronic database of the APS archives, who make a note of it in the entry for Francis Hoskins's second Hiram essay. That knowledge has not, apparently, made its way into scholarship.

31. During the research phase of this book, Campbell Scribner, Nia Soumakis, Eric Strome, Lisa Green, and Benjamin Justice all assisted each other in the identification process.

32. Hoskins published at least two books: *An Introduction to Merchandise. Arithmetick. In whole and broken numbers, designed for the use of Academies. . . * (undated), and *The Beauties and Super-excellency of Freemasonry Attempted* (1801).

33. Hobson published at least five essays in England, which he lists in his only Philadelphia publication, "Prospectus of a Plan of Instruction . . ." (1799). The first tipoff to identification came in the similarity between Hobson's 1799 description of the purposes of education and what Academicus wrote, hastily, two years later. A comparison between Hobson's writing style, habits of punctuation, and spelling, especially in his "Address to the Inhabitants of Birmingham upon the necessity of attending to the philosophy of the mind . . ." (1790), is also compelling, as is an analysis of the substance of the educational arguments of Hobson before and after the Academicus piece, and the piece itself. Strome's computer-based content analysis makes the case beyond a reasonable doubt.

34. APS, Report of the Committee appointed to consider the propriety of offering a premium for the best essay on the subject of education. February 15, 1799.
35. Edmund S. Morgan, *American Slavery, American Freedom* (New York: Norton, 1975).
36. The most aggressive and inaccurate claim of this sort may be found in Clarence Thomas's opinion in *Mitchell v. Helms* (2000). For an overview, and correction, of this trend in scholarship, see Steven K. Green, *The Bible, the School, and the Constitution: The Clash that Shaped Modern Church-State Doctrine* (New York: Oxford University Press, 2012).
37. *Early Proceedings of the American Philosophical Society*, 258–260.

PART I

Methods

CHAPTER 2

The Mysterious No. 3

Lisa Green

From the beginning, essay No. 3 had an air of intrigue about it. All of the essays in the American Philosophical Society Educational Essay Contest of 1795 were submitted anonymously, but No. 3 came with a unique request. If the essay did not win the prize, it was to be returned to the care of Alex Moore, a tavern keeper about two blocks from Philosophical Hall. The author wanted the manuscript back, possibly to use again or to protect his identity. In any case, the original essay is not available, and only the report of the review committee survives.

The report was unusual, too. In contrast to the reviews of Samuel Knox and Samuel Harrison Smith, the report on No. 3 contains direct quotes and summary material, but no commentary. It states, "Your committee have thought it their duty to exhibit the principles and plan of the author, as nearly as possible, in his own language; and that these may appear in the fairest point of view, they withhold every sentiment of applause or censure."[1] Even though the review reflects serious consideration, it has a detached tone that the reviews for the other essays don't. It appears as if the reviewers were trying to distance themselves from essay No. 3. While novel, the contents of No. 3 appeared learned and reasonable, however, and not something to cause alarm.

The plan outlined in No. 3 was comprehensive, and the level of detail indicated that the author may have had first-hand experience with curricular and administrative issues. The plan was unique in placing the most power for educational decisions at the federal level, and expressed the author's "utmost wish, and ardent hope that his part of the System may not appear objectionable."[2] Reviewer Moreau de St. Mery commented that the plan "had been proposed by a man of great ability."[3] Essay No. 3, therefore, was worthy of consideration.

Even the review process for No. 3 was distinctive. Each of the "contenders" was assigned a review committee of three individuals. The original reviewers of No. 3 were Rev. William Smith, Moreau de St. Mery, and W. Abercrombie; but Smith held up the process for at least four months for unknown reasons, and had to be replaced by Jon Williams, a reviewer already serving on another committee. The review committee produced an analysis of No. 3 on November 17, 1797, and the APS scheduled the work to be reviewed at the next meeting. However, consideration of the essays was held up a second time, citing that "certain reasons induce the Society to defer this business a little longer." The final decision was announced on December 15, 1797, and No. 3 lost. The prize was shared by the other two contenders, Samuel Harrison Smith and Samuel Knox.[4] The purpose of this chapter is to try to identify the author of No. 3 by comparing his ideas to other educational writings of the period. Who wrote No. 3, and why was it so mysterious?

METHODOLOGY

In an attempt to identify the author and understand the issues of education that were important at the time, this study compared the directly quoted portions of No. 3 to other writings on education in the period between 1750 and 1800. As a part of the comparison of the essays, themes began to emerge including school organization and governance, the place of religion in education, dead languages, funding, who was to be educated, and the use of honors and rewards. Unusual or unique aspects of each essay were noted as well.

The study was conducted in two phases. In phase I, I compiled a list of people writing about education at the time, and then constructed a comparison grid that showed simplified results for each to see if No. 3 was written by one of these writers. The list included: John Adams, Robert Coram, DuPont de Nemours, Thomas Jefferson, Joseph Priestly, Benjamin Rush, the Reverend William Smith, and Noah Webster. I also included the winners of the contest, Samuel Knox and Samuel Harrison Smith, for comparison, but I did not include Benjamin Franklin, founder of the APS, who was deceased by the time of the contest. Later in the analysis I also considered two French members of the American Philosophical Society, Moreau de St. Mery and Constantin François de Volney, because of some commonalities of language that No. 3 had with French educational reform proposals.

I decided to limit the comparison grid to the following characteristics because of their importance in No. 3 and their promise as discriminating indicators:

1. The use of the term "sacred Legislator"
2. A national moral catechism for the schools
3. Dead languages
4. School hierarchy: national university in the Capitol of the Union, central schools, and free primary schools
5. Dual track central school—some students emphasize literature and eloquence, and others study practical sciences for commerce, navigation, mechanical arts

6. Governance: "Federal Institution"
7. Use of merits and honors
8. Female education—No. 3 mentions equality for school mistresses and the professors, which indicates there must have been female students at some level.

When I constructed the comparison grid, I discovered that some themes proved more discriminating than others. "Dead languages" was the most frequently mentioned indicator in the writings as a whole, and therefore was the most useful in comparing other educational writings to No. 3. By using this main indicator to eliminate a number of possibilities, several writers remained as deserving a "second look." Most of these candidates were also examined by Eric Strome (see chapter 3 in this volume) using computerized author analysis.

Two of the indicators that were not very helpful in this initial phase of analysis were "governance" and "female education." No one besides the author of No. 3 mentioned a "Federal Institution" or suggested quite as strong a federal involvement in schools. Therefore "governance" was too unique to see authors in conversation with each other. Comparisons were also difficult using "female education" as the indicator since this was rarely mentioned and details were lacking.

In phase II of the project, I used the other indicators to compare what is known of the educational views of these remaining writers directly with the views of No. 3. I also explored similarities between No. 3 and the French education plan at the time and considered the possibility of a French writer. I then made a reasoned judgment about who may have authored No. 3. While it may be impossible to ever know for sure, the evidence suggests that the Reverend William Smith is the author of No. 3.

Phase I—The Comparison Grid

The theme I found most useful in the comparison of educational writers was the topic of dead languages (Latin and Greek). Most writers stated an opinion regarding instruction in Latin and Greek; therefore it probably was a common topic of discussion in educational circles at the time. Latin was considered more fundamental than Greek, which was generally started later.

Dead Languages

On one end of the spectrum, writers took a strong position that the dead languages should not be taught at all. Robert Coram argued against any teaching of the dead languages in public schools because it would perpetuate educational and social inequality, and it was unnecessary for understanding obligations to society and therefore not a government responsibility.[5] I placed Samuel Harrison Smith, author of No. 1 and one of the cowinners of the contest, in this category. He does not mention Latin, Greek, or the classics as part of his curricular plans in his essay for the APS contest, yet specifically mentions English and modern languages in regards to college curriculum. The "board of literature and science" he proposed had a position for someone in languages but further specification isn't given.[6]

Other authors exhibited a strong preference for extensive instruction in English rather than Latin or Greek, but seemed to leave room for the study of the dead languages for those for whom this study might be useful; I put Noah Webster in this category. He thought Latin and Greek unnecessary for all students except those who would be entering the learned professions. His own extensive study of Latin and Greek was essential for his work on the English language, and he noted that Latin continued to be useful for epitaphs, inscriptions, treaties, and so on, because it was "everywhere understood by the learned and being a dead language is liable to no change."[7] Nevertheless, Webster was deeply committed to the establishment of an American form of English as a national language, as a way of promoting national unity.[8] This necessitated that grammar study be based in the grammar of English as used in the United States, not on Latin grammar or the grammar of English used in Great Britain.

Benjamin Rush and Joseph Priestley both recognized the necessity of the dead languages for some professions, especially divinity, but wanted English to be of prime importance, even in college.[9] In 1786 Rush published a plan of education for Pennsylvania which called for an academy to teach the learned languages for those preparing for college, but in 1788 he called for French and German to be taught in a national university rather than Latin and Greek.[10] His writings in 1798 again emphasized the study of English, French, and German reflecting the increasing participation of merchants in college education.[11] Rush outlined a plan of liberal instruction without the dead languages, suggesting that Latin and Greek has caused otherwise capable students to become "so disgusted…as to retreat from the drudgery of schools to low company."[12] Latin and Greek were not only a waste of time; they were a cause of moral decrepitude. In 1810, Rush wrote to John Adams:

> It is folly and madness to spend four or five years in teaching boys the Latin and Greek languages. I admit knowledge of the Hebrew to be useful to divines, also as much of the Greek as well enable them to read the Greek Testament, but the Latin is useless and even hurtful to young men in the manner in which it is now taught.[13]

Even though Rush came to despise the teaching of Latin and Greek to boys in grammar school, he left room for the clergy to study Greek and Hebrew to be able to read the Bible in the original languages.

The remaining authors seemed to support the study of Latin and Greek for all students who continued their education past the rudiments of English reading, writing, and basic arithmetic. This was a common pattern of instruction in the early part of the eighteenth century.[14] Samuel Knox, author of

No. 2 and the cowinner of the contest, was a vigorous defender of Latin and Greek instruction, which formed the basis for curriculum in the academies of his educational plan.[15] John Adams believed that a liberal education should be based on studies of Latin, Greek, and the classics. He discussed the education of his own sons as including Latin School, which was part of a typical New England education for those destined for the learned professions.[16] Adams good-naturedly wrote the following to his friend Rush in 1810: "I do most cordially hate you for writing against Latin, Greek, and Hebrew. I never will forgive you until you repent, retract, and reform. No never! It is impossible."[17] Adams argued that the American Revolution stimulated the desire of men of learning to study the language, antiquities, and government of the Greeks, and that Greek was more relevant now than before.[18]

Thomas Jefferson also supported the concept of Latin grammar schools, considering the study of classical languages foundational to the study of the sciences.[19] The University of Virginia, founded by Jefferson, required proficiency in Latin, while higher degrees required demonstrated proficiency in Latin and Greek.[20] Evidence of Jefferson's affection for the classics is seen in his "commonplace book," which he kept as a student and an adult, where he wrote Latin, Greek, and other quotes that appealed to him.[21] Both ancient and modern languages played an important role in Jefferson's conception of secondary schools.[22] Pierre Samuel DuPont de Nemours favored the teaching of Latin, Greek, French, and German in secondary schools. Beyond mere instruction in the languages, DuPont de Nemours advocated teaching subject matter from other areas in the foreign languages.[23]

The plan in No. 3 takes what I would call a "compromise approach." The secondary level of education would have two courses or tracks—a basic course, which was entirely English based, and an extended course, which included instruction in Latin and Greek as preparation for university study. This approach had much to recommend it. Most colleges were controlled by what Franklin called "Latinists," who required students to have at least a basic proficiency in Latin as prerequisite for further study.[24] Those who did not plan on entering the learned professions such as law or divinity really had no need for Latin or Greek, and could spend their time in secondary schools learning more practical arts and sciences such as navigation and commerce. Instruction might also include the study of the classics translated into English, especially for the basic course of study. An important example of this compromise approach was found in the College of Philadelphia prior to 1779. The Reverend William Smith, provost at the time, was a member of the APS (and a member of the review committee for No. 3), so I decided to look at him more closely in Phase II.

By this point, I had eliminated Robert Coram, Noah Webster, Benjamin Rush, and Joseph Priestly as possible authors of No. 3, along with Samuel Knox, Samuel Harrison Smith, and Benjamin Franklin, all impossibilities from the outset who had been included only to enrich my baseline knowledge. Since it was possible that writers who took a traditional approach to the dead languages may also have seen the advantage of a less classics-based education for some students, I decided not to eliminate John Adams, Thomas Jefferson, or DuPont de Nemours at this point. Last, in investigating Thomas Jefferson, I realized that both he and the French reformers used the term "central schools" for secondary education as does No. 3. This led to a consideration of French influence on No. 3.

Phase II: A Second Look

In Phase II, I took a second look at John Adams, Thomas Jefferson, DuPont de Nemours, and the Reverend William Smith. As the French influence on No. 3 became more apparent I also considered several French members of the APS, including Moreau de St. Mery and Constantin François de Volney. Besides looking at these writers' views on dead languages, I looked at the indicators more broadly and tried to determine if these authors could be clearly eliminated on other criteria. Based on available information, John Adams could not be eliminated, and shared an unusual feature with the author of No. 3, who used the term "sacred Legislator," while Adams used a similar reference, "Great Legislator of the Universe," in the Massachusetts Constitution of 1780. I decided to start with John Adams.

John Adams

Founding father John Adams was a member of the APS and was in Philadelphia in December, 1796 for his presidential election.[25] He had been vice president under George Washington, who had advocated a national university to educate the nation's leaders and promote national unity.[26] Adams also placed a high value on education, as seen in the Massachusetts Constitution of 1780 and in his inaugural address in March 1797. Like Washington, Adams was in favor of a national university.[27] Nevertheless, neither letters to his wife nor his diaries during 1796 or 1797 contain any discussion of a national university or an educational essay, which might be expected if Adams was working on an essay for the contest during that time frame. When later asked about education by Thomas Jefferson, Adams replies:

> Education, Oh Education! The greatest Grief of my heart, and the greatest Affliction of my Life! To my mortification I must confess, that I have never closely thought, or very deliberately reflected upon the Subject, which never occurs to me now, without producing a deep Sigh, and heavy groan and sometimes Tears. My cruel Destiny separated me from my Children, almost continually from their Birth to the Manhood. I was compelled to leave them to the ordinary routine of reading writing and Latin School, Accademy and Colledge.[28]

Adams seems to have been so overwhelmed by his duties that even the education of his children, something very dear to his heart, did not get the attention he had desired. His sons followed the regular routine of a New

England liberal education, almost by default. In a later letter he mentions an education essay by Talleyrand Perigord as well as other French and German pamphlets, but mentions none of his own and defers to Jefferson's superior knowledge of educational treatises.[29]

Regarding who should be educated and how it should be paid for, it seems clear that Adams thought that schooling should be available for all classes of people at public expense: "The whole people must take upon themselves the education of the whole people, and must be willing to bear the expenses of it."[30] It seems that Adams would have free public education at all levels, but he did not specify how much education each student should have.

The most difficult part of the comparison between the ideas of John Adams and the author of No. 3 relates to the structure of a national educational hierarchy. Adams favored a strong federal government and therefore he may have entertained a top-down educational structure like the one in No. 3. However, No. 3 has similarities to educational ideas proposed in France during the early 1790s, and it seems unlikely that Adams would have wanted to align himself so closely with the ideals of French education at that time. The hierarchy of schools in No. 3 is reminiscent of the organization of schools under the Daunou Plan in place in France at the time of the APS contest. Neither the Daunou Plan nor No. 3 provide for religious instruction. But Adams was no Francophile, and the alliance with the French that had been forged during the American Revolution was placed under great strain in 1794 by the passage of the Jay Treaty. Adams became increasingly suspicious of the French in America and called for the deportation of some of them—including Constantin François de Volney and Moreau de St. Mery, members of the APS—in July 1798. The latter was a reviewer of No. 3. When St. Mery had a friend ask Adams why he was being deported, Adams replied that he was "too French."[31] Based on the evidence presented, I concluded that John Adams was probably not the author of No. 3.

Thomas Jefferson and DuPont de Nemours

Thomas Jefferson and DuPont de Nemours are sometimes thought of together when it comes to ideas on education since Jefferson is credited with encouraging DuPont de Nemours to write on education. Both Jefferson and DuPont de Nemours thought that Latin and Greek were an important part of a liberal education, although their ideas on this issue appear to be more traditional than that of No. 3. Both were fond of the classics as preparation for a college education.

Jefferson asked DuPont about his views on curriculum in higher education in 1800. In response, DuPont designed a whole system of education, beginning with primary schools, which he published in French as *National Education in the United States*.[32] It is misleading to assume that Jefferson agreed with all of what DuPont wrote, however, even though DuPont may have wanted others to think that way.[33] Jefferson also asked Joseph Priestley to write on higher education at the same time, and Jefferson's vision was that the three of them would form a committee to look at the issue.[34]

With regards to school hierarchy, No. 3 calls for a national university, as does DuPont de Nemours. Jefferson's view on a national university is not so clear, however. In his earlier writings, Jefferson supported education managed by the individual state.[35] James B. Conant states that "Jefferson became increasingly interested in higher education and in 1806 supported a bill for the establishment of a national academy and university in the city of Washington, and district colleges throughout the nation."[36] So it seems that somewhere between Jefferson's earlier writings and this bill in 1806, Jefferson warmed to the idea of a national university. However, No. 3 goes beyond the establishment of a national university to the formation of a Federal Institution with broad powers over national education. Its regulations, once ratified by the president and the Senate, had the rule of law. I think it is unlikely that Jefferson would have supported such a strong federal role in regulation of local schools.

DuPont clearly advocated a national university but his conception appears to be somewhat different than that of No. 3.[37] Of primary importance, there is no indication that No. 3 was submitted in French. DuPont wrote only in French, and Jefferson complained that his writing was very difficult to translate.[38] Also, DuPont did not actually arrive in the United States until 1799, after the contest was finished, so it is unlikely that DuPont authored No. 3.

There are also differences between DuPont, Jefferson, and No. 3 in the treatment of religion. DuPont advocates nondenominational prayers at several points throughout the day, whereas Jefferson and No. 3 distance themselves from religious practice in the schools. All three authors have similarities to French writers during the transformation of schools all through the French Revolution, but their ideas do not appear identical to each other. I do not think it likely that either DuPont de Nemours or Jefferson wrote No. 3.

The French Connection

From the results presented earlier, it appears that there was a possible French connection to No. 3. During the revolutionary period of 1790–1799, a series of educational plans were proposed in France in their own attempt to reform education to better fit the changing nation. Two early plans, one by Talleyrand in 1791 and another by Condorcet in 1792, were not enacted, but provided important stepping stones for the education law passed in 1795, popularly known as the Daunou law.[39] The Daunou Plan was in effect in France during the APS contest, so I will compare and contrast what we know of No. 3 with the Daunou Plan.[40]

The major similarity between No. 3 and the Daunou Plan is the organization of schools. Both include a primary level of education for all citizens in which reading, writing, and arithmetic were taught, in addition to moral instruction. These features are typical of most plans for primary schooling during the period in both France and America.

Both the Daunou Plan and No. 3 also have an intermediate level for students (12–18 years of age in the Daunou Plan) called "central schools," which were intended to replace the existing colleges and universities.[41] There was to be uniformity in course offerings from school to school in the Daunou Plan, but there was quite a great deal of freedom for students within the plan at the local level. No. 3 also called for a uniform plan of instruction among central schools, but it is unlikely that students had the same flexibility as under the Daunou Plan. After giving a list of course offerings for the central schools, No. 3 calls for the division of students into two classes "the one limited, the other extended," which implies the grouping of students based on their learning objectives, and possibly a more regimented sequence of classes.[42] Table 2.1 shows a comparison of the course offerings in the central schools of the Daunou Plan and No. 3.

There is considerable commonality between the two sets of courses for the central schools but they are not identical. There are three important differences. First, No. 3 emphasizes the availability of applied science. The second difference is that legislation is specifically mentioned as a course under the Daunou Plan separate from history. In the third difference, eloquence or rhetoric was unique to No. 3, although aspects of these may have found a place in other courses such as general grammar in the Daunou Plan.

The third level of schooling in No. 3 differs from the Daunou Plan. The Daunou Plan called for 10 advanced "special schools," including medicine, antiquities, and political science.[43] No. 3 called for a national university in

Table 2.1 Curriculum comparison of central schools in the Daunou Plan and No. 3

Daunou Plan	*No. 3*
Ancient languages	Ancient and modern languages
Mathematics	Mathematics
Physics-chemistry	Nat philosophy and chemistry*
Belles lettres	Belles lettres
History	History
Gen grammar†	Philosophy
Natural history	Geography, astronomy
	Sciences adapted to navigation and commerce
Legislation	Eloquence or rhetoric
Drawing	Penmanship

*According to No. 3, the course in natural philosophy and chemistry should be taught annually in each capital city, possibly because not all central schools could afford the necessary scientific apparatus.
†R. R. Palmer, *The Improvement of Humanity: Education and the French Revolution* (Princeton, NJ: Princeton University Press, 1985), 253. "General grammar presented an empirical philosophy derived from Condillac." Under the elective system, few students chose general grammar, and the professors ended up teaching elementary French grammar instead.

the capital of the United States. One of Washington's last wishes as president was to see a national university, and many education writers in the United States picked up that theme. The national university contained a number of schools, but specifics are not given in the reviewer's notes.

Both the Daunou Plan and No. 3 had a national body at the head of the educational pyramid. In the Daunou Plan, this was called the National Institute. Talleyrand had originally proposed a National Institute where the most learned of the country could teach and do research, but in the Daunou Plan, the members of the National Institute were not expected to teach. This National Institute was given the task of "collecting discoveries and improving the arts and sciences," and had more of a pure than applied science emphasis.[44] No. 3 had a parallel body called the Federal Institution, but its primary purpose was the administrative oversight of the national schools. Rather than being chosen by their peers as in the French National Institute, the members of the Federal Institution in No. 3 were to be elected "in the same manner as members of Congress were elected," and the rules they made had force of law once ratified by the president and the Senate. In contrast, the National Institute of the Daunou Plan had some responsibilities but little real political power. The huge amount of power given to the Federal Institution is one of the most unique features of No. 3. The author of No. 3 was well aware of the boldness of his plan in giving the Federal Institution so much power, and states that he hopes his plan would not be "offensive." Moreau de St. Mery, one of the reviewers of No. 3, commented that he thought "the director of the bureau in No. 3 was given too much power."[45] St. Mery also comments that in No. 3 government was too "intimately concerned" with the actual administration of teaching.[46] The Federal Institution of No. 3 was given broad powers over curriculum, regulating expenses, professors' salaries, and acquisition of property.

Another provision in No. 3 grants that "the President [of the national university] and the professors may consult on internal Regulations, but otherwise they shall conform to the Acts of the Federal Institution." Masters and mistresses of the primary schools were also required to take an oath to "observe the Rules enjoined by the Federal Institution." This emphasis on centralized power over academe in No. 3 caused me to question whether the author of No. 3 had an administrative background within a college or university, and had a vested interest in keeping faculty under control. This desire for control made me think again of the Reverend William Smith. Having achieved and lost his position as provost of the College of Philadelphia twice, he may have wanted to create a position for himself that would place him above the academe, which he felt had been so unfair to him.

No. 3 had another distinctive feature, which has a parallel in French education of the period: the call for a universal moral catechism to replace sectarian religious instruction in the schools, especially at the primary level. Before the Revolution in France, most schools were run by the Catholic Church and Catholic catechisms were the basis of moral instruction. Even before the French revolution, however, Baron d'Holbach, an atheist, wrote a secular moral catechism in 1765. This work was not published until 1790.[47] In France in 1796, the same year in which most of the entries were submitted for the American Philosophical Society Contest, the French government held a textbook contest. The winning entry in the category including republican catechisms was reprinted many times. These catechisms in general "showed a deist respectfulness for God, though with a dose of agnosticism."[48] No. 3 also shows this "deist respectfulness for God," by encouraging the acknowledgment of the "Supreme Creator," but makes it clear that religious instruction should be avoided in schools. Instead, the elected Federal Institution would compose a general moral catechism to replace sectarian religious instruction.[49] Another important aspect of French education at this time was the use of public festivals for general education and moral and political indoctrination.[50] Public festivals are conspicuously absent from the accounts of No. 3.

In his personal review of No. 3, Moreau de St. Mery commented that "[e]ducators of other nations had nothing in common with the staff of the Federal Institute," which indicates that St. Mery felt there were important differences between the Federal Institution of No. 3 and national education bodies in other countries.[51] So while similar in name to the national organization in France, the composition and duties of the Federal Institution in No. 3 were significantly different.

As a matter of practicality, it is unlikely that Talleyrand, Condorcet, or Daunou were the authors of No. 3. Talleyrand was a member of the APS and had lived in the United States from 1794 to 1796, but left Philadelphia on June 13, 1796,[52] and was therefore not in Philadelphia when No. 3 was submitted later that year.[53] Condorcet died in 1794. Daunou did not visit the United States to the best of my knowledge. But what about other French intellectuals living within the orbit of the APS?

The APS had a long history of admitting French intellectuals. Talleyrand, Buffon, Condorcet, Lavoisier, and many others were elected to membership.[54] Therefore, the membership included a significant number of Frenchmen who could have authored No. 3, although only a limited number were in Philadelphia at the time of the contest. Some had sought refuge there from the turmoil of the French Revolution or the slave uprisings in the West Indies.[55]

Of particular interest was one of the reviewers of No. 3—Moreau de St. Mery. St. Mery's journal is especially helpful for understanding the French in Philadelphia during this time. On May 25, 1797, St. Mery notes that he reviewed an essay for the APS education contest. Even though he does not identify the essay as No. 3, it was the only committee he belonged to.[56] Of particular interest is St. Mery's criticism that No. 3 required professors of the national university to become naturalized citizens, since "they have [already] been obliged to renounce their countries."[57] None of the other educational essays I read addressed the matter of foreign professors. The requirement for citizenship could either represent a concern over foreign influence on the part of an American author or the support of American nationalism on the part of a French author (see chapter 10 in this volume). However, this requirement would have excluded many French in Philadelphia from being involved in public education, and it is not clear that a Frenchman would have wanted to exclude his fellows from employment in this sector.

Other Frenchmen attending APS meetings during the contest period included Rochefoucauld-Liancourt, Alexander Lerebours, Palisot de Beauvois, Legeaux, and Constantin François de Volney.[58] Volney stood out from the rest on several accounts. He was accepted for membership at the same time as contest-winner Samuel Harrison Smith.[59] Volney was a famous historian and a member of the National Institute in France.[60] He would have been thoroughly familiar with the evolving French educational system during the 1790s. He was able to write in English, as evidenced by his letter of March 10, 1797, to Joseph Priestly.[61] According to St. Mery, Volney was in Philadelphia on September 22, 1796, and on January 20, 1797, so it is likely that Volney was also there in December 1796 when No. 3 was submitted.[62] Volney referred to George Washington as "the great Washington" twice in his book on the United States,[63] as did the author of No. 3.

Of particular interest is Volney's *The Ruins*, in which he examines the origins of various religions and advocates a catechism of morality based on natural law. Remember that No. 3 also advocates a moral catechism to be written by the National Institute for use in the schools. However, Volney discredits all religions in *The Ruins*, and the author of No. 3 seems to have at least a former sympathy for the Christian religion. Because of this affection for Christianity in No. 3 and Volney's more deist disposition, I do not think that No. 3 was written by Volney. It is possible that the author of No. 3 could have had access to Volney's *The Ruins*, which was written in French in 1793 and translated into English soon afterward, and that this book influenced the author to recommend a moral catechism.

Rev. William Smith

Another prominent educator living in Philadelphia at the time was the Reverend William Smith, an Anglican priest and member of the APS. He was born in Scotland in 1727. John Adams called him "soft, polite, insinuating, adulating, sensible, learned, industrious, indefatigable," and Ezra Stiles, president of Yale, labeled him "avaricious and covetous."[64] Although he frequently enraged both friends and enemies, Smith was brilliant, and probably the best orator in Philadelphia at the time.[65]

Smith immigrated to Long Island, New York, in 1751 to teach in the home of Josiah Martin. He returned to England in 1753 to obtain Episcopalian clerical orders, which improved his credentials as a classical educator.[66] Smith loved the classics, and was determined to preserve the time-honored traditions. In 1753 before he left for England, Smith wrote "A General Idea of the College of Mirania" in which he outlines an educational system for a mythical polity of "Mirania."[67] Smith advocated three years of primary school, a mechanics' school (in English), and a Latin school for college preparation, as well as the college.[68] The mechanics' school allowed for greater access to general education for those students who had no need for Latin in their future work. The dual-tiered structure of No. 3 is similar in general structure to Smith's plan for secondary schools, although No. 3 calls these secondary schools "central schools." In Smith's plan for Mirania, five years of Latin, English, and Greek study were necessary for college admission.[69]

In 1754, Benjamin Franklin hired Smith as a professor for his academy in Philadelphia, where Smith developed the College of Pennsylvania and became its first provost. The primary school, or Charity School of the College of Philadelphia, as well as the German schools, which Smith helped to organize in Pennsylvania, emphasized reading, writing, arithmetic, and religious instruction, which was "plain and practical, such as all Christians agree in."[70] This is reminiscent of the discussion in No. 3 of a "universal Christianity" as being previously the most valued source of morality in the schools.

After the Charity Schools, male students could advance to the English Academy, composed of the English, writing, and mathematics schools aimed toward education for practical professions such as navigation and commerce. Those aspiring to a liberal education advanced to Latin School, where Latin and Greek were begun. At the college, also known as the Philosophy School, the emphasis was on the classics and the learned arts and sciences, such as law, medicine, and natural philosophy. This is reminiscent of the dual-track curriculum seen in No. 3. Smith put more emphasis on the classics than Franklin had wanted in the college, which was one of several issues that put them at odds with each other.[71] Franklin was not the only person to dislike Smith. According to Charles J. Stille, Smith "made many enemies in the methods he adopted."[72]

The College of Philadelphia lost its state charter in 1779, and Smith lost his position as provost due to suspicions of his being a Loyalist. He fled to Chester, Maryland, where he started Washington College, named after George Washington. After restitution of the charter of the College of Philadelphia by the State Legislature of Pennsylvania, Smith returned to Philadelphia to once again assume the position of provost in 1789. He was soon released, however, when the College of Philadelphia and the University of the State of Pennsylvania merged in 1791 to form the University of Pennsylvania, and Smith therefore had the distinction of twice losing his position as provost of the College of Philadelphia.[73]

Smith had also been nominated for bishop of Maryland when he resided there, but was never formally consecrated. This also was a source of disappointment for Smith, which left him without the honors in his later years that he had so hoped to attain.

Smith would have had everything to gain by producing a winning essay in the APS contest. The anonymous nature of the contest would have allowed Smith to be recognized for his ideas without the political prejudices of his enemies that had plagued his career as both an educator and churchman. At the same time, he would have suffered additional public humiliation if he lost, so concealing his identity would have been desirable.

The tavern keeper to whom No. 3 was returned to protect the author's identity was Alex Moore. Smith had married into the Moore family of Moore Hall by tying the knot with Rebecca Moore, so Alex Moore could have been a relative of Smith. However, none of the available genealogies of the Moore family of Moore Hall in Pennsylvania contain an Alex or Alexander Moore. There was an Alexander Moore who was a mason in the Grand Lodge of Pennsylvania, as was Smith.[74] Smith was known as a drinker, and Moore's tavern was only two blocks from the APS and a similar distance to the College of Philadelphia, so it is probable that Smith knew Alex Moore whether he was a relative or not.[75]

The admiration the author of No. 3 had for George Washington is seen in his reference to the president as "The great Washington himself." The Reverend William Smith was enamored with Washington and sought many ways to ingratiate himself. Smith was an active member of the APS and secured Washington's membership in the society even though Washington was technically not qualified.[76] While Washington dealt graciously with Smith, the president avoided Smith whenever possible.[77]

Washington was a major proponent of a national university, and Smith supported the national university concept in a commencement speech for the graduates in medicine in 1790.[78] Even though he was now in his late sixties, Smith may have desired a post in the national university since he no longer held an academic appointment at the time of the contest. Smith's family, and possibly Smith himself, also stood to gain financially by the creation of a national university in Washington, DC. Smith's son-in-law, Samuel Blodgett, Jr., had invested "his entire fortune in the founding of the city of Washington and the establishment of a national university."[79] If Smith had coincidentally been assigned to review his own essay in the contest, he would have been in a position that would have forced his withdrawal. In fact, Smith did withdraw as a reviewer for unknown reasons.

There are similarities between Smith's ideas and those in No. 3 in regard to religion as well. Smith was an Anglican clergyman and espoused traditional Christian doctrine in his eloquent sermons. But Smith's desire to see a "short system of religious and civic truths and duties, in the Socratic or catechetic way" used in the German schools in the 1757 does sound similar to the desire for a moral catechism in No. 3.[80] Smith wrote prayers for the College of Philadelphia, and conducted Anglican services there but students of all faiths were encouraged to attend.[81] There were no official religion courses, and "readings focused on ethics and on deist views of the universe authored by a variety of authors."[82] Geiger and Sorber note that the mandatory prayers that began and ended the day at the College of Philadelphia were "merely a formality" and that "revealed religion was as much an afterthought at Philadelphia as at the College of Mirania."[83] So it is possible that while Smith spoke Christian doctrine in his sermons, he desired a more deist approach in the schools to avoid sectarian conflict.

Another possible connection from No. 3 to the Reverend William Smith is a Latin inscription, which was marked on the outside of the envelope for

No. 3. This inscription reads: "Tu modo nascenti puero, quo ferrea primum desinet ac toto surget gens aurea mundo casta fave Lucina." This is a quote from Virgil's most famous Eclogue, Eclogue 4. Here is a translation of this inscription in its immediate context (italics mine):

> The last great age the Sibyl's song foretold
> Rolls around: the centuries are born anew!
> The maid returns, old Saturn's reign returns
> Offspring of heaven, a hero's race descends.
> *Now as the babe is born, with whom iron men*
> *Shall cease, and golden men spread through the world*
> *Bless him, chaste goddess*; now your Apollo reigns.
> Begin their courses, Pollio, with you
> As consul, and all traces of our crimes
> Annulled release earth from continual fear.[84]

Therefore, in the inscription of No. 3, a baby is born and "golden men" will spread through the world. Alpers explains that Virgil beseeches the chaste goddess, Lucina, the goddess of childbirth, to bless this first fruit of a new order.[85] Alpers also points out that Eclogue 4 has been a source of standardized forms from the classical Greek for representing a coming golden age more generally.[86]

Virgil's Eclogue 4 would have been very familiar to the Reverend William Smith as a classics professor, and likely inspired some of his own poetry. In *A General Idea of the College of Mirania*, Smith includes a set of verses used at the opening of the fictional College. These verses employ golden age imagery regarding the coming of a heroic race, including men of science and literature. Rapturously, the poet foresees "Golden Days" featuring future Bacons, Newtons, Lockes, Popes, and Spencers arising as a result of the educational endeavors of the College of Mirania, a fictional place that allegorically represented New York. Wisdom and knowledge would bring peace, civilize the Indian, and abolish slavery, continuing until "Life-endearing Knowledge covers all."[87]

This set of Smith's verses also reappears at the opening of Washington College in 1783 in Maryland.[88] The theme of a golden race remains and is strengthened in the newer rendition of Smith's verses for Washington College. But he alters some of the lines. Rather than "Gospel-Truth," dissipating "Pagan-Error" as in *Mirania*, now "Peace and Science" disperse "War and Error."[89] This is additional evidence that over time Smith may have advocated an increasingly secular view of education.

A footnote to the verses for Washington College makes the interesting observation that these verses, with some changes, were used three times; once at the opening of the fictional College of Mirania, the second time at the opening of another college (probably the College of Philadelphia), and the third time at the opening of Washington College. Therefore, if Smith wrote educational essay No. 3, the verses might be expected to be found there again. But they do not, and one could argue they could not, without giving away the identity of the author. If Smith wrote No. 3, he may have used the Latin inscription from Eclogue 4 as a substitute, since it was likely an inspiration for Smith's own verse and would not by itself identify the author. While this is an intriguing possibility, Virgil's Eclogue 4 was so widely influential that another author could have chosen it as well. Therefore, while the inscription for No. 3 would be highly consistent with authorship by Smith, it is not definitive evidence of his authorship.

When the review committees were assigned, Smith was assigned to review No. 3. One can imagine his chagrin if he was assigned his own essay to review! After a prolonged period of not acting on No. 3, he withdrew from the review committee. This would have been his only choice if he had written No. 3, as it would have eventually become apparent that he was not an impartial reviewer. Of course, this is speculation, but it is consistent with the possibility of Smith's identity as the author of No. 3. There was also a second delay in the contest after Smith withdrew. If the review committee perceived that it was Smith that authored No. 3, they may have had difficulty deciding how to handle an entry from this controversial educator. In the end, the review committee decided to take a detached attitude toward No. 3, and the APS awarded the prize jointly to essays No. 1 and 2.

At the very next meeting, January 5, 1798, the Society appointed a committee to "consider the propriety of drafting an advertisement offering again a Premium for the best essay on Public Education."[90] Apparently the APS was not completely satisfied with the results of the first contest. On March 2, 1798, the committee proposed several principles that should be addressed in the new essays, including the public duty to provide education for the impoverished and attention to Latin and Greek.[91] The committee did not report again until February 15, 1799, when it proposed the following:

1. A five-person essay review committee would be formed through an announced election.
2. No one who wanted to enter the contest should accept election.
3. Committee members could only resign within the first two months after the election.
4. Papers would be held unopened until March 1800, and then be reviewed and reported on within two months.[92]

The specificity of these requirements suggested that they addressed difficulties with the first contest. Apparently the way reviewers were appointed to committees was unsatisfactory in the first contest and a scheduled election was chosen instead. The second requirement suggested that an appointed reviewer in the first contest had also submitted an essay, which I suggest Smith had done. The third requirement suggests that Smith's resignation four months after his appointment was not appreciated, and I have suggested that he resigned because he was inadvertently assigned to review his own essay. The last requirement supports my assertion that the delays in reporting the results were irregular. All of this evidence further suggests that Reverend Smith did indeed write No. 3.

Conclusion

In this study, I explored various themes in educational writing of the early republic and discovered that the subject of dead languages was useful in distinguishing writers from each other since most writers had definitive views on the subject. This criterion was insufficient, however, for an identification of the author of No. 3. Issues of religion, governance, and school hierarchy were useful, but also insufficient to solve the mystery. As the study progressed, the possible French influence on No. 3 became apparent. I think that it is probable that the writer of No. 3 was knowledgeable of French education. I also think it is highly probable that the writer was familiar with the dual curriculum of English and Latin schools as instituted by the Reverend William Smith. Taken together, Smith's positions as a Philadelphia educator, classics scholar, early member of the APS, Charity School founder, twice-ousted college provost, churchman denied consecration as bishop, politically controversial character, likely acquaintance of Alex Moore, and enamored follower of George Washington create a portrait of a man that very well could have authored No. 3 himself.

Notes

1. Benjamin Justice, "'The Great Contest': The American Philosophical Society Education Prize of 1795," *American Journal of Education* 115 (February 2008): 203.
2. Review of Essay No. 3, American Philosophical Society, Philadelphia, PA.
3. Moreau de St. Mery, *Moreau de St. Mery's American Journey 1793–1798*, trans. Kenneth Roberts and Anna Roberts (Garden City, NY: Doubleday & Company, Inc., 1947), 232.
4. American Philosophical Society, Early Proceedings of the American Philosophical Society for the Promotion of Useful Knowledge; Complied by One of the Secretaries; from the Manuscript Minutes of its Meetings from 1744 to 1838 (Philadelphia, PA: McCalla & Stavely, 1884), 245–265. http://archive.org/stream/earlyproceedings1884ameruoft#page/244/mode/2up (accessed July 28, 2012).
5. Robert Coram, "Political Inquiries: To Which Is Added, a Plan for the General Establishment of Schools throughout the United States," in *Essays on Education in the Early Republic* (Cambridge, MA: The Belknap Press of Harvard University Press, 1965), 141.
6. Samuel Harrison Smith, "Remarks on Education: Illustrating the Close Connection between Virtue and Wisdom," in *Essays on Education in the Early Republic*, 212.
7. Noah Webster, "On the Education of Youth in America," in *Essays on Education in the Early Republic*, 48.
8. Noah Webster, *Dissertations on the English Language* (Gainesville, FL: Scholars' Facsimiles & Reprints, 1951), 20–21.

9. Ruth Watts, "Joseph Priestley (1733–1804)," *Prospects: The Quarterly Review of Comparative Education* (Paris, UNESCO: International Bureau of Education) 24:1–2 (1994): 343–353.

10. Benjamin Rush, "A Plan for the Establishment of Public Schools and the Diffusion of Knowledge in Pennsylvania; To Which Are Added, Thoughts upon the Mode of Education, Proper in a Republic," in *Essays on Education in the Early Republic*, 5. See also Benjamin Rush, "To Friends of the Federal Government: A Plan for a Federal University," in *Letters of Benjamin Rush* (Princeton, NJ: Princeton University Press, 1951), 1:491–495.

11. Benjamin Rush, "Of the Mode of Education Proper in a Republic," in *Essays, Literary, Moral and Philosophical* (Philadelphia, PA: Thomas & Samuel F. Bradford, 1798), 6–20.

12. Benjamin Rush, "Observations Upon the Study of the Latin and Greek Languages, as a Branch of Liberal Education, with Hints of a Plan of Liberal Instruction, without Them, Accommodated to the Present State of Society, Manners, and Government in the United States," in *Essays, Literary, Moral and Philosophical*, 23.

13. Benjamin Rush to John Adams, October 2, 1810, *The Spur of Fame: Dialogues of John Adams and Benjamin Rush 1805–1813*, ed. John A. Schutz and Douglass Adair (Indianapolis, IL: Liberty Fund, 1966), 183.

14. Lawrence A. Cremin, *American Education: The National Experience 1783–1876* (New York: Harper & Row, Publishers, 1980), 388–389.

15. Samuel Knox, "An Essay on the Best System of Liberal Education, Adapted to the Genius of the Government of the United States," in *Essays on Education in the Early Republic*, 338–343.

16. John Adams to Thomas Jefferson, July 16, 1814, in *The Adams-Jefferson Letters, Vol. II*, ed. Lester J. Cappon (Chapel Hill, NC: The University of North Carolina Press, 1959), 438.

17. John Adams to Benjamin Rush, September 16, 1810, in *The Spur of Fame*, 182.

18. John Adams to Benjamin Rush, January 18, 1811, in *The Spur of Fame*, 192.

19. Carl J. Richard, *The Founders and the Classics: Greece, Rome, and the American Enlightenment* (Cambridge, MA: Harvard University Press, 1994), 34.

20. Cameron Addis, *Jefferson's Vision for Education 1740–1845* (New York: Peter Lang, 2003), 62, 116.

21. Richard, *The Founders and the Classics*, 24–26.

22. James B. Conant, *Thomas Jefferson and the Development of American Public Education* (Berkeley, CA: University of California Press, 1962), 15.

23. According to historian Kim Tolley, the classics persisted as a central part of male education because of four reasons: they remained part of the entrance requirements at most colleges; prestige was associated with that knowledge; professors perpetuated the status quo since they were not trained in the sciences themselves; and there were limited job prospects in science at the time. See Kim Tolley, *The Science Education of American Girls: A Historical Perspective* (New York: RoutledgeFalmer, 2003), 49–50.

24. Benjamin Franklin, "Observations Relative to the Intentions of the Original Founders of the Academy in Philadelphia, June, 1789," in Jared Sparks

(ed.), *The Works of Benjamin Franklin* (Boston, MA: Hilliard, Gray and Company, 1840), 147.

25. American Philosophical Society, "About the APS," American Philosophical Society website, http://www.amphilsoc.org/about/ (accessed September 22, 2010). See also John Adams, *Diary and Autobiography of John Adams Volume 3*, ed. L. H. Butterfield (Cambridge, MA: Belknap Press of Harvard University Press, 1962), 248, fn1. No. 3 was submitted in December 1796.

26. Albert Castel, "The Founding Fathers and the Vision of a National University," *History of Education Quarterly* 4:4 (1964): 283.

27. Ibid., 288.

28. John Adams to Thomas Jefferson, July 15, 1814, in *The Adams-Jefferson Letters Vol. II*, 438.

29. John Adams to Thomas Jefferson, July 19, 1815, in *The Adams-Jefferson Letters, Vol. II*, 444.

30. John Adams to John Jebb, September 10, 1785, in *The Works of John Adams, Second President of the United States: Official Letters, Messages, and Public Papers, 1797–1801*, Vol. IX, ed. Charles Francis Adams (Boston, MA: Little Brown and Company, 1854), 540.

31. St. Mery, *Moreau de St. Mery's American Journey*, 253.

32. Pierre Samuel DuPont de Nemours, *National Education in the United States*, trans. B. G. DuPont (Newark, DE: University of Delaware Press, 1923).

33. DuPont de Nemours states in his preface that "[t]his treatise, was written in 1800, at the request of Mr. Jefferson…it had the approval of that great statesman and of his worthy successor." This implies that Jefferson agreed with everything written therein, which may have been wishful thinking on the part of DuPont. *National Education in the United States of America* was not printed in English until 1923.

34. Jefferson to DuPont de Nemours, April 12, 1800, in Correspondence between Thomas Jefferson and Pierre Samuel Du Pont de Nemours 1798–1817, 8–9.

35. See B. G. Du Pont's "Introduction" in Pierre Samuel Du Pont de Nemours, *National Education in the United States*, xiii. Also see Ian Bartram, "The Political Origins of Secular Public Education: The New York School Controversy, 1840–1842," *N. Y. U. Journal of Law and Liberty* 3:2 (2008): 275. Also at http://works.bepress.com/cgi/viewcontent.cgi?article=1000&context=ian_bartrum (accessed September 23, 2012).

36. Conant, *Thomas Jefferson and the Development of American Public Education*, 24–25. This bill died in committee. See also Castel, "The Founding Fathers and the Vision of a National University," 288.

37. DuPont de Nemours, National Education in the United States.

38. Jefferson to Nemours, December 12, 1800, Correspondence between Thomas Jefferson and Pierre Samuel DuPont de Nemours 1798–1817, 26.

39. R. R. Palmer, *The Improvement of Humanity: Education and the French Revolution* (Princeton, NJ: Princeton University Press, 1985), 230. The Daunou law is formally entitled the Law of 3 Brumaire of the Year IV.

40. Information in this section regarding the Daunou Plan as well as the plans of Talleyrand and Condorcet were taken from Palmer, *The Improvement of Humanity*.

41. The French central schools were decreed by the Convention in February 1795 and were incorporated into the Daunou Plan later that year.

42. Talleyrand asserted that after primary school, it would be "a real madness, or a cruel kindness, to make them all go through the several levels of an instruction that would be useless and hence harmful to most" (ibid., 97).

43. Ibid., 232.

44. Ibid., 231.

45. St. Mery, *Moreau de St. Mery's American Journey*, 232.

46. Ibid.

47. Baron d'Holbach, *Elements de la Morale Universelle, ou Catechism Universelle*. (Paris: Chez De Bure, 1790). Translation for marxists.org by Mitch Abidor, 2006. http://www.marxists.org/reference/archive/holbach/1765/catechism.htm (accessed June 29, 2010).

48. Palmer, *The Improvement of Humanity*, 239.

49. Interestingly, Noah Webster published his own Federal and Moral Catechism in 1798 as part of *The American Spelling Book*. http://edweb.sdsu.edu/people/DKitchen/new_655/webster_catechism.htm (accessed July 10, 2010).

50. Palmer, *The Improvement of Humanity*, 231.

51. St. Mery, *Moreau de St. Mery's American Journey*, 232–233.

52. Ibid., 214.

53. Of course, Talleyrand could have written No. 3 in France and sent it to a friend in Philadelphia to submit, but Moreau de St. Mery was a very close friend of Talleyrand, and nothing in St. Mery's memoir indicates Talleyrand's involvement with the APS contest.

54. Rosengarten, "The Early French Members of the American Philosophical Society," 87–93. See also: Gilbert Chinard, "The American Philosophical Society and the World of Science (1768–1800)," *Proceedings of the American Philosophical Society* 87:1 (July 14, 1943): 1–11.

55. Allan Potofsky, "The 'Non-Aligned Status' of French Émigrés and Refugees in Philadelphia, 1793–1798," *Transatlantica* 2 (2006), http://transatlantica.revues.org/index1147.html (accessed June 30, 2010).

56. Since St. Mery critically reviewed No. 3 in his journal it follows that St. Mery was not the author of No. 3.

57. St. Mery, *Moreau de St. Mery's American Journey*, 232.

58. American Philosophical Society, Minute Book, Entries for December 30, 1796, to December 15, 1797, APS Archives.

59. Rosengarten erroneously states that Volney was elected in 1799. See Rosengarten, "The Early French Members of the American Philosophical Society," 87–93.

60. St. Mery, *Moreau de St. Mery's American Journey*, 221.

61. Joseph Priestly wrote a pamphlet in opposition to Volney's *The Ruins*, and Volney's reply can be found at http://knarf.english.upenn.edu/Volney/vanswer.html (accessed September 23, 2012).

62. Institut Français de L'Éducation, "Volney," http://translate.googleusercontent.com/translate_c?hl=en&sl=fr&u=http://www.inrp.fr/edition-electronique/lodel/dictionnaire-ferdinand-buisson/document.php?id=3805 (accessed October 2, 2010).

63. C. F. Volney, *A View of Climate and Soil of the United States of America: to which are annexed some accounts of Florida, the French colony on the Scioto,*

certain Canadian colonies and the savages or natives (London, C. Mercier and Co. 6, Northumberland-Court, 1804): vii, 465.

64. Thomas Firth Jones, *A Pair of Lawn Sleeves: A Biography of William Smith (1727–1803)* (Philadelphia, PA: Chilton Book Company, 1972), 2–3.

65. The Reverend William Smith, known for his oratory skills, was chosen to deliver a eulogy for Benjamin Franklin by the American Philosophical Society in 1791, a year after Franklin's death. This is ironic because Franklin and Smith had been political enemies for decades according to Nian-Sheng Huang, *Benjamin Franklin in American Thought and Culture, 1790–1900* (Philadelphia, PA: American Philosophical Society, 1994), 28–30.

66. Mary D. McConaghy, Michael Silberman, and Irina Kalashnikova, "Penn in the 18th Century: William Smith," University of Pennsylvania Archives, http://www.archives.upenn.edu/people/1700s/smith_wm.html (accessed January 26, 2010).

67. William Smith, *A General Idea of the College of Mirania* (New York: J. Parker and W. Weyman, 1753), http://sceti.library.upenn.edu/sceti/printedbooksNew/index.cfm?textID=ac7_sm683_753g&PagePosition=1 (accessed February 27, 2012).

68. Franklin had published a plan for an English school in Philadelphia to which Smith referred in his treatise on Mirania. It was entitled *Idea of an English School* (Philadelphia, PA: B. Franklin and D. Hall, at the Post Office, 1751). Also at http://www.historycarper.com/resources/twobf2/school.htm (accessed February 27, 2012).

69. William Smith, *A General Idea of the College of Mirania*, 16..

70. Horace Wemyss Smith, *Life and Correspondence of the Rev. William Smith, D.D.*, Vol. I and II (New York: Arno Press, 1972), I 39.

71. McConaghy, Silberman, and Kalashnikova, "Penn in the 18th Century."

72. Charles J. Stille, *A Memoir of The Rev. William Smith, D.D., Provost of the College, Academy and Charitable School of Philadelphia* (Philadelphia, PA: Moore & Bond, 1860), 61.

73. John Ewing, the provost of the University of the State of Pennsylvania, became the head of the new University of Pennsylvania. See Mary D. McConaghy, Michael Silberman, and Irina Kalashnikova, "Penn in the 18th Century: Introduction," University of Pennsylvania Archives, http://www.archives.upenn.edu//histy/features/1700s/penn1700s.html____(accessed September 28, 2010).

74. Reprint of the Minutes of the Grand Lodge of Free and Accepted Masons of Pennsylvania Volume 1 (Philadelphia, PA: Grand Lodge of Pennsylvania, 1875), 418.

75. Jones, *A Pair of Lawn Sleeves*, 53–54.

76. Ibid., 136.

77. Ibid., 133–137.

78. William Reiss Peters, "The Contribution of William Smith, 1727–1803, to the Development of Higher Education in the United States" (PhD diss., University of Michigan, 1968), 213. In 1790, both the College of Philadelphia and the University of Pennsylvannia had medical programs, and it is not clear from Peters's dissertation at which one Smith spoke.

79. Smith, *Life and Correspondence of the Rev. William Smith, D.D.*, II:514–519.

80. Rev. William Smith to the Society for the Propagation of the Gospel, December 13, 1757. In ibid., I:34.
81. Roger L. Geiger and Nathan M. Sorber, "Tarnished Icon: William Smith and the College of Philadelphia," *Iconic Leaders in Higher Education* (Piscataway, NJ: Transaction Publishers, 2011), 6, http://books.google.com/books?vid=978-1-4128-1859-9&printsec=frontcover#v=snippet&q=Prayers%20for%20the%20Use%20of%20the%20Philadelphia%20Academy%20&f=false (accessed March 1, 2012).
82. McConaghy, Silberman, and Kalashnikova, "Penn in the 18th Century."
83. Geiger and Sorber, "Tarnished Icon," 9.
84. Virgil, Eclogue 4. See Paul Alpers, *The Singer of the Eclogues: A Study of Virgilian Pastoral* (Berkeley, CA: University of California Press, 1979), 27. http://books.google.com/books?id=wXxmU8a2tMEC&pg=PA4&lpg=PA4&dq=the+singer+of+the+eclogue&source=bl&ots=gGJ9XtYdMW&sig=mSXu-A_uvY3qrCot02eRhxuYqBY&hl=en&ei=QoNbTcS7CpOssAP1nrGdCg&sa=156#v=onepage&q=the%20singer%20of%20the%20eclogue&f=false (accessed January 27, 2012).
85. Alpers, *The Singer of the Eclogues*, 162. This Eclogue was written between 42 and 38 BC, and was considered by Dante and others to be a prophesy of Jesus Christ.
86. Ibid., 161.
87. Smith, *A General Idea of the College of Mirania*, 7.
88. Charles Smith, "The Valedictory Oration," delivered at the first Commencement at Washington College, May 14, 1793, An Account of Washington College, in the State of Maryland, published by order of the Visitors and Governors of the said college, for the information of its friends and benefactors (printed by Joseph Crukshank, 1784), 31–36.
89. Ibid., 34.
90. American Philosophical Society, Early Proceedings of the American Philosophical Society for the Promotion of Useful Knowledge; Complied by One of the Secretaries; from the Manuscript Minutes of its Meetings from 1744 to 1838 (Philadelphia, PA: McCalla & Stavely, 1884), 266. http://archive.org/stream/earlyproceedings1884ameruoft#page/266 (accessed July 28, 2012).
91. American Philosophical Society. Minute Book, Entry for March 2, 1798. APS Archives.
92. American Philosophical Society. Minute Book, Entry for February 15, 1799. APS Archives.

CHAPTER 3

"Raked from the Rubbish": Stylometric Authorship Attribution and the 1795 American Philosophical Society Education Contest

Eric Strome

This study attributes two pseudonymous entries to the American Philosophical Society's 1795 education essay contest by employing conventional historical methods for the first, and a progression of stylometric measures and statistical techniques for the second. New knowledge of who participated in the educational conversation of the early republic is worthwhile in its own right, but it is also offered with a view toward understanding how stylometric analysis and corpus linguistics can contribute to historical argumentation and debate. It reports its methods and conclusions with a transparency characteristic of only the most recent stylometric studies, with the threefold hope that (1) standardization and even replicability will characterize future efforts; (2) nonspecialists will be emboldened to undertake similar work; and (3) recommendations for best practices will prove useful.

INTRODUCTION

The postrevolutionary period was pregnant with new possibilities in all aspects of the American experiment, and intellectually and politically engaged citizens from the Founding Fathers echelon to the franchised and beyond were absorbed with the question of whether and how the fragile American experiment might perpetuate itself. Given republican ideals about democracy and an intelligent and informed citizenry, few possibilities were understood to be as momentous as the opportunity to reconsider, revise, even rewrite, the educational landscape of the emerging nation. As Bernard Bailyn put it, "Education had been dislodged from its ancient position in the social order...and cast as a matter for deliberation into the forefront of consciousness."[1] It was from within this critical moment that the American Philosophical Society (APS), via its 1795 education essay contest premium, solicited proposals for a system of education equal to the unprecedented and angst-ridden historical task felt so keenly by the postrevolutionary generation.

The prompt drafted by the APS requested "an essay on a system of liberal education, and literary instruction, adapted to the genius of the government, and best calculated to promote the general welfare of the United States; comprehending, also, a plan for instituting and conducting public schools in this country on principles of the most extensive utility."[2] The APS received only seven submissions; none were judged ideal. The entries fell into two groups—three real contenders for the premium, and four pretenders of dubious quality. Of the contenders, the entries by Samuel Knox and Samuel Harrison Smith were judged by the review committees to be worthy enough to split the premium and a third, dubbed No. 3, received a positive review. The four remaining entries were the pretenders, submitted under the pseudonyms Academicus, Freedom, Hand,[3] and Hiram. The five entries not awarded the APS premium languished in varying levels of historical obscurity, mentioned only in the most exhaustive surveys of educational history.[4] The import of the contest itself rather than the winning efforts has been recently demonstrated, but of the losing entries only the four pseudonymous essays survive, their authors unknown due to the manner in which the APS conducted blind reviews.[5]

Much has been made of the two winning essays in the educational history of the early republic, such that Knox and Smith have been regarded as among the canonical educational thinkers of the period.[6] The place of these winning essayists in such a canon, indeed the very notion of a meaningful canonical standard for early republican educational thought, has been challenged convincingly. A handful of men should not be understood as representative of the scope of educational thought, especially given counterevidence unknown or ignored by early educational historians claiming representative status.[7] Yet the notion of a canonical expression or set of expressions of republican educational thought differs from a claim of representativeness, however conflated these claims were in the historians' judgments establishing and perpetuating canonical or representative status. This begs the question: who else contributed to the conversation beyond the elite men whose thoughts and publications survive? How did their contributions compare with those who have become canonical figures in early republican educational thought?

The contributions to this volume address these questions and more, but even before leaving the APS archives some new knowledge was already discovered. Just like other learned societies of the transatlantic world, the APS offered many premiums, and few were as lofty as its education premium. One gets a sense of the abject scientific applications with which its members were occupied when Jefferson refers to one of the papers on agricultural practices that made it to the Society's table as "a charming treatise on manures."[8] Among such submissions for other premiums I found a proposal for a method of calculating longitude submitted for the 1800 APS Magellanic premium under the pseudonym Hiram. A second version also survives dated 1803 that included the author's name, Francis Hoskins.[9] Having cooperatively judged the handwriting of these proposals as identical to Hiram's contest essay handwriting, the first attribution was achieved without leaving the archive. Hiram was Francis Hoskins, a local Philadelphia accountant and Freemason, who published only two other works known to the world's libraries.[10]

That Hoskins does not publish further on educational matters is unsurprising given that his submission for the APS premium was rather poor. As noted derisively in his review, Hoskins made overly practical suggestions such as a physical building with doors and windows. While the considerable variation in schools as well as the existence of itinerant schoolmasters in this period may be reason to forgive the simplicity of his proposals, Hoskins certainly had not appreciated the purpose or scope of the APS essay prompt. His recommendation to allot a plot of land as a funding scheme was characteristic of a seventeenth-century English system in which rents were paid for scarce plots; such an arrangement had no lasting potential in an eighteenth-century America with practically limitless acreage.

By virtue of length Hoskins's essay was the least serious, being one-fourth as long as the other submissions derided by the committee assigned to review the pretenders. Nevertheless it stands with the remaining anonymous entries as a counterpoint to the lofty vision of the overly specific essay prompt. It also provides evidence that even an accountant was concerned with education and its purpose in a republic. If the remaining anonymous authors could also be identified, what other occupations or demographic categories might be represented among them, and with what implications for knowledge about who contributed to educational thought in the early republic?

To provide further new evidence for this question, this study employed computer-aided statistical methods to attempt to identify the four remaining anonymous authors. Beyond that, a second aim was to try to bridge the gap between traditional and nontraditional authorship attribution studies, and in so doing address the question of whether statistical differentiation among authors produces substantive knowledge worth having.[11]

A First Pass: Content Analysis

Tilting at this particular windmill required some decidedly nonhistorical work. The most general method for quantifying a spoken or written communication is content analysis, an "empirically grounded method" that "entails a systematic reading of a body of texts, images, and symbolic matter" most often used during the twentieth century in the analysis of newspapers and propaganda. It is not so much a method as an entire field that has proliferated to such an extent over the twentieth century as to render its name practically meaningless. Four subfields, namely, discourse analysis, rhetorical analysis, conversation analysis, and corpus linguistics, have emerged that are tailored for use with their eponymous modes of communication.[12] Corpus linguistics, with its construction of a body of text against which another text is compared, is the most consistent with traditional historical methods and initially seemed the most appropriate for solving the riddle of APS essay authorship.

After compiling a small pilot corpus of educational writing from the period I used the Wordsmith[13] program to make the systematic count of the words in the corpus characteristic of content analysis, including word lists for the entire corpus along with each text, varied groups of texts, and subdivisions of texts necessary for some of the tests described in subsequent sections. Based upon these word lists Wordsmith can then make concordances, that is, lists of selected words and all their occurrences within the corpus or chosen text. It can also compute keyness, a simple measure largely of subject used in determining the key words that figure prominently in the metadata on which database subject searches rely. The preliminary results of an analysis based on such direct counts of contextual words were disappointing. While one could accurately state that Academicus used "knowledge" 16 times versus Freedom's 11, or that the terms from the APS essay prompt such as "liberal" or "government" figure more prominently in a list of key words for those responding to the APS prompt than those writing in other contexts, there is little use to be made of such comparisons when the task is authorship attribution.

STYLOMETRY

Thankfully, another possibility more closely tailored to the needs of identifying the anonymous authors emerged—stylometry, or the mathematical measuring of literary style. Indeed there have been many authorship attribution studies that aimed to settle authorship disputes, following both traditional literary methods and nontraditional methods admitting the use of statistical procedures on measured textual features, including the recent and increasing use of computers.

There have been three large-scale episodes to the use of these methods. First were the earliest rudimentary efforts of the nineteenth century to apply the new discipline of probabilistic statistics to anything and everything, including words. The almost prohibitive labor required for hand counts kept text lengths short and sample sizes small. This first period lacked meaningful results other than Zipf's Law, which established a basic log-linear relationship between the ordinal ranks and frequencies of a word list in any natural language.[14] Second came the comparatively powerful computing machines and an era of few, yet substantial and high-profile results, the Federalist Papers attribution by Mosteller and Wallace being the classic.[15] Currently, the possibilities have never been greater, limited only by the still laborious preparation of data. The preparation of texts for analysis is becoming more automated, as evidenced by data mining scripts scouring the Internet for consumer preferences and attitude research, or by the ready availability of scanners and optical character recognition software routinely operating at high levels of accuracy that are only increasing. Of course, the preparation of literary and historical data is not high on the priority list of analyses put to marketing or political purposes, so anything unpublished, and consequently most historical sources, must still be transcribed. But there is little stopping the assembly and maintenance of a text archive that, speaking relative to the history of the discipline, is larger and more powerful by orders of magnitude than anything for which early stylometers might have wished.

If stylometry measures textual variables from a corpus of text, what constitutes a corpus and how is it compiled? Some of the oldest corpora are those used in the analysis of the Pentateuch and its authors, or the Pauline Epistles, and these are followed by literary corpora such as the Shakespeare Corpus among others. Relatively recent additions, notably the million-word Brown Corpus of the early 1960s, aimed to be systematic and, as editing continued, as transparent as possible, revealing coding schemes for parts of speech and the like. As the discipline developed, corpora proliferated, and there are now standard usage sets for both British and American English whose word counts run upward of one hundred million words. Available since 2011, the Google Books Ngram Corpus compiled words from eight million *books*—over 861 *billion* words—from eight languages over five centuries, which by their reckoning constitutes 6 percent of all books ever published.[16] These promising developments for researchers are not limited to the practically infinite; there are ready-to-download niche corpora, which virtually eliminate the upfront labor involved should one wish to study further a set of texts already compiled—say German versus Polish novels (among many other possible languages and genres). There are even benchmark data sets for use in artificial studies whose sole purpose is experimenting with or refining methods.[17]

Because of this unprecedented availability of data, contemporary methods demand larger counts of words per text, and more texts per author, but these demands have not yet coalesced into best practices for data collection because they are outpaced by the next bigger digitization project. Unfortunately for historians, increasing data availability does not extend to corpora assembled for historical as opposed to linguistic purposes. Historical corpora are comparatively harder, if not impossible, to find, and if found are unlikely to be appropriate to the period(s) and place(s) of any given research question(s). Furthermore, the indexing of readily available data is not yet standardized, such that separating discrete authors or texts from such gargantuan sets as Google's does not seem possible, and in any case would be more laborious than assembling a corpus tailored to one's research needs.

The Corpus

I compiled the corpus used in this authorship attribution study specifically for it, and in keeping with the literature, all word counts referred to here use the distinction between tokens and types. Each unique word is a type, and each discrete occurrence of any type is a token, such that adding the raw frequencies of each type gives the total token count. The token count cannot be less than the type count, is almost always much larger, and would be identical for a text, say a short poem, made up entirely of single-occurring words. It should be noted that the boundary of a word is not without debate. The simplest examples are a place name, such as New York City, or any contraction, for which arguments can be made to count as either one or separate tokens. The way programs deal with hyphens and apostrophes also affects word counts. In keeping with the practice of the field, the counts in this corpus have worried only about internal consistency rather than trying to match the varied practices of other studies.

Not counting the anonymous entries to the contest, the corpus comprises 940,471 tokens across 24,493 types from 27 authors and 64 texts, excerpts, or groups of letters. Almost all of the texts fall between 1790 and 1803 with a handful necessary to augment authorial sets extending as early as 1753.[18] In theory, a corpus is limited only to the literary or philosophical connections among texts and authors, and the rationale for including texts began with educational writings of respectable length, that is, several thousand words at a minimum, that were as close as possible to the APS contest years. In practice, compiling a corpus remains limited by obstacles, the first of which in this case is that the ideal text is almost invariably not the one that an online full text resource has already digitized. A second difficulty is that limiting texts to explicitly educational writing left some authorial sets too small. Therefore, supplemental texts for the authors in question were chosen to fill out the authorial sets, and the attempt was made to keep these within the essay genre. The danger of genre effects being statistically more prominent than the desired authorial effects is real, and so many shorter letters were added to authorial sets in order to even those genre effects out.

For example, one feature of the Addisonian essay genre popular at the time was the enumeration and discussion of historical examples, best exemplified in this corpus by John Adams's discussion of Sparta. Occurring 67 times across the noun, adjective, and plural forms in which it appears, Adams's discussion of that example far outpaces anyone else in the corpus: Joseph Priestley uses it 10 times in roughly the same length of text, and others use it once or not at all. Were one to construct a probability table comparing Adams's rate to the rate in the corpus based on the appropriate statistical distribution—the Poisson distribution for rare events—the probabilities would be so skewed as to indicate an alarming authorial marker. Doing the same for Hand's essay, which refers to the "Spartan model" once in roughly three thousand words, would produce a similarly outrageous Poisson probability leading to a facile and erroneous attribution of Hand's essay to Adams, especially considering that others make use of that conventional example as well.

Among the authors (followed by their corresponding token counts) included in the corpus are canonical figures in the history of education in the early republic: Robert Coram (11,792), Samuel DuPont deNemours

(31,443), Simeon Doggett (5,792), Louis Amable-Rose Lafite duCorteil (15,808), Benjamin Rush (20,074), Noah Webster (47,193), and the two APS education premium winners Samuel Knox (33,268) and Samuel Harrison Smith (17,828). Adding to the canonical material from Europe are excerpts from David Hume (7,758) and a later English translation of Immanuel Kant (6,114). Representing the Founding Fathers are Thomas Jefferson (65,771), John Adams (98,014), George Washington (16,237), and Benjamin Franklin (2,308), all of whom are included as less likely candidates (or in Franklin's case, an impossible candidate, given that he died five years prior to the contest) in order to provide a robust check on the attributions. Federalist Papers authors Alexander Hamilton (53,687), James Madison (47,391), and John Jay (6,088) are present, all of whom Douglas Adair calls masters "of that Addisonian prose style which had all but standardized the tone of eighteenth century essays."[19] Joseph Priestley (100,406) is included as a likely attribution candidate, along with William Smith (43,770), Constantin-Francois de Volney (49,269), and John Hobson (26,640). Adding to the transatlantic character of the corpus are John Brand (61,114), Edmund Burke (12,156), Thomas Dutton (26,177), and James Mill (22,923). Given the attention paid to female education among the anonymous entries, Hannah More (105,907) and Mary Wollstonecraft (5,543) are also included.[20]

Plainly there are differences, some quite large, in the token counts among these authors, and the casual observer should not be blamed for asking whether those should be more similar. Relative frequency is the important measure, however, and in the interest of having as thorough an authorial baseline as practicable, texts were not truncated to the lowest common word count. As much textual information as practical was also important given that most texts were in the end headed for an analysis relying on several hundred to several thousand word-variables. For the few texts originally composed in a language other than English, it should be noted that stylometric analysis of translated material identifies the original author in most cases rather than a translator, although that may depend on the translator.[21]

Wherever possible these texts were collected from full text Internet sources, notably the Oxford Text Archive, Eighteenth Century Collections Online, and the Online Library of Liberty.[22] Texts or authors unavailable via the Internet were obtained as images or scanned from books to produce pdfs, each of which was then converted to machine-readable text by the optical character recognition (OCR) tool in Adobe Acrobat Pro. It is critical to note that even with ongoing improvements in the accuracy rates of such tools the resulting text had to be examined line by line to correct OCR mistakes, which limits how many additions requiring such attention can be made to the corpus. Optical character misrecognitions are already common enough with printed materials in standard typography, the most frequent in this case being the letter "m" recognized as "rn" and vice versa. For images of text with script fonts, ligatures, or nonstandard characters one will have considerably more corrections to make, including the script letter "s" being mistaken for "f."

Measuring Textual Features to Identify the Anonymous Authors

With Hiram identified as Francis Hoskins without recourse to stylometric or statistical methods, the three losing entries of Academicus, Freedom, and Hand remained, along with the special case of the review committee's quotes from No. 3. This actual historical attribution problem is a difficult case. In much stylometric work the methods employed are tested on known benchmark texts of considerable length, which are taken to be anonymous in order to see how well the methods perform rather than to solve an ersatz historical question, and a tidy up or down assessment of success can be had.[23] This case has no such luxury. Difficulties include that the popular essay style of the period was, as Mosteller characterized it, "complicated and oratorical." Two principles of the style are: "Never use a short word if a long one will do" and "Double negatives are good, triple even better."[24] Second, one is frustratingly limited by the actual count of words from the pseudonymous authors. Not only that, but the differences among them are varied: the entries by Academicus and Hand are of similar length, more than three times the quoted material from No. 3, and less than half of Freedom's length. A set of simple descriptive statistics provides a useful orientation to the data, and in the earliest days of stylometry, these measures or ratios derived from them were compared in the hope that they would successfully discriminate among authors. All the techniques depend on creating variables and there is a long history of attempts and failures at mathematical expressions of textual features.[25]

For the corpus and all the contestants, table 3.1 shows the token and type counts, their ratio, and two means, one for characters per word and another for words per sentence.

Note the stark difference in mean words per sentence, due to run-ons and the like, between Freedom or Hand and the rest of the entries, a ratification of the APS review committee's inclusion of their entries with the pretenders. Inspecting the word length values in the table shows considerable similarity, with the largest value for No. 3, which makes perfect sense given that his material is quoted outside of its original context and to capture its main ideas, tending to lower the relative rate of the shorter, functional words and hence the average. The authors from the corpus closest to these mean characters per word values are as follows: for Academicus, Dutton (4.66), Hobson (4.65), or duCorteil (4.67); for Freedom, Adams (4.75) or Wollstonecraft (4.77); for Hand, Hume (4.79) or Franklin (4.83), whose value is highest in the corpus and so is also closest to No. 3. Although the Dutton, Hobson, and Wollstonecraft similarities were intriguing, just as in the Federalist case with Madison and Hamilton, different authors appear almost identical as judged by these simple measures.[26] It seems that averages, while providing some useful information—in this case a confirmation of the review committee's views on the poor compositional quality of the pretenders versus the contenders—are not adequate discriminators among authors on their own.

Table 3.1 Raw counts and descriptive statistics

	Academicus	Freedom	Hand	No. 3	Hiram	Samuel Knox	S. H. Smith	Corpus
Tokens	2,842	6,050	2,886	778	740	33,259	17,786	953,767
Types	856	1,299	983	326	299	3,555	2,923	24,493
Type/token ratio (TTR)	0.3012	0.2147	0.3406	0.4190	0.4041	0.1069	0.1643	0.0257
Mean characters per word (st. dev.)	4.66 (2.68)	4.76 (2.74)	4.82 (2.80)	5.05 (2.69)	4.46 (2.51)	4.94 (2.81)	4.86 (2.79)	4.69 (2.66)
Mean words in sentence (st. dev.)	31.61 (19.28)	121.04 (82.02)	125.83 (93.02)	27.79 (13.13)	26.46 (24.41)	39.23 (19.08)	23.46 (15.46)	32.17 (26.71)

The final measure from table 3.1, type-to-token ratio, or TTR, has a long, if checkered, history. Theoretically it has a meaningful interpretation as lexical density, or the richness of vocabulary, but it varies too much with the length of a text, as evidenced by the exceedingly low value for the entire corpus. This means that from a statistical point of view, it is not an unbiased measure. A measure called "pace"—supposedly the rate at which new words enter a text—has been suggested, and it is claimed "to be extremely characteristic of an author's style." Its inventor claims that pace is the inverse of the TTR, that is, 1/TTR, yet does not state any statistical idea behind it, and, unbelievably, conflates his proposal of pace with the very TTR of which it is meant to be the inverse. Indeed the texts ranked in the table are ranked by TTR, and furthermore authors are shown to have substantially different values within the table. For example, Shakespeare's lowest ratio is 0.1422 for *Much Ado About Nothing* and his highest is 0.2645 for *Venus & Adonis*, while Marlowe's varies even more, from 0.149 for *Edward II* to 0.3108 for *Hero & Leander*.[27]

Despite this limitation of TTR as a variable, Brainerd has shown good agreement between predicted and observed distributions of the standardized TTR (STTR) in the works of Soren Kierkegaard, and claims that STTR is likely consistent within a small range for a given author.[28] The crucial difference is that the predicted STTR is based on models using repeated sections of identical size, rather than a single value for an entire text. On the strength of that work the STTR was also investigated for this corpus where possible, but given that standard sections are usually at least one thousand tokens, only authors with at least ten thousand tokens have a useable STTR. As shown in table 3.1, Academicus has 856 types over 2,842 tokens, giving a TTR of 0.3012. The TTR for Freedom is 0.2147 and for Hand 0.3406. Of authors in the corpus, Mill is the closest to all of these, with a STTR of 0.3769. As with the descriptive statistics, TTR and even STTR cannot serve as a lone discriminator among authors, yet the value of either or both as one of many variables in a multivariate analysis remains an open question.

A measure that, unlike TTR, is stable with respect to text lengths from one thousand to four hundred thousand tokens is the percentage of twice-occurring words in a text. Called *dis legomena*, literally "twice-said" in Greek, the remarkable stability of this percent for an exceedingly large range of tokens is a statistical and stylometric holy grail. The explanation for its robust property is that as the text lengthens there are as many once-occurring types, or *hapax legomena*, becoming *dis legomena* as there are *dis legomena* becoming *tris legomena*, or thrice-occurring types.[29] While the stability of the measure is confirmed with this corpus, stability does not necessarily equate to an authorial marker, as shown by the similarity of the percentages in table 3.2.

The usefulness of particular measures remains relative to the authors and texts in question, and perhaps this relatedness is ultimately appropriate to the extent that unique historical circumstances or corpora require custom analyses.

It is easy to imagine other measures of increasingly larger sections, such as mean sentences per paragraph or paragraphs per chapter, yet given the poor discriminatory value of these types of averages it is doubtful whether they

Table 3.2 Percentages of once- and twice-occurring types

	Hapax Legomena (%)	Dis Legomena (%)	% of Total
No. 3	65.95	16.56	82.52
Academicus	62.97	15.65	78.62
Freedom	57.74	14.93	72.67
Hand	68.06	15.06	83.11
Wm. Smith	52.09	16.64	68.72
Volney	47.56	17.63	65.19
Hobson	52.78	16.92	69.70
More	43.62	16.06	59.68
Priestley	41.39	16.58	57.98
Rush	52.73	16.94	69.67
Corpus	36.17	13.33	49.51

could serve as reliable authorial markers. From a compositional point of view, the ratio of one part of speech to another is interesting, and had we known prior to our transcription work in the archives that such categories could prove useful it might have been feasible to produce these hand counts as we transcribed, but the manual tagging and disambiguation of occurrences is quite labor intensive even for a team of researchers, and this was not pursued here.

Curves of Composition

If relying on one or a handful of measures cannot differentiate among authors, perhaps inspecting the entire distributions underlying such averages fares better. This is just the approach taken in the seminal work of stylometry, T. C. Mendenhall's 1887 presentation of "The Characteristic Curves of Composition."[30] Proceeding from an earlier suggestion by Augustus DeMorgan that average word length might differentiate authors, Mendenhall proposed a literary analogy to the spectroscopic analysis of matter done in physics, in which light emitted from intensely heated matter never fails to indicate the particular signature unique to particular elements. In the literary case, Mendenhall proposed "what may be called a 'word-spectrum,' or 'characteristic curve,' which shall be a graphic representation of an arrangement of words according to their length and to the relative frequency of their occurrence."[31] After hand counting the words, and letters per word, of Dickens's *Oliver Twist* and Thackeray's *Vanity Fair* in one thousand, five thousand, and ten thousand word increments, these were plotted and the two authors were found, for the first two samples, largely to agree with themselves. Yet for the ten-thousand-word samples Mendenhall finds the curve of these works at least as similar to each other as the smaller samples were to themselves, especially in the tail of the curve where they were identical for eleven- and thirteen-letter words, and differed by just a single occurrence for twelve-letter words. Curiously, Mendenhall claims that "this closeness to identity must be largely the result of accident, and it would not be likely to repeat itself in another analysis" rather than take this result as counterevidence for his spectroscopic analogy. To be fair, he considered his piece a demonstration of the idea rather than any conclusive test of its validity, and suggested that authorial samples of one hundred thousand words might be sufficiently large to invariably identify authors.

Whereas the hand counting of words into the hundreds of thousands, let alone the letters therein, proved prohibitively laborious, the computer processing of texts makes the construction of Mendenhall's curves almost a by-product of compiling a word list. While the current consensus is that his idea may be more characteristic of genre or, even less usefully, a particular language (English having its own signature curve versus, say, French), the method was included as part of the evidence in the Federalist Papers study. To examine its validity against the final method to be presented later in this chapter, and by virtue of the relative ease with which it can be done, the curves are shown in figure 3.1 for the corpus, our anonymous authors, and those candidates who were likely according to other tests or for substantive reasons presented in other contributions to this volume.

It is clear to see that Academicus, Freedom, and Hand peak with two-letter words, while Smith and Volney peak with three-letter words. The Corpus, Hobson, No. 3, and Wollstonecraft are flat between two- and three-letter words. One also sees in the lower relative rates for No. 3 an expression of the fact that his words were quoted out of their original context, limiting to a certain extent the normal amount of grammatical words relative to others. Both Hobson and Wollstonecraft are proportionally high in four-letter words. Having noted these differences, the salient fact is that these curves appear more similar than different, and for each place on the curve where

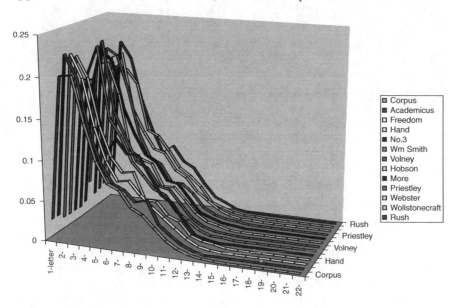

Figure 3.1   Mendenhall's curves of composition for select authors

slopes might compare favorably, another can be found to differ. Perhaps because it goes against his idea of the entire curve being an authorial indicator, Mendenhall never mentions separating these curves into sections. Yet it may be meaningful to break these curves into several strata that can be said to have distinct characteristics. For the most part function words have four or fewer letters, the linguistic chameleon "which" and several other five-letter pronouns and prepositions being illustrative exceptions. Therefore the one-letter through five-letter shape may characterize an author's functional habits, while the tail of the curves may relate to vocabulary sophistication, or perhaps genre, given that technical works often have fatter tails due to scientific jargon. With their use uncertain in this case, such attempts will have to be repeated in other studies to ascertain their usefulness.

When these attempts proved to be unreliable or inconsistent discriminators, what other methods exist to meet the challenge of text attribution? There are methods, in pursuit of analyzing only the elements of compositional style not in the conscious control of the author, which take as their variables strings of characters with no regard to word, sentence, or paragraph boundaries. Like STTR, these rely on sampling the text, which subdivides a text into equal, or as nearly equal as possible, token counts, usually of one to several thousand tokens. Statistical operations performed on these samples enable inferences from them to the population.[32] From a compositional point of view this does not model the act of writing well because they are open to the objection that, statistically speaking, they treat composition as if it occurred by drawing words one at a time with replacement from an authorial urn. Given the difficulty of meaningfully interpreting strings of characters disassociated from words as a marker string of a particular author, these seemed best suited to the forensic uses to which they are put, most famously the attribution of the Unabomber Manifesto to Ted Kaczynski. More interpretable ideas that aim to quantify vocabulary richness by the repeat rate of types, namely, Simpson's Index or Yule's Characteristic K, have been improved since midcentury, but again, as with STTR, our anonymous texts were not sufficiently long to be subdivided into respectably sized samples, and these versions of computational stylistics were unable to help in this case.

Delta

Within the last decade a benchmark method has emerged for so-called open games, in which candidates for a closer, traditional scrutiny are sorted from others whose contextual differences are often small, especially relative to the spread of contextual views in a corpus of respectable size.[33] Developed by John Burrows, it is called Delta and was first presented in 2001.[34] Delta makes use of the most frequently occurring words (MFWs) in a given text or corpus, to which stylometric theory ascribes a unique significance. A cursory look at any word list ranked in descending order of frequency reveals that grammatical necessities, or function words, invariably top the list. Indeed, for English prose, if the word "the" is not ranked first one already has quite a rare difference in relative frequency from any likely corpus that it could be decisive on its own. These MFWs are understood to be either (1) outside the conscious control of an author and revealing of characteristic authorial habits or (2) so functionally necessary as to constrain within definite limits the possible variations an author might consciously try to choose among. Those choices characterize the authorial signature.

The focus on MFWs is in part driven by the stylometer's obsession with having her method fooled by a talented parodist who scribbles in some dimly lit room conniving ever more devious stylistic doppelgangers.[35] But it has mathematical justification as well, given that it is a multivariate method relying on far more variables than those already mentioned. It also, somewhat controversially from a literary or historical point of view, aims to "let the data speak for themselves" rather than rely on researcher inputs such as tagged grammatical features or phrases. Delta's focus on MFWs is also serendipitous for this or any case limited by short texts, because although Burrows recommends a minimum of 1,500 tokens, the relative frequencies for MFWs are high enough even in shorter texts to allow them to be included, albeit with this caveat, in Delta analyses.

Delta is defined as "the mean of the absolute differences between the z-scores for a set of word-variables in a given text-group and the z-scores for the same set of word variables in a target text."[36] This means that for a ranked list of most frequently occurring words, each understood as a "word-variable," there is for each author or text some difference between the relative rate of occurrence of each MFW from its rate in the corpus, expressed as a standardized z-score.[37] Because Delta wants to measure simple difference, the absolute value of all these differences are summed over the chosen number of most frequent words to arrive at a Delta score for each author or text. The small type counts of the pseudonymous authors limit the number of MFWs appropriate, even though ideally one would follow recently suggested improvements to extend the number of MFWs as high as 8,000 due to reported increases in accuracy. There are studies in which type counts are increased by disambiguating homographs, for example, the varied functions of "to" leading to its token count being subdivided accordingly. David Hoover's recent work forgoes this most time-consuming step with no appreciable loss of accuracy, and his recommendation was largely followed here.[38] The exception was to standardize spellings, which of course should not be altered in the original instances given their importance in revealing characteristic misspellings or preferences, but for the purposes of accurate type counts, multiple spellings should collapse into a single type. For example, Freedom spells chemical and related variations with a y—chymical, chymistry, and so on—which was unique in the corpus. Accounting for that in the word lists used with Delta, but not editing the texts, allows correct type counts without the loss of a possible idiosyncratic marker.

Table 3.3 shows the attribution candidates ranked by their Delta scores based on the one hundred MFWs in the corpus, expressing their level of similarity to the anonymous contestant's difference from the corpus.

Table 3.3 Sample Delta results for 100 MFWs

MAX	261.98		MAX	171.88	
MIN	224.92		MIN	138.33	
MEAN	240.23		MEAN	154.75	
STDEV	11.34		STDEV	12.66	
Three	**100.00**	**MFW**	**Academicus**	**100.00**	**MFW**
three	Delta-scores	Deltaz-scores	Acad	Delta-scores	Deltaz-scores
Dutton	224.92	−1.35	Hobson	138.33	−1.30
Volney	225.84	−1.27	Smith	139.38	−1.21
Hobson	227.28	−1.14	Webster	141.10	−1.08
Smith	235.17	−0.45	Dutton	141.56	−1.04
Jefferson	235.96	−0.38	Rush	142.50	−0.97
Rush	235.97	−0.38	Adams	154.96	0.02
Brand	239.16	−0.09	Brand	155.08	0.03
Adams	239.57	−0.06	More	160.71	0.47
More	246.17	0.52	Jefferson	163.70	0.71
Webster	246.23	0.53	Volney	165.58	0.86
Mill	248.31	0.71	Priestley	168.08	1.05
Burke	256.37	1.42	Mill	168.94	1.12
Priestley	261.98	1.92	Burke	171.88	1.35
MAX	214.20		MAX	215.36	
MIN	171.43		MIN	181.12	
MEAN	186.40		MEAN	200.91	
STDEV	12.49		STDEV	11.24	
Freedom	**100.00**	**MFW**	**Hand**	**100.00**	**MFW**
free	Delta-scores	Deltaz-scores	hand	Delta-scores	Deltaz-scores
Rush	171.43	−1.20	More	181.12	−1.76
Adams	171.68	−1.18	Dutton	188.54	−1.10
Smith	172.19	−1.14	Adams	189.14	−1.05
Mill	177.40	−0.72	Smith	190.58	−0.92
Priestley	182.65	−0.30	Hobson	196.40	−0.40
Dutton	184.04	−0.19	Rush	196.78	−0.37
More	185.71	−0.06	Jefferson	202.60	0.15
Hobson	185.77	−0.05	Volney	207.57	0.59
Webster	190.29	0.31	Priestley	207.92	0.62
Brand	191.15	0.38	Webster	208.45	0.67
Jefferson	194.16	0.62	Mill	213.28	1.10
Burke	202.45	1.29	Brand	214.06	1.17
Volney	214.20	2.23	Burke	215.36	1.29

MFW: Most frequently occurringwords.

The full Delta results are considerably wider and longer, but for the sake of space only a sample is included. It is important to note that each of these is a separate test, such that different Delta scores for the same candidate author are not directly comparable across different tests, for example, Jefferson's 100 MFWs score of 163.70 in the Academicus test and 194.16 in the Freedom test are not directly about Jefferson's texts, but rather their difference from the test author's texts, respectively. Also, because Delta rank-orders candidate authors, it must be calibrated.[39] This involves including false anonymous authors along with the set of actual test pieces to make sure that one is in fact capturing authorial signatures. Two sample calibration Delta z-scores not shown here are for Brand -2.80, and for Burke -2.79. Using the probabilities from the normal curve (which is the purpose of standardization), these calibration scores express that only 0.26 percent of texts would be expected to be more similar to these authors' differences from their own writing based on chance alone. These typical calibration results indicate that Delta is correctly attributing the false anonymous authors and that confidence in its actual anonymous attributions is well founded. The choice of how many MFWs to use is not straightforward, and Delta calculations from thirty to four thousand MFWs were made during calibrations. A perplexing result reported in the literature is that increasing the number of MFWs increases the accuracy of Delta even for texts whose total types are fewer than the number of word-variables chosen.[40] This was true on occasion for this corpus, but certainly not for all iterations of MFWs, and needs further study.

Turning to the interpretation of the Delta results and their implications for attribution, it is worth noting that with statistical procedures one deals not in certainties but probabilities. In the one hundred MFWs sample shown earlier, Hobson ranks first for Academicus, Rush ranks first for Freedom, and More ranks first for Hand, with Dutton first in the special case of No. 3. The easiest way to understand the rankings is by examining the standard deviations and a second set of z-scores from the Delta scores themselves, called Delta z-scores and shown in each anonymous author's third column. These are calculated using the same form as the word-variable z-scores whose absolute values are summed to produce the Delta score itself. Taking the result with the largest gap between the first and second ranks, that for More's from Hand's essay, the Delta z-score is -1.76. Again, based on the normal curve, this means that 3.92 percent of texts would be expected to rank higher by chance alone. Among first-ranked candidates, Rush's score is least significant, with a delta z-score in the Freedom test of -1.20, for which 11.5 percent of texts could be expected to rank higher. The first-ranked candidate for No. 3 is Dutton at -1.35 and for Academicus it is Hobson at -1.30, with 8.85 percent and 9.68 percent of texts expected to rank higher, respectively.

Inspecting these first-ranked candidates for one hundred MFWs against the probabilities of the sample calibration results shows a significant difference, and certainly any test on only one count of MFWs should not be regarded as conclusive, for example, Rush's authorship of Hand's essay or More's of Freedom's, both of which can be disproved for historical reasons.

The true inferential strength of Delta results has to do with how consistently high a particular author ranks over a wide range of MFWs. Delta calculations were performed on larger numbers of MFWs, increasing by one hundred word increments up to one thousand MFWs, and from there by two hundred word increments up to four thousand MFWs, such that twenty-five tables including table 3.3 comprise the total procedure. The first ranked author of all the pseudonymous authors varies to some extent as the MFWs are increased, yet Hobson as Academicus varies least and is the top-ranked candidate in all save one (in which he is second) of the MFWs appropriate to Academicus's type count. Statistically speaking, that constitutes a strong case for attributing the Academicus essay to Hobson. In conjunction with the traditional case for Hobson made elsewhere in this volume, it can be concluded with confidence that Academicus is John Hobson.

As for the unique case of No. 3 and the statistical likelihood of its author being William Smith, he is most often the fourth-ranked candidate behind Rush, Volney, and a rotating third-ranked author depending on the MFWs in question. Interestingly, Rush appears among the top-ranking candidates for Freedom and Hand as well, although there is more rotation of other authors in and out of the top few spots for these two essayists. As Justice noted, the almost verbatim similarity of the essay prompt to two of Rush's own essay titles indicates that he may have directly composed the essay prompt, or at the least exercised an outsized influence on it.[41] The fact that in many tests Rush figures as the first result for No. 3 (as for Hand and Freedom) may find an explanation in the overwrought question having a similarly outsized and contextual effect on the word choices or other authorial habits of the essayists. Two other facts regarding William Smith's candidacy bear repeating: first, that his authorial set was augmented with the text furthest removed both stylistically and chronologically from the otherwise tightly focused corpus; and second, that only the review committee's quotes from No. 3 survive, severely limiting the authorial signature to which these authors are compared. The continual presence of both Smith and Volney despite these difficulties bears out the historical work on those candidates presented elsewhere in this volume.

CONCLUSION

While knowing the identities of Hiram and Academicus as Francis Hoskins and John Hobson provides new information about the characteristics of contributors to the early republican educational conversation, such attributions do not (yet) add to the larger question of whether there can be an empirical basis for considerations of canonical status. Initially I was hopeful that some quantitative expression of canonical significance could be found around the notion of how thinkers of the period understood the conscious uses to which education could be put, and that this might be revealed by the occurrences within the corpus of terms such as "use," "useful," "utility," and the like. This hope was in part based on familiar expressions of men understood as leaders—for instance, Webster's line that "[t]he virtues of men are of more consequence to society than their abilities," or Rush's claim that it was necessary "to convert men into republican machines...if we expect them to perform their parts properly in the great machine of the state."[42] The inability to do so in this corpus should not necessarily be understood as proof that it cannot be done, although recent work shows that the idea of usefulness may be particularly thorny, and should not be understood in a simple dichotomy with "ornamental."[43] But it also points anew to the problem: canonical status, however established, tends to reinforce itself through scholars acting according to it.

Expansions of both scope and depth are required if corpus linguistics and statistical methods are to make contributions to historical argumentation on questions of canonical status, periodization, and so on. One promising idea is to create "phrase-variables" as suggested by Mosteller and Wallace.[44] While reliant on researcher tagging and thus exceedingly labor intensive, this promises to be the way forward for historical work utilizing these methods, with a Delta-inspired multivariate analysis of comparative differences in most frequent phrases rather than words. A cooperatively constructed and empirically grounded intellectual citation network of such phrases would be a powerful research and teaching tool indeed.

A second improvement in a methodological vein is to stop avoiding contextually sensitive terms as textual variables. This simplification of the attribution or classification problem was understandable in early attempts in order to establish the possibilities of new methods, but as a matter of principle there can be no writing without context, no authorial signature abstracted from the set of contexts represented in the author's body of work. However difficult incorporating such contextual material is, it needs to be included rather than ignored if these methods are to prove robust enough for historical use. Understanding contextual effects is an avenue for further work that could make comparative use of already compiled corpora, and would have direct benefits on the applicability of these methods to traditional historical and literary arguments.

Even after these or other improvements, quantitative analyses such as this study must be regarded only as supplemental to the painstaking and specialized work of historians. That being said, denials of their power and growing potential are untenable. There was a time when defensive, even panicked, humanists derided these and similar methods as running roughshod over intricate literary methods, as evidenced by Burrow's 1992 rebuttal that "[l]iterary theorists...are not entitled to deny that literary works are marked by the particular stylistic habits and, by a not unreasonable inference, the intellectual propensities of their authors."[45] Yet the strength of the final inference, the one from computer-aided counts and statistically derived features to "intellectual propensities" of authors, is one to be determined by conventional historical means. The trend away from needing special knowledge to perform these analyses toward notions of so-called plug and play tools do serve useful scientific purposes of standardization and replicability, and of adoptability by nontechnical scholars. But there remains and will always remain a need, especially for any questions of significance such as canon or period studies, for historians to wed their unique knowledge to the power of these methods.

NOTES

I would like to thank Bob Scott, director of Columbia University's Digital Humanities Center, for access to Wordsmith, the program used to compute the word lists and concordances for this study, and also Christine Jacknick for a productive conversation on the affordances of corpus-based work for historical purposes. Thanks also to the editor for indispensible advice from the project's beginning to end.

1. Bernard Bailyn, *Education in the Forming of American Society: Needs and Opportunities for Study* (Chapel Hill: UNC Press, 1960), 21; *The Ideological Origins of the American Revolution* (Cambridge: Belknap Press, 1967); Gordon Wood, *The Creation of the American Republic* (Chapel Hill: UNC Press, 1969); J. G. A. Pocock, *The Machiavellian Moment: Florentine Political Thought and the Atlantic Republican Tradition* (Princeton: PUP, 1975); Carl Kaestle, *Pillars of the Republic: Common Schools and American Society, 1780–1860* (New York: Hill & Wang, 1983).
2. APS minute book, May 1, 1795, APS Archives.
3. This was in fact a drawing of a hand, referred to by the reviewers and throughout this chapter as "Hand."
4. Lawrence Cremin, *American Education: The National Experience, 1783–1876* (New York: Harper & Row, 1980).
5. Benjamin Justice, "'The Great Contest': The American Philosophical Society Education Prize of 1795 and the Problem of American Education," *American Journal of Education* 114 (2008): 191–213.
6. Frederick Rudolph, *Essays on Education in the Early Republic* (Cambridge: Belknap Press, 1965).
7. Siobhan Moroney, "Birth of a Canon: The Historiography of Early Republican Educational Thought," *History of Education Quarterly* 39:4 (1999): 476–449.
8. Quoted in Meyer Reinhold, "The Quest for 'Useful Knowledge' in Eighteenth-Century America," *Proceedings of the American Philosophical Society* 119:2 (1975): 108–132.
9. Francis Hoskins, *Navigation Made Easy, or a Mariners Complete Guide, May 2nd, 1800*, APS Archives II.1.
10. Francis Hoskins, *An Introduction to Merchandise. Arithmetick. In whole and broken numbers, designed for the use of Academies and Schools adapted to the trade of the United States of America* (Philadelphia, 18–?); *The Beauties and Super-excellency of Free Masonry Attempted* (Philadelphia, Coughlin & M'Laughlin: 1801). Thanks to Campbell Scribner for pointing to these. I consulted the latter work at the New York Historical Society in the hope of using it to calibrate a stylometric method described later: did it predict authorship known to be true? Unfortunately, neither was suitable for calibration: the first was an arithmetic text book while the second was predominantly biblical passages and Masonic hymns.

11. Hugh Craig, "Authorial Attribution and Computational Stylistics: If You Can Tell Authors Apart, Have You Learned Anything About Them?" *Literary and Linguistic Computing* 14:1 (1999): 103–113.
12. Klaus Krippendorff, *Content Analysis: An Introduction to Its Methodology* (Thousand Oaks: Sage, 2004), xvii–17.
13. Wordsmith is a concordance program developed by Tim Smith in connection with Oxford University Press: http://www.lexically.net/wordsmith/ (last accessed October 1, 2012).
14. G. K. Zipf, *Psycho-Biology of Language* (Boston: Houghton Mifflin, 1935).
15. Frederick Mosteller and David Wallace, *Inference and Disputed Authorship: The Federalist* (Reading: Addison-Wesley, 1964).
16. http://aclweb.org/anthology-new/P/P12/P12–3029.pdf (last accessed October 1, 2012).
17. Richard S. Forsyth and David I. Holmes, "Feature-Finding for Text Classification," *Literary and Linguistic Computing* 11:4 (1996): 163–174.
18. Given limited space, an exhaustive list of works or excerpts thereof is impractical; students or researchers interested in the list should contact the author at ecs2110@columbia.edu.
19. Douglas Adair, "The Authorship of the Disputed Federalist Papers," *William and Mary Quarterly*, Third Series 1:2 (1944): 98.
20. Thanks to Lisa Green and Ben Justice for providing some of these texts.
21. John Burrows, "The Englishing of Juvenal: Computational Stylistics and Translated Texts," *Style* 36 (2002): 677–699; Jan Rybicki, "Translation and Delta Revisited: When We Read Translations, Is It the Author or the Translator that We Really Read?" (paper presented at the annual conference of the Alliance of Digital Humanities Organizations, London, July 7–10, 2010).
22. http://ota.ahds.ac.uk/, http://quod.lib.umich.edu/e/ecco/, http://oll .libertyfund.org/.
23. Patrick Juola, John Sofko, and Patrick Brennan, "A Prototype for Authorship Attribution Studies," *Literary and Linguistic Computing* 21:2 (2004): 169–178.
24. Frederick Mosteller, "A Statistical Study of the Writing Styles of the Authors of 'The Federalist' Papers," *Proceedings of the American Philosophical Society* 131:2 (1987): 133.
25. David Holmes provides an excellent survey of measures used over the twentieth century and reviews the success or lack thereof with which they have been demonstrated: "Authorship Attribution," *Computers and the Humanities* 28:2 (1994): 87–106.
26. Mosteller, "Statistical Study," 132–140.
27. J. C. Baker, "Pace: A Test of Authorship Based on the Rate at which New Words Enter an Author's Text," *Literary and Linguistic Computing* 3:1 (1988): 36–39.
28. Barron Brainerd, "The Type to Token Ratio in the Works of S. Kierkegaard," in Richard W. Bailey (ed.), *Computing and the Humanities: Papers from the Fifth International Conference on Computing in the Humanities* (New York: North-Holland, 1982), 97–109.
29. H. S. Sichel, "Word Frequency Distributions and Type-Token Characteristics," *Mathematical Scientist* 11 (1986): 45–72.

30. T. C. Mendenhall, "The Characteristic Curves of Composition," *Science* 9:214 (1887): 237–249.
31. Ibid, 238.
32. Gerard R. Ledger, *Re-Counting Plato: A Computer Analysis of Plato's Style* (Oxford: Clarendon Press, 1989).
33. More precisely there are several possibilities about which expert stylometers continue to experiment, including both cluster analysis and principal component analysis, which are more sensitive to multidimensional distances. Burrow's Delta has the advantage of having passed repeated rigorous tests, and, significantly for historians or other nonexperts, being mathematically straightforward.
34. John Burrows, "Questions of Authorship: Attribution and Beyond—A Lecture Delivered on the Occasion of the Roberto Busa Award ACH-ALLC 2001, New York," *Computers and the Humanities* 37:1 (2003): 5–32.
35. John Burrows, "Who wrote *Shemela*? Verifying the Authorship of a Parodic Text," *Literary and Linguistic Computing* 20:4 (2005): 437–450.
36. John Burrows, "'Delta': A Measure of Stylistic Difference and a Guide to Likely Authorship," *Literary and Linguistic Computing* 17:3 (2002): 267–287.
37. The basic form of a standardized score can be found in introductory statistics textbooks. Most generally it is a random variable's observed value minus its expected value, divided by the standard deviation. In this case the z-scores are each word's observed rate in a text minus the average rate in the corpus, over the standard deviation in the corpus, or $z = (x-\mu)/\sigma$.
38. David Hoover, "Testing Burrows's Delta," *Literary and Linguistic Computing* 19:4 (2004): 453–475.
39. I have become well acquainted with Burrows's "exhaustive and possibly fruitless series of iterations" required to calibrate stylistic methods such that false anonymous authors are correctly attributed—a make or break process for any study without which one can have little to no confidence in the actual anonymous attributions. Despite not finding David Hoover's Delta Calculation Spreadsheets until after much manual calculation, I am indebted to and grateful for his programming of the Delta procedure into easy-to-use spreadsheets that offer a great deal of user control of parameters, and including improvements discussed in Shlomo Argamon, "Interpreting Burrows's Delta: Geometric and Probabilistic Foundations," *Literary and Linguistic Computing* 23:2 (2008): 131–147.
40. Burrows, "Delta," 277.
41. Justice, "Great Contest," 196.
42. Quoted in Kaestle, *Pillars*, 7–8.
43. Margaret Nash, *Women's Education in the United States, 1780–1840* (New York: Palgrave Macmillan, 2005).
44. Mosteller and Wallace, *Inference*, 45.
45. Quoted in Holmes, "The Evolution of Stylometry in Humanities Scholarship," *Literary and Linguistic Computing* 13:3 (1998): 111–117.

PART II

Meanings

CHAPTER 4

False Start: The Failure of an Early "Race to the Top"

Campbell Scribner

We all know that there are many of the circumstances of the times we live in, which differ widely from those of former times, as well as our local situation does, [and] in both these respects we stand upon very different ground.

—*"Freedom," Philadelphia, 1797*[1]

Histories of education in the early United States tend to divide sharply between national and local reforms. On one hand, they describe the Founders' plans to create virtuous citizens through a national, hierarchical, publicly funded school system; on the other, they describe the chaotic marketplace of privately run academies and charity schools that actually sprang up in urban areas. Almost as a rule these stories do not overlap.[2] The push for a national school system fell victim to popular fears about taxes and centralized control while the private sector successfully provided mass education, attracted tax support, and paved the way for public schools a generation later. Yet these divergent outcomes were not preordained and the divide between them was never absolute. At one time, national and local reforms both seemed viable and shared many assumptions about the best practices of teaching, curriculum design, and school organization. In fact, many proposals for national education built on institutions and reforms from particular cities, hoping (in modern terms) to "scale up" those that succeeded. Why, then, did such proposals fail? While localism and parsimony are partly to blame, we tend to overlook the fact that, for ideological reasons, the Founders, too, rejected potentially workable models of national education.

Education played a prominent but very particular role in the republican ideology of the late eighteenth century. In their respective proposals for public schools in Virginia and Pennsylvania, Thomas Jefferson and Benjamin Rush famously argued that the stability of the new republic required not merely widespread literacy but a centralized school system to "render the mass of people more homogenous...for uniform and peaceable government" and to advance a deserving few on to higher learning and national leadership.[3] In both proposals, Enlightenment ideals of order and natural merit found form in tiered systems of local elementary schools, regional academies, and state and national universities.[4] As historian J. M. Opal notes, a centralized school system would abstract governance from local voters and instill competition among students—replacing communitarian values in rural schools and the competition *for* students among urban schools—thus creating an engine of progress and "utility to the Publick." However, the virtues of this system were not self-evident to most Americans. Because most academies and colleges, unlike rural district schools, "did not rely on [local] taxpayers' funds and did not serve every taxpayer's child," their supporters had to "redefine the relationship between school and community" in order to win public support. Thus, Opal observes, the "publickness [of centralized education] had to be proclaimed and contrived."[5]

A number of tracts were written between 1790 and 1820 with just that end in mind—enough for historians to pronounce a widespread consensus around the tiered model of public education.[6] Yet the era's educational consensus was less uniform than current literature suggests. To proclaim the importance of nationalized education, proponents had to continually refine its definition. The vision of a national system of education did not spring fully formed from the minds of the Founders and was not immediately apprehended by their supporters in the public. Many proposals for national schools deviated from the top-down model of reform by relying on market forces, preserving vestiges of local control, or stopping short of a national university. Bringing them into line with plans like Jefferson's and Rush's required educational and media elites to reward imitators and correct or punish nonconformists. Yet historian Margaret Nash notes that most historians ignore this process of ideological construction and negotiation. Instead, they follow a model "in which political leaders articulate an agenda that is [simply] adopted by the public." Nash suggests that future research should explore the "space in between the elite and the average person" and the ways in which writers were "responsive to local loyalties and values at least as much as to nationalistic ideologies."[7]

The American Philosophical Society (APS) essay contest provides an excellent opportunity to examine the interplay between local and national visions of eighteenth-century school reform. In 1795, the APS offered a hundred-dollar premium for the best essay on "a system of liberal education, and literary instruction, adapted to the genius of the government, and best calculated to promote the general welfare of the United States: comprehending, also, a plan for instituting and conducting public schools in this country on principles of the most extensive utility."[8] The premium failed to generate much interest. Even after the deadline was extended it received only seven submissions and did not spur any major reforms. Nonetheless, historians frequently cite the two winning essays—by Samuel Knox, a minister and schoolteacher in Maryland, and Samuel Harrison Smith, a newspaper editor in Philadelphia—as important examples of the era's educational thought. Like Jefferson and Rush, both Knox and Smith argued that "the general welfare" of the country required a hierarchical system of state-run schools and colleges, beginning with regional academies and culminating in a national university.[9]

The contest's other essays, which remain anonymous and are less well known, have been presented in the same light. Historian Lawrence Cremin, for example, writes that all seven expressed a "widely articulated and widely accepted" view of education that "cut across partisan lines in politics and religion...surely transcended regional boundaries, and...may even have transcended social-class boundaries."[10] At a basic level, Cremin is correct. All the contestants understood that when the APS asked for a system of "liberal education," it referred to the classical curriculum taught in the nation's few colleges; "utility" meant the modern languages, mathematics, and clerical skills taught at its rapidly proliferating academies; and "public schools" referred either to academies or the free primary schools then provided by rural communities and urban charities. How to systematize these disparate elements, however, remained unclear and elicited surprisingly diverse propositions from the writers. As one of them noted at the beginning of his essay, a workable answer had "to distinguish between [the question's] preceding clauses & its last"—liberal and public education—"as about objects differing from each other in degree at least" and not easily integrated.[11] Other questions were implicit in this observation. For example, should the public schools be free for everyone, for everyone in need, or for only a few of the deserving poor? Should they be administered by a central governmental agency or by local trustees? What sort of education would be of the greatest "utility" for the middling classes? What about the poor? And, perhaps most importantly, how could one ensure the schools' greatest impact at the least cost?

The remainder of this essay will consider the five losing essays in the APS contest—submitted under the pseudonyms Academicus, Hand, Freedom, Hiram, and No. 3—and compare them to the era's better-known models of school systemization. It will pay particular attention to their reliance on examples of local educational reform. For while these authors, like the winners, drew on the European Enlightenment for notions of citizenship and the public good, several of them were residents of Philadelphia and specifically referenced changes in that city's schools. Some limited their recommendations to local or state reforms altogether, which was a significant reason that they lost.[12]

Notwithstanding William Penn's wish that all residents have access to free schooling, public provisions for education were virtually nonexistent in colonial Pennsylvania and only sporadic in the years after the Revolution. The state constitution of 1790 included two sections pertaining to education.

The first decreed that "the arts and sciences shall be promoted in one or more Seminaries of learning."[13] At the time, Pennsylvania was one of the only states with any constitutional provisions at all for higher education. It had already chartered three colleges: the University of Pennsylvania (1755), Dickinson College (1783), and Franklin and Marshall College (1787).[14] Yet there was an acute lack of funding for these institutions. The state assembly promised to support the University of Pennsylvania, for example, with land grants and the sale of estates confiscated during the Revolutionary War but generally reneged on both promises after the 1780s.[15] The second section of the 1790 constitution declared that "a school or schools shall be established in each county for the instruction of youth, and the State shall pay to the masters such salaries as shall enable them to teach at low prices." Some state representatives hoped that these county schools would also provide free education for the poor, but they could only secure a weak resolution ordering counties to accommodate paupers "as soon as conveniently may be."[16] Thus, the state's patchwork system of locally controlled schools remained largely undisturbed until the middle of the nineteenth century.

Despite these shaky public foundations, there was a drastic expansion in Pennsylvania's educational capacity during the 1780s and 1790s. The number of teachers in the Philadelphia directory—most of them widows operating "dame" and "venture" schools, fee-based tutorials operated ad hoc out of the home or rented rooms—doubled between 1785 and 1800, from one hundred to two hundred.[17] The colony chartered its first academy in 1751 and the state chartered at least twelve more by 1800, including an Episcopal Academy that APS judges Samuel Magaw and James Abercrombie opened shortly after the essay contest.[18] The number of charity schools expanded as well. The Friends Public School and Philadelphia Academy both supported charity schools by the middle of the eighteenth century. In the years after the Revolution, poor children could also attend St. Mary's Catholic School (1783), the Negro Charity School (1786), a School for Poor Boys in the Northern Liberties (1787), the Free School (1788), or a string of Sunday schools for both white and Negro students (1791).[19] Less than a decade after the APS contest, another Negro free school appeared (1800), as did the first school operated by the Philadelphia Society for the Establishment and Support of Charity Schools (1799), and the Adelphi School (1807), the second institution in the country to use the Lancaster system of monitorial instruction.[20]

The rate at which these institutions appeared troubled some of the essayists, who, like many republican thinkers, were skeptical of the market's ability to ensure the sort of education that would produce civic virtue.[21] Academicus lamented that academies and venture schools "accommodated to the larger bulk of people...[but] so much neglected...are often erected, and as often destroyed again, by the capricious humours of a few individuals, which renders their permanence unstable & precarious."[22] Hand likewise observed a "want of respectability" and "burlesque" in the colleges and academies of the day.[23] Freedom argued that low standards were to be expected "when this business of finishing an education is left totally to teachers." "We cannot expect that their credentials should do much honour to the young candidates," he wrote, because one "may expect something like that partiality between a father and son" between a teacher and his students. It was little surprise, then, that "diplomas have fallen into disrepute."[24]

Although the essayists bemoaned the disorganized collection of schools surrounding them, all five believed that it could provide the components of a future, centralized system. The best model for such a system was the University of Pennsylvania, which opened as an academy in 1751—inspired by a pamphlet circulated by Ben Franklin—and almost immediately developed a charity school (1751) and a college (1755), constituting a three-tiered system in itself and expanding its enrollment proportionately.[25] The same group of trustees administered all three branches and frequently sought ways to extend education (and their own influence) to new segments of society. For example, when the Society for the Propagation of the Gospel, an arm of the Church of England, established a statewide system of charity schools in the late 1750s, the trustees became its strongest supporters.[26]

The Anglican charity school system hardly offered universal education: at its peak in 1760, 12 schools served only seven hundred students.[27] Nor was it designed to identify and advance talent in a Jeffersonian sense. But its backers believed that it could nonetheless become an engine of improvement, binding the English city and largely German countryside in a shared sense of colonial identity. At the very least, they hoped, the charity schools' demand for college-educated teachers would increase investment in the University of Pennsylvania. William Smith, the university's first president (and, later, the likely author of essay No. 3), wrote, "It is a happy circumstance that there is a flourishing Seminary, where such [teachers] may be educated; and happier still that the honorable proprietary is to make a foundation for maintaining and educating constantly some promising children of poor Germans as a Supply of well-principled Schoolmasters, that must be acceptable among their friends."[28] One of the first teachers the charity schools hired was Samuel Magaw, a recent University of Pennsylvania graduate who would later return as a professor and provost and go on to lead the review committee for the APS premium.[29]

The Anglican charity schools closed shortly before the Revolution, but reformers in the early national period believed that the same sort of institutions could provide the basis for an integrated school system. Magaw, for instance, in 1787 noted that the Young Ladies' Academy of Philadelphia "[met] our ideas, and accords with our wishes [for female education]" and hoped it would "enlarge its system yet farther, and spread extensively its goodly influences."[30] Benjamin Rush, who was closely involved with the support of Sunday schools and charity schools in Philadelphia, believed that making those institutions public would "[diminish] the number of the poor and of course the sum of the tax paid for their maintenance . . . by lessening the expenses of jails."[31] The APS essayists likewise saw potential in Pennsylvania's existing academies and colleges. Freedom based his recommendations for public education on the "studies and modes of instruction which exist at present" and planned to "[carry] these methods to a greater degree of perfection than they have hitherto acquired."[32] No. 3 intended "universities now established" to become "the Central Schools" of a public system, and expected that a national university would hire current university professors.[33] Hand also hoped that "as state institutions," existing colleges would "remain much on their present footing for usual collegiate studies—but add to them the province of solely qualifying...for the learned professions & higher public offices." Much as they had under the German charity school system, he expected colleges to provide "moral-politic missionaries" for neighborhood schools.[34]

The losing essays echoed the era's conventional wisdom about public education in many other respects as well. They were divided on the practicality of teaching Greek and Latin but unanimous on the importance of religious toleration, arguing, as No. 3 did, that "to teach no other morals to [one's] youth than those of [one's] own creed, introduces dangerous effects, foments divisions amongst mankind, & subjects liberal and solid sentiments to religious prejudices."[35] They all believed in a general diffusion of knowledge among the "mass of...common citizens, [who were] not only the most numerous description of any in society" but the ones who would "decide eventually that of its representation & government."[36] Most wanted the state or federal government to reimburse teachers for taking on poor scholars, although they expected that, after the children of workingmen had been exposed to the rudiments of republicanism, "the number of our Pupils will be naturally diminished in the second class of public Schools, which become central."[37]

All foresaw local trustees controlling neighborhood schools, "[using] their influence to suppress popular passions and control the society in which they lived."[38] For Freedom, putting teacher selection in the hands of "the most competent judges" would remedy the problem of quality in the market-based system.[39] Hand also believed that if the state would "pay & choose"—or, he equivocated, "at least choose or approve"—each neighborhood schoolmaster, higher professional standards would allow for a regime of identifying and advancing talent. To determine "the after occupation of each son," he hoped, "the proper officers, his past instructors...[would] discuss & determine openly among themselves at a Board for that purpose, the kind of genius & turn of mind of the youth & select employment for him accordingly"—and this would all occur "to the exclusion of the parent."[40] No. 3 took the farthest steps toward centralized control, putting primary schools "under the immediate authority of Corporations or Justices of the Peace" and recommending that they "be inspected by the Provost delegated by [a central] Federal Institution."[41]

Several of the writers hoped to disseminate useful knowledge with reading circles and traveling lecturers, much like the literary and debating clubs of the day or lyceums later in the nineteenth century. Freedom advised that

> in distant parts of the country where teachers cannot well be supported, young
> men and youths may very advantageously form themselves into Societies, to

meet weekly or oftener, and by this means follow their Studies, by this means they will stimulate one another to improvement...If they can have a teacher to come periodically or other men of information to give them instruction...so much the better.[42]

Hand likewise proposed that neighborhood schools receive "plain, easy, familiar discourses regularly delivered several times a year by fit persons sent round to perform circuits for the purpose."[43]

The authors recommended other sorts of public exhibition as well. No. 3 hoped to see "provision for a public & annual Course of natural Philosophy & experimental Chemistry in each [state's] capital City."[44] His call for public science instruction echoed that of Charles Wilson Peale, who had just founded the Philadelphia Museum to encourage broader public understanding of medicine and natural history.[45] Freedom sought "to render the science, and the practice of the healing art, more extensively usefull" through "a course of lecturers...at every eminent seminary of learning." This proposal almost certainly drew from the writings of Benjamin Rush, who advocated a similar dissemination of medical knowledge—as well, perhaps, from the 1765 adoption of the Edinburgh Plan of medical instruction at the University of Pennsylvania, under which lectures were open to all the university's students and the learned public.[46]

While there were small variations in these suggestions, all were fairly conventional responses to the era's educational debates. And their conformity should come as no surprise: the Society's turgidly written, overly specific question was intended to limit the range of ideas submitted. Indeed, the contest was not, as some have suggested, a "search for alternatives" to the prevailing republican ideology so much as an attempt to popularize and reinforce it.[47] Shortly after the contest began, however, an accident set some of the essayists on a slightly different path. As historian Benjamin Justice notes, there was a transcription error in one of the advertisements that the APS published in the *American Monthly Review*, Samuel Harrison Smith's journal. Instead of "instituting and conducting" public schools, the *Review* asked for plans on "instructing and conducting" them. All five of the losing essays arrived after the announcement's publication and several of them, it seems, followed its cue to emphasize contemporary innovations in pedagogy.[48]

Freedom, for example, noted that rather than merely reciting letters by rote, schools in London had begun teaching children to read and write at the same time "in order to impress [the letters] better on their memories."[49] Academicus, too, argued for more holistic instruction and less memorization in the classroom. His remedy was to encourage the use of dictionaries and a thorough understanding of etymology.[50] As an Englishman he was less intent than Noah Webster on developing a particularly American canon, complaining that "the best English writers, Milton, Pope, Young, Dayton, Templeton...[were frequently] condemned by the bar of modern grammarians." Like Webster, however, he grumbled that "almost every year, for ten or twelve years past, we have seen a new grammar offered forth," and argued for a more systematic approach to the language.[51]

The Society's judges responded harshly to these proposals, making it clear that they were interested in comprehensive arguments for systemization, not digressions into piecemeal reforms. The single most important factor in how the judges arrayed the entries seems to be the establishment of a national university. The authors that prominently discussed such a university (Knox, Smith, and No. 3) received positive reviews. Those that limited their proposals to district- or state-level reforms (Academicus, Hand, and Hiram) received criticism and scorn.[52]

Academicus, the judges wrote,

> having spent rather too much time, and wasted too much paper, on a fruitless attempt to prove the absolute necessity of our learning Some language in order to be able to communicate our ideas and thoughts, and having next advanced a few very tattered arguments in favour of the proposition "that a knowledge of the Latin language as an essential ingredient" in the constitution of a complete English or American Education...ventures to propose a plan for the more respectable establishment of English schools.

Yet his plan did not discuss "to what extent [the poor's] education is to be earned" and concluded with "a very languid [eulogium] on the effects that would probably result from a general dissemination of knowledge, in a republican government."[53] The reviewers similarly dismissed Hand's argument that "'[l]iterary instruction'...[be] not confined in its acceptation, to any precise formulary" but be pursued "by emulation, the strongest of all incitements [and] by frequent public exhibitions," as "some general tho obscure Observations on the Importance of Liberal Education."[54]

Even more interesting was the judges' response to Hiram's essay, the shortest of the seven and the least national in scope. Hiram suggested only that teachers and students attend "a Commodious [and] lightsome schoolhouse" rather than the dank and drafty district schools of the day, and that small grants of land would "be of great Benefit" to schoolmasters because they would allow them to "[i]nstruct [their] pupils, at one third or one fourth less than the Usual Charge Or else to Instruct or teach, one third of [their] Scholars gratis."[55] He also outlined a brief plan to improve student performance while lowering the costs and expanding the capacity of public schools. "I know a master," he wrote, who

> when his Scholars increased to more in Number than he could Instruct, and not being able to hire an Usher, Chose two of his best Scholars to assist him, who spent half their School hours Instructing the younger Scholars, under his View whereby they gave great assistance to their Master and the Young Scholars learned as well as from their Master who at Certain times examined & taught them also. The two Youths, Improved by Instructing others...And the Master gave them every proper indulgence, the Use of his Books, and

> Instructions after school Hours. Whereby in a Short time by application and Study [they] became better Scholars than their Master.[56]

While the use of paid ushers and assistants was a centuries-old practice in preparatory schools, systematically using older students to teach younger ones was new and (although more modest in scope) was precisely the method that Joseph Lancaster would use in London a year later.[57] Like Lancaster, Hiram clearly understood that devolving instructional responsibility to pupils allowed for larger class sizes, lower costs, and emulative advancement. It was the sort of bottom-up, self-perpetuating system that would later trigger the expansion of American public education.

The judges did not see it that way. Responding to Hiram's concern for architectural improvements, they sarcastically noted that a "school-house [should be] furnished with doors, or windows...as he conceives it wholly impracticable for either master or scholars to read in darkness." Hiram's point about the "[necessity] for the teacher to be provided with lodging-rooms with a garden and with a grass-lot as a pasture" elicited similar jibes about it being "equally impossible for school-masters as for other men, to live without *eating* and *sleeping*." The judges went on to lampoon Hiram's system of monitorial instruction, ignoring its systematic aspect altogether with the comment that "scholars may, at times, become more learned than masters, that an instance of this kind fell...under [Hiram's] own observation; and that the master was even so ingenious as to acknowledge the fact."[58] In each of these points, the APS judges perceived only piecemeal reforms, not the sort of integrated system that was "well adapted to the present state of Society in this Country."[59] As a result, they dismissed Hiram's essay out of hand.

The "great contest" of 1795 was a failure in several respects. It obviously failed to popularize the public system that so many of the Founders supported. More broadly, as Justice observes, its critical reviews "[reveal] an important and, as it turns out, dubious assumption on the part of the APS: that a uniquely American education necessarily needed to be systematic in design and national in scale." The contest's central irony was that the scholarly body most intent on the "practical application of ideas" in American society ultimately sacrificed practicality for ideological purity. Not only did its judges misunderstand the "genius of American government" by posing an overly specific question for top-down reform, as Justice argues, but in their rejection of lecture circuits, curricular reform, and monitorial instruction, they rejected the very solutions that would go on to success scarcely a decade later.[60]

This hardly implies that national education would have flourished if the reviewers had simply responded differently. Issues of cost and centralization remained daunting political hurdles. Yet while the systems proposed by Smith, Knox, Rush, and others failed both of these tests, the losing essays at least passed the first: what they lacked in grandiosity and "intellectual consistency" they made up for with affordability. Hiram framed his recommendations for garden plots and student assistants as necessary cost-cutting measures. Freedom made the same argument for circuit riders, which would allow "one teacher in different branches of learning to attend ten or twelve of these small [student] associations in rotation."[61] Academicus lamented that neighborhood schools taught reading, writing, and arithmetic "in so ineffectual a manner, as to be of little use to the learners, and at so expensive a rate, as to put it out of the power of the poorer class of citizens to gain any advantage from them."[62] None of them advocated a purely market-driven approach, but all hoped to "scale up" and publicly finance reforms that had worked locally. We will never know whether any of their proposals would have been cheap enough to satisfy taxpayers, whether the infrastructure existed for their implementation, or whether affordability alone would have led to the rising standards and centralization that they envisioned. Nevertheless, it is worth considering what might have happened if opinion-makers like those at the APS had recognized their merits.

Members of the prize committee seemed to arrive at a tantalizingly similar conclusion themselves when, just a month after the education premium was awarded, they suggested a second contest almost identical to the first. Propagation remained the basic purpose. "In order to obtain...the establishment of a proper system of public education, for the whole community," they wrote, "it seems necessary that certain principles should be impressed upon the minds of our fellow citizens in general, & Legislative Bodies in particular." Again they outlined the principles, but this time with not only specificity but practicality in mind. In addition to questions about classical languages and the role of sectarian religion, for example, they focused on issues of accessibility and popular opinion. "Youth deprived of the means of education by the poverty, or neglect of their parents, have a just claim upon the community for education," they found, and "[p]ublic Seminaries ought to be equally acceptable to every description of citizens, and therefore in as much as the youth in the vicinity of colleges and academies have advantages superior to those at greater distance, provision ought to be made as far as possible for equal advantages in this respect." Most importantly, the committee envisioned a broader range of answers, cautioning that its report should not be seen "as comprizing all the principles which might be attended to, but [expecting] that upon an examination of the subject some others will occur to the Society." This caveat was not an open solicitation of ideas—once the APS settled on its principles it would still require "the Candidates to illustrate & enforce their principles which are regarded as fixed"—but it at least left room for proposals "to ascertain and determine those questions which may be considered as doubtful."[63]

Indeed, the second contest might have signaled a first step toward ideological compromise or experimentation, toward a synthesis of republican and market ideals. But, unfortunately, there is no way to gauge its extent. The idea seems to have died in committee and the Philosophical Society launched no more educational initiatives over the coming years. Traditional conceptions of a properly republican school system remained intact but impotent while the demand for local provisions surged ahead, steadily widening the gap between the pure and the possible.

NOTES

1. Freedom, "The Best Plan for Conducting a Liberal Education," 1797, American Philosophical Society Archives.
2. This is evident in Carl Kaestle, *The Pillars of the Republic: Common Schools and American Society, 1780–1960* (New York: Hill and Wang, 1983), Chapter 1; and Bernard Bailyn, *Education in the Forming of American Society: Needs and Opportunities for Study* (Chapel Hill: University of North Carolina Press, 1960), 113–114.
3. Gordon S. Wood, *Empire of Liberty: A History of the Early Republic* (New York: Oxford University Press, 2009), 473–474.
4. Thomas Jefferson, "A Bill for the More General Diffusion of Knowledge," in Merrill D. Peterson (ed.), *Jefferson: Writings* (New York: Library of America, 1984), 365; Benjamin Rush, "Plan for the Establishment of Public Schools," Frederick Rudolph, *Essays on Education in the Early Republic* (Cambridge: Harvard University Press, 1965), 3–23.
5. J. M. Opal, "Exciting Emulation: Academies and the Transformation of the Rural North, 1780s-1820s," *Journal of American History* 91:2 (September 2004): 4.
6. On the debatable degree of educational consensus during the early national period, see Siobhan Moroney, "Birth of a Canon: The Historiography of Early Republican Education," *History of Education Quarterly* 39:4 (Winter 1999); and Eldon L. Johnson, "The 'Other Jeffersons' and the State University Idea," *The Journal of Higher Education* 58:2 (March–April, 1987): 127–150.
7. Margaret Nash, "Contested Identities: Nationalism, Regionalism, and Patriotism in Early American Textbooks," *History of Education Quarterly* 49:4 (November 2009): 418. Several other historians have made similar arguments about the interplay of local and national contexts. See Kim Tolley, "'Let the Education of Children Become a Common Charge': Democratic-Republican Newspaper Printers and the Question of Public Education, 1787–1828," Paper presented at ISCHE, Newark, New Jersey, 2008; Nancy Beadie, *Education and the Creation of Capital in the Early American Republic* (New York: Cambridge University Press, 2010); and Rita Koganzon, "'Producing a Reconciliation of Disinterestedness and Commerce': The Political Rhetoric of Education in the Early Republic," *History of Education Quarterly* 52:3 (August 2012): 403–429.
8. The announcement was clearly based on Benjamin Rush's ideas and may have been written by Rush himself, who was an active member of the APS. Benjamin Justice, "'The Great Contest': The American Philosophical Society Education Prize of 1795 and the Problem of American Education," *American Journal of Education* 114 (February 2008): 196.
9. Ibid., 192.
10. Lawrence Cremin, *American Education: The National Experience, 1783–1876* (New York: Harper & Row, 1980), 124.
11. Hand, "On Education and Public Schools," 1, American Philosophical Society Archives. This observation belies the assumption that, "as theorists,

[Republican educators] did not have to make hard-and-fast choices between different levels of education—for example, between primary and grammar schools or between grammar schools and colleges—and as a corollary they were under little pressure to choose between universal and liberal education." Joseph Kett, *The Pursuit of Knowledge under Difficulties: From Self-Improvement to Adult Education in America, 1750–1990* (Stanford: Stanford University Press, 1994), 78.

12. Only two of the essayists were definitely not from Philadelphia. As noted earlier, Samuel Knox was from Maryland. Academicus was most likely a pseudonym for John Hobson, an English clergyman, who nevertheless spent several years in Philadelphia as a private tutor; see chapter 9 in this volume. If William Smith was No. 3, as seems to be the case, he had been a fixture of the city's political and educational establishment for decades. Francis Hoskins (Hiram) was a Philadelphia clerk at the time of his submission, but would later go on to business success and marry a wealthy Virginian. Hand and Freedom remain unclear, but the latter's references to the "local situation" suggest a resident of the city.

13. The word "universities" was purposefully omitted, lest critics find it too elitist. J. P. Wickersham, *A History of Education in Pennsylvania* (New York: Arno Press, 1969), 258–259.

14. David W. Robson, *Educating Republicans: The College in the Era of the American Revolution, 1750, 1800* (Westport, CT: Greenwood Press, 1985), 237; Donald Tewksbury, *The Founding of American Colleges and Universities before the Civil War* (New York: Arno Press, 1969), 218; Frederick Rudolph, *Essays on Education in the Early Republic* (Cambridge: Harvard University Press, 1965), 3–8.

15. Robson, *Educating Republicans*, 243.

16. Thomas McKean and James Findley, the strongest proponents of public education in the legislature, fell on opposite ends of the political spectrum. McKean, as the state's chief justice in the 1780s, had become a federalist and renounced its original constitution. Findley, representing rural interests in the western part of the state, became an antifederalist but, like Jefferson, remained interested in the cause of public education. George B. Wood, *Early History of the University of Pennsylvania*, 3rd ed. (Philadelphia: Historical Society of Pennsylvania, 1896), 67–117.

17. Kim Tolley, "Mapping the Landscape of Higher Schooling, 1727–1850," in Kim Tolley and Nancy Beady (eds.), *Chartered Schools: Two Hundred Years of Independent Academies in the United States, 1727–1925* (New York: Routledge Farmer, 2002), 20–24.

18. James Mulhern, *A History of Secondary Education in Pennsylvania* (New York: Arno Press, 1969), 252.

19. Wickersham, *Education in Pennsylvania*, 281.

20. William C. Kashatus, *A Virtuous Education: Penn's Vision for Philadelphia Schools* (Wallingford, PA: Pendle Hill Publications, 1997), 98; "Sketch of the Origin and Present State of the Philadelphia Society for the Establishment and Support of Charity Schools," [*ca.* 1817], American Philosophical Society Archives.

21. Recommending schools for Thomas Jefferson's nephews a decade earlier, James Madison had written, "In the recommendation of these Seminaries I was much governed by the probable permanency of them; nothing being

more ruinous to *education* than the frequent interruptions & change of masters & methods incident to the private schools of this Country." James Madison to Thomas Jefferson, April 27, 1785, in *Letters and Other Writings of James Madison*, vol. 1 (New York: R. Worthington, 1884), 150.

22. Academicus, "Outlines of a Plan for the Education of Youth," 13. John Hobson, the likely author of the Academicus essay, elsewhere wrote that a public system would obviate "the evils of our common day schools," particularly their chaotic scheduling and poor instruction. John Hobson, *Prospectus of a Plan of Instruction for the Young of Both Sexes* (Philadelphia: D. Hogan, 1799), 16.

23. Hand, "On Education," 2.

24. It seems noteworthy that educational theorists were worried about teachers' accountability and the corresponding worth of academic credentials even before public schools existed. Freedom, "The Best Plan for Conducting a Liberal Education," 17.

25. Mulhern, *Secondary Education in Pennsylvania*, 186.

26. For more on Anglican educational and missions work, see E. Jennifer Monaghan, *Learning to Read and Write in Colonial America* (Amherst: University of Massachusetts Press, 2005), Chapter 5.

27. More than mere Christian charity, the Anglican Society for the Propagation of the Gospel hoped to undermine Quaker political power by winning the support of poor Germans. A similar challenge later came from within the Quaker establishment in the 1830s, when a group of young businessmen leveraged their work in charity schools to usurp their parents' generation and successfully implement public schools in Philadelphia. Samuel Edwin Weber, *The Charity School Movement in Colonial Pennsylvania* (New York: Arno Press and the New York Times, 1969), 45–48.

28. The same thinking led to the foundation of Franklin College (later Franklin and Marshall), which opened with a bilingual faculty and sought to integrate Germans into the state's political fabric. Benjamin Rush was a strong promoter of the new college. Weber, *The Charity School Movement in Colonial Pennsylvania*, 28–30; Benjamin Rush, "To the Citizens of Pennsylvania of German Birth and Extraction: Proposal of a German College" (August 31, 1785), in L. H. Butterfield (ed.), *Letters of Benjamin Rush* (Princeton: Princeton University Press, 1951), vol. 1, 364–368.

29. Weber, *The Charity School Movement in Colonial Pennsylvania*, 33. For more on the connections between the Anglican charity schools and the APS premium, see Benjamin Justice, "Beyond Nationalism: The Founding Fathers and Educational Universalism in the New Republic," in Doyle Stevick and Bradley Levinson (eds.), *Advancing Democracy through Education? U.S. Influence Abroad and Domestic Practices* (New York: Information Age Publishing), 1–27.

30. Samuel Magaw, "An Address Delivered in The Young Ladies Academy, at Philadelphia on February 8, 1787" (Philadelphia: Printed for Thomas Dobson, 1787), 11.

31. Benjamin Rush, "To the Citizens of Philadelphia," March 28, 1787, in Butterfield, *Letters of Benjamin Rush*, 412–415. Like Magaw, Rush was also a strong proponent of women's education. Benjamin Rush, *Thoughts Upon Female Education* (Philadelphia: Prichard & Hall, 1787).

32. Freedom, "The Best Plan for Conducting a Liberal Education," 1.
33. "Report of the committee appointed to make an analysis of the third piece on education, submitted for the premium, 23 July 1797," 10, American Philosophical Society Archives. Hereafter cited as "No. 3." Not everyone assumed that America's colleges could provide qualified university professors. Thomas Jefferson once tried to hire the entire faculty of Geneva to staff a national university. Neil McDowell Shawen, "Thomas Jefferson and a 'National' University: The Hidden Agenda for Virginia," *Virginia Magazine of History of Biography* 92:3 (July 1984): 316.
34. Hand, revealing his federalist sympathies, continues "that as many of those or other of our general civil officers as shall be found conveniently practicable to be thence only appointable, of the use of which restriction, to secure at least tolerable competency, we may yet be convinced, under a less prudent & judicious administration than we have hitherto been blessed with" (Hand, "On Education," 12).
35. The proper role of classical languages remained a live debate throughout the nineteenth century. Benjamin Rush opposed their use, while many others continued to equate them with refinement and "mental discipline." Benjamin Rush, "Of the Mode of Education Proper in a Republic," in Rudolph, *Essays on Education in the Early Republic*, 3–8.
36. Hand, "On Education," 12.
37. Academicus, "Outlines of a Plan for the Education of Youth," 14–16. No. 3, 3–4.
38. Wood, *Empire of Liberty*, 109.
39. For Freedom, quality teaching was part of a broader preoccupation with credentialing. He argued for higher standards for doctors, as well. Freedom, "The Best Plan for Conducting a Liberal Education," 16.
40. Hand, "On Education," 3, 12.
41. "No. 3," 10.
42. Freedom, "The Best Plan for Conducting a Liberal Education," 11–12. For more on eighteenth-century reading circles, see Richard Brown, *Knowledge Is Power: The Diffusion of Information in Early America, 1700–1865* (New York: Oxford University Press, 1989), Chapters 6, 8.
43. Hand, "On Education," 5.
44. "No. 3," 10.
45. David C. Ward, *Charles Wilson Peale: Art and Selfhood in the Early Republic* (Berkeley: University of California Press, 2004), 95–110.
46. Freedom, "The Best Plan for Conducting a Liberal Education," 20; Lisa Rosner, "Thistle on the Delaware: Edinburgh Medical Education and Philadelphia Practice, 1800–1825," *The Social History of Medicine* 5:1 (1992): 19–42.
47. Johnson, "The 'Other Jeffersons,'" 5.
48. Justice, "The Great Contest," 200; "Premiums," *American Monthly Review; or, Literary Journal* 2:1 (May 1795): 98. *Early Proceedings of the American Philosophical Society...1744–1838* (Philadelphia: McCalla & Stavely, 1844), 253.
49. Freedom, "The Best Plan for Conducting a Liberal Education," 4. See also Monaghan, *Learning to Read and Write*, Chapters 7, 8, and 12.
50. In one of the more inept lines of the contest, he pointed out that students might be confused when "the word *jus* in law, or a tract of jurisprudence,

signifies a *Right*; but in cookery it signifies a *broth* or *gravy*" (Academicus, "Outlines of a Plan for the Education of Youth," 11).

51. Academicus, "Outlines of a Plan for the Education of Youth," 6; Jill Lepore, *A is for American: Letters and Other Characters in the Newly United States* (New York: Knopf, 2002).

52. Such criticism was hardly unique to the APS essay contest. The judges for a contemporary literary journal in New York made similarly "dismissive comments about authors' poor 'stile' or lack of originality, [and] examiners expressed huffy frustration with poor grammar and spelling as well as 'indecent' subject matter" (Carolyn Eastman, *A Nation of Speechifiers: Making an American Public after the Revolution* [Chicago: University of Chicago Press, 2009], 121).

53. "Report of the committee appointed to make an analysis of the paper on education, submitted for the premium by 'Academicus,'" April 15, 1797, American Philosophical Society Archives.

54. Hand, "On Education," 2–3. "Report of committee upon an anonymous paper on education and public schools," American Philosophical Society Archives

55. In 1787, the Northwest Ordinances established federal land grants for the construction of schools and other internal improvements. For more on land grants, see Gordon Lee, *The Struggle for Federal Aid: The First Phase* (New York: Teachers College Press, 1949), 9–13; and Robert S. Hill, "Federalism, Republicanism, and the Northwest Ordinance," *Publius* 18:4 (Autumn 1988): 41–52.

56. Hiram, "A Plan for Establishing Schools, &c," 1–2.

57. For a discussion of monitors in medieval and early modern schools, see Philippe Ariès, *Centuries of Childhood: A Social History of Family Life* (New York: Vintage Books, 1962), 256–257. For a history of the Lancaster system, see David Hogan, "The Market Revolution and Disciplinary Power: Joseph Lancaster and the Psychology of the Early Classroom System," *History of Education Quarterly* 29:3 (Autumn 1989): 381–417.

58. "Report of the committee appointed to make an analysis of the paper on education, submitted for the premium by 'Hiram,'" April 17, 1797, American Philosophical Society Archives.

59. Justice, "The Great Contest," 207.

60. Ibid., 206–208.

61. Freedom, "The Best Plan for Conducting a Liberal Education," 11–12.

62. Academicus, "Outlines of a Plan for the Education of Youth," 14.

63. "Respecting a Prize Question on Education [Back Matter]," *Proceedings of the American Philosophical Society*, February 15, 1799.

CHAPTER 5

"Encouraging Useful Knowledge" in the Early Republic: The Roles of State Governments and Voluntary Organizations

Nancy Beadie

*That a school or schools should be established in each county by the legis-
lature for the convenient instruction of youth, with such salaries to the
masters paid by the publick, as may enable them to instruct youth at low
prices; and all useful learning shall be duly encouraged and promoted in
one or more universities.*

—*Section 44, Pennsylvania Constitution of 1776*[1]

As to their STUDIES, it would be well if they could be taught **every Thing**
that is useful, and **every Thing** *that is ornamental: But as Art is long,
and their time is short, it is therefore propos'd that they learn those Things
that are likely to be* **most useful** *and* **most ornamental**, *Regard being
had to the several Professions for which they are intended.*

—*Benjamin Franklin,* Proposals Relating to the
Education of Youth in Pensilvania, 1749[2]

Perhaps no phrase better captures the enlightenment educational project
than that of "encouraging useful knowledge." With its implied reference to
the agency of the learner, its apparent favoring of active trades and professions, its unspoken contrast with the purely theological, and its veiled critique of mere markers of social status, the phrase seems to suggest a world in
which new learning and innovative practices were breaking out everywhere,
including government itself, which in many ways they were. Some version
of the phrase appeared in virtually every educational essay and manifesto of
the late colonial and early republican eras, including the statement of purpose for the American Philosophical Society, which defined its mission as

"promoting useful knowledge." And no person or place better represented the notion of encouraging useful knowledge than Benjamin Franklin, the city of Philadelphia, and the state of Pennsylvania, where Franklin used the language to promote the founding not only of the APS but also of the institution that became the University of Pennsylvania, both in the 1740s.

To try to define what counted as useful knowledge and what did not, however, was a very difficult task at the time and continues to challenge the historian today. As Benjamin Franklin himself demonstrated in his discussion of the curriculum for the proposed Academy of Philadelphia, and as the scholar Margaret Nash has documented in a wide-ranging analysis of similar writings of the period, virtually any subject could be defined as "useful" with respect to some end.[3] What I suggest here, however, is that there was greater clarity and consensus about the practical means by which useful knowledge could be promoted than there was about the substantive content of that knowledge. Specifically, I focus on the roles of two entities in the enlightenment educational project: state governments and voluntary organizations.

In the previous essay and in the opening chapter of this book, Campbell Scribner and Benjamin Justice highlight the gap between the broad national scale of the educational proposals that the sponsors and judges of the American Philosophical Society contest apparently favored, on the one hand, and the intensely local scale at which most schooling and educational innovation actually occurred, on the other.[4] They suggest that a historical alternative to the nationalist framework favored by APS judges might have focused on "scaling up" existing educational provisions rather than on imposing new systems or institutions from the top down.

State governments and translocal voluntary organizations operated at this intermediate scale. What follows is a discussion of common ideas about the roles that state governments and voluntary organizations could play in encouraging useful knowledge, as represented first in the language of educational provisions in early state constitutions and second by the educational ideas, structure, and practices of Freemasonry. Although at first glance this dual focus on the role of early state governments and of Freemasonry in promoting education may seem idiosyncratic, in fact, as I hope to show, the relationship was complementary, even symbiotic. To a degree so far largely unappreciated, Freemasonry aimed precisely at occupying the intermediate space between different scales of government and at forging practical and ideological links between enlightenment educational initiatives at those different scales. State governments, meanwhile, provided the legal and organizational forms that made effective exercise of such educational agency and leadership possible. Together, one could say that state governments, Freemasonry, and other voluntary organizations, often founded in part by Freemasons, provided a kind of ghost system underlying apparently independent local educational initiatives, including those of the APS itself and the University of Pennsylvania.

The discussion proceeds in three parts. In the first part I discuss common understandings about the role of Revolutionary-era state governments in promoting education, as expressed in the language of new state constitutions, with particular emphasis on the State of Pennsylvania. The second part follows with a discussion of the role of voluntary organizations in promoting education, science, and culture in the eighteenth-century Anglo world, with specific attention to how Freemasonry both built upon and distinguished itself from this broader associational culture. Finally, in the third part I provide a brief account of how the American Philosophical Society, the Academy of Philadelphia, and eventually the University of Pennsylvania intersected in this historical context. In the process I also recontextualize the American Philosophical Society Contest of 1795 and suggest a somewhat speculative hypothesis regarding its political significance at the time.

The Role of State Governments: "Rewards" and "Immunities"

State constitution writing was a quintessential enlightenment project. As the eminent historians Pauline Maier and Gordon S. Wood have each made plain in their respective bodies of work, early republican leaders operating at multiple scales—from the local town meeting to colonial, state, and federal legislatures—approached the work of constituting new governments and advancing new political principles in a highly experimental way, studying the evidence of past examples, proposing remedies for existing problems, and subjecting their efforts to the test of experience.[5] In this way, principles such as religious toleration and universal access that became central to the idea of public education effectively developed as syntheses of existing practice. The language of state constitutions provides a window onto how the principles summarizing these practices came to be conceived during the early Republican era.

Scholars and popular writers have typically turned to Massachusetts, in particular, and New England states in general, as historical leaders and exemplars of public support for education. In its constitution of 1780, Massachusetts included a fairly elaborate and felicitously worded declaration about the value of education, which other states imitated and which is certainly deserving of analysis. This provision was more rhetorical than directive, however. For a somewhat earlier and more active statement of the role of the state in promoting education, the Pennsylvania constitution of 1776, which other states also imitated, was arguably the leader.

Three words in particular stand out in the education provisions of the Pennsylvania constitution: "convenient," "useful," and "encouragement." The first of these essentially addressed the distribution of education, suggesting that the state had a role to play in making education geographically accessible and financially affordable. Section 44 of Pennsylvania's constitution of 1776 specified that "a school or schools should be established in each county by the legislature for the convenient instruction of youth"; and that such salaries should be "paid by the public" to the masters of these schools as would enable them to "instruct youth at low prices."[6] The language of this provision was repeated in its entirety in Article XLI (41) of the North Carolina constitution of 1776, framed a few months later. The implication in both cases—as in Georgia's constitution of 1777, which used different language to specify the same basic provision—was that at least one publically subsidized institution of learning should be available in each county, making affordable instruction more "convenient" than if confined only to major coastal cities like Philadelphia.[7]

In addition to these clauses promoting the "convenient" instruction of youth, the Pennsylvania and North Carolina constitutions used the language of "useful" to suggest that the state had a role to play in promoting certain *kinds* of learning. The same article which directed that the legislature establish county schools went on to specify that "all useful learning" be encouraged "in one or more universities."[8] The implication was that in addition to establishing at least one school for the instruction of youth in each county, the legislature would support at least one university in the state, and that the chief purpose or justification for supporting such an institution lay in the "usefulness" of the learning it would promote.

This language of "usefulness," though vague, had considerable currency. In the case of Pennsylvania, it also had substantial precedent and some greater specificity in the colonial charter, or "Frame of Government," drawn up by William Penn in 1682. Article XII of that document specified that the governor and provincial council "encourage and reward the authors of useful science and laudable inventions."[9] In this formulation, then, the language of "usefulness" seems to have referred to a certain practical or applied use, particularly of a sort that might result in improved economic productivity and increased trade.

Note also that in this earlier formulation, the suggested means of "encouraging" useful knowledge was a "reward" or premium much like that offered in the American Philosophical Society contest of 1795. The offer of rewards or premiums for the solution of technical or applied problems was a common practice dating back to at least the early Renaissance, when nations or city-states often gave rewards for problems of engineering and design or navigation and cartography. During the enlightenment, the practice of offering rewards or prizes for scientific invention or navigational feats was taken up as well by various voluntary associations or corporations of individuals, including groups of merchants and gentlemen scientists.[10] In this tradition, the APS in 1786 established the Magellanic Premium for discoveries "relating to navigation, astronomy, or natural philosophy," as well as subsequent contests devoted to the solution of practical and technical problems such as the heating of rooms and the lighting of streets.[11] In the contest of 1795 the APS applied the premium tradition to a problem of what we might call "social" science, that of improving education. Matters of law and social organization in this way also became a kind of "useful" knowledge that could be "encouraged" through "rewards."

But what made it possible for a voluntary association like the American Philosophical Society to do what it did? Another form of "encouragement" besides the direct distribution of funds in the form of "rewards" or premiums was the structural framework that enabled scientific associations like the American Philosophical Society and educational institutions like the Academy of Philadelphia to exist, to do their work, and to achieve a degree of continuity and permanence. In a separate section, the Pennsylvania Constitution of 1776 delineated this structural role that the state played in supporting educational organizations and institutions. "Laws for the encouragement of virtue, and prevention of vice and immorality shall be made and constantly kept in force," Section 45 began, "... [a]nd all religious societies or bodies of men heretofore united or incorporated for the advancement of religion or learning, or for other pious and charitable purposes, shall be encouraged and protected in the enjoyment of the privileges, immunities and estates which they were accustomed to enjoy, or could of right have enjoyed, under the laws and former constitution of this state."[12]

With this provision, the Pennsylvania constitution affirmed the corporate charters of existing educational organizations and institutions, such as the American Philosophical Society and the Academy of Philadelphia. More broadly, it articulated the value of incorporation as a form of "encouragement" for various social enterprises, including education. The importance of the state role in granting acts of incorporation is difficult to recapture now, when it is so far assumed as to be almost invisible, but it was highly significant in the early republican era. Then as now, incorporation was a legal "privilege" that enabled an association of individuals with an interest in a common project to pool their resources, hold the resulting property (or "estates") in common, and dedicate that common wealth to a specified purpose, including "the advancement of religion or learning." It furthermore made it possible to protect that common property from being appropriated to satisfy private debts against the corporation's individual members. In the absence of the "immunities" conferred by incorporation, the future of a school or voluntary association depended on the whims and fortunes of individual teachers or sponsors. Finally, incorporation provided for the continuation of an entity over time, beyond the lives and regardless of the fates of its founders. It thus enabled societies and institutions to achieve a degree of permanence and stability. By reinforcing the power of the state to protect the "privileges, immunities, and estates" of incorporated institutions such as universities, county schools and seminaries, libraries, mechanics' institutes, and philosophical societies, the Pennsylvania constitution of 1776 indirectly but effectively "encouraged useful knowledge" and other educational ends.

Much of the existing literature on corporate legal history focuses on the origins of business corporations such as banks and railroads. Initially, however, the expansion of access to corporate legal power in the United States occurred with regard to social and educational institutions such as churches, schools, and charitable organizations. During the early republican period, acts of incorporation were still presumed to be legitimate only in cases where the resulting organization would perform a recognizable public service. Granting acts of incorporation to associations organized simply for private gain, and in competition with individual households and partnerships, was widely considered a violation of republican principle. In this context, the first organizations to gain broadened access to corporate power were religious, educational, and charitable associations.[13]

In summary, then, the Pennsylvania constitution and its imitators conceived the state's role in encouraging "useful" knowledge in three main ways: (1) by directly establishing "convenient" institutions of learning throughout the state; (2) through direct funding in the form of "rewards"; and (3) through the indirect legal structure of incorporation, which encouraged the formation of voluntary educational organizations and protected the "privileges, immunities and estates" of those associations through corporate law.

These three means of encouraging useful knowledge were not idiosyncratic to Pennsylvania. The educational provision of the Massachusetts constitution of 1780 included some of the same ideas, but expressed in different language. Three words in particular stand out in the Massachusetts provision: "diffusion," "duty," and "cherish." The word "diffusion" enjoyed considerable currency in enlightenment thought and early national statecraft, and was often coupled with words suggestive of education, such as "learning" or "intelligence." As with the notion of "convenience" in the Pennsylvania constitution, the word "diffusion" addressed issues of distribution, both geographically and among different classes of the population. The Massachusetts constitution, however, linked this distribution to an explicit civic purpose. Chapter V, Section 2, of the Massachusetts constitution of 1780, entitled "The encouragement of literature," declared that "[w]isdom and knowledge, as well as virtue, diffused generally among the body of the people" was "necessary for the preservation of their rights and liberties." It then went on to elaborate what it meant by diffusion: that is, "spreading the opportunities and advantages of education in various parts of the country, and among the different orders of the people."[14]

As mentioned previously, the Massachusetts constitution specified a less active role in this process of diffusion than did Pennsylvania. Rather than directing the Commonwealth to establish institutions in counties throughout the state, as did the Pennsylvania constitution, the Massachusetts constitution left the business of "establishment" up to localities and voluntary associations. Nonetheless, Massachusetts appears to be the first state to use the language of "duty" with respect to the state's responsibility for education. After its opening declaration regarding the civic value of diffusing wisdom, knowledge, and virtue widely through the country and the population, the Massachusetts provision went on to state that "it shall be the duty of the legislatures and magistrates, in all future periods of this Commonwealth," to "cherish the interests of literature and the sciences, and all seminaries of them."[15]

But what did it mean to "cherish" the interests of literature and the sciences? It meant to cherish the interests of particular institutions. In this category, the Massachusetts provision specifically included "the university at Cambridge," and the "public schools and grammar schools in the towns." It further specified that officers of the Commonwealth should "encourage private societies and public institutions" and "rewards and immunities." Thus

Massachusetts used similar language to that of Pennsylvania to affirm the value of funding ("rewards") and incorporation ("immunities") as means of "cherishing" literature and the sciences.[16]

The Massachusetts constitution also elaborated the content of the learning and the types of virtue necessary for a good society, and thus the kinds of public institutions and private societies the state should encourage. Among these were all the domains of study that authors of the Pennsylvania constitution probably had in mind when they invoked the value of "useful learning" for economic development: that is, "agriculture, arts, sciences, commerce, trades, manufactures, and a natural history of the country." In addition, however, the Massachusetts education provision, reportedly written by John Adams, articulated the public value (or "usefulness") of an education in virtue and the humanities. It was thus the duty of the Commonwealth not only to promote the kinds of learning that would increase commerce, improve agriculture, or produce inventions, thereby creating financial capital, but that would also "countenance and inculcate the principles of humanity and general benevolence, public and private charity, industry and frugality, honesty and punctuality in their dealings, sincerity, good humor, and all the social affections and generous sentiments among the people"—in other words, the kind of learning that would promote the creation of social and political capital in the form of voluntary associations. Those associations in turn might then organize formal educational institutions that applied to the state for corporate charters.

Versions of these ideas appeared in the provisions of other early state constitutions as well. The Massachusetts education provision was repeated in its entirety in the revised New Hampshire constitution of 1784.[17] Portions were also borrowed by a number of other states.[18] States varied, however, in the degree to which they encouraged the voluntary organization of new institutions through grants of incorporation. As Pauline Meier showed in her survey of the subject, southern states such as Virginia were more likely to rely on individual proprietorships or limited partnerships than corporations to undertake public works. In the North, by contrast, the practice of granting acts of incorporation accelerated in the early republican era. New York and Massachusetts were among the states with the most liberal incorporation policies.[19]

The historical significance of incorporation to the development of the early republic is often underappreciated, but can be glimpsed through international comparison. In England, where the authority to grant acts of incorporation lay with the crown rather than Parliament, the practice was all but abandoned for more than a century, from 1720 to 1825. Similarly, in France, incorporation was regarded as a vestige of pre-Revolutionary government. In the new United States, by contrast, and somewhat paradoxically, incorporation became a tool of republican independence.[20] For a group of ordinary "public-spirited gentlemen" (to use a Franklin phrase) to obtain a charter for an educational institution in the new United States was to gain a power and privilege that in much of Europe was reserved to the hierarchy of a state-controlled church and thus to the Crown. Access to corporate power by voluntary associations in this sense became a practical embodiment of principles of religious and political freedom.

The Role of Voluntary Organizations: Fraternities of "Scientific and Ingenious Men"

No one better understood the powers of incorporation and the value of a corporate charter for promoting useful knowledge than Benjamin Franklin, who made those principles explicit in his famous "Proposals Relating to the Education of Youth in Pennsilvania" in 1749. Although the most commonly cited portion of that document is its extensive discussion of curriculum, the more immediate aim, as the author(s) clearly stated at the outset, was incorporation:

> It is propos'd,
>   THAT some Persons of Leisure and publick Spirit, apply for a CHARTER by which they may be incorporated, with Power to erect an ACADEMY for the Education of Youth, to govern the same, provide Masters, make Rules, receive Donations, purchase Lands &c, and to add to their Number, from Time to Time such other Persons as they shall judge suitable.[21]

As indicated here, a central benefit of incorporation was the power it conferred to acquire corporate property—that is, to receive donations, purchase lands, and erect a building. The *Proposals* themselves were drafted precisely for these purposes, as Franklin explained in his autobiography. Having distributed his pamphlet to inhabitants of the city for free, Franklin waited until he supposed "their Minds a little prepared by the Perusal of it," and then "set on foot a Subscription for Opening and Supporting an Academy."[22] Once sufficient pledges had been collected, the organizers hired a house, engaged masters, enrolled students, and began searching for a piece of real estate to purchase for a more permanent home for the institution. Incorporation was an essential tool for accomplishing these practical tasks of capital creation, investment, and property acquisition.

Just as important as the legal privilege of corporate ownership conferred by the corporate charter, however, was the association of like-minded individuals who initiated and promoted the project, contributed start-up funds, shepherded the charter through the colonial legislature, secured the real estate, and oversaw its actual operation. In his autobiography, Franklin presented himself as the prime mover in launching this and other "public-spirited" enterprises. According to his account, he first solicited the assistance and support of others and then strategically took a backseat as others moved the plan ahead.[23] No doubt there is considerable truth in this, as Franklin clearly had a genius for launching such initiatives. But just as clearly he had a network of willing compatriots. The preamble to the *Proposals* suggests as much, stating that the proposed plan for an academy "is so far approv'd by some publick-Spirited Gentlemen, to whom it has been privately communicated, that they have directed a Number of Copies to be made by the Press, and properly distributed, in order to obtain the Sentiments and Advice of Men of Learning, Understanding, and Experience in these Matters."[24]

Who were the "publick-spirited Gentlemen" who read Franklin's draft *Proposals* in 1749 and lent their support? We do not know precisely, but they definitely included members of the Junto, the society of 12 like-minded men whom Franklin had organized into a club more than 20 years earlier in 1727 or 1728.[25] Members of the Junto had been party to the launching of a number of previous Franklin enterprises, including the founding of the Philadelphia Library Company in 1731 and the American Philosophical Society in 1743 (at least half of the APS's founding members are known to have been members of the Junto).[26] The Junto, among other things, took as its mission the identification of public problems that needed to be addressed. Reportedly, members followed a weekly ritual of posing and discussing a set series of questions, including: "Have you lately observed any defect in the laws of your country of which it would be proper to move the legislature for an amendment? Or do you know any beneficial law that is wanting?"[27] The opening line of the preamble to the *Proposals* could be read as an answer to that question: "It has long been regretted as a Misfortune to the Youth of this Province, that we have no ACADEMY, in which they might receive the Accomplishments of a regular Education."[28] After initial discussion of such an issue, the practice of the Junto was for a member of the group to take up the assignment of writing a paper on the topic, having consulted appropriate literature, and to present the paper to the group for further discussion and critique. One can well imagine the *Proposals* as the product of such a process.

The larger point here, however, is not what precise role the Junto played in founding the Academy of Philadelphia, but the more general role that voluntary organizations played in "encouraging useful knowledge" and establishing educational institutions. The particular societies and clubs in which Franklin assumed leadership were part of a much larger and denser network of associations in Philadelphia and other colonial cities in the eighteenth century and more broadly in the Anglo urban world. The initial locus of this flowering of associational culture was London, but it quickly grew to include other Anglo commercial cities such as Edinburgh and the coastal cities of the colonies. In the 1710s London already hosted an estimated two thousand clubs and societies.[29] As a young journey man who worked in London for 18 months during the 1720s, Benjamin Franklin experienced this flowering of associational culture and it was this culture that he helped reproduce when he returned to Philadelphia.

By the 1740s, this urbane club society had also acquired an apologist in the Scottish Enlightenment thinker David Hume, who argued that the formation of clubs and societies simultaneously increased knowledge and learning and served a public purpose. In such a culture, men and women met on a sociable basis, exchanged ideas, improved each other's minds, and at the same time created a demand for refined goods and other amenities that stimulated invention and improvement in the arts of all kinds, including the art of politics. All this in turn had a beneficial effect on public life, both through the improvements themselves and through the cultivation of better and more thoughtful leaders: "The same age, which produced great philosophers and politicians, renowned generals and poets, usually abounds with skilful weavers, and ship-carpenters. We cannot reasonably expect, that a piece of woollen cloth will be brought to perfection in a nation, which is ignorant of astronomy, or where ethics are neglected."[30]

Most clubs and societies of this urbane age were strictly local. Their membership was of the city and their locality was in many ways their point and purpose. They provided a particular place where people of different trades, geographic origins, and social positions could come together, dine, socialize, and exchange and refine their sensibilities, ideas, and views. They developed distinctive, sometimes deliberately silly, symbols and rituals precisely to distinguish themselves from other local clubs in a convivial, entertaining way. A few older chartered institutions like the Royal Society of London, on which the APS was modeled, originated in an earlier period and had more ambitious purposes and translocal and even international memberships. The Royal Society, which had been chartered in the 1660s directly by the crown, initially operated primarily as a corresponding society, with members who traveled the world. In the eighteenth century, nonetheless, even the Royal Society gained local meaning and significance. It was during the flowering of London's associational culture in the 1710s that the Royal Society first established itself in a permanent building, becoming the site of a library, regular lectures, and a show place for various inventions and natural collections.[31]

Freemasonry had roots in this same associational culture. As it emerged in Britain in the late 1710s and early 1720s, Freemasonry was a fraternal movement of learned gentlemen with a common interest in science, a nostalgic relationship to medieval guilds, and a fascination with ancient mysteries and even magic. In its first decade, its membership overlapped considerably with that of the Royal Society.[32] As it grew over the course of the eighteenth century, Freemasonry became an international federation of clubs with a common body of knowledge, a common set of enlightenment ideas, rituals, and traditions, and a common process of initiation—that is, a common curriculum. What distinguished Freemasonry from most clubs and societies of this period was its simultaneously local and international character. Part of the point of becoming a Mason was precisely the fact that membership transcended locality, that initiation into its rituals in one place made one a member in an international brotherhood, providing a credential that traveled. Through commercial and colonial networks Freemasonry quickly spread through the western world, including the American colonies, where it took root in the 1730s and flourished in the Revolutionary Era. Benjamin Franklin was an agent of this American expansion. Having first become a Mason in 1731, he served as Grand Master of the Masons of Pennsylvania in 1734 and again in 1749, the same year he issued his *Proposals*.

The impact of Freemasonry on American society and culture was substantial, particularly in the period immediately preceding and following the Revolutionary War. There were two dimensions of this influence: the education of new republican leaders and the promotion of education itself. Freemasonry was a highly effective educational organization in its own right. At every level of Masonic membership, from certification as an "Entered Apprentice" to the award of the "Fellow Craft" and "Master's" degrees, men were initiated in the historic traditions, structures, and values of Freemasonry. As framed and explained by Masonic leaders in the Republican era, the rituals themselves were pedagogical in their effects, designed to "impress" Masonic lessons "with greater force upon the mind." To ensure the efficacy of this pedagogy, moreover, the Masons organized a form of teacher training in which traveling agents of the organization, known as "lecturers," drilled members in the texts and meaning of Masonic rituals and symbols. Among the ideas cultivated by these means were the value of civic virtue and the virtue of learning itself.

The particular significance of Freemasonry during the early Republican era derived from the way it coupled an enlightenment educational vision with an extensive and highly effective organizational structure. Once the colonial structure of government was overthrown, leaders of Freemasonry in the United States turned away from tending their British connections and toward the cultivation of new Masonic networks and leaders in the United States. During Franklin's era Freemasonry had thrived primarily in coastal cities such as Boston, New York, Philadelphia, and Charleston. Expansion generally occurred through multiplication of lodges within those cities. In the 1790s, by contrast, expansion occurred in towns and cities in the interior. Between 1790 and 1806, for example, the number of lodges in New York State increased from about 10 to about 100, with new lodges meeting primarily outside New York City. By 1825, the number of lodges in the state would increase to nearly 500, with most in the interior of the state.[33]

The earliest of these new lodges were founded in the new capital cities such as Raleigh, North Carolina, that Revolutionary governments had deliberately established in the interiors of their states, and in the county seats where the division and sale of new land and the commercial development of the early Republic occurred. Not insignificantly, these were the places where new courthouses were being built and new county seminaries and academies were being established to school the children of the associated commercial and professional classes.[34] Masons both literally and figuratively laid the cornerstones of many of these buildings. They also increasingly came to frame their roles in this institution-building process in educational terms.

As the historian Stephen C. Bullock argued in his monumental study of Freemasonry in America from 1730 to 1840, a decided post-Revolutionary shift occurred in Masonic culture in the United States beginning in the 1790s. This new Masonic culture emphasized the significance of Freemasonry as a scientific organization and its mission as one of promoting the diffusion of knowledge and learning throughout the country and across all classes of people. Rhetorically, this meant that Masonic leaders like DeWitt Clinton of New York, giving a major and widely circulated address in 1793, praised the founders of Freemasonry as "scientific and ingenious men" who aimed at sharing the secrets of the arts and sciences with the world and at bringing "the means of instruction to all ranks of the people."[35] Practically, this shift in culture meant that Masonic leaders at all levels of the system began portraying themselves and their organizations as promoters of education and learning in society and as sponsors of educational activities and institutions, including libraries, public schools, and museums. Bullock recounts instances in which particular Masonic lodges housed and financed schools and libraries and referred to lodges themselves as seminaries of learning and places where the sciences were taught. More broadly, Masonic leaders and lodges in the early Republican era began associating themselves with the policy of encouraging "schools and the advancement of knowledge" and of promoting "the general diffusion of education."[36]

The significance that Freemasonry assumed in promoting education in the early Republic should not be underestimated. It would be difficult to assess on a systematic basis the extent of Masonic involvement in school, library, and academy building during the first three decades of Republic, but the evidence from specific cases suggests that that role was substantial. It is not necessary to tie every educational project to the initiative of a Masonic lodge or leader to appreciate the educational significance of Freemasonry, however. More important, perhaps, than the direct role that Masonic Lodges played in such projects was the indirect role that Freemasonry played in the education of local leaders and networks of like-minded compatriots imbued with enlightenment ideas and ideals who sought to "encourage useful knowledge" in their respective counties, cities, and towns in whatever way they could.[37]

This, then, was the invisible system that connected the educational declarations of political leaders at national and state levels with local educational initiatives in counties and towns throughout much of the country. It was not, for the most part, a top-down system of direct support of education by government. Rather, it was a system of "scientific and ingenious men" who could be counted on to help promote useful knowledge wherever they found themselves, whether in Congress, the state legislature, the county seat, or a local board of trustees. Among other things, such networks of "publick-Spirited gentlemen" would well know how to conceive an educational project, enlist the financial and moral support of their fellows, apply for a corporate charter, and organize an educational institution that "encouraged useful knowledge."

Bridging the Gap: The APS Contest as a Local Initiative with National Ambition

The combined significance of state government and voluntary organization in promoting useful knowledge in the early Republic is well illustrated by the early history of the Academy of Philadelphia. Having received its first charter in 1749 and enrolled its first students in 1751, the Academy of Philadelphia developed in the 1750s and 1760s as an amalgam of schools, including a charity school, an English school, a classical school, a college, and eventually a medical school, each effectively operated under its own master, but under a common board of trustees. What held the academy together, in other words, was its common property, the common rules by which the use of that property was administered, and the men who governed that use.

Throughout the Revolutionary period, tension existed among the component schools, their masters, and the models of education that each represented. To some extent this tension reflected a conflict over the relative significance of "classical" versus "useful" knowledge and among the social classes, populations, and occupations those models served. To some extent the tension also represented a conflict over the influence of the Anglican Church in education and over the loyalties of various masters and members of the board of governors during the Revolutionary War.[38] In corporate terms, however, the conflict came down to the question of who controlled the "privileges, immunities, and estates" of the institution and for what purpose—in other words, who served on the board of governors.

In 1779 these conflicts were temporarily resolved, or at least reframed, through the replacement of the original academy and college charters with a new university charter, by which the institution came to be known as the University of the State of Pennsylvania. The issuance of this new charter was itself highly contested and deeply intertwined with events of the Revolution and early Pennsylvania statehood. Ultimately, the transformation of the academy into the University of Pennsylvania involved the passage of two university charters, one in 1779 and another in 1791. Pursuant to Section 44 of the Pennsylvania constitution of 1776, the Revolutionary government in 1779 established the University of the State of Pennsylvania, effectively replacing the existing leadership of the academy and college with men more clearly independent of the Anglican Church and more clearly aligned with the Revolutionary cause. For the next ten years, until 1789, the university operated under that leadership and charter. In 1789, however, the previous provost of the college, William Smith, and his allies temporarily won reinstatement of the old Academy and College charters of the 1750s, briefly regaining control of the old academy and college property and facilities. During this brief two-year period, from 1789 to 1791, there were actually two institutions in operation, one under the old college charter of 1755, located at the original academy facilities, and one under the new university charter of 1779, which occupied rooms in the newly completed facilities of the American Philosophical Society, known as Philosophical Hall and located on State House Square.[39]

The fact that the American Philosophical Society was so closely associated with this Revolutionary-era conflict over the future of the University of Pennsylvania suggests that the Society's 1795 contest, and its apparent preference for a plan that included a national university, should be considered in that context. Although the legal contest over who controlled the original academy property was soon resolved by merging the two institutions under yet another charter in 1791, certain practical problems remained. One of these was the problem of adequate facilities for an institution that included more than one component part. Under the provisions of a five-year lease, portions of the university, probably including its College of Physicians, continued to occupy rooms in APS's building until 1794. At the end of the lease, the APS took on a new, more "desirable tenant" in the form of Charles Willson Peale's art and natural history museum, and the university returned to the now somewhat cramped quarters of the original academy and began searching for new and larger quarters.[40] Thus, in 1794–95, the future of the university—especially the matter of its future facilities—was very much an issue.

It was at this point, in 1795, that a fraternity of scientific and ingenious men in the form of the American Philosophical Society decided to solicit proposals for a national education plan with a clear, though unstated, preference for a plan with a national university at its head. Given the situation of the University of Pennsylvania at the time and the undeniable familiarity of APS with that situation, it would not be surprising if some members imagined the University of Pennsylvania as somehow serving in that new national role.

And who's to say it could not have happened? Recall that in the 1790s Philadelphia served as the nation's capital. Initially, at least, Philadelphia's leading men apparently hoped that somehow the city would hold on to the status of national capital permanently, given the obvious cultural advantages and leadership the city already claimed and the initially slow progress of the new city building project on the shores of the Potomac. In 1792, city leaders endeavored to make that hope tangible by commencing construction of a grand president's house, intended for President Washington, though not completed until 1797, by which time John Adams had been elected president.[41] Throughout this period, including the duration of the Society's contest from May 1795 to April 1797, the American Philosophical Society regularly hosted, entertained, and addressed leaders of the new nation. Regular attendees included Presidents Washington and Adams and Vice President Jefferson, who became president of the APS in 1797, as well as other cabinet members and members of Congress.[42] During this period, members of the American Philosophical Society could reasonably have imagined that Congress might somehow be induced to appropriate the funds that would effectively transform the University of Pennsylvania or some related entity into a national university of the United States. Perhaps, more precisely, what members of the Society hoped in 1795, when they launched the contest, was for a vision that would somehow inspire and legitimize such a move.

Unfortunately for the Philadelphia organizers of the essay contest, however, a significant political shift occurred between May 1795, when the essay contest was announced, and early 1797, when the entries were first due. The presidential election of 1796, in which John Adams defeated Thomas Jefferson in a closely fought contest, significantly reduced the prospects of support for a Philadelphia-based bid for a national university, as it became clear to Adams and those around him that to appear to lend any support whatsoever to the notion that Philadelphia might hold onto a position of influence as a formal or informal capital of the new nation would be political suicide for a New Englander aspiring to the position of president. For this reason, in fact, Adams would refuse to move into the Philadelphia president's house in 1797 once it was completed. By then, indeed, it had become clear that a US president would never occupy the house—that to seem to accept the City of Philadelphia's offer of such a residence, however temporarily, would be politically problematic, given considerable negotiation and compromise between North and South that had gone into the plan of locating and constructing the capitol in the District of Columbia.[43] Political survival for someone like Adams depended on not alienating southerners any more than necessary.

What all this suggests is the possibility that the American Philosophical Society's contest to select a *national* education plan may in fact have been more local than it seems. It may also have been recognized as such by people at the time. Understanding the APS contest in this way may help explain the relatively small number of contest entries the APS received, the relative weakness of some of the proposals it did receive, its failure to attract additional strong entries once the deadline had been extended to 1797, and the decidedly localist character of some of its later entries. Those with political influence and perception may have correctly understood that prudence dictated avoiding a Philadelphia-based bid for national educational leadership.

As for the University of Pennsylvania, its immediate future involved a somewhat ironic twist. In the year 1800, when the national capital in fact moved to the District of Columbia, the University of Pennsylvania took over the building originally intended as the president's house, which had lain dormant since its completion in 1797.[44] Thus the university launched a new life from what was once imagined as a symbolic representation of Philadelphia's status as the national capital, but without designation as a national university. A fraternity of scientific and ingenious men located in the city of Philadelphia had tried to bridge the gap between local and national scales of educational initiative and leadership by building on existing institutions, but ultimately had failed.

NOTES

1. "Constitution of Pennsylvania—1776," Section 44, as printed in Francis Newman Thorpe, ed., *The Federal and State Constitutions, Colonial Charters, and Organic Laws, 1492–1908* (Washington, DC: Government Printing Office, 1909), vol. 5, 3083.

2. Benjamin Franklin, *Proposals Relating to the Education of Youth in Pensilvania* (Philadelphia: Franklin and Hall, 1749), facsimile reprint (Philadelphia: University of Pennsylvania, 1931), 6–7.

3. Margaret A. Nash, *Women's Education in the United States, 1780–1840* (New York: Palgrave MacMillan, 2005), 41–49.

4. See chapters 1 and 4 in this volume. See also Benjamin Justice, "'The Great Contest': The American Philosophical Society Education Prize of 1795 and the Problem of American Education," *American Journal of Education* 114 (February 2008): 191–213.

5. Pauline Maier, *American Scripture: Making the Declaration of Independence* (New York: Vintage, 1998); Gordon S. Wood, *The Creation of the American Republic, 1776–1787* (New York: Norton, 1972, *ca.* 1969).

6. "Constitution of Pennsylvania—1776," Section 44, as printed in Thorpe, *The Federal and State Constitutions*, vol. 5, 3083.

7. Ibid., "Constitution of North Carolina—1776," article XLI, vol. 5, 2794.

8. Ibid.

9. Ibid. "Frame of Government of Pennsylvania—1682," vol. 5, 3056.

10. Several recent popular histories describe examples of such contests. For example, Ross King, *Brunelleschi's Dome: How a Renaissance Genius Reinvented Architecture* (New York: Penguin, 2000); Dava Sobel, *Longitude: The True Story of a Lone Genius Who Solved the Greatest Scientific Problem of His Time* (New York: Walker Publishing, 1995); and Russell Shorto, *The Island at the Center of the World: The Epic Story of Dutch Manhattan and the Forgotten Colony that Shaped America* (New York: Vintage, 2005).

11. Edward C. Carter II, *"One Grand Pursuit": A Brief History of the American Philosophical Society's First 250 Years, 1742–1993* (Philadelphia: American Philosophical Society, 1993).

12. "Constitution of Pennsylvania—1776," Section 45, in Thorpe, *The Federal and State Constitutions*, vol. 5, 3083.

13. See Ronald Seavoy, *The Origins of the American Business Corporation, 1784–1855: Broadening the Concept of Public Service During Industrialization* (Westport, CT: Greenwood Press, 1982).

14. "Constitution or Form of Government for the Commonwealth of Massachusetts—1780," Chapter V, Section II, Thorpe, *The Federal and State Constitutions*, vol. 3, 1907–1908.

15. Ibid.

16. Ibid.

17. Ibid. "Constitution of New Hampshire—1784," vol. 4, 2467.

18. For a comparative analysis of education preambles and provisions in state constitutions, see David Tyack, Thomas James, and Aaron Benavot, *Law and the Shaping of Public Education, 1785–1954* (Madison, WI: University of Wisconsin Press, 1987), esp. Chapter 2, "Education as the Fourth Branch of State Government," 43–76. As Tyack et al. note, one of the most influential statements of the civic value of education was that synthesized in the Northwest Ordinance of 1787, written by John Adams and modeled on the earlier Massachusetts provisions, which specified the terms upon which territories north of the Ohio River would be governed and organized into states. As part of the portion of the document devoted to defining the rights of citizens and the responsibilities and limits of government, the ordinance declared: "Religion, morality, and knowledge, being necessary to good government and the happiness of mankind, schools and the means of education shall forever be encouraged." Coupled with an earlier act of 1785, which specified that certain portions of the lands in western territories should be reserved "for the maintenance of public schools," the Northwest Ordinance set a precedent for subsequent state support of education in the United States. For a relatively concise compilation of texts of education provisions in state constitutions collected in a single volume, see Franklin B. Hough, "Constitutional Provisions Relating to Education, Literature, and Science in the Several States of the American Union," in *Circular of Information of*

the Bureau of Education for the Year 1875 (Washington, DC: Government Printing Office, 1877), 543–672.

19. Pauline Maier, "The Revolutionary Origins of the American Corporation," *William and Mary Quarterly* 3rd. Ser., 50, n. 1, *Law and Society in Early American* (1993): 51–84.

20. Ibid.; Nancy Beadie, "Education, Social Capital and State Formation in Comparative Historical Perspectives: Preliminary Investigations," *Paedagogica Historica* 46:1–2 (February–April 2010): 15–32.

21. Franklin, *Proposals Relating to the Education of Youth in Pensilvania*, 6–7.

22. Benjamin Franklin, *The Autobiography* (New York: Vintage, 1990), 114–116.

23. Ibid.

24. Franklin, *Proposals*, 3.

25. "Peace being concluded, and the Association Business therefore at an End, I turn'd my Thoughts again to the Affair of establishing an Academy. The first Step I took was to associate in the Design a Number of active Friends, of whom the Junto furnished a good Part; the next was to write and publish a Pamphlet intitled, *Proposals in relation to the education of youth in Pennsylvania*" (Franklin, *Autobiography*, 114).

26. Carl Van Doren, *Benjamin Franklin* (New York: Penguin, 1990 [Viking, 1938]), 139.

27. Ibid., 75.

28. Franklin, *Proposals*, 3.

29. Steven C. Bullock, *Revolutionary Brotherhood: Freemasonry and the Transformation of the American Social Order, 1730–1840* (Chapel Hill: University of North Carolina Press, 1996), 29.

30. David Hume, "Of Refinement in the Arts," in Knud Haakonssen (ed.), *Political Essays* (Cambridge: Cambridge University Press, 1994), 107.

31. Bullock, *Revolutionary Brotherhood*, 36; D. C. Martin, "Former Homes of the Royal Society," *Notes and Records of the Royal Society of London* (The Royal Society) 22:1/2 (1967): 12.

32. Bullock, *Revolutionary Brotherhood*, 36. According to Bullock, fellows of the Royal Society made up more than one-quarter of the membership of the Freemasons in the decade after its founding in 1717.

33. Ibid., 187–188.

34. J. M. Opal, "Exciting Emulation: Academies and the Transformation of the Rural North, 1780s-1820s," *Journal of American History* 91:2 (September 2004): 445–470; Edward Herring O'Neil, "Private Schools and Public Vision: A History of Academies in Upstate New York, 1800–1860" (unpublished PhD dissertation, Syracuse University, 1984).

35. Bullock, *Revolutionary Brotherhood*, 139–148.

36. Ibid., 109–133.

37. For an in-depth discussion of the political significance of Freemasonry in the State of New York as well as a case study of its significance for educational initiatives at the local level, see Nancy Beadie, *Education and the Creation of Capital in the Early American Republic* (Cambridge: Cambridge University Press, 2010), especially Chapter 10, 158–175.

38. Edward Potts Cheyney, *History of the University of Pennsylvania, 1740–1940* (Philadelphia: University of Pennsylvania Press, 1940), 129–150.

39. Ibid., 153–162.
40. Carter, *"One Grand Pursuit,"* 20.
41. Ibid.; and also Cheyney, *History of the University of Pennsylvania.*
42. On the culture and politics of Philadelphia during the ten years that it was the location of the nation's capital, see Kenneth R. Bowling, "The Federal Government and the Republican Court Move to Philadelphia, November 1790–March 1791," and Anna Coxe Toogood, "Philadelphia as the Nation's Capital, 1790–1800," in Kenneth R. Bowling and Donald R. Kennon (eds.), *Neither Separate Nor Equal: Congress in the 1790s* (Ohio University Press, 2000), 3–33 and 34–57.
43. Toogood, "Philadelphia as the Nation's Capital."
44. Ibid.; and Cheyney, *History of the University of Pennsylvania.*

CHAPTER 6

Race and Schooling in Early Republican Philadelphia

Hilary Moss

Almost without exception, entrants in the American Philosophical Society education contest eschewed any mention of race in their essays. When devising "a plan for instituting and conducting public schools," winners and losers alike spilled no ink on the question of whether or not African Americans, free or enslaved, should have equal, or any, access to the nation's newly imagined school system. While several authors engaged with issues of class and to a lesser extent gender, all opted to avoid the question of whether or not a national system of public education should—or should not—be truly universal. Why did these essayists remain silent on the subject of race while reflecting on public education in the early American republic? And what, if anything, does their silence say about the present and future place of African Americans in the nation's public schools?

On the one hand, the absence of any discussion of race seems understandable. Perhaps a respondent like Samuel Knox presumed that because the preponderance of black people in his home state of Maryland toiled under the yoke of slavery, they were obviously not part of the public his nation should seek to educate. In which case, to go so far as to affirm that public schools should not admit African Americans would be simply to state the obvious. It is harder to understand, however, how and why the question of whether or not to include free black children in America's public schools escaped Knox's cowinner, Samuel Harrison Smith. As a resident of Philadelphia at the close of the eighteenth century, Smith could not avoid the issue of black education as easily for, simply put, he could not avoid free blacks. Certainly Pennsylvania's enslaved population of 3,700 paled in comparison to that of Knox's Maryland, which had already surpassed 100,000 by 1790. But while fewer than one in ten African Americans in Maryland labored outside of slavery, in Pennsylvania nearly twice as many black people lived in freedom than in bondage.[1]

In Smith's hometown of Philadelphia especially, the free black community was growing at a rapid clip. Historian Gary Nash has dubbed the seaport "a city of refuge" for newly emancipated African Americans. Abandoning the rural hinterlands of the mid-Atlantic and the Upper South, free blacks migrated there en masse at the turn of the nineteenth century, attracted by the city's reputation for antislavery sentiment and its relative tolerance toward free people of color. Between 1790 and 1800 alone, Nash notes, Philadelphia's free black population ballooned from 1,805 to 6,381, an increase of more than 300 percent.[2] While many free black families would later relocate to the southern edge of town, as of 1790, a noticeable number resided just north of the city's "commercial core."[3] Strolling through the city in 1795, Smith would literally have had to avert his eyes to miss free black men working along the wharves as mariners or day laborers. At most any gala or celebration, he would have had to plug his ears to shut out the sounds of free black musicians echoing through the halls.[4]

So why was it, then, that when Smith penned a 90-page treatise on the subject of a national public school system, he, like his cocontestants, made no mention of free blacks? Why did he not weigh in on whether the public schools he envisioned should instruct black children alongside whites, in separate institutions, or not at all? Of course, it is a difficult, if not impossible task to ask a historical document to speak to those thoughts of its creator that did not make it onto the page. But just because Smith remained silent on these issues, it does not also follow that his essay shines no light on the subject of race. While Smith, like his cocontestants, did not speculate about African American inclusion in the nation's public schools, the arguments he advanced, particularly those relating to republicanism and to citizenship, suggested the school system he envisioned would not provide equal educational opportunity to black and white children.

This essay contextualizes Smith's submission against the backdrop of early republican Philadelphia, juxtaposing his musings against the fabric of free black life in the city. Along the way, it asks what the absence of the "race question" in the APS essays might reveal about the future place of black people in American public schools. I argue that Smith's essay portends the kind of rationale that would later undergird state efforts to segregate or exclude black people from public schools. In this way, one can see the groundwork being laid for unequal educational opportunity, despite the fact that all the essayists, winners and losers alike, rarely, if ever, mention race at all.

First, I explore the case that Smith makes for a national system of public education, paying special attention to his ideas about access and diffusion. Next, I try to envision what experience, if any, Smith might have had with African American education in Philadelphia. I do this not because I wish to discuss Smith per se, but rather because I hope to familiarize those who read his essay with the rich and varied tradition of free black schooling occurring in his backyard. In an effort to enhance discussion about the APS contest in particular and the origins of American public schools in general, I highlight a few instances of black Philadelphians' efforts at self-education in the antebellum period. I then recount the emergence of public education in Pennsylvania, when white Philadelphians created segregated schools.

* * *

Just a few references to race lie buried within the hundreds of pages contestants generated on the subject of a national education. Only one entrant, Academicus, even engaged with the subject of black inclusion indirectly. While he never called for public schools to serve whites only, his thoughts on taxation suggest he probably did not envision a national school system that enrolled black students. When reflecting on how to finance public education, Academicus proposed to levy a property tax "not exceeding nine pence, nor less than six pence" on "all single free white male inhabitants above the age of twenty five years"[5] One can assume that if black parents did not pay the school tax, they probably could not send their children to public schools. On this point it is likely most entrants agreed, though no one, Smith included, commented on the subject.

As Smith may or may not have recognized, the essay prompt placed two discrete demands upon respondents. The first part of the question spoke more to the nation's republican sensibilities than to its democratic possibilities. It asked essayists to discuss a "system of liberal education, and literary instruction, adapted to the genius of the government, and best calculated to promote the general welfare of the United States." While this sentence did not reference race, class, or gender, contestants probably recognized its call to engage with the political preparation of elites, namely, white men of property.

Republican ideology, commonplace in post-Revolutionary political thought, posited that a nation would function best if led by those most suited to lead: white male freeholders. By its very definition, a "republican education" excluded African Americans, enslaved and free, because their status as slaves or dependents—to put the point more crudely, their tendency to be property rather than to hold property—precluded them from being virtuous. Unlike free or enslaved laborers who sustained themselves at someone else's behest, property holders possessed the requisite independence to sacrifice their individual needs for those of the commonwealth. It followed that these individuals required a liberal education, one steeped in science, mathematics, the classics, and history, to prepare them to make decisions on behalf of the polity. Smith invoked republican ideology when he ruminated on "Wisdom and Virtue." Republican education, he observed, prepared men to "imbibe a habit of independence, and of self-esteem, which are perhaps the great and only preservatives of virtue."[6] Here virtue connoted both action and character: the wisdom to discern the national interest and the willingness to defer one's own needs for those of the nation.

To Smith, America's very existence hinged upon a republican education, necessary to create good citizens. Americans of this generation were notorious for their fixation on decline. Having just experienced the painful process of breaking away from England, a bloody Revolution, and a contentious Constitutional Convention, the founders did not take America's existence for granted. The fallen republics of Greece and Rome represented a cautionary tale for those who became overconfident in American longevity. Likewise, Smith linked America's existence to an American education. "It is true that some nations have been free without possessing a large portion of illumination," he observed, "but their freedom has been precarious and accidental, and it has fallen as it rose."[7] Or as he explained in a more roundabout fashion: "The diffusion of knowledge, co-extensive with that of virtue, would seem to apply with close precision to a republican system of education, because: An enlightened nation is always most tenacious of its rights," among other things.[8] And who best to protect that nation than "enlightened citizens?"

The second portion of the essay question, more democratic than republican, lent itself more readily to questions of diffusion. This section asked respondents to envision "a plan for instituting and conducting public schools in this country on the principles of the most extensive utility." Such phrasing, in contrast to the previous mention of a "liberal education," referenced what contemporary audiences might consider education for the masses. Question writers made this distinction clear when they asked respondents to "comprehend also" a plan for public education, suggesting that such a system was not synonymous with "literary instruction." With its overt reference to "the public," this section, much more than the previous one, called for serious reflection on accessibility.[9]

Smith's conception of public education here proved more radical than any which would appear in the federal constitution. He made a number of bold claims about the importance of widespread access to public education. First, he asserted that individuals possessed a right to some instruction in reading, writing, mathematics, geography, and history. Second, he contended, the state had an affirmative responsibility to deliver such knowledge, even if it superseded parental authority. "One principal must prevail," he maintained. "Society must establish the right to educate, and acknowledge the duty of having educated, all children."[10] An individual's right to an education existed independent of his innate capabilities. While "all men will never be philosophers," he affirmed, "... all men may be enlightened."[11] With those precepts in mind, Smith qualified his definition of all children to include "every male child, without exception."[12]

Without being able to press him on this assertion, one cannot know if by "every male child" he meant black *and* white boys or white boys alone. The history of education in colonial America suggests Smith may have had some reason to believe public schools should serve both constituencies. From their founding, several northern colonies gestured toward inclusion. As E. Jennifer Monaghan points out, "By the 1670s, all New England colonies, then in existence, except Rhode Island, had passed legislation...mandating that all children be taught to read."[13] As early as 1642, the Massachusetts Bay Colony charged "selectmen of every town" with having a vigilant eye over their brethren & neighbors, to see, first that none of them shall suffer so much barbarism in any of their families as not to indeavor to teach, by themselves or others, their children & apprentices so much learning as may enable them perfectly to read the english tongue, & knowledge of the Capital Lawes: upon penaltie of twentie shillings.[14]

Likewise, in 1656 legislators in the colony of New Haven charged parents and masters with making certain their children and apprentices could "read the scriptures, and other good and profitable printed Books in the English tongue."[15]

At the same time, the particular language Smith employed to champion public education suggests he probably did not intend to enroll black children. Specifically, the concepts he invoked, particularly citizenship, independence, and freedom, ran counter to most whites' expectations for African Americans. Smith concludes his essay by considering the impact an American school system might have upon its citizens, the nation, and the globe. In each instance, he envisioned an education synonymous with liberation, one that would prepare men to protect democracy and to perform freedom. Citizenship, according to Smith, could not exist without freedom; nor could it subsist without education. "The citizen enlightened," he contended,

> will be a freeman in the truest sense. He will know his rights, and he will understand the rights of others; discerning the connection of his interest with the preservation of these rights, he will as firmly support those of his fellow man as his own...Not at one moment the child of patriotism, and at another the slave of despotism, we shall see him in principle forever the same.[16]

While Smith's invocation of slavery here existed apart from race, it could not have escaped him that those with the most tenuous hold on freedom were African Americans. As of 1790, the nation's enslaved population neared 700,000.[17] Nor were even free blacks in his home state of Pennsylvania necessarily citizens. Enslaved African Americans had arrived into Philadelphia as early as 1684, when 150 entered the port aboard the *Isabella*. While colonial Philadelphians may have relied upon enslaved labor less than their counterparts in Baltimore or New York, slaveholding among the city's elite was a common practice. Gary Nash points out that almost half of the estates inventoried in Philadelphia prior to 1750 included human property.[18] Most famously, APS founder Benjamin Franklin held slaves as early as the 1740s.[19] As of 1783, around 400 African Americans remained enslaved in Philadelphia alone.[20]

At the time Smith took pen to paper in the summer of 1796, Pennsylvanians had yet to outlaw race-based slavery. While in the aftermath of the Revolution, Quakers pressured state legislators to advance abolition, the resultant 1780 statute bore the stamp of ambiguity. Historian Richard Newman observes that in contrast to their more radical counterparts in Massachusetts, Pennsylvania abolitionists tended to espouse gradualism.[21] Accordingly, while Pennsylvania may have been the first state in the nation to enact emancipation legislation, the statute did not actually free a single person from slavery. First, it did not apply to those currently enslaved. Second, those born into slavery after 1780 would have to wait for freedom until their twenty-eighth birthday.[22] It would be another 67 years before Pennsylvania outlawed chattel slavery altogether.[23] Moreover, even those whites most sympathetic to abolition did not necessarily favor black equality. Tellingly, the Pennsylvania Abolition Society (PAS), the most prominent antislavery association in the state, denied membership to African Americans.[24]

Thus when Smith declared that "above every other consideration, the system of public education inspires a spirit of independent reflection and conduct," he probably was not advancing a radical call for immediate emancipation.[25] Likewise, when he affirmed his support for a national public school system, he likely did not envision one that would provide equal education to black and white children. In the end, contemporary audiences will never know what Smith thought about black education; because he avoided the subject entirely, his views remain an open question. But because of the centrality of republicanism and citizenship in his claims, there is good reason to suspect African Americans were not to participate in his national school system.

*　*　*

Ultimately, to learn about black education in the early republic, one must look to sources besides the APS essays. References to African American instruction in Philadelphia trace back as far as 1722. That year, an unnamed individual new to the city notified "[a]ll serious Persons, whether *Roman Catholics, Presbyterians, Independents, Water-Baptists,* or People called *Quakers,* who are truly concern'd for their Negro-Servants Salvation, (whether Men or Women)" of his willingness to "teach his poor Brethren the Negroes to read the Holy Scriptures, &c. in a very *uncommon, expeditious* and *delightful Manner,* without any Manner of Expense to their respective Masters or Mistresses." While he did not divulge his identity, he did inform his readers of his whereabouts (at "the Dwelling-House of *John Read,* Carpenter,") suggesting he probably did not anticipate much opposition.[26]

As the 1722 advertisement attests, black schools, while uncommon, did operate in the open. Evidence suggests, however, that at least some whites in Pennsylvania remained uneasy with these institutions. In 1740, a letter in the *South Carolina Gazette* recounted the difficulties one Philadelphia instructor, Mr. Bolton, had encountered upon attempting to provide literary instruction to both white and black students. "[U]pon giving Notice that he would teach Negroes also," the *Gazette* reported, Bolton enrolled some "53 Black Scholars" in but "23 Days." Confusion arose, however, as to the legality of this practice; Bolton was "arraign'd in Court, as a Breaker of the Negro Law," in consequence. Ultimately, the Grand Jury determined Bolton's activities violated no law. It instructed him "to continue his School without Interruption."[27]

White support for black schooling came primarily from Anglicans and Quakers, many of whom were sympathetic to antislavery. Sometime around 1750, Anthony Benezet opened a school for both free and enslaved black children in his Philadelphia home. He challenged others eager to end chattel slavery to prepare bondspeople for freedom. As part of that mission, he provided lessons in reading, writing, and mathematics, and encouraged fellow Friends to do the same.[28] As of 1771, he had raised enough money to build a separate schoolhouse for free blacks. The institution, located in Willing's Alley, later enrolled enslaved students as well.[29] Younger boys and girls studied reading, writing, and arithmetic. When they advanced in age, girls cultivated their domestic skills while boys pursued a more academic curriculum.[30] By 1813, Benezet's school provided free instruction to nearly one hundred students.[31] Alumni included African American ministers Absalom Jones and Richard Allen, and sail-maker James Forten.[32]

Likewise, in 1789, another contingent of Philadelphia Quakers hostile to slavery sought to extend educational opportunity to African American adults. Like Benezet, these individuals espoused enthusiasm for emancipation. In an effort to advance their antislavery agenda, they provided "free instruction" to "orderly Blacks and People of Color."[33] Under the auspices of the Association for the Free Instruction of Adult Colored Persons, the organization sought to prepare African Americans to live and labor independently. The group sponsored Sunday evening classes in reading, writing, and mathematics. As of 1809, it reported 18 students attended weekly.[34]

Anglicans also provided religious and literary instruction to black Philadelphians. In 1757, John Waring, a representative of Dr. Bray's Associates, an English organization dedicated to "Founding Clerical Libraries in England and Wales and Negro Schools in British America" contacted Benjamin Franklin to gage white sentiment toward black religious instruction.[35] Eager to open a school for "black Children," Waring inquired as to the present state of black education in the colonies. "[M]ight Not," Waring suggested, "the black Children born in the Province be taught to read and instructed in the Principles of Christian Morality?"[36] Franklin informed Waring that white attitudes toward black education in Philadelphia appeared discouraging. "At present," Franklin replied, "few or none give their Negro Children any Schooling." White Philadelphians eschewed schooling black people, enslaved and free, for reasons that ranged from apathy to antipathy, or as Franklin described,

> partly from a Prejudice that Reading and Knowledge in a Slave are both useless and dangerous; and partly from an Unwillingness in the Masters and Mistresses of common Schools to take black Scholars, lest the Parents of the white Children should be disgusted and take them away, not chusing to have their Children mix'd with Slaves in Education, Play, &c.[37]

Franklin did, however, give Waring some reason to be optimistic. A segregated school for black children, sensitive to the concerns of slaveholders, might assuage fears about black education, both in Philadelphia and through-out the colonies, he supposed. Franklin continued:

> [A] separate School for Blacks, under the Care of One, of whom People should have an Opinion that he would be careful to imbue the Minds of their young Slaves with good Principles, might probably have a Number of Blacks sent to it; and if on Experience it should be found useful, and not attended with the ill Consequences commonly apprehended, the Example might be followed in the other Colonies, and encouraged by the Inhabitants in general.[38]

A month later, Franklin updated Waring on some specifics. "I am of Opinion that for £30 a Year, Sterling, a good Master might be procur'd that would teach 40 Negro Children to read," Franklin reported. While a school for enslaved blacks might at first have a limited subscription, he posited, "if they were taught some useful Thing besides Reading it might be an Encouragement to Masters and Mistresses to send them." He advised Bray's Associates to employ a female teacher at first "who could teach both Boys and Girls to read, and the Girls to knit, sew and mark; a good One might be had, I believe, for about £20 Sterling, that would well instruct in this Way about 30 Scholars." Once attendance increased "a Master may be procured for the Boys, and the Mistress retained for the Girls; the whole Charge not exceeding £50 Sterling per Annum for 60 or 70 Children." Eventually, Franklin predicted, the school might become self-sufficient. He anticipated that a number of slaveholders in Philadelphia possessed the means and motivation to pay tuition. "Most of the Owners of Negro Children are able to pay for their Schooling," Franklin reported, "and will be willing if they like the Design, see it well manag'd, and find it useful."[39]

Soon after, Bray's Associates did, in fact, open a school for black students in Philadelphia.[40] Years later, Franklin, a slaveholder himself, recalled being so impressed with the institution that it led him to revisit his own assumptions about black people. Upon touring the "Negro School" in 1763, Franklin witnessed children making "considerable Progress in Reading." The majority, he noted, "answer'd readily and well the Questions of the Catechism; they behav'd very orderly, showd a proper Respect and ready Obedience to the Mistress, and seem'd very attentive to, and a good deal affected by, a serious Exhortation." Franklin reported that he was "on the whole much pleas'd, and . . . conceiv'd a higher Opinion of the natural Capacities of the black Race, than [he] had ever before entertained." "Their Apprehension seems as quick, their Memory as strong, and their Docility in every Respect equal to that of white Children," he wrote to Waring. "You will wonder perhaps that I should ever doubt it, and I will not undertake to justify all my Prejudices, nor to account for them."[41] So enthused with what he had seen, Franklin enrolled his own bondsperson Othello in the Anglican institution.[42]

Franklin also lent his energies to the Pennsylvania Abolition Society (PAS), another organization sympathetic to black education.[43] With Franklin as its first president, the PAS originated in 1775 amidst the gathering storm of the

American Revolution. With its emphasis on elite leadership and its respect for legal and political institutions, the PAS championed a conservative style of antislavery activism distinguished by its moderation and gradualism.[44] In 1793, PAS members opened a school for black children on Cherry Street and hired African American Eleanor Harris to instruct them. Four years later, in 1797, it founded a school located in the Northern Liberties section of Philadelphia. Neither institution flourished. As of 1799, PAS members complained of scarce attendance and poor instruction. That same year, it also gave money to free black Philadelphian Absalom Jones to operate a private preschool for black children. As of 1805, a decade after the APS contest, Philadelphia housed at least seven separate schools for African Americans, which collectively enrolled approximately five hundred adults and children.[45]

While documented accounts of black schooling in eighteenth-century Philadelphia generally highlight white involvement, as the nineteenth century advanced, African Americans in the city assumed a more public spirit of educational activism. Black Philadelphians sought out educational opportunity for many of the same reasons articulated in the APS essays. Just as Smith asserted that "the citizen, enlightened, will be a freeman in its truest sense," free blacks in the city championed education as a means to secure citizenship, or full inclusion in the body politic, and freedom, both for themselves and for those American Americans still held in slavery.[46] Just as Academicus observed that "[it] is a matter of the highest importance, to a republican government, to disseminate knowledge, and to keep the avenues of access to it, open to all, and especially to the middle, or even lower class[es]," African Americans with means also endeavored to extend education to those who lacked the resources for private instruction.[47]

As early as 1818, for example, a group of elite free black Philadelphians founded the Pennsylvania Augustine Society for the Education of People of Color. Led by Prince Saunders, one of the first black teachers in Boston's segregated Smith School, the society included wealthy black Philadelphian and former Benezet school student James Forten, and New Yorker Samuel Cornish, editor of the nation's first black newspaper, *Freedom's Journal*. Members urged African Americans to take responsibility for educating their own community. For too long, they asserted, black people had depended upon whites or permitted "the formidable barriers that prejudices, powerful as they are unjust, have reared to impede our progress in the paths of science and of virtue." "[I]t is an unquestionable duty which we owe to ourselves, to our posterity, and to our God, who had endued us with intellectual powers," they maintained, "to use the best energies of our minds and of our hearts, in devising and adapting the most effectual means to procure for our children a more extensive and useful education than we have heretofore had in our power to effect." With these goals in mind, the association set out to build "a Seminary, in which children of colour shall be taught, so far as may be found practicable," "all useful and scientific branches of education."[48]

Black Philadelphians also promoted self-education through a range of associations, including reading clubs, lectures, and lyceums. As of 1826, for a small payment of "one cent per week," African American subscribers could access a collection of books to read at their leisure.[49] In 1833, free black men including Robert Purvis and Frederick Hinton launched the Philadelphia Library Company of Colored Persons, desiring to promote "among our rising youth, a proper cultivation for literary pursuits and improvement of the faculties and power of their minds."[50] In addition to amassing reading materials, the group sponsored weekly talks and occasional debates. Five years after its founding, it had collected some six hundred books and enrolled approximately 150 members, who paid 25 cents a month to support the organization.[51]

Many black women in Philadelphia desired to prepare themselves to uplift their children. Akin to the notion of republican motherhood that championed white female education to enable women to raise good citizens, members of the Female Literary Association, founded in 1831, advocated for their own education to ensure prosperity for the next generation. Their duty also stemmed from the responsibility they held to those who toiled in slavery. Members posited that "as daughters of a despised race" black women had a special obligation "to cultivate the talents entrusted to our keeping; that, by so doing, we may in great measure break down the strong barrier of prejudice, and raise ourselves to an equality with those who differ from us in complexion."[52] Upon the society's first anniversary, one orator affirmed that educated free blacks could serve as an example to alleviate white fears about emancipation. In this respect, free blacks owed it to those still in slavery to avail themselves of all educational opportunities. "[A]s the free people of color become virtuous and intelligent, the character and the condition of the slave will also improve," she predicted. "A[lways] remember that our interests are one, that we rise or fall together, and that we can never be elevated to our proper standing while they are in bondage." Education, moreover, empowered black people to partake in the American narrative of progress and self-sufficiency. The speaker pointed her audience to other Americans who had seized upon education to advance in society. "By perseverance Benjamin Franklin and a host of worthies rose superior to obscure birth and early disadvantages, and acquired lasting fame in the various departments of literature and the mechanic arts," she observed; "with the powerful weapons of religion and education" "we may do the same."[53]

* * *

One should not confuse white tolerance for black self-education with widespread enthusiasm for African Americans' inclusion in the public schools. While a small number of independent religious and antislavery associations provided spiritual and literary instruction to people of color, in general, white Philadelphians showed little inclination to instruct black and white children together in tax-supported institutions.

As early as 1795, when the APS asked contestants to envision a national school system, PAS representatives began to press state legislators to allocate public funds for black education; their efforts, however, met with little success. In 1802, Pennsylvania's General Assembly passed a statute that provided funding to private schools that enrolled impoverished students. While the law did not mention race, few, if any, schools that received public money enrolled black children.[54] In 1813, Arthur Donaldson, who opened a private school for African Americans in 1809, questioned why "the coloured children [who] come under the notice of that law [were] neglected?"[55] PAS members petitioned the legislature to apportion some part of the school fund to African Americans for several years. Finally, in 1820, nearly two decades after Pennsylvania began to finance education publicly, the General Assembly assented. In Philadelphia, however, local controllers charged with overseeing the city's public schools made no effort to comply with the state statute. Only after the PAS agreed to provide the city with a building did controllers allocate public money toward black education. Philadelphia's first tax-supported school for African Americans opened on Mary Street in 1822.[56] In less than a year's time, the school enrolled more than two hundred boys and girls. In 1826, the city opened a second school for black girls on Gaskill Street, leaving the Mary Street School for black boys alone.[57]

African Americans in other northern cities with public school systems fared no better. No American city that created a public school system in the early nineteenth century opted to give white and black children equal educational opportunity. As of 1827, New York City sustained just two schools. Boston operated three separate schools for African American children. Likewise, New Haven provided two schools, but these institutions remained open just three months a year.[58]

Pennsylvania formally established a public school system in 1834, when it passed its "free school law." Technically, black parents could enroll their children; informally, however, towns and cities that provided public education to African Americans generally did so in separate institutions.[59] Thus despite the expansion of public education in Philadelphia, black children remained dependent upon private and philanthropic organizations, and continued to have fewer educational opportunities than their white counterparts. White children both could begin public education earlier and pursue a more advanced curriculum. While the city operated a public infant school for white children between the ages of four and six, it provided no equivalent for black children, leaving the private Infant School Society of Philadelphia in charge of such instruction.[60] Likewise, when the city opened its first "public high school" in 1837, it also denied admission to African Americans.[61] Those in search of advanced education could attend "The High School for the Instruction of Colored Boys," a PAS supported institution.[62]

In 1854, the Pennsylvania legislature further circumscribed black access to public schooling by codifying segregation. While it permitted black children to attend public schools alongside whites in small numbers, it instructed districts with more than 20 black pupils to open separate institutions.[63] No doubt, many black parents found the state's policies galling. For although the General Assembly denied African Americans full access to the state's public schools, it nevertheless continued to assess black and white property holders equally. Unlike Academicus, it did not envision a school tax that applied to whites only. In 1853, Robert Purvis, a wealthy black landholder in Byberry, Pennsylvania, protested the injustice of paying to support a system that excluded his children. In a public letter to tax collector Joseph J. Butcher, Purvis explained that he would suffer the tax no more. He would not "bear any longer this robbery of my rights and property, by those miserable serviles to the slave power, the Directors of the Public Schools." He informed Butcher, "I object to the payment of this tax, on the ground that my rights as a citizen and my feelings as a man and a parent have been grossly outraged in depriving me, in violation of law and justice, of the benefits of the school system, which this tax was designed to sustain." He found the state's decision to bestow upon African Americans all the burdens of public schooling without full access to its privileges undemocratic and insulting. In particular, he resented having to both finance public schools and pay private school tuition: "I have borne this outrage ever since the innovation upon the usual practice of admitting all the children of the Township into the 'Public Schools' and at considerable expense have been obliged to obtain the services of private teachers to instruct my children, while my school tax is greater, with a single exception, than that of any other citizen of the Township." "I shall resist this tax," he determined "which before the unjust exclusion had always afforded me the highest gratification in paying."[64]

And so Purvis's protest circled back to the same arguments Smith had once advanced in support of a national system of public schools. Just as Smith once asserted every man's inherent right to an education, so too did Purvis claim that right to be his as well. Just as Smith once argued that public schools were the responsibility of every citizen, so too did Purvis acknowledge his willingness to assume this burden. Just as Smith once supposed that the state had an affirmative duty to support the education of its citizens, so too did Purvis affirm that the state owed no less to his children. Where Purvis and the APS entrants diverged was not on the importance of public education but rather on the subject of inclusion. When Purvis maintained that segregated public schools violated his rights as a citizen, he assumed others would see him as an American. On this point, he and APS contestants would probably have disagreed.

Purvis's resistance to the school tax also speaks to a fundamental shift in how some Americans understood and articulated black access to public education in the first half of the nineteenth century. At the time of the APS contest, when Smith and his fellow republicans imagined a system of public education, essayists approached the topic of black exclusion as a given. With the end of slavery nowhere in sight and a state-supported school system still decades from fruition, essayists like Smith felt neither compelled nor inspired to engage with the race question. But by the 1850s, as African American calls for citizenship and freedom intensified, those who sought to deny black children access to public schooling needed a rationale for that exclusion. With a common school system in place and emancipation on the horizon, white Americans could not ignore black demands for education or liberation. In consequence, those seeking to exclude African Americans from public institutions now needed to defend that decision. No longer would Americans, white and black, remain silent on the subject of educational equality.

NOTES

1. John Hope Franklin and Evelyn Brooks Higginbotham, *From Slavery to Freedom: A History of African Americans* (New York: McGraw-Hill, 2011), 105.
2. Gary Nash, *Forging Freedom: The Formation of Philadelphia's Black Community, 1720–1840* (Cambridge: Harvard University Press, 1991), 136–137.
3. Ibid., 164.
4. Ibid., 149–150.
5. Academicus, "A Plan for the Education of Youth," pp. 248–249 of this volume.
6. Samuel Harrison Smith, *Remarks on Education* (Philadelphia: 1798), p. 35.
7. Ibid., 80.
8. Ibid., 36.
9. See p. 1 of this volume.
10. Smith, *Remarks on Education*, 39.
11. Ibid., 41.
12. Ibid., 67.
13. E. Jennifer Monaghan, *Learning to Read and Write in Colonial America* (Amherst: University of Massachusetts Press, 2005), 31.
14. As quoted in Mary Ann Connolly, "Boston Schools in the New Republic, 1776–1840" (PhD dissertation, Harvard University, 1963), 7–9.
15. As quoted in Monaghan, *Learning to Read and Write*, 24–25.
16. Smith, *Remarks on Education*, 82.
17. Franklin and Higginbotham, *From Slavery to Freedom*, 105.
18. Nash, *Forging Freedom*, 8–9.
19. David Waldstreicher, *Runaway America: Benjamin Franklin, Slavery, and the American Revolution* (New York: Hill and Wang, 2004), 25–26.
20. Nash, *Forging Freedom*, 65.
21. Richard S. Newman, *The Transformation of American Abolitionism* (Chapel Hill: University of North Carolina Press, 2002), 6.
22. James Oliver Horton and Lois E. Horton, *In Hope of Liberty: Culture, Community and Protest Among Northern Free Blacks, 1700–1860* (New York: Oxford University Press, 1997), 73.
23. Nash, *Forging Freedom*, 62.
24. Newman, *Transformation of American Abolitionism*, 6.
25. Smith, *Remarks on Education*, 63.
26. *American Weekly Mercury*, February 19, 1722.
27. *The South-Carolina Gazette*, July 18, 1740.
28. Nancy Slocum Hornick, "Anthony Benezet and the Africans' School: Toward a Theory of Full Equality," *The Pennsylvania Magazine of History and Biography* 99:4 (October 1975): 399–400.
29. Nash, *Forging Freedom*, 31.
30. Hornick, "Anthony Benezet and the Africans' School," 406.

31. Arthur Donaldson, "Arthur Donaldson's Address to His Pupils: Rules for the Government of the Scholars Belonging to Arthur Donaldson's School for Children of Color," *The Juvenile Magazine* 3, July 1, 1813.
32. Hornick, "Anthony Benezet and the Africans' School," 415–416.
33. *History of the Associations of Friends for the Free Instruction of Adult Colored Persons in Philadelphia* (Philadelphia: Friends' Book Store, 1890), 3.
34. Ibid., 7.
35. *Account of the Institution Established by the Late Rev. Dr. Bray and his Associates for Founding Clerical Libraries in England and Wales and Negro Schools in British America with an Abstract of their Proceedings* (London: R. Gilbert, 1824).
36. John Waring to Benjamin Franklin, January 24, 1757, *The Papers of Benjamin Franklin*: http://franklinpapers.org/franklin/ (accessed November 26, 2012).
37. Benjamin Franklin to John Waring, January 3, 1758, *The Papers of Benjamin Franklin*: http://franklinpapers.org/franklin/ (accessed November 26, 2012).
38. Ibid.
39. Benjamin Franklin to John Waring, February 17, 1758, *The Papers of Benjamin Franklin*: http://franklinpapers.org/franklin (accessed November 26, 2012).
40. Nash, *Forging Freedom*, 22.
41. Benjamin Franklin to John Waring, December 17, 1763, *The Papers of Benjamin Franklin*, accessed November 26, 2012, http://franklinpapers.org/franklin.
42. Nash, *Forging Freedom*, 22.
43. Newman, *Transformation of American Abolitionism*, 21.
44. Ibid., 6, 17.
45. Nash, *Forging Freedom*, 204–205.
46. Smith, *Remarks on Education*, 82.
47. Ibid., 36.
48. Prince Saunders, "An Address Delivered at Bethel Church, Philadelphia, on the 30th of September, 1818, before the Pennsylvania Augustine Society, for the Education of People of Color. To Which is Annexed the Constitution of the Society" (Philadelphia: Joseph Rakestraw, 1818).
49. "Library for Blacks," *African Repository* 1:12 (February 1826): 383.
50. "To the Public," *Genius of Universal Emancipation*, April 1833.
51. Dorothy Porter, "The Organized Educational Activities of Negro Literary Societies, 1828–1846," *Journal of Negro Education* 5:4 (October 1936): 561.
52. "Female Literary Association of Philadelphia," *Genius of Universal Emancipation*, December 1832.
53. "Address to the Female Literary Association of Philadelphia on their First Anniversary, by a Member," *Liberator*, October 13, 1832.
54. Edward Price Jr., "School Segregation in Nineteenth-Century Pennsylvania," *Pennsylvania History* 43:2 (April 1976): 122–123.
55. Donaldson, "Arthur Donaldson's Address to His Pupils."
56. Price Jr., "School Segregation in Nineteenth-Century Pennsylvania," 122–123.

57. Harry C. Silcox, "Delay and Neglect: Negro Public Education in Antebellum Philadelphia, 1800–1860," *The Pennsylvania Magazine of History and Biography* 97:4 (October 1973): 451–452.

58. "African Free Schools in the United States," *Freedom's Journal*, June 1, 1827.

59. Price Jr., "School Segregation in Nineteenth-Century Pennsylvania," 124.

60. "Colored Infant School," *Freedom's Journal*, May 9, 1828; "Travelling Scraps," *Freedom's Journal*, July 11, 1828.

61. Silcox, "Delay and Neglect," 459.

62. "Education," *Liberator*, March 28, 1835.

63. Price Jr., "School Segregation in Nineteenth-Century Pennsylvania," 124.

64. Robert Purvis, "Many Protest Against Wrong," *Liberator*, December 16, 1853.

CHAPTER 7

Gender and Citizenship in Educational Plans in the New Republic

Margaret Nash

In a review of the seminal work on education in the new republic, *The Learning of Liberty* by Lorraine Smith Pangle and Thomas L. Pangle, historian Edith MacMullen wrote that she wished the Pangles "had looked to the second tier of Founding Fathers," those who labored at the state or community level, and to women. Scholars must, MacMullen wrote, "break away from a myopic focus on the great and famous."[1] The publication of the nonwinning essays in the American Philosophical Society contest is an important step toward heeding MacMullen's advice. Some of the essay writers are so far removed from the great and famous that identification is difficult.

The APS asked for plans for a "system of liberal education, and literary instruction, adapted to the genius of the government, and best calculated to promote the general welfare of the United States; comprehending, also, a plan for instituting and conducting public schools in this country on principles of the most extensive utility." The plans, then, needed to be broad in scope, encompassing wide-ranging educational issues such as pedagogy and curriculum, perhaps responding to known or perceived regional differences, and including thoughts regarding multiple levels of education, from primary school through university. The best plans would explain their reasoning, leading the prizewinning essayists, along with some others, to think deeply about the purposes of education in a republic and therefore to think deeply about the responsibilities and meanings of citizenship. In the minds of the essayists, education was not the domain merely of the wealthiest of citizens; rather, the health of the republic depended on the education of poor citizens, too. Virtually all of the contestants wrote about class differences as they described their plans for mass education, and several stressed the importance of providing education for the poor.

Yet as sweeping as their visions were, none of the essay writers discussed race (chapter 6 in this volume), only three mentioned girls or women, and none presented fully developed plans for female education. In this essay, I try to figure out why. So far as we know, no women composed any of the entries, and excluded from membership in the APS, women were neither the judges nor the primary intended audience for the essays. In explicit and implicit ways, gender is infused throughout the contest; here, I set out to understand what meanings gender held to these writers. First, I detail the morsels that the writers did provide about female education. Next, I question why they said so little. Did they dismiss the topic because they didn't believe women's intellect warranted a full discussion? Did they avoid the topic because they felt it was either unimportant, or too controversial? Examining a range of primary sources and secondary arguments, I conclude that none of these explanations accounts fully for the absence of girls and women in these essays. In a historical moment in which citizenship took on new meaning and relevance, and as some women clamored for more respect and increasingly visible roles in the new republic, anxiety about status led some white men to articulate ideals that more clearly separated men from women. For those writers, education was one way to consolidate and perpetuate a definition of white masculinity. However, none of these plans for national education materialized, and neither did a plan for education that set out to make clear distinctions of gender.

*   *   *

Only two of the writers mentioned female education, and they were the two who shared the prize for best essay; a third mentioned women as teachers. All of these mentions were brief. Samuel Knox stipulated that he would find it preferable for girls to be educated separately from boys, under a female teacher. During this period most teachers were men, and Knox's statement presaged the feminization of teaching that would follow, although that is not what Knox had in mind. In this section of the essay, he did not even refer to these women as teachers; rather, he thought that "the teacher's wife" should take charge of the girls, and that ideally, every schoolteacher should be a married man so that there would be someone to teach the girls. If "it were found necessary" that boys and girls had to be educated together, he suggested that they be separated on different pews in the classroom.[2]

Knox mentioned girls only in the context of primary schools, so we do not know from this essay what he thought of more advanced educational opportunities for women. He did not, however, differentiate the curriculum; all the studies that he recommended for boys in the primary schools, he apparently also thought fitting for girls. He also assumed that a "teacher's wife" would be educated enough to be able to teach girls, but that the profession of teaching—or at least, teaching boys—was for men. Coeducation of small children was the norm in "dame schools" throughout the northeastern United States. Taught by a woman in her home, girls and boys in dame schools learned their letters and numbers, perhaps to read a few words, and to memorize a Scripture or two. By the middle of the eighteenth century, coeducation at the primary school level, beyond the rudiments taught in dame schools, frequently occurred during summer sessions.[3] Knox's statements, then, about education for both girls and boys at this level was not radical or uncommon for his time, and the degree to which it was accepted practice might be reflected in Knox's offhand reference to the subject. In fact, the ubiquity of offering rudimentary education to both girls and boys is part of what makes the lack of attention to female education in these essays so surprising.

The anonymous writer of essay No. 3 (probably William Smith; see chapter 2 in this volume) also referred to women as teachers, and in a more egalitarian way than Knox. This writer thought that primary school teachers should swear to adhere to a set of rules that would be set at the federal level, and referred to these teachers as "master [or] mistress." He also specifically mentioned women teachers at the higher level of "central schools" and universities, stipulating that "mistresses shall rank with the Professors."[4] Clearly this essayist knew that there were well-educated women and advocated not only that they should be able to teach, but that they should be given the same rank as male instructors. But who the students should be in these schools, the limited extant material (only the reviewers' summary, not the essay itself) does not indicate. Presumably the essayist included females as students, given that (s)he envisioned female teachers, but nowhere is this made explicit.

The other essayist who mentioned female education was Samuel Harrison Smith, who raised the subject only to acknowledge that he was avoiding it. The reason, Smith said, was that there was too much "diversity of opinion" and that agreement "must absolutely be despaired of. It is sufficient, perhaps, for the present that the improvement of women is marked by a rapid progress, and that a prospect opens equal to their most ambitious desires."[5] These were his only two sentences on female education, in a 92-page essay. Lack of agreement seems like an odd reason not to present a case, given that there was no agreement on a system for male education, either, a situation that had, after all, prompted the essay contest to begin with. Yet Smith did not present himself as hostile to female education, as he seemed to approve both the progress women had made, and women's "ambitious desires."

Smith's essay provides a few other clues about his views of gender and education. Smith noted that infancy and early childhood was under "maternal control," and that it was therefore "fortunate that we have not occasion to regret the unenlightened state of the female mind."[6] The formulation of this sentence, with its double negative, hardly comes across as a vigorous celebration of women's enlightenment, and this "damned with faint praise" approach continues as Smith explains that these early years under the mother's control "do not mark much strength of mind" in children, anyway. A reader can almost hear Smith sigh in resignation when he says that those early years "must be surrendered to the claims of maternal regard," years when the child is not "able to attend to any thing but those external objects which irresistibly force themselves on its notice." Smith sets aside five years for this stage of life, a period he refers to as "unavoidable sacrifices" of time when the child, under maternal care, has not yet arrived "at the period of life most proper for commencing a system of general education."[7] When that proper period for education commences, when children are freed from maternal control, Smith's detailed plan is that of an all-male world.

The other four contestants said nothing about female education. "Academicus" specifically referred to boys in his essay without ever mentioning girls. Most of these essays were long and quite detailed; these were not plans painted in broad brush strokes, but were exhaustive in their specifics regarding curriculum, years of study and at what ages, pedagogy, financing, and governance. Why, in the midst of all of that detail, the writers chose not to include girls is perplexing.

There are several possible explanations. One is that, as essayist Samuel Smith explained, female education simply was too controversial a topic. Perhaps the writers assumed that if they took on this controversy, they lessened their chances of winning the prize, as any stance was likely to alienate someone on the prize committee. As physician and writer George Gregory noted in a 1785 essay,

> There are certain subjects of which it is almost impossible to treat, without inducing censure, or provoking resentment. The author, who, in the present age of gallantry and politeness, should assert the mental inferiority of the female sex, would be upbraided by the one party, as the advocate of tyranny, and the slave of prejudice; and on the other hand, the courteous knight-errant, who maintains the intellectual equality of the sexes, will hardly escape the opprobrium of a traitor to his party, who perfidiously deserts his post, and fights the battles of the enemy.[8]

Clearly, controversy abounded on the question of women's intellect and therefore on the appropriate nature of their education. Yet controversy does not seem like an adequate explanation, for several reasons. For one thing, including girls' education was not the same as claiming intellectual equality. Second, many people did believe in intellectual equality. In addition, the issue of women's rights, including women's education, was getting a lot of attention, so it would not have seemed odd to bring it up in the context of an essay on education. Finally, controversy was not unknown to the APS, and likely would not have been reason enough to eschew a topic or an argument. I will discuss each of these reasons in turn.

Making a case for female education did not require one to argue for intellectual equality. Even those writers in newspapers and books in this era who said that women could not achieve the same intellectual heights as men did not claim that women were incapable of learning anything whatsoever; rather, they argued that female minds were not capable of "intense and severe studies," such as might be included in advanced education.[9] A plan for providing basic literacy and numeracy to all citizens of the republic did not need to make any claims about intellectual equality; such a plan only needed to claim that girls as well as boys needed to be able to read and perhaps to write, perform basic arithmetic, and to think clearly enough to not be taken in by connivers of either a personal or political nature.[10] For instance, Samuel Magaw, vice provost of the University of Pennsylvania and an APS member, published an address in 1787 in which he said that while not "every woman should have a classical education,...unquestionably, all, of every description, should learn to read correctly. All should be taught to write tolerably well. All should be instructed to manage common Numbers, and to keep plain Accounts."[11] The APS contestants whose plans provided for basic education for the poor did so without arguing that *all* men of the lower classes were capable of or would benefit from advanced education. As Thomas Jefferson—a prominent member of the APS—famously phrased it, basic education for poor boys would allow for a few "geniuses [to] be raked from the rubbish."[12] Rudimentary education, either for the poor of either sex or for females of any class, did not imply that all members of that group would or should pursue advanced education. The APS contestants could have suggested basic education for girls without having to enter into a contentious debate about intellectual equality, and they could have been assured that a number of APS members would have agreed with them.

Although there were people who did not believe that women were intellectually as capable as men, a large number of vocal people, influenced by the Enlightenment, did believe that women had intellectual capabilities and that those abilities should be developed. Why "Nature" should have endowed women with intellectual abilities only to have society treat their potential "as a *sealed book* which ought not to be opened, I confess I cannot comprehend," wrote Elizabeth Hamilton.[13] Arguments for women's education included women's civilizing and moral influence on families and on society; the deepened relationship with the deity that would naturally result from studying science and therefore being better able to appreciate God's creations; the personal satisfaction that stems from the pleasure of learning; and the potential for financial independence, critical to many widows in the wake of the Revolution, or for being of assistance in family businesses.[14] If the APS contest essay writers had not thought that women were capable of being educated, they likely would have said so. A plethora of voices argued for women's intellectual abilities—including some members of the APS itself who were directly involved in female education in Philadelphia—and men in the intelligentsia let it be known that they read and published women's writing. Furthermore, education for young women was thriving (chapter 8 in this volume), and it was thriving among the same elite group that belonged to the APS. Therefore it seems unlikely that the APS advocates of national systems of education would have subscribed to an extreme belief in intellectual inferiority that rendered women incapable of any academic learning. The essayists' reticence to address the subject should not be read as their agreement with a belief that women could not benefit from education. Rather than weighing in on any debate about women's intellectual capacity, or the best type of education for women, they chose not to meaningfully engage the subject.

Women's rights was one of "the most debated topics" on both sides of the Atlantic in the 1790s, according to historian Bryan Waterman, and publication of Mary Wollstonecraft's *Vindication of the Rights of Women* in 1792 turned up the volume on that debate. *Vindication* also specifically increased discussion of women's education.[15] The topic of female education appeared regularly in newspapers and periodicals in this period. Judith Sargent Murray, for example, wrote a monthly column for the *Massachusetts Magazine* from 1792 to 1794, in which she championed the cause of women's education, among other issues; these essays were collected and reprinted under the title *The Gleaner* in 1798. Murray was hardly alone. Newspapers and magazines published scores of articles on the topic of female education during the 1780s and 1790s.[16] In the very years of the essay contest, New York City physician Elihu Smith wrote a plan for his vision of a utopian republic; his plan encompassed a state-supported school system that included women on an equal basis up to the university level.[17] The topic may have been controversial, but that did not keep writers from expounding on it on a regular basis. Instead, the frequency of the discussion of the topic makes it all the more noticeable that no essayist for the contest was willing to address it. Were these not bold men of vision, willing to take on an important topic that they deemed critical to the very survival of the new nation? How could they be too squeamish, then, to weigh in on this particular aspect of the need for education, when they were answering a call to thoughtfully offer their opinions on the important subject?

The omission is especially striking in the case of contest cowinner Samuel Smith, who was no blood relation to Elihu Smith, but with whom he had an important link. Samuel's fiancée and later wife, Margaret Bayard, was an integral part of Elihu Smith's intellectual circle. While Samuel was in Philadelphia, Margaret was in New York, happily occupied with a vibrant group of women and men who "ignored sexual distinction" as they discussed philosophy, history, and literature. Moreover, Samuel encouraged Margaret in her intellectual adventures, and "constantly admonish[ed] her to increase her education and her independence."[18] Samuel Smith appears to have valued education for his fiancée, and encouraged her to challenge social conventions by meeting with a mixed-sex social group, yet he did not address this topic in his essay on educational plans for the nation.

The controversy associated with the topic of women's rights generally, or with female education specifically, might have been reason to avoid the topic if the APS were known as a conservative organization. Contestants send entries hoping to win, and they tend to know something about the views of their judges. A radical might send an entry to a conservative organization, or vice versa, just to rile their adversaries, but not with any expectation of winning a contest. But in this case, the APS was not particularly known for political conservatism. According to APS historian Whitfield J. Bell, Jr., some prevalent views of the Society in the 1790s were that it was "dangerous," "a triumph of atheism, deism, and nothingism. The Society was in short, controversial, suspect, and probably subversive."[19] People who were horrified by the Society's associations with the French, for instance, or who viewed the APS as dangerous, might well have also held conservative views of women; but they would not likely have entered the contest. Those who did enter the contest hoping to win and not merely irk the judges were more likely to have had more politically liberal views. During the years of the essay contest, APS welcomed controversial guests, including Joseph Priestley at a time when Priestley was excoriated for his pro-French views; Priestly also was part of Mary Wollstonecraft's circle. Staying away from the topic of female education because it might be too controversial seems unlikely in this context, and the absence of controversy seems an implausible criterion for a winning essay. Besides that, members of the APS were already on record as supporting female education. Benjamin Rush had already published his famous essay, and he and other APS members were associated with Philadelphia female academies.[20] Contestants would have had no reason to suspect that APS judges would have viewed the topic as controversial.

Another possible explanation for the essayists' silence is that they simply did not see women's education as critical to the success of the young republic. This too seems odd, given that historians have told us for decades that in the early national period, many people saw the vital importance of women's influence in their role as "republican mothers."[21] As mothers, according to this viewpoint, women would shape the next generation of virtuous civic leaders. Therefore, women needed education in order to teach their children the appropriate morals, values, and sense of responsibility the republic required. Other historians have argued that many political theorists in the early republic saw important roles for women beyond mothering, and have suggested that an ideology of republican womanhood, rather than republican motherhood, filled newspapers and periodicals.[22] As wives, daughters, and sisters, republican women could exert a civilizing effect on society, making their education essential.[23] Noah Webster, for instance, urged education for females because of women's "influence in controlling the manners of the nation."[24]

Samuel Smith came the closest of any of the contestants to referencing this idea, in the section already noted in which he bemoans the years of childhood that "must be surrendered" to the mother's care. Even here, Smith conveys uneasiness. Rather than acknowledging the mother's importance and sway, Smith implies the opposite. And in an essay in which he barely mentions women, he manages to both diminish their impact and question their morals. Smith writes of early childhood years when "the disposition" is formed, "which seldom fails to receive a virtuous bias from a mother, who, however vicious herself, feels deeply interested in the virtue of her offspring."[25] Proponents of "Republican Motherhood" argued that women needed to be educated in order to know how to instill virtue in their children. But in the view Smith presents, there is no obvious need for female education given that even a "vicious" mother will have the same effect of imparting virtue into her child. In a cultural milieu in which many people spoke of the health of the new republic being dependent on the virtue of its citizens, and in which women were framed as key to instilling that virtue in their children, Smith's comments stand out. Not only did he not use the opportunity of discussing maternal influence as a vehicle for supporting female education, which would have been a familiar line of thought to his audience, but he also planted a seed of doubt regarding women's virtue. In this context of virtue being key to shoring up the fledgling republic, virtue itself has a political meaning. Here, Smith is subtly excising women from that political role.

If a preponderance of the civic-minded citizenry subscribed to an ideology of either republican motherhood or republican womanhood, one would expect to see it show up in these essays, as it did in Benjamin Rush's 1787 publication, "Thoughts Upon Female Education, Accommodated to the Present State of Society, Manners, and Government in the United States of America."[26] Given Rush's prominence (as a Founding Father, a signer of the Declaration of Independence, the surgeon general of the Army during the Revolutionary War, among other accomplishments), his choice to publish an essay on female education certainly carried some weight. Even if people disagreed with Rush's position, or Webster's, or the many other civic leaders who wrote essays on female education, the fact that they took a position connoted that the topic was worthy of attention. If the topic was not too trivial, if women's education was sufficiently important, for Rush to take the time to write about it, why would the contest entrants have seen the topic as unworthy of their time and attention? None of these are compelling explanations.

Perhaps the reason that the essayists didn't include women systematically in their plans for education was not because of the writers' views of women, but because of their views of men. That is, they were not so much deliberately leaving women out (except for Samuel Smith, who did explicitly leave women out) as much as they were responding to and bolstering an ideology of manhood. Political scientist Mark E. Kann articulated several varieties of acceptable manhood (aristocratic, republican, and self-made men) in the early republic, showing the "complex, diverse, and contested" nature of manliness in the era.[27] All the variations were united, however, by a few consensual norms, one of which was manhood's opposition to womanhood, in contrast to an earlier period that saw adulthood as distinct from childhood. Many historians have documented gender opposition in this period, from a discourse that divided up positive and negative characteristics as male and female, to the creation of "gender-specific citizenship."[28] While men were defining themselves against women, they were doing so primarily in cultural rather than political venues: newspaper and journal articles, in plays and other forms of rhetoric. In political forums, men rendered women "almost invisible."[29] Men were nearly completely silent about women's political presence, past or present contributions, or potential roles. According to Kann, in "thousands of pages of founding-era political documents that dwell on virtually every aspect of men's relations," there occurs little more "than a rare reference to women's existence."[30] The APS essay writers fall within this rubric of silence regarding women. If the essay writers were thinking of education in political terms, and they were part of a milieu that refused to see women as political actors in any way, this might explain why they left women out of consideration in their essays.

In some ways, education was obviously and overtly political, but in others education served apolitical functions. Most discourse about education did not frame education as an individual political right; most discourse framed education as a civic obligation, and as a way to protect the republic, or, as the APS essay prompt put it, "to promote the general welfare" of the country. This is why most of the APS essays, for instance, specifically refer to plans to pay for education for the poor. Poor children needed to be educated, not because it was their right to receive an education, but because the cost to the republic of not educating them could be very high. Samuel Smith insists that it is "the duty of a nation to superintend and *even to coerce* the education of children," a compulsion that reflects a belief that education of the masses is critical to the welfare of the country, even if the masses do not want that education.[31] Coercing children into public schools would not be necessary if everyone saw education as a right that they would all want to exercise. Likewise, the contestant "Hand" calls education "wholly a public concern even to the exclusion of the parent from interference therewith," and believes it should be available to "the mass of common citizens." "Hand" and others see education as important for "the masses" because the "character" of the masses "will ever decide" the character of the government.[32] In this way, education was decidedly political, as it had the potential to forge the character of the electorate.

From this point of view, the essayists leaving women out might make sense. Yet much rhetoric of the time placed care of the future character of the republic squarely in the hands of women as well as men, even if most people did not see women as part of the electorate (although, as we will see, some women were).[33] In addition, few people, if any, framed education solely in terms of political needs and the preservation of the republic. Basic needs for literacy and numeracy created practical reasons for education for both sexes, and the APS essayists almost all offer plans for practical, vocationally oriented, education. Education—in practice, if not in theory—may have existed in a conceptual space that was depoliticized, and therefore open to females. In theory, however, especially in political theory, education may have been deeply politicized, and therefore construed by these essayists as part of the tradition of political discourse that kept women invisible. Positioning themselves as political actors, the writers ignored women.

The essayists stressed the political meanings of education. All of the plans are explicit about the relationship between education and the survival of the republic. For a republic to survive, its citizens needed to be well educated to exercise their duties. To make good decisions, whether as voters electing leaders, or as jurors deciding the fate of their peers, citizens needed to be educated enough to see through the smokescreen of duplicitous rhetoric, and to understand the law. Citizens, then, needed to study rhetoric, history, government, and other subjects that would give them the background knowledge and the analytical skills necessary to act as responsible citizens. In these senses of the word, citizenship did not apply to women; a citizen was a free (and therefore usually white) male past a specific age. If the essayists designed their educational plans for these enactments of citizenship, that might explain why they left women out. For many people, the prospect of women as voters or jurors was inconceivable, and therefore women's education did not need to train them for these unlikely events.

Citizenship did not just entail action, though. In addition to thinking rationally, making logical decisions, analyzing legalities, and defending people's rights—all traits associated with manliness—citizenship also included the unmanly behavior of subordination.[34] Lockean views of education linked freedom and subjection: as the child is subject to the parent, the citizen is subject to the law. Freedom comes from willingly submitting to particular forms of civil authority.[35] John Hobson (who may have been "Academicus"), for instance, stipulates that "education *alone* can supply this republic with citizens formed to *subordination*." Proper education will be the basis from which a "spirit of subordination will arise, spontaneous as the fountain, diffusive as light, and harmonious as the solar system."[36] It may be that the unmanly subordination requirement is one of the reasons the essayists didn't talk about women. Education was imperative for getting men to agree to submission to authority. If education—the means toward gaining men's assent in subordination—was itself typed as feminine, then both the means and the ends were emasculating. If, however, education could be reserved for men—not literally reserved only for men, but ideologically and rhetorically reserved for men—then the hoped-for outcome of subordination could be recast as manly, as well.

Some of the essayists did concern themselves with manliness. Samuel Knox fretted over the entertainments indulged in by youth when not studying; those entertainments could "give the mind a frivolous or effeminate bias on the one hand, or if well chosen, a manly and vigorous resolution on the other."[37] For boys, swimming constituted good vigorous exercise. By the time they reached college, their pleasurable activities should become "more manly and dignified." Here, Knox recommends the "manly" arts of dancing, smooth conversation, and manners.[38] References like this might reveal some gender anxiety, a need to shore up the links between and among education, citizenship, and manliness.

The rights and responsibilities of citizenship, such as serving in political office and voting, were arrogated to men; the proper fulfillment of those duties depended on a certain amount of subjugation of individual desires to the common good and to the law; and the ability to perform civic duty was contingent upon education. In these ways, education was heavily related to participation in the political system. Samuel Smith clearly articulates a strong link between education and citizenship. The educated citizen "will know his rights, and he will understand the rights of others," and will increase the "prospect that our political institutions would quickly mature into plans as perfect as human happiness would require."[39] For Smith, participation in the perfection of the nation's political institutions was civic work that needed to be done by educated men. It is possible, then, that the APS writers omitted females from their plans because they framed themselves as writing political tracts about political issues in a culture in which politics was a male pursuit.

Another very different possibility is that some or all of this group of writers saw themselves as distinctly *not* political and therefore all the more defensive of their status as men. Historian Catherine O'Donnell Kaplan, who has written eloquently on masculinity and citizenship in the early republic, analyzed an amorphous group of literati. Kaplan argues that "men of letters" who chose intellectual pursuits rather than political interests may have felt that their claim to manhood was under threat. In a world in which engagement in political rhetoric was the sine qua non of American citizenship, these men instead promoted a view of citizenship based on cultural refinement and sensibility. Their cultural circles included women of letters, an inclusion that, according to Kaplan, further imperiled their masculinity. The men responded by excluding women from their inner circle. They might exchange ideas with women in social settings, read women's intellectual work (as did, for instance, the Friendly Club of New York City that approvingly read Mary Wollstonecraft), and they might even publish women's intellectual writings (for instance, the Anthology Society of the Boston Athenaeum published Mary Moody Emerson in their *Monthly Anthology*), but they would not admit women as members of their clubs.[40] Men of New York's Friendly Club had "daily interactions [in] a mixed-sex intellectual world—including walks, teas, dinner parties, parlor performances, and group readings of recently published novels and poetry."[41] These men clearly valued women's company and their intellectual engagement. Yet when the Club itself held its meetings, these same men prohibited women from attending. This exclusion, writes Kaplan, "emerged from a need to assert the manliness of cultural activities rather than from denigration of women's intellectual capacities."[42]

Such men believed in women's intellectual aptitudes and enjoyed the company of educated women, as we saw, for instance, in the example of Samuel Smith. But they feared that too much interaction with women in the realms of philosophy, science, and literature might "unman" them and their cultural pursuits. If education was the foundation for these cultural pursuits, this might explain, for some of the essayists, why they left women out. These men may have relished social interactions with intellectual women, but rhetorically they needed to associate education itself with manliness in order to bolster their own identities as learned men. Therefore, when writing plans for a system of education, and submitting those plans to the APS—an all-male cultural institution—those plans spoke of education only in terms of male learners.

Clear demarcations of men's and women's roles, if such had ever existed, faded into fuzzy lines in the years of the nation's founding. Women's place in the public and political realms was in flux. As we have seen, discussion of women's rights abounded. Women participated in both political and cultural contexts in new and sometimes dramatic ways. In New Jersey, single women who met the property qualifications were eligible to vote during the time of the APS contest; in fact, for 30 years, from 1776 until 1807, single and widowed women could vote in New Jersey, just a stone's throw from APS.[43] Married women, however, were not eligible, and given that most women married, and that New Jersey's laws had not caught on anywhere else, the small number of "petticoat electors" may have made little impact on the thinking of the essay writers. There was, though, a lot of public and private discussion about women as citizens. Historian Susan Branson documents the wide range of arenas for these discussions, and for increasingly prominent public positions for women. The 1790s saw a burgeoning of printed material discussing "women's authority and responsibilities in marriage, social relations, and participation in public political life [and t]hough opinions on this issue varied, there was a tendency to favor increased female autonomy."[44] In addition to print, women took on greater participation in political salons, public political activities, and in theaters as playwrights and actors. In the 1780s and 1790s, women "clearly were part of the public sphere."[45] Women in Philadelphia were so inspired by the French Revolution that newspaper editor William Cobbett railed against "those bold, daredevil, turban-headed females...these fiery frenchified dames."[46] At least some of the contest entrants had to have been aware of the tensions broiling around gender, politics, and culture.

Essayists for the APS contest on a system of national education may have paid little attention to female education, not because they didn't *think* about it, but because they were more interested in perpetuating particular ideals of manhood and womanhood. The APS positioned itself as a learned society interested in the pursuit of useful knowledge. APS members were scientists and inventors, doctors and geologists, philosophers searching after truth. Yet historian Bernard Fay contends that European and American learned societies in the eighteenth century did not actually accomplish much in any scientific realm. The societies "left relatively few interesting evidences of their scientific work," because their "lack of intellectual discernment and their naïve utilitarianism led them into all sorts of trivial adventures." Although society members "united around a great ideal, 'Science,'...in reality they were busied with other concerns." Instead of holding any major importance in the scientific realm, Fay argues, the learned societies played social, moral, and religious roles.[47] In the case of the APS contest on education, the Society reflected social values, indeed, commenting, through their silence, on issues of gender.

* * *

None of the essays submitted for the APS contest for a plan for national education included girls or women in any significant way in their ideas. Each of the seven contestants surely had his own reasons, and we are not likely ever to know for certain what those reasons were. It is not likely that all seven believed that women were incapable of learning, even if one or two may have. It also is not the case that including females simply did not occur to them; we know it occurred to several of them, if only to make quick reference to separating the girls from the boys, and we know that the topic filled countless newspaper columns. It is, in fact, the quantity of print material dealing with this topic that makes it perplexing that these seven dealt with it not at all.

I suggest two possible explanations that may apply, either together or separately. One explanation is that these men saw this essay-writing venture as part of a political process—either by virtue of the topic (education generally, and education "adapted to the genius" of a republican government, specifically) or the format (entries to a contest sponsored by a well-known society). For most of this founding generation, women were excluded from political discourse; therefore these essayists also excluded women from their plans. The second explanation, and one that could exist in tandem with the first, is that excluding women was a way of bolstering the essayist's claims to manhood. Historians have documented a period of upheaval in gender dynamics in the early republic. Many men felt that their masculinity was threatened by this disruption in gender norms. Further, in an environment in which political engagement was one of the definitions of manhood, men of a certain class background who were more interested in culture than in politics faced another identity crisis. These men set out to define a new manhood: the man of letters. As such, they were triply in jeopardy: they were not involved in politics; they were involved in culture, which was coded as feminine; and their cultural pursuits and circles included a lot of women—and not just any women, but educated, intelligent, freethinking, independent women. In response, these "men of letters" worked to redefine culture as manly, and culture depends on education. They may have excluded women from their plans for education, then, not because they did not value educated women—clearly many did—but because they needed to rhetorically associate both education and culture with manliness. One way they did this was by presenting education as a male domain.

NOTES

1. Edith N. MacMullen, "*The Learning of Liberty,* Book Review," *Journal of the Early Republic* 14 (Spring 1994): 114.
2. Samuel Knox, *An Essay on the Best System of Liberal Education, Adapted to the Genius of the Government of the United States* (Baltimore: Warner & Hanna, 1799), 96.
3. David Tyack and Elisabeth Hansot, *Learning Together: A History of Coeducation in American Public Schools* (New Haven and Long: Yale University Press, 1990), Chapter 1.
4. Review Committee Report, Review of Essay #3, July 23, 1797.
5. Samuel Harrison Smith, *Remarks on Education* (Philadelphia: Ormrod, 1798), 77–78.
6. Ibid., 60.
7. Ibid., 58–59.

8. George Gregory, "Miscellaneous Observations on the History of the Female Sex," in *Essays Historical and Moral* (London: J. Johnson, 1785), 145–146.
9. William Alexander, *The History of Women* (Philadelphia: J. H. Dobelbower, 1796), 66.
10. For other arguments for and against women's education, see Margaret A. Nash, *Women's Education in the United States, 1780–1840* (New York and London: Palgrave, 2005), Chapter 2.
11. Samuel Magaw, *An Address Delivered in the Young Ladies Academy, at Philadelphia, on February 8th, 1787* (Philadelphia: Thomas Dobson, 1787), 9.
12. Thomas Jefferson, *Notes on the State of Virginia* (London: John Stockdale, 1787), 244.
13. Elizabeth Hamilton, *Letters on Education* (Dublin: H. Colbert, 1801), 2–3; emphasis in original.
14. Sarah Fatherly, *Gentlewomen and Learned Ladies: Women and Elite Formation in Eighteenth-Century Philadelphia* (Lehigh University Press, 2008); Caroline Winterer, *The Mirror of Antiquity: American Women and the Classical Tradition, 1750–1900* (Ithaca: Cornell University Press, 2007); Nash, *Women's Education in the United States.*
15. Bryan Waterman, *Republic of Intellect: the Friendly Club of New York City and the Making of American Literature* (Baltimore: Johns Hopkins University Press, 2007), 108.
16. For instance, "An Address to the Ladies," *American Magazine* (March 1788), 446; "Hints on Reading," *Lady's Magazine* (March 1793), 171; "On Female Education," *New York Magazine* (September 1794), 569–70; Mary Hays, "On the Independence and Dignity of the Female Sex," *New York Magazine* (April 1796), 203. See also William C. Dowling, *Literary Federalism in the Age of Jefferson* (Columbia: University of South Carolina Press, 1999); Linda Kerber, *Women of the Republic: Intellect and Ideology in Revolutionary America* (New York, 1985); Mary Beth Norton, *Liberty's Daughters: The Revolutionary Experience of American Women, 1750–1800* (New York: HarperCollins, 1980).
17. Waterman, *Republic of Intellect*, 109; Catherine O. Kaplan, "Elihu Hubbard Smith's 'The Institutions of the Republic of Utopia,'" *Early American Literature* 35 (Fall/Winter 2000): 294–336.
18. Waterman, *Republic of Intellect*, 136, 138.
19. Whitfield J. Bell, Jr., "As Others Saw Us: Notes on the Reputation of the American Philosophical Society," *Proceedings of the American Philosophical Society* 116 (June 1972): 273.
20. Benjamin Rush, "Thoughts Upon Female Education, Accommodated to the Present State of Society, Manners, and Government in the United States of America" [1787], in Frederick Rudolph (ed.), *Essays on Education in the Early Republic* (Cambridge: Belknap Press of Harvard University Press, 1965), 1–23; Ann D. Gordon, "The Young Ladies Academy of Philadelphia," in Carol Ruth Berkin and Mary Beth Norton (eds.), *Women of America: A History* (Boston: Houghton Mifflin, 1979), 68–91. APS members John Andrews, Robert Blackwell, Samuel Magaw, Thomas McKean, and William Smith all were associated with Poor's Young Ladies' Academy, and Samuel Magaw and Rush were associated with Brown's Young Ladies' Academy.

See *The Rise and Progress of the Young Ladies' Academy of Philadelphia* (Philadelphia: Stewart & Cochran, 1794); Samuel Magaw, *An Address Delivered in the Young Ladies Academy at Philadelphia* (Philadelphia: Thomas Dobson, 1787).

21. Kerber, *Women of the Republic*; Gordon Wood, *The Creation of the American Republic, 1776–1787* (Chapel Hill, 1969); Sara M. Evans, *Born for Liberty: A History of Women in America* (New York, 1989).

22. Ruth H. Bloch, "The Gendered Meanings of Virtue in Revolutionary America," *Signs: Journal of Women in Culture and Society* 13 (Autumn 1987): 37–58; Margaret A. Nash, "Rethinking Republican Motherhood: Benjamin Rush and the Young Ladies' Academy of Philadelphia," *Journal of the Early Republic* 17 (Summer 1997): 171–192.

23. Jan Lewis, "The Republican Wife: Virtue and Seduction in the Early Republic," *William and Mary Quarterly* 3rd ser., XLIV (October 1987): 689–721; Margaret A. Nash, *Women's Education in the United States, 1780–1820* (New York: Palgrave, 2005).

24. Noah Webster, "On the Education of Youth in America" [1790], in Rudolph, *Essays on Education in the Early Republic*, 69.

25. Smith, *Remarks*, 60–61.

26. Benjamin Rush, "Thoughts Upon Female Education, Accommodated to the Present State of Society, Manners, and Government in the United States of America" [1787], in Rudolph, *Essays on Education in the Early Republic*, 1–23.

27. Mark E. Kann, *A Republic of Men: The American Founders, Gendered Language, and Patriarchal Politics* (New York and London: New York University Press, 1998), 3, 15–16.

28. Ruth H. Bloch, *Gender and Morality in Anglo-American Culture, 1650–1800* (Berkeley, LA, and London: University of California Press, 2003); Ruth H. Bloch, "The Gendered Meanings of Virtue in Revolutionary America," *Signs: Journal of Women in Culture and Society* 13 (Autumn 1987): 37–58; Joan R. Gunderson, "Independence, Citizenship, and the American Revolution," *Signs: Journal of Women in Culture and Society* 13 (Autumn 1987): 59–77; Linda Kerber, "'History Can Do It No Justice': Women and the Reinterpretation of the American Revolution," in Ronald Hoffman and Peter Albert (eds.), *Women in the Age of the American Revolution* (Charlottesville: University Press of Virginia, 1989); Michael S. Kimmel, *Manhood in America: A Cultural History* (New York: Free Press, 1996).

29. Linda K. Kerber, Nancy F. Cott, Lynn Hunt, Carroll Smith-Rosenberg, and Christine Stansell, "Forum: Beyond Roles, Beyond Spheres: Thinking about Gender in the Early Republic," *William and Mary Quarterly* 3rd ser., 64 (July 1989): 569.

30. Kann, *A Republic of Men*, 17–18.

31. Smith, *Remarks on Education*, 66; emphasis mine.

32. "Hand," "Concerning Education in Public Schools," [1797], 3, 4.

33. Kerber, *Women of the Republic*.

34. Kann, *A Republic of Men*.

35. Sandra M. Gustafson, "Morality and Citizenship in the Early Republic," *American Literary History* 15 (Spring 2003): 172–187; Gillian Brown, *The Consent of the Governed: The Lockean Legacy in Early American Culture*

(Cambridge: Harvard University Press, 2001); Courtney A. Weikle-Mills, "'Learn to Love Your Book': The Child Reader and Affectionate Citizenship," *Early American Literature* 43 (Winter 2008): 35–61.

36. John Hobson, *Prospectus of a Plan of Instruction* (Philadelphia: Hogan, 1799), 10, 11; emphasis in original.
37. Samuel Knox, *An Essay on the Best System of Liberal Education* (Baltimore: Warner & Hanna, 1799), 133.
38. Ibid., 146.
39. Smith, *Remarks*, 82, 84.
40. For women's engagement in intellectual social circles, see David Shields, *Civil Tongues and Polite Letters in British America* (Chapel Hill: University of North Carolina Press, 1997); Catharine Allgor, *Parlor Politics: In Which the Ladies of Washington Help Build a City and a Government* (Charlottesville: University of Virginia Press, 2000); Waterman, *Republic of Intellect*.
41. Waterman, *Republic of Intellect*, 132.
42. Catherine O'Donnell Kaplan, *Men of Letters in the Early Republic: Cultivating Forums of Citizenship* (Chapel Hill: University of North Carolina Press, 2008), 83.
43. Judith Apter Klinghoffer and Lois Elkis, "'The Petticoat Electors': Women's Suffrage in New Jersey, 1776–1807," *Journal of the Early Republic* 12 (Summer 1992): 159–193.
44. Susan Branson, *These Fiery Frenchified Dames: Women and Political Culture in Early National Philadelphia* (Philadelphia: University of Pennsylvania Press, 2001), 9.
45. Ibid., 144.
46. William Cobbett [1798], quoted in ibid., 72.
47. Bernard Fay, "Learned Societies in Europe and America in the Eighteenth Century," *The American Historical Review* 37 (January 1932): 266.

CHAPTER 8

The Significance of the "French School" in Early National Female Education

Kim Tolley

In 1795, when the American Philosophical Society in Philadelphia sponsored an essay contest on the topic of a national system of public schooling, few Americans had begun to consider the place of females in such a system. One prize-winner, Samuel Knox, recommended public elementary schools enrolling both sexes, but the second winner, Samuel H. Smith, decided not to include any mention of female education in his essay, explaining that there was too much "diversity of opinion" to do the issue justice.[1]

Regardless of the diversity of opinion regarding the value of tax-supported education for girls, female schools flourished in Philadelphia's private education market. When the essay contest was under way, this market included a collection of entrepreneurial schools enrolling female students from both northern and southern states. Some of these institutions offered the sort of education that reflected Revolutionary egalitarian ideals, but others provided a traditional form of "polite education" that contemporaries often associated with elite social status. According to historian Daniel Kilbride, many wealthy southern families sent their daughters north to Philadelphia to become refined and polished young ladies in one of the city's thriving French schools.[2]

Most of the scholarship on the history of women's education in the United States has highlighted the role of Revolutionary and British Enlightenment ideology to explain young women's increasing access to schooling during the early republican period. Paradigm shift and institutional change are recurring themes in these historical accounts. The city of Philadelphia is sometimes featured as a sort of intellectual ground zero in this evolutionary process; after all, this is where Benjamin Franklin founded the first academy to receive a colonial charter, where young women threw aside convention after the Revolution and stepped up to deliver public speeches at the Young Ladies Academy, and where Benjamin Rush taught the first known chemistry course for females in 1787 and advocated a "general and uniform system of education," which would "render the mass of the people more homogeneous and thereby fit them more easily for uniform and peaceable government."[3]

Nevertheless, although the evidence of a post-Revolutionary educational shift in published essays and speeches is compelling, there is also evidence of a surprising degree of continuity in female schools, even in a city like Philadelphia. In the absence of any systematic, tax-based funding, an unregulated market in female education developed in all areas of the country alongside an informal system of charity schools established and maintained by various religious and philanthropic groups. As a result, female schools competed for students in a free market by advertising in local newspapers, adding potentially attractive subjects to their courses of study, and adjusting tuition rates to meet changing demand. To understand the diversity of opinion about female schooling during the early republican period, one need only study the changing landscape of entrepreneurial schools.[4]

Christie Anne Farnham was the first historian to provide a relatively extensive discussion of so-called French schools in the United States. In her study of higher education for elite white women in the South, she depicted such schools as conservative institutions that offered an education centered on language, culture, and the arts and emphasized young women's domestic role in the home. Farnham concluded that while French schools could be found all along the Atlantic coast during the colonial period, they had become a distinctly Southern phenomenon by the antebellum period. She argued that there was a difference in the education of Northern and Southern women, because the democratization of the North facilitated a regionally distinctive utilitarian approach to schooling and a "suspicion of gentility as elitist and decadent." However, recent work by Daniel Kilbride has provided documentary evidence of the enduring appeal of French schools in the North. Throughout the early national period, French schools were common in the North and mid-Atlantic states as well as in the South. As Kilbride has shown, the city of Philadelphia was particularly well-known for its French schools, which were very attractive to elite Southern families. Many wealthy Southerners sent their daughters north to receive an education at such schools throughout the early national period, where they studied side by side with the daughters of elite Northern families.[5]

Evidence of a thriving market in French "polite education" raises several questions about the significance of French schools during the early republican period. What distinguished these institutions from other kinds of schools open to young women? Why did they persist for so long in both the North and South? What is the significance of these schools in American education? This chapter addresses these questions through a survey of the secondary literature and a case-study analysis of primary documents from North Carolina, including school newspaper advertisements from a sample of 95 venture schools and 133 academies enrolling females.

ENLIGHTENMENT PHILOSOPHY AND THE "FRENCH SCHOOL"

Some of the earliest arguments for more advanced forms of female education originated in France. As early as 1673, François Poulain de la Barre published an essay in which he argued that females should receive the same education as males, gain access to the university, and be able to acquire professional degrees. Although few contemporaries shared Barre's views, a number of prominent women and men began to promote a more rigorous education for females in the early eighteenth century. In 1728, the French writer and salonnière Mme de Lambert (1647–1733), also known as the Marquise de Lambert, published *Advice from a Mother to her Daughter*, in which she criticized the shallowness of female education and advocated moral training. In 1730, the radical thinker Charles-Irénée Castel, abbé de Saint-Pierre, recommended the creation of female public secondary schools comparable to those that existed for young men.[6]

However, few French philosophers believed that female education should be identical to that of males. Most writers believed that biological differences produced inherent cognitive differences between the sexes. In line with contemporary beliefs, many eighteenth-century French reformers proposed relatively conservative educational models of female education, in which the overarching goal was to train young women to be virtuous wives and mothers. The most famous proponent of this view was the philosopher Jean Jacques Rousseau. In his novel *Emile* (1762), Rousseau wrote, "Thus the whole education for women ought to be relative to men. To please them, to be useful to them, to make themselves loved and honored by them, to educate them when young." Rousseau's gendered vision of female education spread throughout Europe and to the Americas, stimulating the establishment of many "French schools" that provided a more rigorous education in literacy than many of their predecessors.[7]

What was a "French school"? According to historian Rebecca Rogers, elite boarding schools catering to the daughters of wealthy and aristocratic families existed in France throughout the eighteenth century, often run by religious orders. These schools aimed to provide girls a postprimary education and help them acquire the learning and social bearing associated with the lifestyles of the upper classes. A French education was distinguished by an emphasis on culture, language, manners, deportment, and a woman's domestic duties. According to Christina de Bellaigue, English parents often sent their daughters to France to "finish" their education and attain the marks of high social status and cultural sophistication. A specific vision of French female education spread through much of the Western world during this time, and in the Americas and England this form of schooling had clear class overtones with an aristocratic flavor. By the end of the eighteenth century, every accomplished young woman was expected to know French, just as every well-educated young man was expected to know Latin.[8]

French schools were distinguished by their course of study, offering what was known as a polite education through a curriculum that included "accomplishments," or the "ornamental branches." As one advice manual for governesses described it, "There are some [arts and accomplishments], such as music, dancing, drawing, and the like, which are merely, or at least chiefly, ornamental. There are others, which, besides being ornamental, are likewise useful, such as writing, arithmetic, geography, and needlework." In his popular *Lectures on Female Education and Manners*, the Englishman John Burton cited Rousseau in recommending the usefulness of an ornamental education. Burton claimed that accomplishments in needlework were both "useful and ornamental," and that "though it be not necessary for Women to study the learned Languages, or those Arts and Sciences which are called Professional, yet a certain degree of knowledge is both ornamental and useful."[9]

The French schools in the American colonies followed this pedagogical model. French schools appeared in the larger coastal towns during the colonial period, ranging from small day schools to relatively large boarding schools. Historian Christie Anne Farnham has concluded that South Carolina may have had more French schools than large northern cities like New York, Philadelphia, or Boston during the early republican period, because many French immigrants from Haiti settled in the South after the Haitian Revolution, bringing this tradition of female education with them. The smallest institutions offered instruction in French and needlework only, as did the Widow Varnod's school in Charleston, South Carolina, in 1734. Larger institutions, like Mrs. Duneau's school in Charleston in 1770, might provide additional subjects like the three Rs, drawing, dancing, grammar, history, and geography. In 1757, Rebecca Woodin of Charleston, South Carolina, described "the different branches of Polite Education, viz. Reading English and French, Writing and Arithmetic, Needlework; and Music and Dancing, by proper masters."[10]

The thinking of some prominent Americans reflected this philosophy. In 1775, John Adams advised his daughter: "[Form] your heart to goodness and your mind to useful knowledge, as well as to those other accomplishments which are peculiarly necessary and ornamental in your sex." Those accomplishments did not include the classics. In 1776, Adams wrote his daughter, "[I]t is scarcely reputable for young ladies to understand Latin and Greek—French, my dear, French is the language, next to English—this I hope your mamma will teach you." In a letter to his wife Abigail that same year, he explained the importance of French for men as well as women. "It is in your power to teach [the children] French, and I every day see more and more that it will become a necessary accomplishment of an American gentleman or lady."[11] Thomas Jefferson also recommended instruction in French as "an indispensable part of education for both sexes." In a letter to a friend in 1818, Jefferson explained that women should also learn dancing, drawing, music, and domestic skills. "Every affectionate parent should be pleased to see his daughter qualified to participate with her companions & without awkwardness at least in the circles of festivity of which she occasionally becomes a part," he wrote. Learning household skills was also essential.

"The order & economy of a house are as honorable to the mistress as those of the farm to the master & if either be neglected ruin follows, & children are destitute of the means of living." Although Jefferson never used the term "French school," his description of female education matches the overarching goals of a French education. Such schooling provided elite and middling-class American women the polish necessary to move in the highest levels of society, and it also emphasized domesticity and preparation for motherhood as the central aims of female education.[12]

By the early nineteenth century, French schools had spread inland, to smaller towns as well as large cities. For example, the French émigré couple Lucien and Caroline Murat founded Murat's Select Boarding School for Young Ladies in Bordentown, New Jersey, in the 1830s. Murat was the son of Napoleon Bonaporte's cavalry leader Joachim Murat, the grand duke of Berg, and later king of Naples and Sardinia. The Murat's prestigious social credentials attracted elite students from the Carolinas, Kentucky, and Spain.[13]

Not all founders of French schools hailed from France, and not all schools offering a traditional French curriculum called themselves "French schools." British men and women that had been educated in the French tradition in England brought that style of pedagogy with them when they immigrated to the United States. For instance, when Thomas and Elizabeth Sambourne came to Raleigh, North Carolina, to teach music, they placed an advertisement in the *Raleigh Minerva*, offering not only lessons on the piano or violin, but also instruction for "a few Young Ladies...in all or any of the ornamental branches of Education," including French, Italian, drawing, embroidery, and needlework. Their school bore the hallmarks of a traditional French School, but the Sambournes were English, having recently come to the United States in search of a better life after Thomas lost his fortune. In 1813 another English couple opened "Mrs. Falkener's Young Ladies Boarding School" in Warrenton, North Carolina, advertising a course of study in "principles of Morality, domestic Economy, and polite Behavior, as may render [students] Ornament to their Country, Consolation to their Parents and Friends, and happy in themselves."[14]

Along with lay educators like the Sambournes and the Falkeners, the female Catholic teaching orders also brought traditional styles of French female education to America in the form of convent academies. Catholic nuns and priests came to North America with settlers in the French and Spanish territories. In 1801, when Thomas Jefferson began his term as the third president of the United States, the nation's boundaries stretched from the Atlantic Ocean to the Mississippi River, and from the Great Lakes nearly to the Gulf of Mexico. Further west, the Catholic countries of Spain and France expressed claims to an enormous expanse of the continent, and Catholic teaching orders had already begun to establish academies in the western territories. Among the European Catholic teaching orders that regarded America as a vast opportunity for missionary activity were the Ursulines, a French female order. The Ursulines brought convent education to North America in

1727 by establishing a female academy in New Orleans. The school offered a traditional French education and became an important center of female education in Louisiana and the neighboring territory. Catholic communities in the former English colonies increased after the Revolution, when a number of states repealed laws discriminating against Catholic clergy. According to historian Eileen Brewer, between 1790 and 1920, 119 European religious communities established foundations in America, and Catholic communities with roots in America founded 38 orders. After 1820, the number of convents in America roughly doubled each decade until the end of the century. Among the French teaching orders in America were the Sisters of the Sacred Heart, who opened academies for the daughters of wealthy and powerful Catholics and also founded schools for the children of the poor.[15]

PERSISTENCE AND APPEAL

Despite the egalitarian rhetoric of some early republican writers calling for a rigorous form of female schooling more comparable to that offered young men, French female schools persisted throughout the early national period. Their longevity can be explained in terms of their ongoing appeal to middling- and upper-class parents. This appeal could arise from a number of motivations: To maintain or increase the family's class status, to develop and strengthen social ties with like-minded individuals and families, or to acquire the social polish and education necessary to marry into a family of wealth and position. In the case of French schools run by the Catholic teaching orders, an important motivation for many families was to provide their daughters a Catholic education.

French schools were popular because they offered young women the chance to legitimize or enhance their class status. According to Christie Anne Farnham, such schools were particularly attractive to Southern parents, because aristocratic pretensions endured in the antebellum South, bolstered by a hierarchical society based on slavery. Wealthy Southern parents had a vested interest in helping their daughters and sons imitate the lifestyles of the French and English aristocracy. French schools appealed to parents in other regions of the country as well. In fact, as Daniel Kilbride has noted, the popularity of such schools in Philadelphia suggests that both elite Northerners and Southerners shared aristocratic ambitions and an upper-class identity in the antebellum era. In all areas of the country, upwardly mobile middling-class parents viewed a traditional French education as the best means to help their daughters gain the poise and social skills necessary to breach class boundaries.[16]

The larger French boarding schools contributed to the development of what might be called upper-class social networks during the early republican period. As historian Nancy Beadie has pointed out, academies and boarding schools were important sites of peer association, acculturation, and identity formation. They accomplished this by bringing young women from different regions of the country together in one place, offering intimate contact and the opportunity for young women to establish long-standing friendships with others of the same class. The wealthy Southern parents who sent their daughters north to Philadelphia encouraged these friendships, because their families already had personal and business connections with Philadelphians, relationships forged through financial dealings, memberships in scientific societies, and correspondence related to politics and religion. According to Daniel Kilbride, these sorts of preexisting links made cities like Philadelphia a natural destination for the schooling of Southern daughters.[17]

Many parents recognized that an elite French education could improve their daughters' chances in the marriage market. Young American women hoping to attain an upper-class lifestyle after leaving their parents' home remained dependent on men, since virtually no occupations open to single women in the antebellum era provided high levels of wealth or social status. Parents hoping to improve the life chances of their daughters enrolled them in French schools to increase their opportunities for marriage to men of wealth and future prospects. Opportunities to meet potential husbands could arise through the friendships and social ties formed at school, since a young woman could become acquainted with the brothers and male cousins of friends. Additionally, the domestic goals and literary and cultural aspects of a French education helped young women to engage in polite and fashionable conversation with men without seeming to outmatch them in knowledge, making them attractive potential marriage partners for young men from conservative families.[18]

For Catholics, religion played an important role in the appeal of French schools established by the Catholic teaching orders. For example, the North Carolina politician William Gaston sent his daughter Susan to study in Philadelphia during the early 1820s. At first glance, Gaston's decision to send his daughter to a French school in Philadelphia is puzzling, because at the time, he served on the board of trustees of Raleigh Academy, a coeducational Southern school with a highly regarded female department. He could have kept his daughter close to home by enrolling her there, where she might have studied a range of advanced subjects that relatively few schools of that era could match, including geometry, the sciences, and Latin. However, because Gaston was a Catholic, it is likely that he chose a traditional French education for his daughter on religious grounds. He would have been very familiar with Raleigh Academy's evangelical Protestant character. In fact, when he wrote his daughter in 1822, the head of the academy's female department was Susan Nye, an evangelical Presbyterian bent on converting and saving the souls of every young woman under her care. Many Catholic parents feared the effect a Protestant education might have on their children's religious beliefs and chose to enroll their daughters in lay French schools or convent schools to maintain their Catholic identity.[19]

French schools conducted by the Ursulines and the Society of the Sacred Heart sought to produce devout and loyal Catholic women. The highest priority for every teaching order was the salvation of souls through religious teaching. Catholic teachers believed that women played a key role in the successful maintenance and development of the church, because mothers were essential in nurturing the faith of future generations.[20]

Nevertheless, French convent schools attracted Protestant students as well as Catholics. Many non-Catholics attended elite convent schools in Midwestern frontier cities, where there were few alternatives. For example, according to historian Mary J. Oates, at the Academy of the Sacred Heart in St Louis, roughly half of the girls enrolled between 1841 and 1851 were Protestant. Most schools took care to reassure the parents of prospective Protestant students that their children would be able to practice their own religious beliefs without undue influence to convert to Catholicism. Financial concerns as well as cultural sensitivity prompted this tactful approach, since on the antebellum frontier, where the Catholic middle- and upper-class population was relatively small and spread over a large geographic area, the tuition revenues generated by Protestant students could help sustain a school.[21]

CRITICISM

Despite their long-standing appeal to middling- and upper-class families, both lay and Catholic French schools attracted criticism throughout the early national period. Critics complained that lay French schools promoted elitism and lacked the academic rigor and moral training young American women required. Philadelphia's Benjamin Rush, author of *Thoughts upon Female Education* (1787) and a founder of the Philadelphia Young Ladies' Academy, endorsed the study of French but believed that an education focused primarily on ornamental subjects such as embroidery, dancing, music, and art was elitist and incongruent with democratic values. "It is high time..." wrote Rush, "to study our own character—to examine the age of our country—and to adopt manners in every thing, that shall be accommodated to our state of society, and to the forms of our government. In particular it is incumbent upon us to make ornamental accomplishments yield to principles and knowledge, in the education of our women."[22]

In 1817, Philadelphia's Moses Thomas expressed doubt about the form of private female education that had developed in the major cities. "Female education has been sufficiently attended to in this country;—but it has not always been attended to in the right way," he wrote.

> Many useful schools, under the tuition of well educated ladies, have been established in most of our cities, but we have to repeat the standing complaint, that they are devoted in too many instances, to the mere ornamental parts of education...if the system of female education goes on the course which it has now taken, the daughters of our fair countrywomen may make good musicians, good dancers, and good frolickers,—but we are afraid they will never make good wives.[23]

By the 1820s, popular magazines began to print articles and letters praising more rigorous forms of female education. For instance, in 1821, *The*

...nale departments in ...cts in North Carolina	
...1829	1830–1840 (%)
	100
	100
	100
	100
	100
	50
	63
	67
	58
	54
	38
	21
	88
	8
	67
	50
	25
	46
	29
	25
	50
	21
	54
	71
	58
	38
	46
2	n = 24

...d., *North Carolina Schools*
...nd Broughton, 1915), and
...North Carolina Collection,

...ent among a sample
...wn in table 8.2.[31]
...d in North Carolina
...e of the nineteenth
...n a generation later

Ladies' Literary Cabinet reprinted a letter titled "From a father in the country, to his daughter at a city Boarding School," in which the writer urged his daughter to focus on the "more useful and permanent branches of education." In response to her desire for music lessons on the pianoforte, the father admonished, "[B]efore you indulge a wish of becoming accomplished, examine your grammar, geography, history, and even your spelling book." Historian Jonathan Daniel Wells links this shift in perspective to the rise of nineteenth-century Protestant evangelical rhetoric that disparaged elite learning in favor of an education designed to prepare women to serve their families and society at large.[24]

Protestant female reformers such as Catherine Beecher and Emma Willard feared that the superficial and elitist character of the ornamental arts would distract from the utilitarian and religious aims of women's education. In the 1830s, Emma Willard's sister, the well-known writer Almira Hart Lincoln Phelps, supported the study of music and other ornamental subjects but deplored the typical French finishing school. In her influential book titled *Lectures to Young Ladies on Female Education*, she pilloried the "elegant and accomplished French opera dancer, who applie[s] for a position as governess, explaining her qualifications: 'You surely do not doubt my capability—do I not speak French with the true Parisian accent? And as for music and dancing, I can certainly teach these to any young person." Phelps's depiction of a traditional polite French education as superficial and ridiculous suggests that some Americans were still choosing this kind of schooling for their daughters when she published her book in the 1830s.[25]

Some educators drew on egalitarian rhetoric to oppose the perceived elitism of traditional French schools, but in many cases, opposition also arose from religious rivalry. During the decades of the Second Great Awakening (1790–1837), Protestant evangelicals eyed the growing numbers of Catholic French schools with anxiety. Initially, Catholics and Protestants collaborated on early efforts to provide free schooling for the children of the working classes and the poor. As JoEllen McNergney Vinyard has shown, in the French town of Detroit, which became part of Michigan territory in 1805, Protestant immigrants enrolled their daughters in the schools operating under the patronage of St. Anne's Catholic Church without sparking any anxiety among Protestant ministers. Even in predominantly Protestant communities, Catholics and Protestants appeared to set aside their differences for a period. For instance, from 1795 to 1825, the state of New York regularly provided public funds to schools run by the various denominations, and New York City's Catholic schools were among the recipients.[26] However, despite early collaborative efforts in some areas of the country, by midcentury Protestants and Catholics were drawn into bitter and protracted struggles over education. In the northeastern states particularly, the growth of the Catholic Church became a source of anxiety in a predominantly Protestant society. At the annual meeting of the American Education Society in 1835, Connecticut minister W. W. Turner probably voiced a common concern when he proclaimed, "It is known that multitudes of foreign papists are

every year pouring in upon our shores, bringing w
and prejudices of a foreign education."[27]

Whether opposition to a traditional polite fem
anti-Catholicism or from an Enlightenment comm
historians agree that a stronger emphasis on a mo
rather than a predominantly "ornamental" educatic
and wealthy families played a role in the eventua
"French schools." One contributing factor to this s
way Americans came to view "useful" subjects. Alth
British and European writers had rarely considerec
ematics, or scientific subjects as useful for females,
to promote the utility of these subjects for improvi
tal discipline, increasing their knowledge and appre
world, and preparing them to serve as teachers. F
educators in American female schools had added tl
advanced subjects to the curriculum. The trend away
so-called ornamental subjects continued throughou
the curriculum available in antebellum schools and a
ern and southern states demonstrate that during th
1860, more schools added such subjects as algebra
science to their courses of study.[28]

THE TRANSFORMATION OF THE "FRE

Many of the lay "French schools" disappeared ove
forms of French education never really vanished. In
ian and Protestant denominational academies simply
style curriculum and continued to offer French and
as electives, often at extra charge. For example, wher
Woodbridge took charge of a female academy and boal
New Jersey, in 1802, the school advertised a curric
classes that appeared quite similar to that recommer
reformers like Benjamin Rush and Benjamin Frankl
quarter, girls could learn English and plain sewing. Fa
advanced education for their daughters could pay five
instruction in English grammar, reading, writing, ar
history, use of the globes, and the fine branches of nee
parents hoping for the polish of a traditional French
their daughters in French lessons for an additional fi
and they could also add instruction in "Drawing, v
music, on reasonable terms."[29]

This trend can be seen in the surviving newspape
announcements of some North Carolina schools. I
Academy, which opened its doors in 1804, initially ac
for young women that eighteenth-century writers wo
as primarily academic, or "useful." As shown in tabl

Table 8.2 Percentage of female venture schools and fe
coeducational academies advertising specific curriculum subje
newspaper advertisements, 1800–1840, by decade (N=55)

Subjects	Decades		
	1800–1809 (%)	1810–1819 (%)	1820 (
Reading	100	100	100
Writing	100	100	100
Arithmetic	100	94	100
Grammar	100	100	100
Geography	70	100	86
Spelling	50	44	64
Needlework	60	94	86
Music	40	67	59
Painting	20	94	86
Drawing	30	83	64
Embroidery	40	78	45
Other arts and crafts	30	22	18
History	20	44	55
Belles Lettres	10	28	27
French	20	2	14
Moral philosophy	0	28	32
Natural theology	0	1	9
Rhetoric	10	22	45
Logic	0	0	27
Composition	10	1	18
Latin	0	2	23
Other modern languages	0	0	9
Astronomy	10	39	64
Natural philosophy	10	33	73
Chemistry	0	22	55
Botany	0	0	45
Math/geom/algebra	0	1	18
Number of schools in sample per decade	n = 10	n = 18	n =

Source: Data derived from newspaper advertisements in Charles L. Coon,
and Academies, 1790–1840: A Documentary History (Raleigh, NC: Edwards
from advertisements and announcements in *The Raleigh Register, 1800–1840*
Wilson Library, University of North Carolina, Chapel Hill.

the South as well as the North. This trend is clearly evic
of 55 schools enrolling females in North Carolina, as sh

A comparison of the subjects most frequently mention
school newspaper advertisements during the first deca
century with the courses of study advertised more tha
makes this shift more apparent, as shown in figure 8.1.

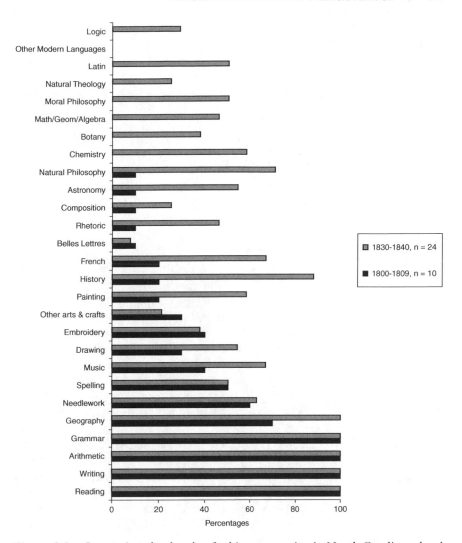

Figure 8.1 Comparison by decade of subjects appearing in North Carolina school newspaper advertisements, 1800–1809 and 1830–1840

Across the United States, schools that had begun their careers as traditional French schools underwent a similar sort of transition. For example, by the 1830s the female academies of the Society of the Sacred Heart had begun to offer instruction in natural philosophy, astronomy, and chemistry along with the other usual branches of a solid education. By the 1840s, this trend was evident in the female academies of the other teaching orders. Historian Nikola Baumgarten has attributed the inclusion of scientific subjects in the curriculum of the academy of the Sacred Heart in St. Louis, Missouri, to the widespread influence of such female educators as Catharine and Mary Beecher. When the Beecher sisters opened their first school in Hartford

Connecticut in April 1823, their advertised course of study included no mention of ornamentals; instead, they offered only the sciences, geometry and algebra, Latin, and other subjects commonly found only in male academies. As more Americans came to endorse the idea of a more advanced education for their daughters, schools offering only a traditional French education either updated their curricula to meet the demand or faced declining enrollments.[32]

CONCLUSIONS

The eighteenth-century French schools left several significant legacies in American society and culture. In both the North and the South, they were among the first institutions to offer middling- and upper-class free women access to postprimary education outside the home, and they played an important role in increasing women's literacy during the eighteenth century. As boarding schools drawing students from different geographic regions, French schools also facilitated the growth of friendships and social networks that transcended political boundaries and helped to create a common American culture during the early republican period. Finally, although the academic courses in the French schools were relatively elementary compared to the courses available to young men at the time, the traditional French emphasis on language, culture, and the arts continued in the later academies, which in many cases, simply appropriated and built on the earlier model.

The evidence of French schools in early national cities like Philadelphia sheds light on American attitudes toward female education in the early republican period.

Educational entrepreneurs conducted dozens of successful French schools geared to provide the daughters of America's powerful families with a very conservative education, one designed to ensure the marriageability of young women to young men of equal social status. New ideas about egalitarianism and women's social equality may have appeared in the speeches and essays of early republican reformers like Benjamin Franklin and Benjamin Rush, but most elite families maintained their traditional focus on the conservation and transfer of wealth from one generation to the next. For the social historian, the evidence of thriving French schools in the early national era underscores the importance of taking early republican rhetoric with a grain of salt.

The thriving education market in early republican Philadelphia may also explain the resistance of many American citizens to proposals for a national, standardized approach to schooling. The disparity of opinion evident in the compositions submitted to the American Philosophical Society's essay contest reflects the lack of agreement in society at large, not only over the content of schooling, but also over its appropriate scope and organization. When it came to the sons and daughters of poor and working-class parents, most middling- and upper-class Americans probably agreed with Benjamin Rush that rendering "the mass of the people more homogeneous" and thereby more governable was a desirable educational outcome. By the end of the nineteenth century, American voters in every state of the Union came to view this goal as worthy of tax-supported funding. But few individuals with actual voting power in the early republican period—white, middling- and upper-class property owners—chose to enroll their daughters in classrooms alongside the children of the poor. Such parents did not value an education that would render their daughters more homogeneous; instead, they sought schools that would help their daughters become more distinctive. To this end, parents turned to the private education market, where they could choose from a diverse range of institutions catering to young women from different income levels, cultural backgrounds, and religious beliefs.

During later decades, as common schools spread across the country, many wealthy families continued to enroll their children in private schools. Some parents made this choice for religious or ideological reasons; others primarily sought more elite forms of schooling for their daughters. Many of the later nineteenth-century day and boarding schools, whether religious or nonsectarian, carried traces of the traditional French education, now merged with a relatively advanced, utilitarian curriculum. The spirit of social egalitarianism in the new republic may have been strong, but so was the desire to retain personal choice, privilege, and social status.

NOTES

1. See Frederick Rudolph, ed., *Essays on Education in the Early Republic* (Cambridge, MA: Harvard University Press, 1965), 217.
2. Daniel Kilbride, *An American Aristocracy: Southern Planters in Antebellum Philadelphia* (Columbia: University of South Carolina Press, 2006), 53–77.
3. Dr. [Benjamin] Rush, "On the Mode of Education Proper in a Republic," *The New England Quarterly Magazine; Comprehending Literature, Morals, and Amusement* 1 (April, May, and June 1802): 133–138. The quote is on page 133. Referring to the discourse supporting female education during the early republican period, Linda K. Kerber coined the term "republican motherhood" in a highly influential essay. See Kerber, "The Republican Mother: Women and the Enlightenment—An American Perspective," *American Quarterly* 28 (Summer 1976): 187–205. Also see Kerber, *Women of the Republic: Intellect & Ideology in Revolutionary America* (Chapel Hill, NC: University of North Carolina Press, 1980). For decades, most historical accounts of this period followed Kerber, explaining that an ideology of "republican motherhood" fueled the development of women's education. See Rosemarie Zagarri, "Morals, Manners, and the Republican Mother," *American Quarterly* 44 (1992): 192–215; Carol Berkin, *Revolutionary Mothers: Women in the Struggle for America's Independence* (New York: Random House, 2006). Margaret A. Nash documented a much broader range of contemporary rationales for female education in "Rethinking Republican Motherhood: Benjamin Rush and the Young Ladies' Academy of Philadelphia," *Journal of the Early Republic* 17 (Summer 1997): 171–191; and *Women's Education in the United States, 1780–1840* (New York: Palgrave Macmillan, 2005), 15–34. For a recent overview of Enlightenment

and secular early republican thinking about female education, see Lucia McMahon, "'Of the Utmost Importance to Our Country': Women, Education, and Society, 1780–1820," *Journal of the Early Republic* 29 (Fall 2009): 475–506.

4. For a general overview, see Kim Tolley, "Mapping the Landscape of Higher Schooling, 1727–1850," in Nancy Beadie and Kim Tolley (eds.), *Chartered Schools: Two Hundred Years of Independent Academies in the United States, 1727–1925* (New York: Routledge, 2002), 19–43.

5. For discussion of French schools in the South, see Christie Anne Farnham, *Education of the Southern Belle: Higher Education and Student Socialization in the Antebellum South* (New York University Press, 1994), 37–50. The quote is from page 31. For French schools in Philadelphia, see Kilbride, *An American Aristocracy*, 53–77.

6. For discussion of eighteenth-century debates over female education in France, see Rebecca Rogers, "Culture and Catholicism: France," in James C. Albisetti, Joyce Goodman, and Rebecca Rogers (eds.), *Girls' Secondary Education in the Western World: From the 18th to the 20th Century* (New York: Palgrave Macmillan, 2010), 25–40. See also Samia Spencer, ed., *French Women and the Age of Enlightenment* (Bloomington: Indiana University Press, 1984); Jennifer J. Popiel, *Rousseau's Daughters: Domesticity, Education, and Autonomy in Modern France* (Lebanon: University of New Hampshire Press, 2008), 140–164.

7. Jean-Jacques Rousseau, *Rousseau's Émile: or, Treatise on Education*, trans. William H. Payne (New York: D. Appleton and Co., 1909), 263. See Rebecca Rogers, *From the Salon to the Schoolroom: Educating Bourgeois Girls in Nineteenth-Century France* (University Park: Pennsylvania State University Press, 2005), 227–252.

8. Rogers, *From the Salon to the Schoolroom*, 227–252; Christina De Bellaigue, *Educating Women: Schooling and Identity in England and France, 1800–1867* (New York: Oxford University Pres, 2007), 203.

9. Charles Allen, *The Polite Lady; or, A Course of Female Education: In a Series of Letters, from a Mother to her Daughter* (Philadelphia: Mathew Carey, 1798), 132–133. This first American edition was originally published in Britain and dedicated "To the Governesses of Ladies' Boarding Schools, in Great Britain and Ireland" (John Burton, *Lectures on Female Education and Manners* [Dublin: J. Milliken, 1794], 148). References to Rousseau appear on pages 118 and 143. This is the third edition of Burton's book, which commonly appeared in American bookstores. For discussion of the ways contemporaries viewed some subjects as both useful and ornamental, see Nash, *Women's Education in the United States*, 41–49.

10. See Farnham, *Education of the Southern Belle*, 37–50. The quote is from page 39. Also see Julia Cherry Spruill, *Women's Life and Work in the Southern Colonies* (Chapel Hill: University of North Carolina Press, 1938), 197–201; Catherine Clinton, "Equally Their Due: The Education of the Planter Daughter in the Early Republic," *Journal of the Early Republic* 2 (April 1982): 39–60.

11. Abigail Adams Smith and Caroline Abigail Smith De Windt, *Correspondence of Miss Adams: Daughter of John Adams, Second President of the United States*, vol. 2 (New York: Wiley and Putnam, 1842, 3–5; John and Abigail

Adams, *The Letters of John and Abigail Adams*, ed. Frank Shuffelton (London: Penguin 1876), 135.

12. Thomas Jefferson to N. Burwell, March 14, 1818. Two pages of this letter are reproduced in Henry Stephens Randall, *The Life of Thomas Jefferson*, vol. 3 (Philadelphia: J. B. Lippincott & Co., 1871), 447–448.

13. Murat's school is described in Laura Battle Phillips, "School Days at Bordentown," in *Charles Phillips Papers* #2462, fol. 34, 1–2. Southern Historical Collection, Wilson Library, University of North Carolina at Chapel Hill [hereafter SHC]. The Sambournes' newspaper advertisement is in Charles L. Coon, ed., *North Carolina Schools and Academies, 1790–1840: A Documentary History* (Raleigh, NC: Edwards and Broughton, 1915), 410.

14. For the Sambournes' experience in North Carolina, see Kim Tolley, "Music Teachers in the North Carolina Education Market, 1800–1840: How Mrs. Sambourne Earned a 'Comfortable Living for Herself and Her Children,'" *Social Science History* 32 (Spring 2008): 75–106. The Sambournes' and Faulkners' newspaper advertisements are found in Coon, *North Carolina Schools and Academies*, 410, 590. For discussion of the Faulkners' school, see Farnham, *Education of the Southern Belle*, 41–44.

15. Eileen Mary Brewer, *Nuns and the Education of American Catholic Women, 1860–1920* (Chicago: Loyola University Press, 1987), 25, 36–37. See also Mary J. Oates, "Catholic Female Academies on the Frontier," *U.S. Catholic Historian* 12 (Fall 1994): 121–136. For an overview of the research literature on the rise of Catholic academies and parish schools, see Kim Tolley, "'Many Years before the Mayflower': Catholic Academies and the Development of Parish High Schools in the United States, 1727–1925," in Beadie and Kim Tolley, *Chartered Schools*, 304–330.

16. Farnham, *Education of the Southern Belle*, 38–43; Kilbride, *An American Aristocracy*, 53–77.

17. Nancy Beadie, "Internal Improvement: The Structure and Culture of Academy Expansion in New York State in the Antebellum Era, 1820–1860," in Beadie and Kim Tolley, *Chartered Schools*, 89–115. See also Kilbride, *An American Aristocracy*, 53–77.

18. Farnham, *Education of the Southern Belle*, 39–43.

19. For discussion of Gaston's daughter in Philadelphia, see Kilbride, *An American Aristocracy*, 60–61. Kilbride does not mention Gaston's Catholicism or his association with Raleigh Academy. William Gaston is listed as a trustee of Raleigh Academy in an 1822 newspaper announcement in Coon, *North Carolina Schools and Academies*, 493. For Raleigh Academy's evangelical Protestant approach to education, see Kim Tolley, "A Chartered School in a Free Market: The Case of Raleigh Academy, 1801–1828," *Teachers College Record* 107 (January 2005): 59–88. Journal of Susan Nye Hutchison, the Southern Historical Collection, Wilson Library, University of North Carolina, Chapel Hill. My conclusions about Susan Nye's evangelism are based on the journal she kept while teaching in Raleigh and elsewhere.

20. Brewer, *Nuns and the Education of American Catholic Women*.

21. Oates, "Catholic Female Academies on the Frontier," 121–136. See also Nikola Baumgarten, "Education and Democracy in Frontier St. Louis: The

Society of the Sacred Heart," *History of Education Quarterly* 34 (Summer 1994): 172–173.

22. Benjamin Rush, *Thoughts upon Female Education, Accommodated to the Present State of Society, Manners, and Government in the U.S. A.* (Philadelphia: Prichard and Hall, 1787), 87.

23. *The Analectic Magazine, and Naval Chronicle*, vol. 9 (Philadelphia: Moses Thomas, 1817), 290.

24. "From a father in the country, to his daughter at a city Boarding School," *The Ladies' Literary Cabinet*, vol. 4 (New York: Nathaniel-Smith, 1821), 34. For discussion of the role evangelicals played in a Southern backlash against elite forms of female education, see Jonathan Daniel Wells, *Women Writers and Journalists in the Nineteenth-Century South* (New York: Cambridge University Press, 2011), 17–54.

25. Mrs. Lincoln Phelps, *The Female Student: Or, Lectures to Young Ladies on Female Education* (New York: Leavitt, Lord & Col, 1836), 50–51n. See Heidi Brayman Hackel and Catherine E. Kelly, *Reading Women: Literacy, Authorship, and Culture in the Atlantic World, 1500–1800* (Philadelphia: University of Pennsylvania Press, 2009), 73–144.

26. JoEllen McNergney Vinyard, *For Faith and Fortune: The Education of Catholic Immigrants in Detroit, 1805–1912* (Urbana: University of Illinois Press, 1998), 4–12. For New York's early funding of Catholic schools, see Harold A. Buetow, *Of Singular Benefit: The Story of Catholic Education in the United States* (London: Macmillan, 1970), 86.

27. W. W. Turner, "Connecticut Branch," *The American Quarterly Register* 8 (Boston, MA: Perkins and Marvin, 1836), 94. For Protestant anxiety about Catholic immigration, see Lloyd P. Jorgensen, *The State and the Non-Public School, 1825–1925* (Columbia: University of Missouri Press, 1987), 31–34; Charles R. Morris, *American Catholic: The Saints and Sinners Who Built America's Most Powerful Church* (New York: Random House, 1997), 58–59.

28. See Kim Tolley, *The Science Education of American Girls: A Historical Perspective* (New York: Routledge, 2003); Farnham, *Education of the Southern Belle*, 33–67; Nash, *Women's Education in the United States*.

29. "Education," *The Port Folio, by Oliver OldSchool, Esq.*, vol. 2 (Philadelphia, PA: H. Maxwell, 1802), 116.

30. A similar trend can be seen in several other North Carolina institutions that left behind documents describing their courses of study over a sustained period, including Fayetteville Academy, Salisbury Academy, Williamsborough Female Academy, and Shocco Female Academy. For a history of Raleigh Academy, see Kim Tolley, "A Chartered School in a Free Market: The Case of Raleigh Academy, 1801–1823," *Teachers College Record* 107 (January 2005): 59–88. For discussion of the rise of academies open to females in every geographic region in the country, see Beadie and Tolley, *Chartered Schools*, 3–43. See also Margaret A. Nash, "'A Triumph of Reason': Female Education in Academies in the New Republic," in Beadie and Tolley, *Chartered Schools*, 64–88.

31. Sources included newspaper advertisements in Coon, *North Carolina Schools and Academies*, and all extant advertisements and announcements in *The Raleigh Register*, 1800–1840, North Carolina Collection, Wilson Library, University of North Carolina, Chapel Hill. From an initial sample

of 95 venture schools and 133 academies, I selected schools that met two criteria: (1) Enrollment of females, either as a single-sex institution or as a female department in a coeducational school; (2) description of the course of study in extant newspapers. This selection yielded a smaller sample of 55 institutions, of which 43 were single-sex venture schools and 12 were coeducational academies.

32. Baumgarten, "Education and Democracy in Frontier St. Louis," 171–192. See "Carmelite Sisters' Academy" in the *Baltimore Sun*, August 12, 1842. The trend toward increased rigor in female schools is evident in school advertisements in this newspaper throughout the 1830s. For the Beecher sisters' advertisement, see "Misses C & M Beecher," in *American Mercury*, Hartford, Connecticut, April 20, 1824. The Beechers did not maintain this emphasis in female education during later years. For Catharine Beecher's embrace of a more domestic education for women in the late 1830s, see Kathryn Kish Sklar, *Catharine Beecher: A Study in American Domesticity* (New York: Norton, 1976).

CHAPTER 9

The Place of Religion in
Early National School Plans

Benjamin Justice

In January 1788, Satan contributed a series of letters to Noah Webster's *American Magazine*. Addressing the rising tide of educational reform proposals in the United States and abroad, the Devil wished to offer his own plan for instructing American youth. Not surprisingly, he focused on moral education. He was especially enthusiastic about the sensational book *Emile* (1762), and especially hostile to that sturdy New England Calvinism espoused by, among other people, the droll young editor of the magazine. "Follow my paradoxical friend Rousseau's advice as to religion," he urged readers. "Let all instruction on this subject come as late as possible. Children who learn with wonderful facility all other branches of knowledge, cannot conceive that they shall be accountable for their actions; that the Diety is witness to all they do, and will reward the good, and punish the bad." If children learned to behave and think long enough without religious teaching, Satan enthused, "you may then preach religion as much as you please; for it will have little effect."[1]

What to teach children about religion proved to be one of the most challenging problems facing would-be creators of national, or even statewide systems of education during the early national period. Writers on both sides of the Atlantic agreed that the success of the American republic would rest on the intelligence and virtue of citizens. And the radical Frenchman Rousseau aside, most writers agreed that education rooted in religious traditions provided the base of moral development. In fact, religion had been the backbone of most formal education in the American colonies for centuries. After the revolution, general pronouncements about the importance of religion and education were easy enough to make, and appeared in state and federal documents as well as in the popular press; but the context of a new politics of religion in American civic life posed considerable challenges for those who cared about the specifics.

Even as Webster penned his satanic satire, state governments debated whether to ratify the new federal constitution instituting a wholly secular design of government (which they did), an unprecedented achievement. Three years later, in December of 1791, the states also ratified ten amendments to that constitution, the first among them declaring that "Congress shall make no law respecting an establishment of religion, or prohibiting the free exercise thereof." All the states were ratifying state constitutions, too, that disestablished religion to some degree, although Connecticut and Massachusetts created, for a time, a system of multiple establishment that clearly favored the Congregational Church, even as they protected some measure of private religious freedom. By the end of the 1790s, controversy over the place of religion in government led to one of the bitterest presidential campaigns in American history between Massachusetts native John Adams and the Virginian Thomas Jefferson.

And therein lay a fundamental problem in school plans of the 1780s and 1790s: how to create republicans who were both virtuous as individuals and patriotic as citizens in a religiously pluralistic society. On the one hand, without common bonds of affection, the many factions in America so carefully balanced by the Constitution of 1789 would soon fly apart. Statesmen and philosophers argued that Americans needed a common history and identity—even a common tongue. Whether accomplished at the federal, state, or local level, leading intellectuals believed that formal education was the way to knit a diverse people into a single nation, *e pluribus unum*, along the lines of a pan-American republican ideology. Noah Webster went so far as to design an *American* version of the English language for just this reason. Benjamin Rush explained, "By producing one general, and uniform system of education, [our schools] will render the mass of people more homogeneous, and thereby fit them more easily for uniform and peaceable government."[2]

On the other hand, American religion was diverse, divisive, political, and particular. With the Second Great Awakening just beginning to stir, church memberships were still low and selective during the 1790s, while religious authority was deeply entrenched and conservative. Religious leaders, historian Jon Butler has observed, would not have called America a Christian nation. Everywhere they looked they saw moral declension, godlessness, and diminished state support (lamented by those who lost it, not the Baptists who championed it).[3] Few faiths conceded the moral validity of their competitors. Moreover, many American intellectuals believed that history proved that some types of religion could be dangerous to free peoples. Each state had its own unique recent history with political strife over organized religion—with disestablishment of state religion, the requiring of religious oaths, barring ministers from office, and the protection of individual religious rights being deeply contentious issues. Insofar as they imagined school systems for the masses to serve a unifying political purpose, educational reformers had to reconcile the politics of religion.

Their solutions clustered around three interrelated aspects of the problem. The first was organizational. How, and by whom, should schools for the

American masses be set up, supervised, and funded in an era of disestablishment? Nearly every author placed schools in the hands of public, secular bodies, while all saw the need for land grants and/or tax support to supplement or replace parental tuition for the poor. In an age where particular religious bodies traditionally worked with the state to ensure the virtue of the people, this was a radical move, although in an increasingly diverse nation with rapidly expanding settlement, a pragmatic one.

The second problem was curricular. How could a country or states without an established church include religion in a national curriculum? Conversely, how could a country that depended on the virtue of its citizens *not* include religion? In resolving this problem, authors came up with a range of solutions, although nearly all posited that there could be such a thing as moral instruction that was at once religious but not sectarian. Nonsectarian religious instruction figured centrally in such plans. More importantly, purpose of schooling was to make citizens first, and Christians of a particular faith second, although most saw the two as related. This move toward nonsectarian moral instruction, too, was a significant departure from tradition.

Finally, many essay writers at the time addressed a particular Enlightenment-era concern about the compatibility between religion and republicanism. Were all religious views equally useful for a republic or were some better than others? Were some dangerous? In searching for an appropriate role for religion, all authors who considered religious questions contended that some religion and republicanism went hand-in-hand. Yet clearly, and at length, many authors identified religious traditions that were incompatible with science and religious toleration—in short, religious traditions that were bad for the republic.

Not on the table in nearly every national or statewide plan, of course, was a place for free or enslaved African Americans, who as a socially branded underclass served as exploitable, although difficult-to-control labor force whose toil fueled the very economic prosperity so commonly associated with American freedom. Nor did national or state plans for education consider any systematic inclusion of Native Americans, whose ancestral lands had been, and would continue to be, necessary for the spread of European settlement. And while they enjoyed greater access to popular discourse in print—and used it—women, too, fought with limited success to find a place in the gendered political conversation about mass education during the 1780s and 1790s. It would be the next generation of women writers and leaders who would successfully frame the girl's right to a public education as a student and the woman's right to employment as teacher—both in terms of a separate gendered sphere of republican motherhood. Religion played a critical role in each of these groups—African Americans, Indians, and women—as a source of empowerment, as well as outside them as a rationalization for their oppression.[4]

This chapter examines the problems of organization and curriculum in plans for statewide or national systems of education between 1783 and 1800. While proposals and pronouncements regarding educational reform could be found in state constitutions, federal ordinances governing territories, essays, sermons, speeches, and public and private letters, the vast majority of writings on education did not take on the utopian task of fully imagining state or federal systems of education, but instead focused on very specific matters (arguing over the teaching of Latin and Greek in college or whether girls should go to school, exhorting parents to raise their children in some particular way, or touting a new school or textbook) or very general ones. Imagining fully formed social policies for instructing every child in the basics (including defining who was meant by "every child," and the basics) proved to be a challenging task, and one that required a good deal of education in itself. Most of such plans were crafted by statesmen, intellectuals, newspaper editors, and ambitious middle-class up-and-comers—essentially the same group of men who framed the federal and state constitutions. Taken together, their plans for educating American citizens do not show us a single view of the role of religion in American political life, but instead gravitate toward a common concept: creating citizens in a religiously diverse society through publicly run, nonsectarian systems of mass schooling.

ORGANIZATION

Many education writers in the early republican period were unsparing critics of the formal educational opportunities available to American citizens. Delaware's Robert Coram put it most plainly in 1791, "The country schools through most of the United States, whether we consider the buildings, the teachers, or the regulations, are in every respect completely despicable, wretched, and contemptible."[5] The revolution had contributed to the problem, disrupting local economies, drawing academies and colleges into battle and young men away to fight. "Since the war began, [public town] schools have been neglected so that but few towns have any such among them," lamented an anonymous contributor to the *Boston Magazine* in 1784."What patriot does not tremble at the prospect?"[6] A 1786 Pennsylvania education law referred to the present state of education as "embarrassed."[7] Given the needs of the new form of government, it was axiomatic among founding fathers that the citizenry must be made more intelligent and virtuous, and both required major reforms in education, including making it more widely available to all free social classes, sometimes including women. It was also clear to such men that the invisible hand of the marketplace alone would not be enough to ensure that citizens received enough formal education—on this even Adam Smith agreed.[8]

What place should religion have in this new American education? Before they wrestled with the problems of content, would-be reformers had to resolve logistical questions: how should schools be organized, funded, staffed, and maintained? Should churches be put in charge? On this question, planners of statewide or national systems of education were nearly unanimous: No. That said, reformers showed a range of solutions to the challenge of "disestablishing" public education, from a strict separationist approach, to a state-encouraged participation, to (in one case) paying all churches directly to run city schools.

One reason for not putting churches in charge of mass education was obvious in most parts of the United States: they could not do it even if they wanted to. Unlike France and England, with their millennium-old parish systems of churches (which included buildings and an administrative apparatus), relatively high population density, and well-worn networks of transportation and government, churches in the United States as a whole lacked the infrastructure to house, pay for, oversee, and staff schools for the masses. Settlement patterns varied by region, making the organization of school districts much easier in Congregational New England, say (where they largely already existed), than in the trans-Appalachian backcountry. In 1790 only 5 percent of Americans lived in places with 2,500 people or more.[9] Indeed churches themselves, observers at the time noted, were struggling against their own ideal worse than schools were. No more than 20 percent of free American adults belonged to churches at the time.[10] Only in cities and "the old and thick-settled counties," as Benjamin Rush put it, could churches provide a systematic approach toward assisting in the provision of free education for the masses. And not surprisingly, it was in cities where such arrangements were proposed (by Rush, for example), and actually attempted in the coming decades.

Yet even if churches could do it, many writers on the subject argued that they should not—or at the very least, that the state, not churches, should take primary responsibility for the education of the masses. Just as the principle of separation of church and state rose dramatically in the United States at the end of the eighteenth century, so too did most school plan authors evince a strong belief that mass education must be disestablished. Schools for the masses should be managed in the public sphere by elected or appointed secular bodies. In the introduction to the published (1799) version of his prize-winning essay on education, Rev. Samuel Knox lectured the Maryland state legislature on why:

> It is true that, agreeably to the spirit or genius of our government, every particular religious denomination has a well-founded right to erect such particular, private seminaries as they may consider most consonant with the spirit of that particular religious system they profess. It should, however, become a free and enlightened people, as much as possible to separate the pursuits of science and literary knowledge from that narrow restriction and contracted influence of peculiar religious opinions; or ecclesiastical policies, by which they have been, too long, and too generally obstructed.[11]

Why separate the particulars of religious doctrinal belief from the universality of science? Disregarding science and literary knowledge, Knox warned, would encourage "those civil broils, national prejudices, and religious feuds and jealousies that, hitherto, have stained the historic page of the otherwise most enlightened nations on earth."[12]

Knox's views were not idiosyncratic, but represented the view of religion and politics consistent with the 1776 Constitution of the state of Maryland. On the one hand, that document protected the "duty" of all Christians to their personal religious beliefs and practices, and ended state support for particular religious bodies, including banning clergy from office. But the constitution reserved the right of the state to levy a tax to support Christianity in general, leaving it to individuals to pick where their money went. Knox's proposal mirrored the state constitutional principle of promoting Christianity generally for the public good without compelling children to support a particular church-run school, although it did not imagine a system where scholars could choose among church-run schools. Jews and other non-Christians did not enjoy constitutional protections.[13]

A sampling of other states' proposed or enacted education plans shows similar connection to particular patterns of disestablishment. Thomas Jefferson submitted his famous educational proposal—the Bill for the General Diffusion of Knowledge—along with his Statute for Religious Freedom to the General Assembly in 1779 in a wave of bills to remake the laws of Virginia upon a republican framework—including plans for the gradual abolition of slavery.[14] Both the education and religion proposals shared a consistent orientation toward the role of churches in managing the public education of citizens—which is to say, they envisioned no role at all. Jefferson's religious freedom statute, adopted by the Virginia General Assembly in 1786, took the strict view that any use of government authority to support organized religion through taxation or compulsion was harmful to the interests of the individual *and* religion. In its interpretation of the statute, the Virginia General Assembly would not even allow the legal incorporation of churches, because that would involve the state using its power to confer a privilege.[15] Jefferson also attempted to disestablish the College of William and Mary by eliminating its Anglican orientation. Succeeding only partially, he resolved to found a new school instead—the University of Virginia.

Jefferson considered his Bill for the General Profusion of Knowledge to be his most important proposal, however, even more important than his precious university. The bill proposed an entirely secular system of education: dividing the state into districts or "hundreds," each of which would support a school open to all white children (male and female) for up to three years gratis, and more if they paid tuition. Above these he imagined a system of grammar schools, with free spots for promising boys from the lower schools, and a third tier capped by the a state university (at first William and Mary, but later, he hoped, the University of Virginia). Jefferson made no mention of religion in his plans for a uniform, state curriculum or in its management. The General Assembly eventually passed a watered-down version of the bill in 1796 and that effectively killed it—a death that Jefferson and his ally James Madison attributed to its expense and difficulty of implementation in sparsely settled regions of the state.[16]

The State of Massachusetts took an entirely different approach, insisting that private conscience deserved protection, but that each community must maintain a default, "publick religion" for the common good. Under colonial law, Massachusetts required that all townships levy taxes to maintain a Congregational minister, while occasionally granting exceptions for some sects to support their own churches instead. The 1780 Constitution, drafted principally by John Adams, broke the legal monopoly of the Congregational Church on tax support from the state, empowering each town to decide for itself whether to levy a religious tax, and to approve alternate churches for receiving that local money if their membership was big enough and their faith deemed legitimate. The law was deeply contentious, and the new form of local, multiple establishment was, in some ways, less liberal than the colonial model (especially in practice); but it did also guarantee freedom to hold private religious views of one's choice, even if one had no choice but to pay for the support of the town's church.[17]

In 1789 the Massachusetts State Legislature passed a comprehensive education law that created a secular framework for managing the two-tiered system of precollegiate schools—district "English schools" for teaching the 3Rs, and Latin grammar schools to prepare boys for college. The law dictated a minimum number of months of schooling each township was obligated to provide its citizens, which depended on its overall population size, and included provisions for teacher certification, governance, taxation, and penalties for noncompliance. The law allowed (and even encouraged) secular authorities to use ministers to encourage attendance, inspect, and oversee these schools, but stipulated that "no settled minister shall be deemed, held, or accepted to be a School-Master within the intent of this act." The law actually cut back on how much free education towns were required to give compared to prerevolutionary laws—no doubt a tax-cut welcomed by many—and placed stronger responsibility on individual parents to pay for schooling.[18] As with the 1780 Constitution's devolution of establishment to the local level, the Massachusetts law formally terminated the legal connection between church and state in education, although in practice Ministers continued to play a significant role in many of these district schools.[19]

Connecticut's approach to disestablishment was similar. The State did not create a new constitution after the revolution, but relied instead on its seventeenth-century colonial charter until 1818. That later constitution would protect "the exercise and enjoyment of religious profession and worship," and ban legal preference for "any Christian sect or mode of worship."[20] During the 1790s, however the Connecticut General Assembly passed a series of laws resembling those of the Massachusetts constitution: protecting private religious freedom but not abandoning the practice of religious establishment. In order to reform schooling along republican principles, the Assembly sold off its Western Reserve lands to create a fund, the interest of which would support a system of mass education or, if a two-third vote approved the decision, "the Christian Ministry or the Public Worship of God." The state enabled the creation of local, secular school societies to run this system at the local level, subject to election by all eligible voters, in replacement of the ecclesiastical societies who once ran the state's tax-supported schools.

These societies could levy taxes, set standards, create school districts, hire teachers, and appoint "civil authorities" to inspect and oversee the schools. Ecclesiastical societies, the law declared, "shall have no power to Act on the Subject of Schooling; and Law, Usage, or Custom, to the contrary."[21] Local Civil Authorities could support the general cause of religion, even through schooling, but the secular, not the sacred, ruled the schools.

In Pennsylvania, colonial patterns of church-state relations and formal education resulted in yet another relationship between church and state in conceptions of the "public school." Certainly the state contained far more diversity—educational, religious, and otherwise—than New England or Virginia, and unlike Virginia or New England had a tradition of religious freedom and no established church. (As an example, the state constitutional convention of 1790 printed its proposals in English and German.) While lacking a comprehensive statewide mandate for tax-supported district schools, the state nevertheless had a colorful (if declining) network of charity schools for German-speakers, Quaker "public schools," Franklin's famed Academy, district schools founded by settlers from New England, and various private, sectarian, informally organized "neighborhood" schools.[22]

The state managed only vague plans for mass schooling, and the issue of religious disestablishment did have the same gravitas as it did elsewhere. The 1776 constitution directed that "[a] school or schools shall be established in each county by the legislature...with such salaries to the masters paid by the public, as may enable them to instruct youth at low prices," but provided no legal framework and had little result.[23] Likewise, a 1786 education law directed the sale of state lands to create a fund to support public schools, but the money went to county academies instead.[24] The State Constitution of 1790 stated simply that "[t]he legislature shall, as soon as conveniently may be, provide, by law, for the establishment of schools throughout the state, in such a manner that the poor may be taught gratis."[25] The legislature did not do so, however, throughout the 1790s, despite various proposals.[26] Significantly, the role of religious bodies in this process was not mentioned either in the language of the constitution or in the recorded minutes, and does not appear to have been contentious; the question was *whether* to support mass education, not how.[27]

It was in this context that Philadelphia's Benjamin Rush wrote a series of proposals for the state that bucked the broader national trend toward disestablishment in plans for mass education. A prolific and thoughtful scholar, Rush wrote several private letters and public essays on various aspects of education, including comprehensive plans for universal education: a plan for a state system of education for Pennsylvania (1786, revised in 1798), and a free charity school proposal for the city of Philadelphia (1787). For the state as a whole, most of which was sparsely populated, Rush proposed a four-tiered system of state-supported schools, including one university, four regional colleges, an academy in each county for college preparation, and free schools in every township or district containing 150 families. Graduates from the university would teach at the colleges, while graduates of the colleges would teach at the academies and free schools. A combination of property taxes and land grants (generating rents) would pay for them. Importantly, Rush did not specify how these schools should be governed, but he did express a clear desire that the law support "the modes of determining the characters and qualifications of schoolmasters, and the arrangement of families in each district, so that children of the same religious sect and nation, may be educated as much as possible together."

In a 1787 proposal for free schools in Philadelphia, he explained what such religious grouping would look like in places that had the population density to support it. The state legislature should levy a city-wide property tax to pay the salary for schoolmasters, rent for schoolhouses, and other connected expenses of a citywide system of free elementary schools for both sexes, in English as well as German if the parents wished. "Above all," he wrote, "let both sexes be carefully instructed in the principles and obligations of the Christian religion." He explained, "This is the most essential part of education—this will make them dutiful children, teachable scholars, and, afterwards, good apprentices, good husbands, good wives, honest mechanics, industrious farmers, peaceable sailors, and, in everything that relates to this country, good citizens."[28] To that end, Rush proposed paying a per-pupil voucher to any religious society that maintained a school of minimum size. "I had rather see the opinions of Confucious or Mahomed inculcated upon our youth, than see them grow up wholly devoid of a system of religious principles," he wrote elsewhere. "But the religion I mean to recommend in this place, is that of the New Testament...A Christian cannot fail of being a republican."[29] Rush's commitment to sharing the responsibility for mass education with specific churches—a direct form of multiple religious establishment—made sense in a state where there was no immediate animus toward religious establishment, and a long, strong tradition of cultural and religious pluralism within schooling and within government. As we shall see, however, even Rush's pluralistic vision had limits when it came to the actual curriculum.

NONSECTARIAN RELIGIOUS INSTRUCTION

What role should religion play in the actual curriculum of schools? Setting aside the content of existing textbooks (which, traditionally, were steeped in Protestant ethics and biblical references), planners for mass, public education highlighted the moral benefits of their schools. To that end, many favored the presence of religion in the school curriculum, but took pains to explain how such religion would favor no particular sect and would further the political aims of the republic. This nonsectarian view of religion specifically, and moral education generally, brought together three interrelated streams of Enlightenment thought: The first stream flowed logically from the movement to disestablish religious control of mass education—a move that required a positive, inclusive, a one-size-fits-all approach to moral instruction and reflected the broader Enlightenment embrace of naturalist and Unitarian and deist views of theology. The second and third streams flowed out of the Enlightenment's negative view of traditional, sectarian religion—both its historical role in supporting tyranny while encouraging bigotry and strife, and its promotion of superstition, enthusiasm, and the suppression of science and reason.[30]

Most comprehensive plans for education proposed a course of study in "useful knowledge." Learning to read, write, and do basic math were the sine qua non of mass education, although most public school promoters lauded the school's role in promoting a useful moral instruction of youth, too. "Religion, morality and knowledge, being necessary to good government and the happiness of mankind," declared the oft-quoted Article III of the Northwest Ordinance of 1787, "schools and the means of education shall forever be encouraged." As historian Nancy Beadie shows, rhetoric was common in state constitutions and school plans.[31] But when it came to the specifics, religion usually gave way to platitudes. An anonymous contributor to the American Philosophical Society (probably former University of Pennsylvania provost Rev. William Smith) explained one facet of the problem. "If Christianity were uniform, it would be difficult to adopt in Politics a better code of morality than that of an universal Christian Religion."[32] But of course American Christianity was not uniform, nor were all Americans Christian.

How to solve this problem? Thomas Jefferson and Samuel Harrison Smith were unusual in their avoidance of religion, each suggesting an elementary school curriculum of the three Rs plus (in Jefferson's case) history or (in Smith's case) "the commission to memory and delivery of select pieces, inculcating moral duties, describing natural phenomena, or displaying correct fancy." More common was the development of nonsectarian religious readings, exercises, or other forms of instruction. William Smith proposed "[a] Catechism or Treatise on universal morality"; Noah Webster actually published one. De Nemours hazarded a daily prayer for secondary students "so worded as to be acceptable to all religious opinions and to offend no one." An anonymous essayist to the APS contest proposed that public schools host public lectures by "moral-politic missionaries" sent by the colleges. And so on.[33]

Authors were aware that a school serving children of varying faiths must, in good faith, strike a balance between teaching the principles of religion and morality to all while offending none. Samuel Knox recognized the importance of "preserving that liberty of conscience in religious matters which various denominations of Christians...justly claim." Nevertheless, he argued it would "be no infringement of this liberty for the public teacher to begin and end the business of the day with a short and suitable prayer and address the great source of all knowledge and instruction." He also favored a "concise moral catechism."[34] These attempts at a nonsectarian moral instruction in public education mirrored the much more painful negotiations that federal and state constitutional conventions had over the suitability of religious oaths for officeholders, which, in the end, were either abolished or gradually reduced, state-by state, to general, nonsectarian (although sometimes anti-Catholic) pronouncements on what kind of belief was necessary to be a full citizen of the republic.

Few comprehensive planners mentioned the practice of Bible reading. Before the Revolution, children commonly used the Bible for reading practice, it being the only book that many families owned. Noah Webster later recalled, "[I] had, in [my] early years, no other education that that which a common school offered, when rarely a book was used in the schools, except a spelling book, a Psalter, testament or Bible."[35] In 1798 Connecticut passed a law requiring its newly created school societies "to direct the daily reading of the bible by such of the youth as are capable of it, and the weekly instruction in some catechism by them approved, and to recommend that the master conclude the exercises each day with a prayer."[36] Massachusetts had no such requirement, nor did proposals by Jefferson, Coram, Hobson, Du Corteil, DuPont de Nemours, the anonymous author of a 1787 "Plan for establishing Schools in a new country, where inhabitants are thinly settled...," or any of the seven contestants in the American Philosophical Society essay contest of 1795. We simply do not know whether the Bible continued to be as ubiquitous in schools after the revolution—given the increasing availability of alternatives (like the spellers and readers of Noah Webster), the degree to which the practice was regional, and whether people chose the practice out of necessity or preference. Given the prominence of religious and moral themes in colonial-era readers like the New England Primer and horn books, it's unlikely that the removal of the Bible for more user-friendly reading materials would have been as controversial as it would become in the nineteenth century.

Not surprisingly, Rush offered the most prominent argument in favor of using the Bible as a schoolbook, while Webster joined Jefferson in the most spirited criticisms of the practice, although for very different reasons. In an essay letter devoted wholly to the subject, Rush made an unusually Machiavellian version of a Lockean argument: Since children are more impressionable than adults, they should learn the literal "truths" of the Bible as much as possible. Even if they learn later, as adults, that Bible stories were not actually true, "no man ever did so, without having been made *wiser* or *better*, by the early operation of these prejudices upon his mind."[37] Jefferson argued the opposite: children were too young to understand the Bible, and most of it was untrue anyway, so they should not be exposed to unreasonable, confusing, counterproductive lessons and lies. He excluded any systematic religious instruction from his public school proposals for Virginia. "Instead...of putting the Bible and Testament into the hands of the children, at an age when their judgments are not sufficiently matured for religious enquiries," he wrote, let their memories "be stored with the most useful facts from Grecian, Roman, European and American history."[38] Noah Webster shared Rush's preference for teaching religion to the young, but argued that frequent references to God cheapened religion and taught children (and teachers) to treat their faith casually. For that reason, as well its awkwardness and difficulty as a teaching tool, he opposed the practice of using the Bible as a regular schoolbook, but encouraged infrequent readings for specific occasions.[39] Of course, as a man who sold school textbooks, he might well make such an argument.

In fact, Webster's view on the place of religion in American civic life, and in the public school, changed radically over the course of his life. During the 1780s and 1790s, young Noah Webster insisted on a strict separation of church and state, religious toleration, the abolition of slavery, and the equal distribution of property. The revolutionary Webster published numerous essays and newspaper articles advocating education for all American children—even, to some extent, girls, all while developing a new distinctly American textbook series for schools.[40] In his 1788 essay "On the Education of Youth in America" he described plans for states outside of New England: "In several States, we find laws passed, establishing provision for colleges and academies, where people of property may educate their sons; but no provision is made for instructing the poorer rank of people, even in reading and writing." This effort, he argued, should be essentially secular in design, built on a district system, and assisted by the federal government. Education was primarily for the diffusion of knowledge, including the development of moral virtue and some nonsectarian religion.[41] Webster's speller stood out from his competitor Dilworth's in its lack of explicit references to God. Webster's *Reader* offered children a collection of secular works as an alternative to sacred ones. He even revised the *New England Primer*, designed for young ABCdarians, replacing religious references with fun, familiar ones. For example, "A. In Adams Fall, We sinned all" became "A. Was an Apple-pie made by the cook."[42]

Webster experienced a powerful religious conversion in the first decade of the 1800s that led him to repudiate many of his earlier republican positions, although one can sense a gradual shift in his religious enthusiasm even by the late 1790s. In 1801 he rerevised his *New England Primer* to include the original, Calvinistic rhymes. Over time he grew skeptical of American democracy, critical of abolitionists, and advocated the use of Christian education as a way to control the masses.[43]

The Dangers of Sectarianism

In addition to developing the idea of nonsectarian moral instruction as a positive affirmation of religious diversity in the civic sphere, authors of some comprehensive school plans expressed fears about the negative consequences of sect-specific education for the young. The first of these was that sectarian religion encouraged bigotry and threatened the stability of society. In his anonymous APS essay, Rev. William Smith wrote, "The perpetual practice in all sects to teach no other morals to their youth than those of their own creed, introduces dangerous effects, foments divisions amongst mankind, [and] subjects liberal and solid sentiments to religious prejudices." These were Madisonian concerns; and although the author of the US Constitution made no education plan at the time, outside of promoting Jefferson's Bill for the Diffusion of Knowledge, he did recommend, some years later, keeping public schools and universities free from sectarian influence, lest, in the latter case, they become "Arenas of Theological Gladiators."[44]

Following Locke, many Enlightenment writers understood that attachments learned in childhood were powerful, and prejudicial. John Adams, who championed the role of religion in the cultivation of virtue— "Statesmen...may plan and speculate for Liberty, but it is Religion and Morality alone, which can establish the Principles upon which Freedom can securely stand"[45]—nevertheless saw dangers in inculcating too-strong prejudice in children. "There is, in the human Breast, a social Affection, which extends to our whole Species," he wrote to his wife Abigail.

> The Nation, Kingdom, or Community to which We belong is embraced by it more vigorously...It is stronger and stronger, as We descend to the County, Town, Parish, Neighbourhood, and Family, which We call our own.—And here We find it often so powerfull as to become partial, to blind our Eyes, to darken our Understandings and pervert our Wills.[46]

Later to Jefferson he wrote, "Every Species of these Christians would persecute Deists, as soon as either Sect would persecute another, if it had unchecked and unbalanced Power. Know thyself, human Nature!"[47] Although no favorite of John Adams, Rousseau understood as much in *Emile*, arguing that a child in pre-Revolutionary France was much better growing up in a state of nature than with the corruption of religious prejudice. Noah Webster, who thought this a devilish idea, promoted an alternative solution to the problem: writing nonsectarian textbooks teaching moral lessons and general religious principles, intending to bring Americans together rather than tear them apart.

Even Benjamin Rush, who favored paying tax money to support church-run charity schools in Philadelphia, and claimed that all religions were preferable to none at all, felt he had to justify his plan as being "friendly to religion, inasmuch as it assists in removing prejudice, superstition and enthusiasm, in promoting just notions of the Diety, and in enlarging our knowledge of his works."[48] Indeed, Rush also advocated teaching children that they do not belong to their parents but to their state, and must become politically homogeneous "republican machines," although he did not explain how to reconcile this identity with their diverse religious attachments.[49]

Divisiveness was only half the problem with sectarian religion, however. In Part I of his best-selling deist manifesto, *The Age of Reason* (1794), Thomas Paine explained the other half: "All national institutions of churches, whether Jewish, Christian or Turkish, appear to me no other than human inventions, set up to terrify and enslave mankind, and monopolize power and profit." While no authors of school plans in the age of Paine wrote with quite such bombast, many—especially Jefferson—wrestled with a contradiction they saw between certain forms of religious belief and expression and two of the fundamental goals of mass education: the cultivation of reason and spread of useful knowledge.

Arguably it was John Adams who first made the link between the American Revolution, the issue of education, and the evils of medieval European religious tradition. In his 1765 diatribe "A Dissertation on Canon and Feudal Law," Adams charged that the Stamp Act was an attack on American institutions, including its schools. Sketching an Americanized version of British history (and drawing on Montesquieu's *The Spirit of Laws*), Adams argued that the development of civilization in Europe boiled down to a struggle between the forces of intellectual darkness and oppression, the Roman Catholic and High Anglican Churches and Feudal government on one side of the pond, and the forces of liberty and intellectual freedom on the other. What made America unique in history was its rejection of both—Americans were free to own and develop property; and they were equally free to own and develop their minds. "A native of America who cannot read and write is as rare an appearance as a Jacobite or a Roman Catholic, that is, as rare as a comet or an Earthquake," he explained. Adams credited the Puritan heritage of New England with its emphasis on mass education and progressive government. By targeting newspapers and pamphlets Parliament was aligning itself with certain High Church (Anglican) and High Court interests in America that sought to keep people ignorant in order to keep them under control. He warned,

> There have been among us a party for some years, consisting chiefly not of the descendants of the first settlers of the country, but of high churchmen and high statesmen imported since, who affect to censure this provision for the education of our youth as a needless expense, and an imposition upon the rich in favor of the poor.[50]

The Stamp Act, then, was an attempt by the forces of medieval government and religion to rob American colonists of their birthright. Any move against education struck a blow to liberty and was, well, *un*-American. Adams wrote like a hotheaded nationalist, although he had no nation yet.

After the revolution, some authors of education plans tended to be general in their critiques of sectarian religion, making references to the Enlightenment view of medieval European religious practices that readers would have known well. Those in the orbit of the American Philosophical Society would have known the work of Joseph Priestley, the polymath English Unitarian minister and scientist who wrote extensively on the subject of education before emigrating to Philadelphia in 1794. Priestley's controversial *An History of the Corruptions of Christianity* (1782) clearly influenced Jefferson. Samuel Smith, who did not discuss religion directly in his essay, described the attacks by "superstition" against the field of astronomy and the immorality of "monastic seclusion."[51] In his anonymous APS essay, William Smith warned that "[t]he History of Superstition inspires horror and disgust of error." While claiming to respect "all modes of faith," he nevertheless hoped that "by shedding the general influence of instruction on the mind, that the gloom of error will soon disperse among those who are guided by reason and a Love of Truth." Robert Coram, whose primary concern was poverty, posited that "[i]n France, if one hundredth part of the money expended in the maintenance of legions [of] fat, lazy, lubberly ecclesiastics had been employed in instructing the people in public schools, the nation would be a nation of men instead of a rude and ignorant rabble.[52] The Reverend Samuel Knox wrote that, "It is a happy circumstance…that this country hath excluded ecclesiastical from civil policy, and emancipated the human mind from the tyranny of church authority; and church establishments. Theology should be entirely excluded from public schools."[53] According to these authors, old-time religion, both in its public role vis-à-vis the state, and in its intellectual role as a cradle of superstition, had no place in the education of a citizen. Any religion that should be taught, Benjamin Rush also conceded, must be consistent with science, reason, and above all, republicanism.

Thomas Jefferson's Bill for The More General Diffusion of Knowledge did not offer an historical or epistemological attack on Christian orthodoxy; but it is easy enough to see these positions in his other writings. In *Notes on the State of Virginia*, for example, he sketched a blistering history of religious sectarianism: "Millions of innocent men, women, and children, since the introduction of Christianity, have been burnt, tortured, fined, imprisoned; yet we have not advanced an inch toward uniformity." The effect of religious coercion, he continued, was "[t]o make one half the world fools, and the other half hypocrites. To support roguery and error all over the earth."[54] More generally, he saw legitimacy in only those religious beliefs and practices that were consistent with science and reason, rejecting, for example, the authority of the Bible and the divinity of Christ. Later in life, as the Second Great Awakening reshaped American religion along more enthusiastic lines, he commiserated with his old rival John Adams on the decline of reason. He also celebrated with Adams in 1817 the impending disestablishment of religion in Connecticut, formerly, "the last retreat of Monkish darkness, bigotry, and abhorrence of those advances of the mind which had carried the other states a century ahead of them." Adams replied, gloomy, "Oh! Lord! Do you think that a Protestant Popedom is annihilated in America?" He warned, "Do you recollect, or have you ever attended to the ecclesiastical Strifes in Maryland Pensilvania [*sic*], New York, and every part of New England? What a mercy it is that these People cannot whip and crop, pillory and roast, *as yet* in the U.S.! If they could they would." Despite his serious concerns about the threats of religious sectarianism, Jefferson claimed throughout his life to be a man of faith, believing in what historian Eugene Sheridan calls a "demythologized Christianity," in which the moral teachings of Jesus were the best guide for individual virtue in a republic.[55]

CONCLUSION

In 1795 the American Philosophical Society launched an essay contest challenging writers to develop a system of mass education adapted to the "genius" of the American government. Among the seven entries it received, not a single one proposed a system of church-run schools (indeed, five explicitly rejected such a plan, opting for a state-run system). Likewise, none proposed that schools instruct children in the tenets of any particular religion, although five proposed various forms of a nonsectarian moral instruction. None proposed using the Bible. Three, which were the most substantial, sought to inoculate children against superstition and unreasonable religion. Such responses were consistent with the broader landscape of thought on the proper role of religion in a "public" system of education, although in their details were less like the public systems existent in New England, and more like other plans (even those *by* New Englanders) for the states without public school systems or for the nation as a whole. Read into the politics of their day, the APS contest essays tended to be more Democratic-Republican than Federalist—not surprising for a body led by Thomas Jefferson.

The separation of church and state in these and other school plans reflected the complex and changing politics of religion in the American political sphere. The problem of religion in government was partially practical, balancing factions by removing religion from the design of government. The problem was also understood as substantive: sectarian, traditionalist religion was corrosive to the mind and the morals of a republic, as much as good religion was necessary to preserve them.

Notably, planners of state or national educational systems did not celebrate local variation or herald the genius of deregulated educational markets. On the other hand, one could argue that the lack of comprehensive plans did just that implicitly. Expanding the power of the state in the name of saving the republic came easily to the essayists, and may well explain their failure.

How the typical American (if there was such a thing) felt about the disestablishment of American public schooling and the development of nonsectarian moral instruction is impossible to say, especially since the twin advents of the Second Great Awakening and Jacksonian democracy would radically alter the American religious and political landscapes, hastening the common school reform movement and building the foundation of modern state systems of public education. Both reading the 1790s forward and reading the 1830s backward is tricky business. Nevertheless, what writers of the 1780s and 1790s made clear was that the intellectual foundation of nonsectarian mass schooling was strong by the end of the eighteenth century, rooted in contemporary politics and Enlightenment theories of government, human nature, and knowledge.

The unattainable utopianism of most plans outside of New England was, perhaps, not as lost on education planners of the 1780s and 1790s as it might seem. One month after the conclusion of the American Philosophical Society essay contest, a special committee was formed to investigate the propriety of having a second one. The committee report stated: "In order to obtain the object so much wished for, the establishment of a proper system of public education, for the whole community, it seems necessary that certain principles should be impressed upon the minds of our fellow citizens in general,

& Legislative Bodies in particular." The third of these three principles was crossed out some time after it was written. It read: "In the United States, as the Citizens are divided into different Religious sects, & are in the habit of inculcating some of their particular tenets at Schools, it will be necessary that the doctrines of Religion taught at the public Schools, should be such as all agree on; & will be satisfied with."[56] There are multiple meanings in this statement. The author framed the issue as being relative, as opposed to absolute: "*As* the Citizens are divided [emphasis mine]" suggested that they need not be. Second, because of religious diversity and the expectation that schools teach what families cherished, public schools must inculcate religion as the least common denominator, not to the advancement of any one set of beliefs or denigration of others. And third, taken in the broader context of the report, the committee seems aware that "the Citizens in general" actually need convincing.

Why this statement was struck after it was written is a mystery. Was it too controversial? Too obvious? What it said was entirely consistent with what writers on the subject had been arguing all along: any system of universal public education had to contend with the conflicting meanings of religion in American civic life. It was a hell of a problem.

NOTES

1. *The American Magazine, Containing a selection of original and other valuable essays, prose, and verse, calculated both for instruction and amusement,* vol. II (January 1788), New York, 86.
2. Benjamin Rush, "A Plan for the Establishment of Public Schools and the Diffusion of Knowledge in Pennsylvania; to which are added Thoughts Upon the Mode of Education, Proper in a Republic" (Philadelphia: 1786), 14.
3. Jon Butler, "Why Revolutionary America Wasn't a 'Christian Nation,'" in James H. Hutson (ed.), *Religion and the New Republic: Faith in the Founding of America* (New York: Rowman and Littlefield, 2000), 187–202.
4. See chapters 6 and 7 in this volume; Hilary Moss, *Schooling Citizens: The Struggle for African-American Education in Antebellum America* (Chicago: University of Chicago Press, 2009); Margaret A. Nash, *Women's Education in the United States, 1780–1840* (New York: Palgrave MacMillan, 2005).
5. Robert Coram, *Political Inquiries, to which is Added a Plan for Establishing Schools throughout the United States* (Wilmington, 1791), Chapter V.
6. On Education (March 1784), *The Boston Magazine, Containing, a Collection of Instructive and Entertaining Essays, in the Various Branches of Useful, and Polite Literature. Together With, Foreign and Domestick Occurrences, Anecdotes, Observations on the Weather, & c., & c. (1783–1786),* 1, 176. Retrieved July 25, 2012, from American Periodicals Series Online (Document ID: 592584342).
7. As cited in James Pyle Wickersham, *A History of Education in Pennsylvania, Private and Public, Elementary and Higher* (Lancaster: 1886), 257.
8. Adam Smith, *An Inquiry into the Nature and Causes of the Wealth of Nations* (1776), book V, Chapter 1.

9. US Census. Table 4: http://www.census.gov/population/censusdata/table-4.pdf.
10. Butler, "Why Revolutionary America Wasn't a 'Christian Nation,'" 187–198, 191.
11. Samuel Knox, *An Essay on the Best System of Liberal Education* (Baltimore: Warner and Hanna, 1799), 12.
12. Ibid.
13. The Maryland State Constitution of 1776 may be found online at the Avalon Project of Yale University: http://avalon.law.yale.edu/17th_century/ma02.asp.
14. Jennings L. Wagoner, Jr., *Jefferson and Education* (Thomas Jefferson Foundation, 2004), 32–34.
15. Thomas E. Buckley, "The Use and Abuse of Jefferson's Statute: Separating Church and State in Nineteenth-Century Virginia," in Hutson, *Religion and the New Republic*, 41–64.
16. Thomas Jefferson, "A Bill for the More General Diffusion of Knowledge," in Merrill D. Peterson (ed.), *Thomas Jefferson: Writings* (Washington, DC: Library of America, 1984), 365–373; Wagoner, *Jefferson and Education*, 40–42. Pangle and Pangle argue that Madison's view of the role for religion in civic education was even more radical than Jefferson's: Madison saw no role whatsoever, while Jefferson conceded the need for a very narrow, deist interpretation of Christianity as sound basis for moral instruction. Lorraine Smith Pangle and Thomas L. Pangle, *The Learning of Liberty: The Educational Ideas of the Founders* (Lawrence: University Press of Kansas, 1993), 188–194.
17. John Witte, "'A Most Mild and Equitable Establishment of Religion': John Adams and the Massachusetts Experiment," in Hutson, *Religion and the New Republic*, 1–40.
18. "An Act to Provide for the Instruction of Youth, and for the Promotion of Good Education," passed June 25, 1789, reprinted in *The Laws of the Commonwealth of Massachusetts, passed from the year 1780, to the end of the year 1800, with the constitutions of the United States of America, and of the commonwealth, prefixed…*, vol. I. Published by Order of the General Court (Boston: Manning and Loring, 1801), 469–473; "An Act in Addition to an Act to Provide for the Instruction of Youth, and for the Promotion of Good Education," passed March 4, 1800, in ibid., vol. II, 906–908. Downloaded from: https://play.google.com/books/reader?id=IRkwAAAAYAAJ&printsec=frontcover&output=reader&authuser=0&hl=en&pg=GBS.PA469.
19. William T. Harris speculated that the scaling back of educational requirements was a political response to the unpopularity of entrenched "ecclesiastical control." See "Editor's Preface," in George H. Martin, *The Evolution of the Massachusetts Public School System: A Historical Sketch* (New York: D. Appleton, 1894), xi. Carl Kaestle and Maris Vinovskis have argued that in its first few decades of existence, a significant private market in education existed alongside this public system, the latter of which had uneven effects depending on the size of a community. Carl F. Kaestle and Maris A. Vinovskis, *Education and Social Change in Nineteenth-Century Massachusetts* (London: Cambridge University Press, 1980).
20. Constitution of the State of Connecticut (1818), available online at the website of the Connecticut Secretary of State's Office: http://www.ct.gov/sots/cwp/view.asp?a=3188&q=392280.

21. An Act appropriating the Monies which shall arise on the Sale of Western Lands, belonging to this State [enacted in May 1795], part 6, in Acts and Laws of the State of Connecticut in America (Hartford: Hudson and Goodwin, 1796), 31–33; Title CXLI, Chapter I. "An Act for appointing, regulating and encouraging Schools [compiled in May 1799], in *The Public Statute Laws of the State of Connecticut. Book I. Published by the Authority of the General Assembly* (Hartford: Hudson and Goodwin, 1808), 581–586.

22. Wickersham, *A History of Education in Pennsylvania*, 179–180. Wickersham argues that schooling was in severe decline, based on anecdotal evidence. Claims of the general decline of schooling during the revolutionary period are so ubiquitous that, barring statistical data to the contrary (which would be difficult to obtain), the argument seems reasonable.

23. The 1776 Constitution text may be found online at the Avalon Project at Yale University: http://avalon.law.yale.edu/18th_century/pa08.asp.

24. Wickersham, *A History of Education in Pennsylvania*, 257.

25. Art. Vii, sec. 1 in ibid., and online at http://en.wikisource.org/wiki/Constitution_of_the_Commonwealth_of_Pennsylvania_1790.

26. Wickersham, *A History of Education in Pennsylvania*, 260–263.

27. *The Proceedings relative to calling the conventions of 1776 and 1790, the minutes of the convention that formed the present constitution of Pennsylvania, together with the charter to William Penn*...(Harrisburg, 1825).

28. *To the Citizens of Philadelphia: a Plan for Free Schools* (Philadelphia, March 28, 1787), reprinted in *Letters of Benjamin Rush*. L. H. Butterfield (ed.), 2 vol. American Philosophical Society 1951, 412–415.

29. Benjamin Rush, *Essays, Literary, Moral, and Philosophical* (Philadelphia: Bradfords, 1798), 9.

30. Northwest Ordinance may be found online at the Library of Congress website: http://memory.loc.gov/cgi-bin/query/r?ammem/bdsdcc:@field(DOCID+@lit(bdsdcc22501)). On the significance of "useful knowledge," see chapter 5 in this volume. The critique and reformation of Christianity figured centrally in Enlightenment. See generally, Peter Gay, *The Enlightenment: An Interpretation. The Rise of Modern Paganism* (1966); Henry F. May, *The Enlightenment in America* (1976).

31. See chapter 5 of this volume.

32. "Review of Essay No. 3," p. 234 of this volume.

33. Jefferson, "A Bill for the More General Diffusion of Knowledge," 367; Smith, *Remarks on Education*, p. 213 of this volume; "Review of Essay No. 3," p. 235 of this volume; DuPont de Nemours, *National Education in the United States of America. Translated from the Second French Edition of 1812 and with an Introduction by B. G. Du Pont* (Newark, DE: University of Delaware Press, 1923), 73; Hand, "Concerning Education in Public Schools," p. 257 of this volume.

34. Knox, *An Essay on the Best System*, pp. 226–227 of this volume.

35. Webster's unpublished memoir in Webster Family Papers, Box 1 folder 10, 3. Yale University Manuscripts and Archives.

36. Title CXLI, Chapter I. "An Act for appointing, regulating and encouraging Schools [compiled in May 1799], sec. 9, in *The Public Statute Laws of the State of Connecticut. Book I. Published by the Authority of the General Assembly* (Hartford: Hudson and Goodwin, 1808), 585.

37. Rush, "Essays, Literary, Moral, and Philosophical," 95.

38. Thomas Jefferson, *Notes on the State of Virginia*, Query XIV, reprinted in Peterson, *Thomas Jefferson*, 273.

39. January 1788, 80–82, "Education, some Defects in the Mode," *American Magazine* (1787–1788), Beinecke Rare Books Library, Yale University.

40. On the education of girls, see "Education—Importance of Female Education, with a brief Sketch of a plan," *American Magazine* (May 1788), 367–374, at Beinecke Rare Books Library.

41. *On the Education of Youth in America* (1788).

42. Richard M. Rollins, *The Long Journey of Noah Webster* (Philadelphia: University of Pennsylvania Press, 1980), 109.

43. Ibid., 139–142.

44. Letter to William T. Barry, August 4, 1822, and letter to Edward Everett, March 19, 1823, in Jack Rakove (ed.), *James Madison. Writings* (Library of America, 1999), 790–798.

45. Letter to Zabdiel Adams, June 21, 1776 (Letters of Delegates to Congress: Volume 4, May 16, 1776–August 15, 1776, John Adams to Zabdiel Adams).

46. Letter to Abigail, October 29, 1775 (Adams Family, vol. 1), 318.

47. Letter to Jefferson, June 25, 1813, in Lester J. Cappon (ed.), *The Adams-Jefferson Letters: The Complete Correspondence between Thomas Jefferson and Abigail and John Adams*, 2 vols (Chapel Hill: University of North Carolina Press, 1959), 334.

48. Rush, "Essays, Literary, Moral, and Philosophical," 1.

49. Rush, "Thoughts upon the Mode of Education Proper in a Republic."

50. John Adams, *A Dissertation on Canon and Feudal Law* (1765), downloaded from the Massachusetts Historical Society Website at http://www.masshist.org/publications/apde/portia.php?mode=p&id=PJA01p108.

51. Samuel Smith, *Remarks on Education* (Philadelphia: 1798), pp. 23, 26.

52. "Review of Essay No. 3," p. 235 of this volume; Coram, *Political Inquiries, to which is Added a Plan for Establishing Schools Throughout the United States*, Chapter III.

53. Knox, *An Essay on the Best System*, p. 223 of this volume.

54. Thomas Jefferson, Notes on the State of Virginia, Query XVII, in Peterson, *Thomas Jefferson*, 286.

55. Cappon, *The Adams-Jefferson Letters*, 509, 512, 515; Eugene Sheridan, "Liberty and Virtue: Religion and Republicanism in Jeffersonian Thought," in James Gilreath (ed.), *Thomas Jefferson and the Education of a Citizen* (Honolulu: University Press of the Pacific, 2002), 242–263.

56. Report of the Committee appointed to consider the propriety of offering a premium for the best essay on the subject of education, Read March 2, 1798. APS Archives.

The Perceived Dangers of Study Abroad, 1780–1800: Nationalism, Internationalism, and the Origins of the American University

Adam R. Nelson

INTRODUCTION

In transitions from colonialism to independence, political leaders often look to education as a tool of national development. Schools and colleges become favored sites for the cultivation of national identity, national loyalty, and national unity; the "uses" of education become tightly interwoven with the pursuit of national prosperity, national security, and national harmony; institutions of learning become places to imagine the nation's future, to embrace—and enforce—a clean break with the colonial past. Hoping to pass the ideals of independence to future generations, political leaders see in schools and colleges an efficient means to instill core values. Certainly, the history of the United States is replete with examples of leaders using, or attempting to use, education as a tool of nation-building.[1]

Yet, in the early years of American independence, the uses of education for nation-building raised a number of key questions. Could the new United States really make a clean break with colonial forms of education? Could its schools and colleges successfully consolidate a new sense of national identity? Particularly at the college level, could the nation justify sending its most talented youth abroad for advanced training, or should it develop new institutions to educate them at home? Could the United States rely on foreign scholars for new discoveries in the arts, sciences, and professions, or must it develop an extensive research infrastructure of its own? How could the nation achieve genuine educational "independence"? These and other questions weighed heavily on educators' minds during the early American republic.

In the period from 1780 to 1800, national leaders entertained a flurry of proposals concerning the development of education in the United States.

George Washington, Thomas Jefferson, Benjamin Franklin, Benjamin Rush, and others figured prominently in these debates. Whether reforming old institutions or creating new ones, they held that education—including higher education—would play a key role in the political, cultural, and economic development of the nation. Among other plans, they welcomed proposals for a so-called national university, a postgraduate institution designed to secure the United States' place among the enlightened nations of the world. Rooted in visions of national greatness as well as international glory, the idea of a national university attracted widespread support.[2]

Within each plan for a national university, however, lay a certain tension between the pursuit of national independence and an awareness of the United States' continued dependence on European ties. Even as Washington, Jefferson, Franklin, and Rush worked to reform higher education in the United States, they sought input from overseas. Many held that Europe offered the best opportunity for advanced education; others cautioned that Americans faced political corruption and intellectual contamination abroad. Indeed, the greatest dilemma facing American colleges in the early republic was the perceived *danger* of study abroad. From 1780 to 1800, it seems, the principal motive driving the development of American higher education was a desire to deter future leaders from studying overseas.

THE DANGERS OF STUDY ABROAD

In the fall of 1785, Thomas Jefferson wrote to John Bannister, Jr., a fellow Virginian who had asked for advice on the subject of study abroad. Jefferson, who had recently taken up his diplomatic post in Paris, scoffed at the idea. "Let us view the disadvantages of sending a youth to Europe," he noted, warning that his list of disadvantages was long. "He acquires a fondness for European luxury and dissipation and a contempt for the simplicity of his own country; he is fascinated by the privileges of the European aristocrats, and sees with abhorrence the lowly equality which the poor enjoy with the rich in his own country." Foreign study, Jefferson held, led not only to "a partiality for aristocracy and monarchy" but also to a disdain for wholesome American values; it was therefore anathema to republican citizenship in the United States.[3]

Jefferson continued. A young American who studied overseas, he wrote, might return home "speaking and writing his native tongue as a foreigner, and therefore unqualified to obtain those distinctions, which eloquence of the pen and tongue ensures in a free country; for I would observe to you, that what is called *style* in writing or speaking is formed early in life, while the imagination is warm, and impressions are permanent." This possibility of linguistic corruption was serious. "I am of the opinion," Jefferson argued,

that there never was an instance of a man's writing or speaking his native tongue with elegance who passed from fifteen to twenty years of age out of the country where it was spoken. Thus, no instance exists of a person writing two languages perfectly. That [language] will always appear to be his native language which was most familiar to him in his youth.[4]

The Virginian's counsel was unequivocal. "It appears to me," he concluded, "that an American coming to Europe for education loses in his knowledge, in his morals, in his health, in his habits, and in his happiness." He strongly discouraged study abroad for anyone who aspired to eminence in American society.[5] He was not alone. The very year he wrote to Bannister condemning study abroad, for example, legislators in Georgia restricted access to public office for anyone who had studied overseas, until the offender had spent an equivalent number of years back home.[6]

Hoping to protect the nation's best and brightest from ideological harm, Jefferson looked for ways to keep them at home. One way to do so, he and others felt, was to improve the United States' own colleges and, thus, to remove any incentive to study abroad. As governor of Virginia during the early stages of the revolution, Jefferson personally engaged in the reform of his alma mater, the College of William and Mary. He called on legislators to reform the college along republican lines. Given "the late change in the form of our government as well as the contest of arms in which we are at present engaged," he wrote, "it becomes the peculiar duty of the legislature . . . to aid and improve the seminary in which those who are to be the future guardians of the rights and liberties of their country may be endowed with science and virtue." Jefferson pursued this "improvement," first, by cutting ties between the college and the church and, second, by filling the board with politically acceptable members—appointed only after each had pledged allegiance to the new United States.[7]

At first, Virginia's legislators declined to accept Jefferson's reforms, citing a lack of resources, but Jefferson pushed forward. He later noted, "I effected, during my residence at Williamsburg that year, a change in the organization of that institution." When all was said and done, he abolished the college's professorships in divinity and classical languages and created new positions in modern languages, medicine, and law; he also expanded an existing professorship in natural philosophy to include natural history and enlarged a professorship in moral philosophy to include "the law of nature and nations" as well as the fine arts. These changes, he noted, would make William and Mary a truly modern college, equipped to educate leaders for a republican society—and, most importantly, in their native country.[8]

BENJAMIN RUSH AND COLLEGES FOR THE REPUBLIC

Jefferson was not the only leader to press for higher education reforms in this period. Arguably the most active reformer was Benjamin Rush, who launched the first new college to be founded after the war. Dickinson College opened in Carlisle, Pennsylvania, in 1784 with 60 students (40 in the preparatory department). Rush marked the occasion with a famous address *On the Mode of Education Proper in a Republic*. "I consider it possible to convert men into republican machines," he declared. "This must be done if we expect them to perform their part properly in the great machine of the government of the state." Each pupil at Dickinson would learn "to love his fellow creatures in every part of the world," he noted, but would "cherish with a more intense and peculiar affection the citizens of... the United States."[9]

On the advantages of study at home (and the disadvantages of study abroad), Rush echoed Jefferson. "It is well known," he maintained, "that our strongest prejudices in favor of our country are formed in the first one and twenty years of our lives." In these years, he argued, the cultivation of national loyalty must be the first priority of every American college. "The business of education has acquired a new complexion by the independence of our country," Rush stated. "It becomes us, therefore, to examine our former habits... and, in laying the foundation for nurseries of wise and good men, to adapt our modes of teaching to the peculiar form of our government." Of the "former habits" Rush examined, that of sending youth abroad for advanced education was, for him, certainly the most wrong-headed.[10] If colleges failed to instill a sense of national identity and national loyalty in their young charges, Rush asserted, the republic would quickly collapse.[11]

Rush designed every aspect of Dickinson's curriculum to cultivate students' dedication to the ideal of American independence. With courses in "the history of the ancient republics" as well as "the progress of liberty and tyranny in the different states of Europe," they learned what it would take for the United States to survive. Besides the science of government, Dickinson also taught modern languages, notably French and German, with special emphasis on English as the language of American political culture. Each student at Dickinson had to master "our American language," Rush held, for a refined and cultivated eloquence in one's national tongue was "the first accomplishment in a republic." Moreover, he added, a capacity for patriotic oratory was needed to set "the whole machine of [republican] government in motion."[12]

This view applied not only to Dickinson but also to another college Rush helped to create in this period—a college specifically for German-speaking immigrants. As early as 1780, the University of the State of Pennsylvania (which temporarily coexisted with the University of Pennsylvania) opened a special department for German immigrant youth. Under the supervision of Professor Justus Christian Heinrich Helmuth, a scholar from Brunschweig, this department enrolled perhaps five dozen students. But it did not last. According to one historian, the "German students at the university appear to have suffered some social derision," including derogatory names such as "Dutchman" and "Sour Crout." Persistent anti-German discrimination led, in 1787, to the creation of an entirely new institution known as Franklin College (later called Franklin and Marshall).[13]

Located in Lancaster, with its large German immigrant population, the new institution boasted a bilingual faculty and courses taught in both English and German. Rush, a trustee, hoped the bilingual college would promote the cause of national unity. "By means of this seminary," he told his fellow board members, the partition wall which has long separated the English and German inhabitants of the state will be broken down. By meeting occasionally in this board, we shall form connections with each other that will be alike useful to ourselves and to the state. Our children will be bound together by the ties of marriage, as we shall be by the ties of friendship, and, in the course of a few years, by means of the college, the names of German, Irishman, and Englishman will be lost in the general name of Pennsylvanian.[14]

Rush saw the new bilingual college as an agent of linguistic assimilation. "By means of this college," he argued, "the *English* language will be introduced among our German fellow citizens. In a state where all legal proceedings as well as commerce are carried on in English, a knowledge of it must be of the utmost consequence for the preservation of property." At the same time, Rush argued, bilingual instruction would protect the German language from corrosion and, simultaneously, provide access to cutting-edge German scholarship. In the new college, he promised, "the German language will be preserved from extinction and corruption by being taught in a grammatical manner. The advantages we shall derive from it will be very great, in as much as it will enable us to understand and adopt all the discoveries in science that shall hereafter be made by one of the most learned nations in Europe."[15]

Rush considered the bilingual college to be an *international* institution serving *national* aims. "By means of this college," he wrote, "the sons of the Germans will be qualified to shine in our legislatures and to fill with reputation the professions of law, physic, and divinity. Their ministers of the gospel and schoolmasters will no longer be strangers to American habits and manners but will be prepared for immediate usefulness by an education in this college." Affirming this ideal, guests at the college's opening convocation raised their classes not only to George Washington and the democratic legislature of Pennsylvania but also to "the friends of science, liberty, and religion in Germany" as well as military allies in France, Spain, Holland, and "other friendly European powers" whose recent support made possible the independence of the United States.

THE IDEA OF A NATIONAL UNIVERSITY

Rush worked hard to develop new colleges in rural Pennsylvania, but he also pressed for a more centrally located university in Philadelphia, the nation's capital. In the fall of 1786, he contacted his friend Richard Price, a republican and supporter of the United States in London, to say that he anticipated the imminent creation of a "federal university" to be funded "by the patronage of Congress." Offering a full range of lectures on "the common law of our country, the different systems of government, history, and everything else connected with the advancement of republican knowledge and principles," this new university promised to become an essential gathering place for republican-minded students and scholars not only from the United States but, according to Rush, from all over the world.[16]

A year later, Rush elaborated on the idea of a "federal university" in a brief essay for *The American Museum*, whose subscribers included Thomas Jefferson, George Washington, James Madison, Alexander Hamilton, and others. He followed this article with another titled simply "A Plan for a Federal University," which outlined his plan. Drafted amid the excitement of the Constitutional Convention in Philadelphia, it cast the university as the best way to educate American youth for national leadership.[17] Building on the curriculum he developed for Dickinson, Rush proposed a series of courses he considered indispensable for American statesmanship. Above all, the federal university would stress "the construction and pronunciation of the English language." While knowledge of French, German, and Spanish all had their uses, familiarity with English—specifically, *American* English—was essential for political leadership.[18]

Rush's concern for American English was not unique in this era. As early as 1780, John Adams had proposed an American Academy for Refining, Improving, and Ascertaining the English Language; a few years later, Noah Webster published his *Grammatical Institute of the English Language*, meant to render all foreign spellers obsolete. Writing for the *American Magazine* in 1788, Webster observed:

> [O]ur honor as an independent nation is concerned in the establishment of lit-
> erary institutions adequate to all our own purposes without sending our youth
> abroad or depending on other nations for books and instructors. It is very
> little to the reputation of America to have it said abroad that, after the heroic
> achievements of the late war, this independent people are obliged to send to
> Europe for men and books to teach their children A B C.[19]

Echoing the views of Rush and others, Webster noted the dangers of study abroad. He noted especially the dangers of forming cultural and political attachments to other nations. "An attachment to a *foreign* government, or rather a want of attachment to our *own*, is the natural effect of a residence abroad during the period of youth," he commented.

> Ninety-nine persons of a hundred who pass that period in England or France
> will prefer the people, their manners, their laws, and their government to
> those of their native country...A man should always form his habits and
> attachments in the country where he is to reside for life. When these habits are
> formed, young men may travel without danger of losing their patriotism.[20]

Webster understood why students went abroad but, noting the appeal of foreign universities, called on American colleges to improve their *own* educational offerings. "If this country, therefore, should long be indebted to Europe for opportunities of acquiring any branch of science in perfection," he chided, "it must be by means of a criminal neglect of its inhabitants."[21]

Webster saw no benefit in study abroad, but Rush's plan was less dogmatic. Concerned about intellectual isolation, Rush recommended that, every year, "four young men of good education and active minds be sent abroad at public expense to collect and transmit to the professors of the [federal university] all the improvements that are daily made in Europe in agriculture, manufactures, and commerce, and in the arts of war and practical government." By *men of a good education*, of course, Rush meant only the most patriotic students—those unlikely to lose their republican values abroad.[22]

According to Rush, the establishment of a national university was essential to American development. "Should this plan of a federal university, or one like it, be adopted," he concluded, "then will begin the golden age of the United States." Such an institution would advance the nation ahead of all competitors.

> While the business of education in Europe consists in…disputes about Hebrew points, Greek particles, or the accent and quantity of the Roman language, the youth of America will be employed in acquiring those branches of knowledge which increase the conveniences of life, lessen human misery, improve our country, promote population, exalt human understanding, and establish domestic, social, and political happiness.

A national university, in short, would propel the United States to international greatness.[23]

University Proposals from Abroad

Rush had high expectations for the role a national university could play in building national strength, and he was not alone. At the Constitutional Convention in 1787, both James Madison and Charles Pinckney offered proposals to give Congress the authority to establish a national university. Delegates from at least four states—Pennsylvania, Virginia, North Carolina, and South Carolina—favored the plan. But delegates from six other states—Massachusetts, New Hampshire, New Jersey, Delaware, Maryland, and Georgia—opposed the idea, and others were divided (William Samuel Johnson of Connecticut endorsed the proposal while Roger Sherman, also of Connecticut, held that states alone had the authority to charter new colleges). Just before the end of the convention, a motion to allow the establishment of a national university was defeated.[24]

This vote did not spell the end of the national university idea, however. Several proposals circulated over the course of the next decade. Some of them even originated abroad. As early as 1783, professor Johann Reinhold Forster of the University of Halle released a pamphlet titled *Remarks Relative to a Plan for the Foundation of a New National Extensive and Useful Institution for the Education of Youth in America*. Forster—who, among other adventures, had accompanied Captain Cook on his second voyage around the world—taught for several years in England at the dissenting Warrington Academy near Birmingham. (His predecessor at Warrington had been the influential chemist, theologian, and republican Joseph Priestley, who later immigrated to Pennsylvania and offered his own plan for a national university.)[25]

As historian David Robson notes, Forster intended to deliver his *Remarks* to Benjamin Franklin in France during the negotiations over the Treaty of Paris, but his emissary, Benjamin Vaughan (who had attended Warrington and later immigrated to the United States with his brothers, including John Vaughan, later president of the American Philosophical Society), failed to make the delivery. Nonetheless, the institution described in his *Remarks* was intriguing. With one "residential college" funded by each state, the campus was to be located outside Philadelphia. With a 40-person faculty, including 13 professors capable of teaching "the whole cyclopedia of human knowledge," the institution was to be supervised by a rector appointed by Congress.[26]

Forster's plan for a national university never reached the United States, but another European plan did. Chevalier Alexandre Quesnay de Beaurepaire, a French soldier who had fought in the revolutionary war, offered a plan for a national academy of arts and sciences. His plan followed the model of the Royal Academy in Paris and shared a number of features with the American Academy of Arts and Sciences established in Massachusetts in 1780. In his *Mémoire, Statuts et Prospectus concernant l'Académie des Sciences et Beaux-Arts des Etats-Unis de l'Amérique, étable è Richmond, Capitale de la Virginie*, Beaurepaire—the grandson of the well-known physiocrat Francois Quesnay—described an elaborate postgraduate institution to be located in Richmond and complemented with branch campuses in Baltimore, Philadelphia, and New York.[27]

Benjamin Franklin learned of Beaurepaire's *Mémoire* in 1783 when his daughter Sara wrote him in Paris to describe the proposal. "It is a very extensive plan and will do honor to the gentleman who has designed it as well as to America," she wrote. "If it can be executed, it will in no way interfere with the plans of the colleges; it will be solely for the completion of the education of young men after they have graduated from college." Sara—known as Sally—stressed the opportunities such an institution could offer her own children as they grew up in the United States, writing, "[A]s a mother who desires to give her children a useful and polite education and who will be especially proud to have them trained in their own country and under her own eyes, I pray you to give M. Quesnay all the assistance that may lie in your power."[28]

Linked with learned societies in Paris and London, Beaurepaire's academy included a full slate of professorships in mineralogy, chemistry, physics, astronomy, mathematics, zoology, botany, anatomy, sculpture, architecture, painting, engraving, and modern languages. As one historian noted, "[S]tress was laid upon the importance of introducing into America, French mineralogists and mining engineers who were to fully develop the natural resources of the United States." To support his plan, Beaurepaire launched a transatlantic subscription drive, recruiting shareholders from France, Britain, Holland, Germany, Poland, and the United States. With letters of endorsement from Lafayette, Condorcet, Beaumarchais, Lavoisier, and Rouchefoucauld, he collected more than 60,000 francs to support the school, including donations from both Franklin and Jefferson.[29] This money was to be spent on research materials "which are for the most part lacking in America, such as utensils pertaining to the arts and trades, books, models, machines, printing presses in type and copper-plates, instruments for astronomy, chemistry, and experimental physics."

Anticipating that most of the academy's faculty would come from Europe, Beaurepaire appealed for resources to pay advance salaries "to professors, masters, and artists, before their departure as well as after their arrival in Virginia." Yet, as historian Richard Heyward Gaines has found, the only scholar hired for the academy was Jean Rouelle, an expert in the natural sciences. Assigned the chair in chemistry and natural history, Rouelle was to meet Beaurepaire in Richmond in the winter of 1788.[30]

But he never arrived. The eruption of the French Revolution the following year foiled Beaurepaire's plans for a French-style academy in the United States. The spread of war threw France, indeed all of Europe, into political turmoil. By the spring of 1792, revolutionary forces had started their eastward march, radicalizing local populations as they went. Aiming to "secure" the revolution by exporting its principles to neighboring areas, the armies of France joined radicals in Switzerland and Italy to establish what they hoped would soon become a European federation of republics.

TRANSPLANTING THE UNIVERSITY OF GENEVA

Events in Europe were not disconnected from debates in the United States— including debates over higher-education reform. In one famous case, these events touched directly on the question of founding a national university. The plan, hatched in 1793, involved a proposal to relocate the entire faculty of the University of Geneva from Switzerland to the United States. This idea— prompted by the French invasion of Geneva—came from a wealthy Swiss named Francois D'Invernois and captured the attention of several prominent Americans, including George Washington, Thomas Jefferson, John Adams, and Albert Gallatin. In various ways, D'Invernois's plan revealed not only the strength of cross-national scholarly ties in this period but also the seriousness brought to the task of "improving" American higher education while relying on European ties.

The main characters in this drama were D'Invernois and Gallatin, who had been classmates at the University of Geneva in the late 1770s. Both men were enthusiastic republicans, and both embraced the cause of American independence. Gallatin had immigrated to Massachusetts in 1780 to join the Continental Army and, following the war, taught French at Harvard for a year. He then moved to Pennsylvania, where he was elected to the state legislature and, later, to the US House of Representatives. (A partisan Republican, he served as secretary of the treasury under presidents Jefferson and Madison and minister to France and Britain under presidents Monroe and John Quincy Adams.) D'Invernois, meanwhile, remained in Europe and directed his republican zeal toward reforms in his native city.[31]

By the summer of 1794, with French assistance, radicals in Geneva overthrew the city's government. Setting up a revolutionary assembly, the radicals rounded up their opponents, issuing more than five hundred convictions, including thirty-seven sentences of death by guillotine. Among those hunted by the revolutionaries were the professors of the University of Geneva, considered a branch of the aristocracy. Horrified by these developments at his alma mater, D'Invernois launched a campaign to save the faculty. Specifically, he proposed transferring the university, with all its assets, to a new location. A month after the radicals took control, he published *La Révolution française à Genève*, which described the violent attacks on the university and called urgently for help.[32]

Dedicating his pamphlet to vice president John Adams (then also president of the American Academy of Arts and Sciences), he sent copies to Thomas Jefferson and his friend Gallatin. The refugee scholars of Geneva, he explained, were prepared "to embark for America in confidence of finding there, the liberty and security which they have lost at home." These learned men, he told his American correspondents, would "bring your habits of acting and thinking, truly republican and perfectly conformable to your own." D'Invernois asked if Congress (or perhaps a wealthy private donor) might be willing to build a campus for the university and establish an endowment for salaries. The whole faculty in Geneva, he explained, was ready and eager to move.[33]

At first, D'Invernois found considerable support for his proposal in the United States. John Adams reported to D'Invernois that all his acquaintances in Congress acknowledged "the honor it would do us, and the advantages it would result to us." Adams brought the proposal to George Washington, who, according to historian James Hutson, "pronounced the situation in Geneva 'afflicting' and D'Invernois's ideas 'important.'" Meanwhile, secretary of state Edmund Randolph promised that "to the utmost of my faculties, I would welcome [the University of Geneva faculty] to our country with the most zealous hospitality." Randolph said that shifting the university to America "would fill up a vast chasm in the education of the United States." The implication was clear: Americans would no longer seek to study abroad if a distinguished European university could be reestablished in the United States.[34]

Jefferson, like Adams, carried the case to George Washington, assuring the president that Geneva's faculty was equal to that of the esteemed University of Edinburgh. If located in Virginia, he told his fellow resident of that state, such a renowned group of scholars would become the envy of all other states. "I would have seen with peculiar satisfaction the establishment of such a mass of science in my country," Jefferson told Washington, "and should probably have been tempted to [connect] myself to it by procuring a residence in its neighborhood." But it was not to be.[35]

Despite the support D'Invernois received from Jefferson, Washington, Adams, and Randolph, he faced opposition from his old friend Gallatin, then engaged in open conflict with Washington over the politics of the Whiskey

Rebellion on the Pennsylvania frontier. Gallatin—a radical democrat enamored of the French Revolution—criticized D'Invernois's plan as a form of government aid to aristocratic scholars. Similarly, a friend of Gallatin's named Jean Badellot, also from Geneva, condemned D'Invernois's proposal as "welfare for the wealthy" and called the professors an elite group of "linguists and rhetors, and a set of babblers in politics." Such criticisms struck a chord with popular democratic sentiment in the United States, particularly in Virginia, where state legislators rejected a personal request from Jefferson to aid the Swiss exiles.[36]

According to historian David Madsen, even Washington expressed growing hesitation over the D'Invernois plan. He worried that he might incur "popular wrath" over what might be "interpreted as an 'aristocratic' move—one that would have prevented worthy professors from other countries from participating in the affairs of the new [federally supported] university. Another consideration was that many members of the Geneva faculty might have been unacquainted with English." Would these professors be as republican in their political outlook as they promised to be? Would they lecture in a pure and patriotic American English? Madsen suggests that "Washington may have had a suspicion that American youth could acquire the taint of anti-republicanism from an exclusively foreign faculty teaching in the United States almost as readily as they could by studying with a foreign faculty abroad."[37]

The whole idea finally collapsed in 1796 when enemies of D'Invernois in London revealed that he collected a royal pension—a fact that immediately alienated him from his American friends. While still favored by John Adams (who had become increasingly antagonistic toward Jefferson in the lead-up to their presidential contest in 1796), D'Invernois reluctantly abandoned his plan. By 1796, political dangers in Geneva had begun to subside, and wholesale relocation of the university no longer seemed necessary. In the wake of this episode, it was clear that any successful plan to create a "national" university would have to originate with *Americans*.[38]

George Washington and the National University Idea

In the 1790s, calls for a national university continued. In 1795, George Washington shared his own fears about the corruption of Americans who pursued advanced education abroad. "We ought to deprecate the hazards attending ardent and susceptible minds from being too strongly and too early prepossessed in favor of other political systems before they are capable of appreciating their own," he warned.[39] In a letter to Jefferson, Washington explained that his chief reason for supporting a national university was "to supersede the necessity of sending the youth of this country abroad, for the purpose of education (where too often principles and habits not friendly to republican government are imbibed, which are not easily discarded) by instituting such an one of our own, as will answer the end." To another friend he wrote, "It is with indescribable regret that I have seen the youth of the United States migrating to foreign countries in order to acquire the higher branches of erudition and to obtain a knowledge of the sciences." To stop the flow of students to Europe, he noted, the United States needed a national university—and soon.[40]

The next year, Washington outlined his ideas for a national university in a letter to Alexander Hamilton, then drafting the president's farewell address. He asked Hamilton to insert in this speech a proposal for a national institution

> where the youth from all parts of the United States might receive the polish of erudition in the arts, sciences, and belles letters and where those who were disposed to run a political course might not only be instructed in the theory and principles [of republican government] but (this seminary being at the seat of the general government) where the legislature would be in session half the year and the interests and politics of the nation of course would be discussed.

Such an institution, located in the nation's capital, would lay "the surest foundation" for leadership in a large republic.[41]

National unity was, for Washington, a principal argument for the creation of a national university. He told Hamilton:

> That which would render it of the highest importance in my opinion is that [during] the juvenile period of life, when friendships are formed and habits established…, the youth or young men from different parts of the United States would be assembled together and would, by degrees, discover that there was not that cause for those jealousies and prejudices which one part of the Union had imbibed against another part.

By instilling a sense of shared national identity, Washington hoped, a national university would safeguard the unity of the republic. Shortly before the elections of 1796, he warned that political and sectional factions were "beginning to revive and never will be eradicated so effectually by any other means as the intimate intercourse of characters in early life."[42]

To spur the creation of a national university, Washington bequeathed 50 shares in the Potomac River Company—shares the Virginia assembly had given in gratitude for his wartime service. James Madison, in turn, assembled a committee to solicit additional donations for the proposed institution. Among the advantages of a national university the committee listed not only "the diminution of those local prejudices which at present exist in the several states" but also "the drawing to our shores [of] the youth of other countries, particularly those attached to republican governments." This hope of drawing foreign students to America became increasingly popular in this era. Was it not time, many asked, to reverse the flow of students, to bring Europeans to America rather than sending Americans to Europe?[43]

While many saw advantages in drawing foreign students to American colleges, others cautioned against it. Washington, for example, doubted the wisdom of any plan to bring large numbers of foreign scholars to the United States. "My opinion with respect to emigration [of foreign scholars]," Washington explained at the height of the D'Invernois affair, "is that, except for useful mechanics and some particular descriptions of men or professions, there is no need of encouragement." He added that any

> policy…of settling them in a body [i.e., in a single institution] may be much questioned; for, by so doing, they retain the language, habits, and principles (good or bad) which they bring with them. Whereas by an intermixture with our people, they or their descendants get assimilated to our customs, measures, and laws: in a word, [they] soon become one people.[44]

The nation's learned societies did not hesitate to welcome foreign scholars as *corresponding* members. Between 1771 and 1799, for example, the American Philosophical Society elected more than 150 corresponding members from abroad, including scholars from Britain, France, Germany, Sweden, Italy, Russia, Spain, Austria, the Netherlands, and other countries. In the same years, the American Academy of Arts and Sciences elected foreign members from Britain, France, Russia, Italy, and elsewhere. These contacts had tremendous benefits for American scholarly development. The exchange of books and specimens otherwise unavailable in the United States helped to build new institutions for advanced research—institutions that enabled American youth to pursue their studies at home. As historian Gilbert Chinard has noted, "Long before governments had thought of creating posts of 'intellectual or cultural attaches,' long before the *Institut de Cooperation Intellectuelle* of the Society of Nations, these men…wove across the ocean and all over Europe a real network of intellectual bonds." Of course, the underlying purpose of cross-national exchange was, in large part, the development of *national* institutions, including a national university.[45]

IMAGINING THE IDEAL UNIVERSITY

Discussion of a national university was not limited to figures such as Washington, Jefferson, Hamilton, Adams, and Rush. In 1795, the American Philosophical Society offered a $100 premium for the best essay on a national system of education "adapted to the genius of the government, and best calculated to promote the general welfare of the United States." The Society, led jointly in these years by Jefferson and Rush, accepted submissions for two years before announcing cowinners in the winter of 1797. The winning essays by Samuel Knox, a minister in Maryland, and Samuel Harrison Smith, a newspaper editor in Philadelphia, both outlined complete systems of education with common schools, academies, and colleges—all leading toward "university" attendance for the best and brightest.[46]

Knox stressed the unifying role of education in a country with "a wide extent of territory, inhabited by citizens blending together almost all of the various manners and customs of every country in Europe." Every school and college, he asserted, was a potential nation-building institution.[47] At the apex of this system was a magnificent, indeed massive, national university, its faculty more extensive than any other in the United States. He wrote:

> There ought to be a professor of classical learning or belles lettres and composition; a professor of Latin and Roman antiquities; a professor of Greek and Grecian antiquities; a professor of Hebrew and Oriental languages; a professor of rhetoric, logic, and moral philosophy; a professor [as well as] an assistant professor of natural philosophy; a professor of mathematics; a professor of astronomy; a professor of history and chronology; a professor of law and the principles of government; and a professor of elocution and oratory,

as well as a professor of medicine and a professor of "the various ornamental arts." The way to keep American students at home, Knox implied, was to build a university superior to any institution abroad.[48]

Knox's university came equipped with a chemical laboratory, a botanic garden "containing a house for the gardener," a rooftop observatory "sufficiently large to admit of an astronomical apparatus in the first style of improvement," a printing house, a bookstore, a public library, a natural history museum, and, to accommodate the professor of fine arts, "a hall for painting, another for music, and a third for statuary." Knox even made room for "kitchens and spacious dining rooms, and over these, lodging rooms for the students." This grand institution, he noted, would "constitute the fountainhead of science, that center to which all the literary genius of the commonwealth would tend; and from which, when matured by its instructive influence, would diffuse the rays of knowledge and science to the remotest situations of the united government."[49]

Given its scale, it was not surprising that Knox's university never came to fruition. Nor did an equally fantastical institution outlined by Samuel Harrison Smith, cowinner of the American Philosophical Society essay contest. Smith, like Knox, proposed a sprawling national university with courses in "1. Languages. 2. Mathematics. 3. Geography and History. 4. Natural Philosophy in general. 5. Moral Philosophy. 6. English Language, Belle Lettres, and Criticism. 7. Agriculture. 8. Manufactures. 9. Government and Laws. 10. Medicine. 11. Theology. 12. Elements of Taste ... Music, Architecture, Gardening, Drawing, etc. [and finally] 13. Military Tactics," all led by "a person eminently skilled in science, who shall be president of the board."[50]

Like his fellow essayist, Smith promised great things from his university, which he saw as the best vehicle to keep American students at home and, thus, protected from an increasingly war-torn Europe. He wrote: "Should the principles then be established, which have been contemplated..., we may expect to see America too enlightened and virtuous to spread the horror of war over the face of any country...and too magnanimous and powerful to suffer [war's] existence where she can prevent it." It was an optimistic view—too optimistic, perhaps, to be sustained in light of events unfolding abroad.[51]

By the time Smith and Knox's essays were published in 1798, the "horror of war" had spread rapidly through France and had put the United States in a precarious diplomatic position. A year earlier, the French Directory answered the controversial Jay Treaty by instructing French warships to seize both British and American vessels trading in the Atlantic, a move that prompted the newly elected president Adams to dispatch an embassy to Paris to restore harmony. This mission, however, was a disaster. The outcome was the infamous X Y Z Affair in which the French promised to meet with the Americans only if the American delegation paid a bribe of $250,000 and gave the French a loan of $12 million. The Americans refused, leading to a year-long undeclared naval war between the two countries.

THE NATIONAL UNIVERSITY IN INTERNATIONAL CONTEXT

Political and military developments in Europe indirectly shaped the debate over a national university for the United States. In 1800, Thomas Jefferson asked French exile Pierre Samuel duPont de Nemours to offer a general plan for American education. Jefferson had known duPont since his residence in Paris in 1785 and had long shared duPont's view of the close ties between scholarship and national development. A physiocrat and expert in political economy, duPont had served as commissioner of commerce under Louis XVI before assuming the presidency of the National Assembly after the revolution. With the rise of Robespierre, however, duPont's fate took a different turn. Captured by secret police, duPont was deemed a counterrevolutionary, and it was only Robespierre's own demise in 1794 that saved duPont's life.[52]

In 1799, after five years in hiding, duPont fled to New York, where Jefferson, then vice president, welcomed him with open arms. Hoping to draw on his friend's administrative experience, Jefferson asked him to develop a plan for national education. DuPont obliged with a three-pronged scheme for primary, secondary, and higher education, including a so-called University of North America to be located in the nation's capital, then under construction. DuPont's university featured a school of medicine, a school of law (or school of "social science and legislation"), a school of mines, and a school of engineering (or school of "higher geometry and the sciences it explains"). This "palace of science," outfitted with its own philosophical society, botanic garden, and natural history museum, would show the world "that youth can be as well taught in America as in Europe."[53]

Indeed, as far as duPont was concerned, the United States had a chance to establish the greatest university ever to exist on earth. With a great university, the District of Columbia would become "the Bokhara, the Benares, the Byblas, the Cariath-Sepher, the City of Knowledge." He added: "[M]en of the highest reputation will be assembled there as professors; perhaps Europeans will not be considered properly educated unless they have studied in its schools." Anticipating the day when the United States would replace all other countries as the mecca of learning, duPont asserted that, to obtain such fame, America needed only "to secure the most illustrious scholars of Göttingen, Edinburgh, and other scholastic cities, promising them a brilliant future that can be attained only by the perfection of their knowledge and that can be secured only by sustained preeminence."[54]

For duPont, the day of American preeminence was not far off, and for his friend Jefferson, the foundation of a great national university would become a lifelong obsession. Both imagined the creation of a truly modern university, a university devoted to national service and deserving international respect. Both foresaw an institution of such excellence that it would reverse the flow of scholars—and scholarship—forever. Once this university came into being, Americans would no longer need, or want, to study abroad. Instead, their European counterparts would study in the United States. The center of intellectual gravity would shift, the direction of scholarly exchange would turn, and the United States would control the immense power that derives from the production, dissemination, and application of knowledge.

DuPont's plan was not the only new proposal for a national university to circulate in this period. The same year, Jefferson solicited a plan from the renowned scientist Joseph Priestley, then settled on a farm outside Philadelphia. Listing the subjects he believed should have a place in the new university—botany, chemistry, zoology, anatomy, surgery, medicine, natural philosophy, agriculture, mathematics, astronomy, geography, politics, commerce, history, ethics, law, and fine arts—Jefferson explained that he planned "to draw from Europe the first characters in science, by considerable temptations, [a recruitment process] which would not need to be repeated after the first set should have prepared fit successors and given reputation to the institution." Once the initial generation passed, the institution's faculty could be entirely native born and bred.[55]

A few months later, Priestley replied to Jefferson with some "Hints Concerning Public Education." He noted, first and foremost, that he would *not* advise recruiting professors abroad. "I would not without necessity have recourse to any foreign country for professors," he wrote. "They will expect too much deference, and the natives will be jealous of them." Having dismissed the idea of hiring foreign professors, Priestley went on to outline two institutions of higher education, one for Americans destined for public office, the other for aspiring professionals. Corresponding roughly to undergraduate and postgraduate institutions, these schools together would constitute a national university. Once such a system was in place, Priestley suggested, American youth would no longer have any reason to study abroad.[56]

Priestley's brief "Hints" in some ways echoed yet another proposal, summarized earlier by Swedish immigrant Nicholas Collin, a graduate of the University of Uppsala, correspondent of the Academy of Sciences in Stockholm, and member of the American Philosophical Society (which made him curator, secretary, and later vice president). Indeed, as Collin, Priestley, and DuPont all showed, many of the most innovative plans for the institutionalization of scholarship came *not* from native-born citizens but from immigrants (or, in the case of Forster and Beaurepaire, from pro-American scholars abroad)—an indication that educational reformers in the United States were not averse to "foreign" ideas as long as these ideas were "naturalized" in American institutions. The perceived danger, it seemed, was not ideas per se but the national *setting* in which ideas took institutional form.

As Collin noted, scholarship was—and perhaps always had been—international, but its pursuit was, first and foremost, a *national* endeavor. "Philosophers are citizens of the world," he acknowledged,

> the fruits of their labors are freely distributed among all nations; what they sow is reaped by the antipodes and blooms through future generations. It is, however, their duty to cultivate with peculiar attention those parts of science which are most beneficial to that country in which Providence has appointed their earthly stations. Patriotic affections are in this, as in other instances, conducive to the general happiness of mankind, because we have the best means of investigating those objects which are most interesting to us.

Americans had learned much from Europeans over the years, Collin admitted, but national differences necessitated the establishment of national institutions.[57]

CONCLUSION

The plans of Collin, Priestley, and DuPont, Knox and Smith, Forster, and Beaurepaire culminated in 1800 in one final plan, that of American diplomat Joel Barlow, then living in Paris, who sent Jefferson a sketch of a national university modeled on the *Institut de France*. Later published as "A Prospectus of a National Institution to be Established in the United States," Barlow's proposal was the most elaborate of all the university plans that surfaced in the early republic. In addition to all the usual arts and sciences, it called for a school of medicine, a school of veterinary medicine, a school of mines, and a school of engineering, as well as a national laboratory, a national bureau of astronomy, a national library, a national publication agency, a national patent office, and a national mint—not to mention extensive museums of natural history and fine arts.[58]

Barlow, whose extensive travels had carried him from Amsterdam to Algiers, drew on his experiences overseas to bolster his case for a national university. He wrote: "a central institution of this kind in the United States would not only remove the numerous disadvantages that our young men now experience in being obliged to obtain a European education, but it would federalize, as well as republicanize, their education at home." A national university, he added, would establish the United States' place among the world's leading scientific nations. "Mankind have a right to expect this example from us," Barlow asserted, "we alone are in a situation to hold it up before them, to command their esteem, and perhaps their imitation."[59]

Barlow drew on political connections to advance his plan for a national university. He gave his "Prospectus" to Samuel Harrison Smith, who, since winning the American Philosophical Society contest had gone on to become editor of *The National Intelligencer* (the primary mouthpiece of Jefferson's Democratic-Republican Party). A year later, he persuaded Senator George Logan, a Democratic-Republican from Pennsylvania, to bring "A Bill to Incorporate a National Academy" to the Senate floor. Logan—whose free-lance negotiations in France had led to the so-called Logan Act of 1799 (which barred private diplomacy)—became a helpful ally in the push for a national university. Speaking for Barlow's proposal, he urged the Senate to "promote...the cultivation of the sciences which...are...necessary to pro-mote the peace, happiness, and prosperity of our country."[60]

Barlow's proposal received enthusiastic support from Jefferson and oth-ers, but in the end it did not win support from Congress. As historian Albert Castel has noted, the subcommittee to which Logan's bill was submitted reported the bill without amendment, but the Senate, voting to strike the word *National* from the institution's name, returned the bill to the sub-committee, where it died. Severely disappointed, Barlow attributed the fail-ure of his proposal to the "opposition of the schools and colleges already established, and the indifference of the great majority of Congressmen to anything but the material development of the country." Jefferson agreed, writing to Barlow that members of Congress seemed to have "more feeling for canals and roads than education."[61]

The push for a national university did not end once and for all with this defeat. It returned many times over the course of the nineteenth century. But this episode did mark the conclusion of an early phase in the debate. Barlow was right to note the opposition of "colleges already established," for, by the first decade of the nineteenth century, many had begun to implement the very improvements that he and others had recommended. Although none yet approached the lavishly outfitted institution that Barlow described, several colleges had begun to move in that direction. The idea of a college equipped for postgraduate research with its own botanic garden, mineralogical cabi-net, or chemical laboratory no longer seemed far-fetched.

Nor did the idea of a college sufficiently excellent to keep the nation's best and brightest students at home. Particularly in light of ongoing military conflicts in Europe, the goal of educating future leaders in American col-leges seemed more necessary than ever. Perhaps no one felt more strongly about this goal than Joel Barlow himself. Upon his return to America after a 17-year hiatus, he echoed the advice that Jefferson, Rush, Washington, and others had given many times. Writing to a brother who planned to send his own sons overseas for advanced education, Barlow wrote: "Do not give them a taste for roving over the world. There are very few young men who are sent to Europe for the sake of seeing the world who are not ruined."[62]

The chief motive driving higher education reform in this period was a desire to deter future leaders from studying abroad. Perhaps no one stated this motive more clearly than Noah Webster, who implored his countrymen to improve their own colleges. "Americans," he wrote, unshackle your minds, and act like independent beings. You have been children long enough, subject to the control, and subservient to the interest of a haughty parent. You have now an interest of your own to augment and defend—you have an empire to raise and support by your exertions—and a national character to establish and extend by your wisdom and virtues. To effect these great changes, it is necessary to frame a liberal plan of policy, and to build it on a broad system of education. Before this system can be formed and embraced, the Americans must believe and act from the belief that it is dishonorable to waste life in mimicking the follies of other nations and basking the sunshine of foreign glory.[63]

Yet, to emphasize the role of nationalism in the emergence of the American university is to emphasize only half the story. The rise of the American university depended just as fundamentally on *international* collaboration and exchange. Drawing ideas and input from abroad, higher education reformers did not work in geographic isolation (much as some may have wished they could). Instead, they looked overseas for models as well as motivation. Even as they sought to keep American youth from crossing the Atlantic, they welcomed examples as well as encouragement from Europe; even as they worried about contamination and corruption, they accepted patterns and prototypes from abroad; even as they demanded intellectual autonomy, they depended heavily on foreign colleagues for ideas. In colleges of the early American republic, nationalism and internationalism went hand in hand.

NOTES

An earlier version of this essay appeared in the *Peking University Education Review*. Adam R. Nelson, "The Perceived Dangers of Study Abroad, 1780–1800: Nationalism, Internationalism, and the Origins of the American University," trans. Zhixiang Zhu, *Peking University Education Review*, CHINA, vol. 31 (2010–13); available online at http://www.jypl.pku.edu.cn/before_e.asp?nian=2010&qihao=3# This chapter is printed with permission.

1. See, e.g., Carl F. Kaestle, *Pillars of the Republic: Common Schools and American Society, 1780–1860* (New York, 1983).
2. For more on the national university debate, see G. Brown Goode, "The Origin of the National Scientific and Educational Institutions of the United States," *Papers of the American Historical Association* 4 (April 1890); H. G. Good, "Who First Proposed a National University?" *School and Society* III (March 11, 1916): 387–391; Allen Oscar Hansen, *Liberalism and American Education in the Eighteenth Century* (New York, 1926); Edgar Brice Wesley, *Proposed: The University of the United States* (Minneapolis, 1936); James W. Hill, "The Movement to Establish a National University Prior to 1860: A Documentary History" (Unpublished MA thesis, University of North Carolina-Chapel Hill, 1946); David Madsen, *The National University: Enduring Dream of the USA* (Detroit, 1966); Edward H. Reisner, *Nationalism and Education since 1789* (New York, 1922); and Neil McDowell Shawen, "Thomas Jefferson and a 'National' University: The

Hidden Agenda for Virginia," *Virginia Magazine of History and Biography* 92:3 (July 1984): 309–335.

3. Thomas Jefferson to John Bannister, Jr. (October 15, 1785), in Adrienne Koch and William Peden, eds., *The Life and Selected Writings of Thomas Jefferson* (New York, 1944), 385–388.

4. Ibid.

5. Ibid. See also Thomas Jefferson to Peter Carr (August 10, 1787) in Koch and Peden, eds., *The Life and Selected Writings of Thomas Jefferson*, 429–434.

6. See "The Legislature of Georgia Makes Aliens of Georgians Who Study in Europe, 1785," quoted in Edgar W. Knight and Clifton L. Hall, eds., *Readings in American Educational History* (New York, 1951), 93.

7. "A Bill for Amending the Constitution of William and Mary, and Substituting More Certain Revenues for Its Support; Proposed by the Committee of Revisors of the Laws of Virginia, Appointed by the General Assembly in the Year 1776" (1779), in Knight and Hall, 186–191. See also Roy J. Honeywell, *The Educational Work of Thomas Jefferson* (Cambridge, MA, 1931), 205–210.

8. Thomas Jefferson, *Autobiography of Thomas Jefferson*, ed. Paul Leicester Ford (New York, 1914), 78. See also Davison M. Douglas, "The Jeffersonian Vision of Legal Education" (American Association of Law Schools, 2001), 11n60; and Susan H. Godson et al., *The College of William and Mary: A History* (Williamsburg, 1993), 133, 135.

9. Benjamin Rush, "Of the Mode of Education Proper in a Republic" (1784), in Dagobert D. Runes, *The Selected Writings of Benjamin Rush* (New York, 1947), 87–96. See also Benjamin Rush, *The Autobiography of Benjamin Rush, His "Travels through Life," Together with His Commonplace Book for 1789–1913*, ed. George W. Corner (Princeton, 1948); and James Henry Morgan, *Dickinson College: The History of One Hundred and Fifty Years, 1783–1933* (Carlisle, PA, 1933).

10. Rush, "Of the Mode of Education Proper in a Republic" (1784).

11 .Ibid. A similar emphasis on educating Americans at home came from European friends. See John Coakley Lettsom to Benjamin Rush (September 7, 1785), quoted in Whitfield J. Bell, Jr., "The Scientific Environment of Philadelphia, 1775–1790," *Proceedings of the American Philosophical Society* 92:1 (March 1948): 12.

12. Rush, "Of the Mode of Education Proper in a Republic" (1784).

13. J. O. Knauss, *Social Conditions among the Pennsylvania Germans in the Eighteenth Century, as Revealed in the German Newspapers Published in America* (Lancaster, PA, 1922; 2001), 86–95 (quotation from page 92).

14. Benjamin Rush to Annis Boudinot Stockton (June 19, 1787), in L. H. Butterfield, *Letters of Benjamin Rush*, vol. I (Princeton, 1951), 420–429. See also David Freeman Hawke, *Benjamin Rush: Revolutionary Gadfly* (Indianapolis, 1971), 318–319.

15. Benjamin Rush to Annis Boudinot Stockton (June 19, 1787). See also Rush, "To the Citizens of Pennsylvania of German Birth and Extraction: Proposal of a German College" (August 31, 1785), in Butterfield, *Letters of Benjamin Rush*, I:364–368. Rush learned to read German on his trip back to Philadelphia (after studying abroad) in 1769. See also Rush, "A Letter by Dr. Benjamin Rush Describing the Consecration of the German College at Lancaster in June, 1787" (Lancaster, PA, 1945);

Account of the Manners of the German Inhabitants of Pennsylvania (1789) (Collegeville, MN, 1974); and "To the Ministers of the Gospel of All Denominations: An Address upon Subjects Interesting to Morals" (1788), quoted in Donald J. D'Elia, "Benjamin Rush: Philosopher of the American Revolution," *Transactions of the American Philosophical Society*, New Series 64:5 (1974): 67; Joseph Hutchins, "Sermon Preached in the Lutheran Church, on the Opening of Franklin College, in the Borough of Lancaster, Pennsylvania: July 17th [sic] 1787" (Philadelphia, 1806), quoted in Butterfield, "Introduction" to Benjamin Rush, "A Letter by Dr. Benjamin Rush Describing the Consecration of the German College at Lancaster in June, 1787," 33–34n26; and Frederic S. Klein, *The Spiritual and Educational Background of Franklin and Marshall College* (Lancaster, PA, 1939).

16. Benjamin Rush to Richard Price (May 25, 1786), in Butterfield, *Letters of Benjamin Rush*, I:388–390. Rush echoed these ideas in his "Address to the People of the United States," *The American Museum* (January 1787), appended in Goode, "The Origin of the National Scientific and Educational Institutions," 82–85.

17. Benjamin Rush, "To Friends of the Federal Government: A Plan for a Federal University," *Federal Gazette* (October 29, 1788).

18. Ibid., in Butterfield, *Letters of Benjamin Rush*, I:491–495.

19. Noah Webster, *The American Magazine* I (May 1788), 370–373, in Knight and Hall, 93–96. In later years, Webster followed the work of the Association of American Patriots for the Purpose of Forming a National Character. See also Jill Lepore, *A Is for American: Letters and Other Characters in the Newly United States* (New York: Knopf, 2002).

20. Webster, *The American Magazine* I (May 1788).

21. Webster, *The American Museum* I (May 1788).

22. Rush, "A Plan for a Federal University" (1788).

23. .Ibid.

24. Madsen, *The National University*, 22–23.

25. David W. Robson, "Pennsylvania's 'Lost' National University: Johann Forster's Plan," *Pennsylvania Magazine of History and Biography* 102 (July 1978): 364–374.

26. Ibid., 371.

27. Chevalier Alexandre Quesnay de Beaurepaire, *Mémoire, Statuts et Prospectus concernant l'Académie des Sciences et Beaux-Arts des Etats-Unis de l'Amérique, établie è Richmond, Capitale de la Virginie* (Paris 1788); abridged version in Knight and Hall, 129–132. See also Richard Heyward Gaines, "Richmond's First Academy, Projected by M. Quesnay de Beaurepaire": http://www. newrivernotes.com/va/richacad.htm.

28. Sara Bache to Benjamin Franklin (February 27, 1783), in Knight and Hall, 127–128.

29. Roland G. Paulston, "French Influence in American Institutions of Higher Learning, 1784–1825," *History of Education Quarterly* 8:2 (Summer 1968): 234. See also Paul M. Spurlin, "The World of the Founding Fathers and France," *The French Review* 49:6 (May 1976): 909–925.

30. Beaurepaire, *Mémoire*, quoted in Knight and Hall, 130. See also John G. Roberts, "The American Career of Quesnay de Beaurepaire," *French Review* 20:6 (1947): 463–470.

31. James H. Hutson, *The Sister Republics: Switzerland and the United States from 1776 to the Present* (Washington, DC, 1991), 70.
32. See ibid., 71.
33. Ibid.
34. Ibid., 73.
35. Ibid., 73–74. See also Thomas Jefferson to George Washington (February 23, 1795), in Albert Ellery Bergh, ed., *The Writings of Thomas Jefferson*, vol. 19 (Washington, DC, 1905), 108–114.
36. Hutson, *The Sister Republics*, 73.
37. Madsen, *The National University*, 28–29. See George Washington to Thomas Jefferson (March 15, 1795), in John C. Fitzpatrick, *The Writings of George Washington from the Original Manuscript Sources, 1745–1799*, vol. 34 (Washington, DC, 1931), 146–148.
38. Hutson, *The Sister Republics*, 75–76.
39. Jared Sparks, ed., *The Writings of George Washington: Being His Correspondence, Addresses, Messages, and Other Papers, Official and Private, Selected and Published from the Original Manuscripts*, vol. I (Boston, 1855), 572. See also George Washington to the Commissioners of the District of Columbia (January 28, 1795), in Fitzpatrick, *Writings of George Washington*, 34:106–108; and Charles Kendall Adams, "Washington and the Higher Education, An Address Delivered before Cornell University, February 22, 1888" (Ithaca, NY, 1888).
40. George Washington to Thomas Jefferson (March 15, 1795) and George Washington to Robert Brooke (March 16, 1795) in Fitzpatrick, *Writings of George Washington*, 34:146–151.
41. George Washington to Alexander Hamilton (September 1, 1796), in Fitzpatrick, *Writings of George Washington*, 35:199.
42. George Washington to Alexander Hamilton (September 1, 1796).
43. Quoted in John W. Hoyt, *Memorial in Regard to a National University* (Washington, DC, 1892), 39–40. See also Madsen, *The National University*, 33.
44. George Washington to John Adams (November 15, 1794) in Fitzpatrick, *Writings of George Washington*, 34:22–23.
45. Gilbert Chinard, "The American Philosophical Society and the World of Science (1768–1800)," *Proceedings of the American Philosophical Society* 87:1 (July 14, 1943): 5–6.
46. Merle M. Odgers, "Education and the American Philosophical Society," *Proceedings of the American Philosophical Society* 87:1 (July 14, 1943): 13–19. See also Benjamin Justice, "'The Great Contest': The American Philosophical Society Education Prize of 1795 and the Problem of American Education," *American Journal of Education* 114 (February 2008): 191–213.
47. Samuel Knox, *Essay on the Best System of Liberal Education, Adapted to the Genius of the Government of the United States; Comprehending Also, a Uniform, General Plan for Instituting and Conducting Public Schools, in This Country, on Principles of the Most Extensive Utility* (Baltimore 1799), 167, quoted in Odgers, "Education and the American Philosophical Society," 15.
48. Knox, *Essay on the Best System of Liberal Education*, 157–158.
49. Ibid., 153–156, 149.

50. Samuel Harrison Smith, *Remarks on Education: Illustrating the Close Connection between Virtue and Wisdom, to Which Is Annexed a System of Liberal Education* (Philadelphia, 1798), quoted in Odgers, "Education and the American Philosophical Society," 17.

51. Smith, *Remarks on Education*, quoted in Odgers, "Education and the American Philosophical Society," 17.

52. See James Woodress, *A Yankee's Odyssey: The Life of Joel Barlow* (Philadelphia, 1958).

53. Bessie Gardner DuPont, trans. of DuPont de Nemours, *National Education in the United States of America* (1800, trans. 1923), 126, 125. See also Odgers, "Education and the American Philosophical Society," 21.

54. DuPont de Nemours, *National Education in the United States of America*, 146.

55. Thomas Jefferson to Joseph Priestley (January 18, 1800), in H. A. Washington, *The Writings of Thomas Jefferson*, vol. 4 (Washington, DC, 1854), 311–314.

56. Joseph Priestley, "Hints Concerning Public Education" (1800), in Edgar F. Smith, *Priestley in America, 1794–1804* (Philadelphia, 1920), 117–122.

57. Nicholas Collin, "Essay on Those Inquiries in Natural Philosophy Which At Present Are Most Beneficial to the United States of North America," *Transactions of the American Philosophical Society* 3 (1793): iii–xxvii, reprinted in Whitfield J. Bell and Nicholas Collin, "Nicholas Collin's Appeal to American Scientists," *William and Mary Quarterly* 13:4 (October 1956): 519–550.

58. Joel Barlow, *Prospectus of a National Institution to Be Established in the United States* (Washington, DC, 1806), appended in Goode, "The Origin of the National Scientific and Educational Institutions," 85–97.

59. Barlow, *Prospectus of a National Institution*, 87.

60. Albert E. Castel, "The Founding Fathers and the Vision of a National University," *History of Education Quarterly* 4:4 (December 1964): 289–290. See also Frederick B. Tolles, *George Logan of Philadelphia* (New York, 1953), 270–272.

61. Castel, "The Founding Fathers," 290. See also Joel Barlow to Abraham Baldwin (September 15, 1800), quoted in Charles Burr Todd, *Life and Letters of Joel Barlow, LL.D., Poet, Statesman, Philosopher* (New York, 1886), 208.

62. Woodress, *A Yankee's Odyssey*, 234.

63. Noah Webster, *The American Magazine* I (May 1788), 370–374, in Knight and Hall, 93–96. See also John C. Greene, "American Science Comes of Age," *Journal of American History* 55:1 (June 1968): 34–35.

PART III

Materials: Essays from the American Philosophical Society Education Contest, 1795–1797

Introduction to the Essays:
Reading the Late Eighteenth Century
in the Early Twenty-First

Benjamin Justice

The challenge was to write:

> An essay on a system of liberal education, and literary instruction, adapted
> to the genius of the government, and best calculated to promote the general
> welfare of the United States; comprehending, also, a plan for instituting and
> conducting public schools in this country on principles of the most extensive
> utility.

What follows are the seven essays of the APS Education Prize contest,
launched in 1795 and decided in 1797. Samuel Smith and Samuel Knox,
cowinners of the contest, had their extensive essays printed and reprinted
through the centuries, and eventually put online. The others have never
before been transcribed or published, and may be found filed away in
the Archives of the American Philosophical Society. One essay, known as
"No. 3" does not survive, having been duly returned to a nearby tavern
keeper according to the instructions of its author. But while the original
essay is lost, its peer review quotes the essay extensively, allowing us to see
the ideas and outline of the essay, as well as the actual words and style of
the author.

Contestants for the prize sent their name in a separate envelope, to be
opened only if they won. Thus the losing essays remained anonymous.
Nevertheless, using a variety of methods, we now can identity three of the
five losers. Hiram was beyond a doubt Francis Hoskins, a clerk at the Rolls
Office of Philadelphia. The author of No. 3 was probably Rev. William Smith,
former provost of the University of Pennsylvania, while the Academicus
essay was probably written by Rev. John Hobson, a Unitarian minister from

Birmingham, England. Freedom and Hand remain anonymous, but both appear to be connected to the University of Pennsylvania, perhaps to medical education.

The winning essays by Smith and Knox were especially complex, detailed, and at times long-winded. Thanks to the digital revolution, there is no need to reprint either essay here in its complete form. Both may be found online. But there is still a need to provide readers with versions they can more easily read. What follows are extensive excerpts from those two essays, which retain, as far as possible, every major idea or issue of historical or contemporary significance. My goal, in the spirit of the contest itself, has been utility. Interested readers will, I hope, find a new appreciation for these otherwise obscure documents.

The authors of these essays lived at a time where the modern concept of public education did not exist. Part of their challenge, as framed by the contest question, was to imagine what public education should be, in ways that were consistent with the form of government of the United States. Some make a case for public education, others assume it. As they imagine how to ensure the education of all citizens, even the poor, the authors anticipate what remain some of the enduring dilemmas in American education: Is public education for the public or private good? How should it be paid for? How should it be managed and organized? What should the children learn? To what end?

Underneath these institution-centric questions were deeper ones still that run throughout American social and political history: Who is a citizen? What place should religious tradition have in a pluralistic republic? What is knowledge and who controls it? Should public institutions exist at all, and if so, should they serve to protect the status quo or improve it according to abstract principles? At their heart, these essays engaged the question of what it meant to be an American.

The winning essays were published by the APS, and it is from the published versions that these excerpted transcriptions come. The remaining essays, however, were drafts—complete with crossed-out words, spelling errors, ink spills, and other infelicities. What matters is not the authors' small mistakes, but their larger ideas about the role of formal education in the new republic. For the remaining four losing essays and the review of No. 3, each transcription is complete. I have retained original spelling except in cases where particular words are abbreviated, obscured, or unintentionally misspelled by the author according to the standards of their own day. I have retained the often eclectic and unpredictable usage of punctuation and grammar as well, except that I have added periods and capitalized the first letter of new sentences when the author forgot to do so (Freedom was guilty of this), and uncapitalized first letters where the author did not intend them (Hiram never used a lowercase "s" or "i" to start a word!). In rare cases where a word is entirely illegible, I have offered my best guess in brackets. To aid readers, each essay begins with a brief biographical note on the author.

NOTE

These essays were transcribed and rechecked by a team of people: Benjamin Justice, Christina Davis, Lisa Green, Eric Strome, Campbell Scribner, Michael Hevel, Nia Soumakis, and Carly Turner. They were reproduced with permission of the American Philosophical Society.

Remarks on Education: Illustrating the Close Connection Between Virtue and Wisdom: To which is Annexed, a System of Liberal Education

Samuel Harrison Smith

Samuel Harrison Smith (1772–1845) was born to a Philadelphia merchant family and educated in Philadelphia schools, earning a BA (1787) and MΛ (1790) from the University of Pennsylvania. Ambitious and financially secure, Smith launched a printing business at the age of 19, which included the *American Universal Magazine,* the *New World,* and the *Independent Gazetteer,* which he renamed the *Universal Gazette.* In recognition of his accomplishments in publishing, the APS elected Smith to membership in 1797 before the announcement of his victory in the essay contest. After the contest, Smith donated his prize winnings to the APS to fund a second contest and became an active member in the organization. In 1800, Smith married his cousin, Margaret Bayard, and moved to Washington, DC at the invitation of Thomas Jefferson to found what would become the mouthpiece of Jefferson's Democratic-Republican Party: the triweekly *National Intelligencer and Washington Advisor.*[1]

REMARKS ON EDUCATION

The diffusion of knowledge, co-extensive with that of virtue, would seem to apply with close precision to a republican system of education, because;

1. An enlightened nation is always most tenacious of its rights.
2. It is not the interest of such a society to perpetuate error; as it undoubtedly is the interest of many societies differently organized.
3. In a republic, the sources of happiness are open to all without injuring any.

4. If happiness be made at all to depend on the improvement of the mind, and the collusion of mind with mind, the happiness of an individual will greatly depend upon the general diffusion of knowledge and a capacity to think and speak correctly.
5. Under a republic, duly constructed, man feels a strong bias to improvement, as under a despotism he feels an impulse to ignorance and depression.

But as knowledge is infinite, and as its complete attainment requires more time than man has at his command, it becomes interesting to assign;

    I.   The time fit to be devoted to education.
   II.   The objects proper to be accomplished; and
  III.   The manner of accomplishing them.

I. The Time Fit to be Devoted to Education

Previously to any prospect of success, one principle must prevail. Society must establish the right to educate, and acknowledge the duty of having educated, all children. A circumstance, so momentously important, must not be left to the negligence of individuals. It is believed, that this principle is recognized in almost all our state constitutions. If so, the exercise of it would not be contested. Indeed, whether at present acknowledged or not, it would produce such beneficial effects, as well in reference to the parent as the child, that a general acquiescence might be relied on.

Having contemplated [earlier in this essay] in reference to [adult men] an abatement of two hours of labour [for daily intellectual improvement], the next object of enquiry is what time should be devoted to the education of youth. It should unquestionably be much larger; as during this period the mind is unimproved; as impressions of the greatest strength are rapidly made; and as the future biass [*sic*] of the mind entirely depends upon the improvement of these impressions. The period, however, should have its limits. Study should never be continued after it becomes oppressive. The preceptor should be as cautious in using every mean necessary to prevent disgust, as he ought to be zealous in exciting a thirst of knowledge. Without aiming at rigid [precision], in considering the claims of labour and study, we shall not, perhaps, materially err in assigning four hours each day to education.

II. The Objects Proper to be Accomplished

It is necessary that the principle of an universal diffusion of knowledge should be in the highest degree energetic. This is a principle which cannot be too extensively embraced; for it is too true, that all the efforts of an enlightened zeal will never make a whole nation as well informed as its interests would prescribe.

But this necessary limit forms no objection to every practicable extension of it. We shall be furnished with irrefragable evidence of its beneficial tendency, on considering that knowledge has only produced injurious effects, when it has been the subject of monopoly. The efforts of ignorance to oppress science have excited a spirit of retaliation, which we must not be surprised at beholding, in its turn, its own avenger. The moment, however, which marks the universal diffusion of science, by withdrawing the temptation to, as well as the means of, injury, will restore knowledge to its original purity and lustre. It is with knowledge, as with every other thing which influences the human mind. It acts precisely in proportion to the force of the object acted upon. As the beggar cannot corrupt by gold the beggar; so neither can opulence corrupt opulence. In the same manner, equality of intellectual attainments is a foe to oppression; and just as mankind shall advance in its possession, the means as well as the inducement to oppress will be annihilated. We are correct, therefore, in declaring a diffusion of knowledge, the best, perhaps the only pledge of virtue, of equality, and of independence.

Let us, then, with mental inflexibility, believe that though all men will never be philosophers, yet that all men may be enlightened; and that folly, unless arising from physical origin, may be banished from the society of men.

The ideas already expressed, and those which succeed, must be understood as applicable to a system of general education. They only prescribe what it is necessary every man should know. They do not attempt to limit his acquisitions. Wealth and genius will always possess great advantages. It will be their prerogatives, if properly directed, to carry improvement to its highest eminences.

In forming a system of liberal education, it is necessary to avoid ideas of too general a character, as well as those which involve too minute a specification. Considerable latitude must be allowed for the different degrees of natural capacity, and the varying shades of temper and biass. It seems, therefore, fit to lay down principles which possess properties common to every mind, and which will, of course, in their application, admit of few, if any, exceptions.

The first great object of a liberal system of education should be, the admission into the young mind of such ideas only as are either absolutely true, or in the highest degree probable; and the cautious execution of all error.

Were man able to trace every effect to its cause, he would probably find that the virtue or the vice of an individual, the happiness or the misery of a family, the glory or infamy of a nation, have had their sources in the cradle, over which the prejudice of a nurse or a mother have presided. The years of infancy are those in which the chains of virtue or vice are generally forged...

If this view be correct, should it not be thought treason against truth and virtue, to instill prejudice and error into the young mind? If this be treason against truth and virtue, what shall we say of those who inculcate principles which they know to be false, and attempt in this way to establish systems that only exist in the midst of human carnage and destruction?

Whether we consider man's existence as terminated by the grave, or view him, as he doubtless is, the heir of a future life, we must consider his happiness as altogether dependent on the observance of certain moral principles. The universality with which these have been received may be considered as the test of their truth...

Let those truths in which all men agree be firmly impressed; let those which are probable be inculcated with caution, and let doubt always hang over those respecting which the good and the wise disagree. Above all things let the infant mind be protected from conviction without proof.

But is will be said that in almost all the departments of a general plan of education, the perusal of approved books must be chiefly relied on. The indispensable economy of arrangements which are to pervade a whole society, will prohibit the employment of preceptors of either great or original talents. It will therefore be fit that the preceptor, instead of inculcating his own immature ideas, should be guided by prescribed works. It is asked, where performances explaining and enforcing plain and undeniable truths, and avoiding prejudices or falsehoods, are to be found? Such productions are acknowledged to be rare. It is also granted that this difficulty presents one of the most serious obstacles to successful education. But it is not insurmountable. It is attempted to be removed, hereafter, by offering large rewards for books of this nature, and by inciting the learned by other inducements to embark in so noble a service. At present, we must be satisfied in giving the preference to those works which abound most with truth and are the most exempt from error.

The elements of education, viz. reading and writing, are so obviously necessary, that it is useless to do more than enumerate them.

Of nearly equal importance are the first principles of mathematics, as at present almost universally taught.

A tolerably correct idea of Geography would seem, in a Republic especially, to involve great advantages. The interest of the mercantile part of the community is closely connected with correct geographical knowledge. Many important departments of science include an accurate knowledge of it. But the most important consideration is that which contemplates the United States as either allied in friendship, or arrayed in hostility, with the other nations of the earth. In both which cases, it becomes the duty of the citizen to have just ideas of the position, size, and strength, of nations...A most interesting part of Geography relates to a knowledge of our own country. Correct information on this subject will always conduce to strengthen the bands of friendship, and dissipate the misrepresentations of party prejudice.

The cultivation of natural philosophy, particularly so far as it relates to agriculture and manufactures, has been heretofore almost entirely neglected. The benefits, however, which it would produce, are great...

If we reverse the scene, and behold the farmer enlightened by the knowledge of chemistry, how wide a field of reflection and pleasure, as well as profit, would acknowledge his empire?

The ingenuity of the mechanic would not long remain passive. Repeated efforts at improvement would often prove successful, and be the source of new and rapid wealth.

The circumscribed advantages, attending Geographical knowledge, will be greatly enlarged by a liberal acquaintance with History...It will be distinctly seen, that ambition has generally risen on a destruction of every sentiment of virtue, and that it much oftener merits execration than applause. Power, long enjoyed, will appear to be hostile to the happiness, and subversive of the integrity, of the individual in whom it centres. Fanaticism and superstition will appear surrounded with blood and torture. War will stand forth with the boldest prominence of vice and folly, and make it, for a while, doubtful, whether man is most a villain or a fool. In short the mirror which history presents will manifest to man what, it is probable, he will become, should he surrender himself up to...selfish pursuits.

The second leading object of education, should be to inspire the mind with a strong disposition to improvement.

It is acknowledged that science is still in its infancy. The combination of ideas is infinite. As this combination advances the circle of knowledge is enlarged, and of course, the sphere of happiness extended. At present science is only cultivated by a few recluse students, too apt to mingle the illusions of imagination with the results of indistinct observation. Hence the reproach that theory and practice oppose each other. But no sooner shall a whole nation be tributary to science, than it will dawn with new lustre...

This progressive improvement would be promoted, in the third place, by inspiring youth with a taste for, and an attachment to, science, so firm, that it should be almost impossible to eradicate it in the subsequent periods of life.

For this purpose, studies which address themselves to the heart, as well as those which require strong mental attention, should invite the exercise of their thoughts...

But this great object would be assisted, more than by any other consideration, by—

Rendering, in the fourth place, knowledge as highly practical as possible.

This idea has been already noticed. But it merits more discussion...

All science ought to derive its rank from its utility. The real good which it actually does, or is capable of doing, is the only genuine criterion of its value...

He is the best friend of man, who makes discoveries involving effects which benefit mankind the most extensively. Moral truths are therefore of importance but little short of infinite. For they apply to numbers which almost evade enumeration, and to time which loses itself in eternity...

In physics, the happiness of mankind is in the highest degree increased by discoveries and improvements connected with agriculture and manufactures. These two occupations employ nine-tenths of most communities, and a much larger proportion of others. Does it not then become an interesting enquiry, whether it be not expedient in infancy and youth to communicate to the mind the leading principles of nature and art in these departments of labour, not only by a theoretic exposition of them, but also by their practical development?

If almost the whole community be defined to pursue one or other of these avocations from necessity, and if it be the duty of an individual to support himself, whenever he can, by an exertion of his own powers; and if these can only yield a sure support from an ability to be acquired in youth to prosecute a particular branch of agriculture or mechanics, does it not seem to be the duty of society to control education in such a way as to secure to every individual this ability? If this ability existed, how much misery would be annihilated, how much crime would be destroyed?

The <u>fifth</u> object should be inspiring youth with an ardent love for mankind. To accomplish this end, the preceptor should cautiously avoid instilling into the mind of his pupil a mean idea of human nature. The pages of the moralist by debasing man have aided that degeneracy which they deprecate....Those who have led the public mind, so far from attending to this maxim, have almost universally pourtrayed [*sic*] the heart and conduct of man as infinitely depraved...The child [however] has no doubt of the honesty of those about him, until his mind has received an artificial biass. Having received this unfortunate biass, and looking upon his fellow-beings as hostile, as he enters on life, he treats them with suspicion; and perhaps, on the supposition that they would pursue their own interest even to his injury, he hesitates not to pursue his to theirs...

We know, in our intercourse with the world, that confidence is the parent of friendship, which forbids its subject to do an act base or dishonourable...

III. The Manner of Accomplishing The Objects of Education:

Before we proceed to adjust the several parts of the system, two interesting enquiries present themselves for solution.

At what age education should commence?

Should education be public or private?

I. Every Correct View of Human Nature Shews The Young Mind, Though Tender, to be Capable of Great Improvement...

... It appears, that the earlier the mind is placed under a proper regimen, the greater is the probability of producing the desired effects. Some years must be surrendered to the claims of maternal regard; some will elapse before the child is able to attend to anything but those external objects which irresistibly force themselves on its notice.

Making an allowance of five years, for these unavoidable sacrifices, and for the acquisition of those elements of knowledge which are with facility acquired in any situation, we arrive at the period of life most proper for commencing a system of general education.

II. Should Education be Public or Private?

The most distinguished talents have been engaged in the discussion of this subject; and here, as in most controversies of a speculative cast, we find a great diversity of sentiment. Quintillian and Milton are warm in their eulogium on a public, while Locke is equally animated in his praise of a private system of education. The great argument, which may be called the centre of all others argued, is the production of emulation by a public education; while the great objection made to public education, is the sacrifice, alleged to be produced, of morality and honesty.

As there is, undoubtedly, truth on both sides, it becomes necessary to consider what weight the alleged advantages and disadvantages ought to possess in determining the preference of the judgment to one over the other system. It will, perhaps, be possible to reconcile the apparently conflicting ideas...

The early period of life is under parental and especially maternal control. The solicitude of a mother is now the best, the only protection, which the child can receive.... It is fortunate that we have not occasion to regret the unenlightened state of the female mind. But though these years do not mark much strength of mind, yet they rapidly unfold and form the disposition, which seldom fails to receive a virtuous bias from a mother who, however vicious herself, feels deeply interested in the virtue of her offspring. Hence those amiable affections are excited which are the ornament of human nature. Before the age of five the child seldom feels a disposition to do an immoral thing...

The young mind, having passed five years of its existence, free from much corruption, and a plan of education being now commenced, it becomes an object of consideration whether the child should remain with its parents, or be separated from them.

... It seems highly important that the child should still remain under the immediate control of parental authority. That affection which, on the part of the child, is but half formed, will have time and opportunity to gain strength, a love of domestic tranquility will be produced, and both these principles will form a firm shield of virtue.

On the other hand, daily attendance at school will withdraw the mind of the child from an *entire* dependence on its parents; will place it in situations demanding the exercise of its faculties; and will strengthen, instead of weakening, its attachment to domestic scenes. To be deprived of that which we love is in some degree painful to us all; to children it is painful in the highest degree. Yet a habit of voluntary or compulsory abstinence from pleasure is absolutely necessary to human happiness.

The child, in this situation, having its time divided between school, the hours of diversion, and those spend in the house of its parents, will, perhaps, remain as free from prostration of morals as can be expected in infancy. This, indeed, is the plan, which universally prevails in the civilized world, and its universality is certainly some argument in its favour.

Let this plan, partly domestic and partly public, be pursued till the mind begins boldly to expand itself, and to indicate an ability and an inclination to think for itself. The commencement of this capacity of combining ideas takes place about the age of ten. We have now reached the period which claims the closest attention. The mind not feels its vigour, and delights in displaying it. Ambition is kindled, emulation burns, a desire of superiority and distinction are roused.

This, then, appears to be the era, if ever, of public education. The indulgence of parental tenderness should now be exchanged for the patient and unobstructed exercise of mental powers. Let us now attend to the advantages of the two rival systems at this period.

With regard to the plan of public Education;

1. Emulation is excited. Without numbers there can be no emulation. It is founded on the love of distinction. In a private family this distinction cannot be acquired.
2. Attention to study, when the child is removed from the house of its parent, may be uninterrupted...[by] a thousand trifling, menial, avocations.
3. But above every other consideration, the system of public education inspires a spirit of independent reflection and conduct. Removed from a scene, where it has little occasion to think, and less to act, the child now finds itself placed in a situation free from rigid parental authority.

Error is never more dangerous than in the mouth of a parent...Hence prejudices are as hereditary as titles; and you may almost universally know the sentiments of the son by those of the father. Now, by education remote from parental influence, the errors of the father cease to be entailed upon the child.

When we consider the argument urged against public education (for only one is urged with any tenacity) we shall find that the evil it deprecates arises from the imperfection of human nature, more than from any appropriate and exclusive property of public education.

"Wherever there are numbers of children assembled together, there will be mischief and immorality." This is true; but is it so extensively true as to countervail the numerous advantages...? Is it equal to the injury sustained by the mechanical adoption of parental error or vice? More mischief, more immorality, have sprung from this source, than from the one complained of...

The discussion of this subject appears in some measure superseded, and the preference unequivocally established of the public over the private plan, by the small expense of the first, compared with the impracticable expense of the last. If parents educated their children, the hours withdrawn from business would alone impoverish them.

Guided by these principles, it is proposed;

I. That the period of education be from 5 to 18.

II. That every male child, without exception, be educated.

III. That the instructor in every district be directed to attend to the faithful execution of this injunction. That it be made punishable by law in a parent to neglect offering his child to the preceptor for instruction.

IV. That every parent, who wishes to deviate in the education of his children from the established system, be made responsible for devoting to the education of his children as much time as the established system prescribes.

V. That a fund be raised from the citizens in the ratio of their property.

VI. That the system be composed of primary schools; of colleges; and of a *University*.

VII. That the primary schools be divided into two classes; the first consisting of boys from 5 to 10 years old; the second consisting of boys from 10 to 18. –And that these classes be subdivided, if necessary, into smaller ones.

VIII. That the instruction given to the first class be the rudiments of the English Language, Writing, Arithmetic, the commission to memory and delivery of select pieces, inculcating moral duties, describing natural phenomena, or displaying correct fancy.

IX. ... should rapid acquisitions be made in the above branches of knowledge at an earlier age than that of 10, the boy is to be promoted into the second class.

X. The most solemn attention must be paid to avoid instilling into the young mind any ideas or sentiments whose truth is not unequivocally established by the undissenting suffrage of the enlightened and virtuous part of mankind.

XI. That the instruction given to the second class be an extended and more correct knowledge of Arithmetic; of the English language, comprising plain rules of criticism and composition; the concise study of General History and a more detailed acquaintance with the history of our own country; of Geography; of the laws of nature, practically illustrated...[in] agriculture and mechanics...[and] to commit to memory, and frequently to repeat, the constitution and the fundamental laws of the United States.

XII. That each primary school consist of 50 boys.

XIII. That such boys be admitted into the college as shall be deemed by the preceptor to be worthy, from a manifestation of industry and talents...That one boy be annually chosen out of the second class of each primary school for this preferment.

XIV. That the students at college so promoted be supported at public expense, but that other students may be received as shall be maintained by their parents.

XV. That the studies of the college consist in a still more extended acquaintance with the above stated branches of knowledge, together with the cultivation of polite literature.

XVI. That each college admit 200 students.

XVII. That an opportunity be furnished to those who have the ability, without interfering with the established studies, of acquiring a knowledge of the modern languages, music, drawing, dancing, and fencing; and that the permission to cultivate these accomplishments [be] held forth as the reward of diligence and talents.

XVIII. That a National University be established, in which the highest branches of science and literature shall be taught. That it consist of students promoted from the colleges. That one student out of ten be annually chosen for this promotion by a majority of the suffrages of the professors of the college to which he may belong.

XIX. That the student so promoted be supported at the public expense, and be lodged within the walls of the University; remaining so long as he please on a salary, in consideration of his devoting his time to the cultivation of science or literature, in which last case he shall become a fellow of the University.

XX. The number of professors in the College and the University is not fixed; but it is proposed that the last contain a professor of every branch of useful knowledge.

XXI. It is proposed that the professors be in the first instance designated by law; that afterwards, in all cases of vacancy, the professors of the college chuse [sic] the preceptors of the primary schools, and that the professors of the University chuse the professors of the colleges.

XXII. For the promotion of literature and science, it is proposed that a board of literature and science be established on the following principles:

It shall consist of fourteen persons skilled in the several branches of, 1. Languages. 2. Mathematics. 3. Geography and History. 4. Natural Philosophy in general. 5. Moral Philosophy. 6. English Language, Belle Letters, and Criticism. 7. Agriculture. 8. Manufactures. 9. Government and Laws. 10. Medicine. 11. Theology. 12 Elements of taste, including principles of Music, Architecture, Gardening, Drawing, etc. 13. Military Tactics. And in addition, 14. A person eminently skilled in Science, who shall be President of the board.

The persons, so elected, shall hold their offices during life, and receive a liberal salary, which shall render them independent in their circumstances. No removal shall take place unless approved by the suffrages of three-fourths of the colleges, three-fourths of the professors of the University, and three-fourths of the fellows of the University.

It shall be the duty of this board to form a system of national education to be observed in the University, the colleges, and the primary schools; to chuse the professors of the University; to fix the salaries of the several officers; and superintend the general interests of the institution.

As merit and talents are best secured by liberal rewards, a fund shall be established under the control of this board, out of which premiums shall be paid to such persons as shall, by their writings, excel in the treatment of the subjects proposed by the board for discussion, or such as shall make any valuable discovery.

It shall further be the duty of this board to peruse all literary or scientific productions submitted to them by any citizen, and in case they shall pronounce any such work worthy of general perusal and calculated to extend the sphere of useful knowledge, it shall be printed at the public expense, and the author rewarded.

It shall be the especial duty of the board to determine what authors shall be read or studied in the several institutions, and at any time to substitute one author for another.

As the extensive diffusion of knowledge is admirably promoted by libraries, it shall be in the power of the board to establish them...

Our seminaries of learning have heretofore been under the management of men, either incompetent to their superintendence, or not interested in a sufficient degree in their welfare. Voluntary and disinterested services, however honorable, are but rarely to be obtained. The zeal, which embarks a man of talents in the promotion of any object, will cool, unless sustained by some substantial benefits, either received or expected. It is almost impossible in this country for the case to be different. Affluence is so uncommon that few are to be found who possess it in union with intellectual attainments. Independent of this consideration, it is generally conceded that more knowledge is to be expected from men in a subordinate sphere of life, who are constrained to cultivate their minds, than from those who can live, without such cultivation, in ease and affluence. From this combination of acknowledged, it must clearly appear that every advantage will flow from the institution of the proposed board, which either does or can proceed from those formed on the existing plans, and that great and exclusive additional benefits may be expected.

In considering the objections likely to be urged against embracing the plan of education here proposed, only two of much importance are foreseen. The first is its extensiveness, the second its expense.

As extensiveness can only be objectionable in reference to the expense, this alone seems to require examination.

To give a fair trial to the system, liberal compensation should be allowed to the preceptors and professors. Their offices should be esteemed as honorable as any employments, either public or private, in the community; and one sure way of rendering them so is to attach to them independence...

Two subjects connected with a general system of education, viz. female instruction, and that which has been called ornamental, have been avoided. Both of these certainly involve very important considerations. But in the existing diversity of opinion respecting the nature and extent of the first, such coincidence and agreement as to produce a system must absolutely be despaired of. It is sufficient, perhaps, for the present that the improvement of women is marked by a rapid progress, and that a prospect opens equal to their most ambitious desires.—With regard to ornamental instruction, it would seem to rest more on principles of expediency than of necessity...

Such is the system proposed.

Let us contemplate the effects of [this] system,

   I.   On the individual citizen.
  II.   On the United States.
 III.   On the World.

I. The citizen, enlightened, will be a freeman in its truest sense. He will know his rights, and he will understand the rights of others; discerning the connection of his interest with the preservation of these rights, he will as firmly support those of his fellow men as his own. Too well informed to be misled, too virtuous to be corrupted, we shall behold man consistent and inflexible. Not at one moment the child of patriotism, and at another the slave of despotism, we shall see him in principle forever the same...

The love of knowledge, which even a moderate portion of information never fails to inspire, would at the same time shut up many sources of misery, and open more sources of happiness. The love of wealth would cease to be the predominant passion of the heart; other objects would divide the attention and perhaps challenge and receive a more constant regard.

II. Viewing the effects of such a system on the United States, the first result would be the giving perpetuity to those political principles so closely connected with our present happiness. In addition to these might be expected numerous improvements in our political economy.

By these means government without oppression and protection without danger, will exist in their necessary strength.

This state of things could not fail to elevate the United States far above other nations. Possessed of every source of happiness, under the guardianship of all necessary power, she would soon become a model for the nations of earth. This leads in the third place to,

III. The consideration of the effects of such a system on the world.

Nation is influenced as powerfully by nation, as one individual is influenced by another. Hence no sooner shall any one nation demonstrate by practical illustration the goodness of her political institutions, than other nations will imperceptibly introduce corresponding features in their systems.

But more important, still, will be the example of the most powerful nation on earth, if that example exhibit dignity, humility and intelligence. Scarcely a century can elapse, before the population of America will be equal, and her power superior, to that of Europe. Should the principles be then established, which have been contemplated, and the connection be demonstrated between human happiness and the peaceable enjoyment of industry and the indulgence of reflection, we may expect to see America too enlightened and virtuous to spread the horrors of war over the face of any country, and too magnanimous and powerful to suffer its existence where she can prevent it. Let us, then, with rapture anticipate the aera [*sic*], when the triumph of peace and the prevalence of virtue shall be rendered secure by the diffusion of useful knowledge.

NOTE

1. Joseph P. McKerns, "Smith, Samuel Harrison"; http://www.anb.org/articles/16/16–01534.html; *American National Biography Online*, February 2000 (accessed on September 18, 2012).

An Essay on the Best System of Liberal Education, Adapted to the Genius of the Government of the United States. Comprehending Also, an Uniform, General Plan for Instituting and Conducting Public Schools, in this Country, on the Principles of the Most Extensive Utility

Samuel Knox

The Reverend Samuel Knox (1756–1832) was born in County Armagh, Ireland, the son of poor farmers. He studied in Dublin, married, and had four children before emigrating to Bladensburg, Maryland, in 1786. There he worked as a master at the local grammar school, publishing poetry in the *Maryland Gazette and Baltimore Advertiser* and Matthew Carey's *American Museum*. In 1789 he enrolled at the University of Glasgow, Scotland, where he earned his MA and received awards for his outstanding scholarship in translation and Latin composition. From 1792 to 1795, Knox moved to Belfast, Ireland, where he received his minister's license from the Belfast Presbytery and preached for a year. He returned to Maryland to work as a minister, while taking the position of head of Frederick Academy from 1797 to 1803. Knox had a penchant for political and religious controversy and, by some accounts, an overbearing personality. After resigning from Frederick Academy, he continued to find work as a supply (interim) minister, publish controversial statements, and for a time, cofounded and presided over the Baltimore College. Just as the college was folding, Thomas Jefferson considered Knox for a founding position at the College (later University) of Virginia in 1817 as "Professor of Languages, Belles Lettres, Rhetoric, History and Geography," at a princely salary. Unfortunately for Knox, by the time he heard of the offer, Jefferson had moved on. Knox returned for a time to Frederick Academy, and continued to teach and publish on educational issues throughout the 1820s.[1]

Section First

Education is the training up of the human mind by the acquisition of sciences calculated to extend its knowledge and promote its improvement. It seldom fails to elevate the powers of the mind above their natural state. According to the attention paid to it, and the plan on which it is conducted, it becomes more or less useful to society, but it seldom fails to improve and elevate the powers of the mind above their natural state.

Though we have been eminently endowed by the great Author of our existence with a structure of body and soul superior to all other animals; yet experience evidently manifests that, without the aid of education, communicated by some means or other, mankind, instead of improving their mental faculties, too soon degenerate to a state of deplorable ignorance...

For a confirmation of this truth, were any necessary, we have only to observe the uninstructed conduct of human life where gross ignorance and barbarism prevail...It would require considerable progress in education, to be able even to describe the difference between the mind of an Esquimaux Indian and the late Benjamin Franklin's; between that of an Hottentot and Sir Isaac Newton's.

It may not require, however, much explanation to delineate its advantages to mankind in general; the most ignorant are in some degree sensible of these, and are often heard to regret the want of means of education or improvement.

From considering the various faculties of the human mind, it would appear that its great author had formed it for a progressive course of improvement. Even in the infantine state curiosity prompts, and that earnestly, to inquiry and knowledge. –The external senses are so many inlets to the treasures of the mind; and are in every respect suited to its most ardent researches, its most industrious application.

During the childhood of life the faculties of the mind have not attained sufficient vigour or maturity for the higher departments of literature, or a close investigation of the more abstruse sciences. During this period, therefore, the study of speech or language is not only the best suited to this state; but is also most proper as a preparation for scientific improvement.

The study of the native language ought to be the leading consideration...

But without a proper knowledge of the learned languages, from which so considerable a share of ours is derived, it is impossible it can be acquired to the highest degree of perfection...

It is a hackneyed argument against classical education, that all the authors in the dead languages, of any eminence, have been translated into English, and consequently that the scholar's time has been ill applied in translating what has been already done...

In many parts of this country, owing either to want of proper seminaries of instruction; to the mistaken fond indulgence of parents; or to both, youth have the greatest part of their education to acquire when it ought to be nearly compleated [*sic*]...Indeed nothing can be more hostile in any country to the interests of the education of youth than the pampered treatment and imprudent fondness of luxurious and indulgent parents. A public, patriotic or general sense of the importance of education may lead to the establishment of proper seminaries, and suggest plans or systems of instruction; but unless these laudable institutions be seconded by the wise authority of parents and guardians, much of their real advantage must be lost to the community.

Section Second

On the Question, Whether Public be Preferable to Private Education

... The enlightened part of the ancient world were no less sensible of the great advantages of public education, than those of the same description in the modern. Though they sometimes encouraged private tuition; yet we find from the reputation of the famous academy at Athens, that public education was most approved. Many are the illustrious characters of antiquity that bear witness to the truth of this observation...

In modern times, also, we find few who of those who have distinguished themselves in the higher walks of science have been educated on some familiar[2] plan. The superior advantages of academical instruction are sufficiently obvious...

Education would diffuse its happy influence to a very contracted extent, indeed, were there no public schools or universities established by national or public encouragement.

... Emulation, with hath so powerful an influence on the human mind, especially in the season of youth, would lose its effects in promoting improvement and the love of excellence, on any other plan than that of the academical. Indeed this consideration alone ought to be sufficiently decisive in its favor.

Granting that something resembling emulation may be excited even on a private plan of education, yet it is manifest that the great variety of abilities and genius which the university or academy exhibits must afford a much greater field for competition; as well as such public and flattering prospects of reward as are the principal incitements to a laudable emulation and love of excellence.

Another argument in favour of academic education is, that such as are tutored in private are apt to form too high an opinion of their own attainments or abilities.

The academic school has, also, the peculiar means of affording youth an opportunity of forming such friendships and connections as often in a literary and interested view contribute eminently to their future prosperity and happiness.

It is true that many object to public plans of education, because that from their situation in populous towns, and the various complexion of the many students who attend, opportunities for corruption, by scenes of vice and examples of debauchery.

... But it requires no very elaborate proof to manifest that the most dangerous temptations to vice more effectually succeed in the private and retired shades of bad example than in the social scene, bustling crowd, or public assembly.

The celebrated Locke himself not excepted, we find very few who have attempted to offer any plausible objections to a public education...who were not themselves indebted to some academical institution even for being qualified to reason on the subject....Upon the whole, it appears that there are many and various arguments in favor of an academical, as preferable to a private education; and that any objections against the former, are almost all, in equal degree, applicable to the latter. One conclusive argument, however, in favor of public education, arises from its becoming an object of national patronage and encouragement. It is from this view that education might be made to assume a still higher degree of importance in its influence on human happiness...

Section Third

The Importance of Establishing a System of National Education

When we take into consideration the many great exertions, and laudable institutions which various commonwealths or nations have devised and adopted for the general benefit, in framing and maintaining wholesome laws and government, it would appear, in some degree, unaccountable that little hath yet been done in promoting some general plan of education equally suitable and salutary to the various citizens of the same state or community.

In our own times and language, we have been favored by ingenious men with several excellent treatises on the subject of education. The greater part of these, however, are rather speculative theories...What has lately been done in France excepted, I know of no plan devised by individuals or attempted by any commonwealth in modern times, that effectually tends to the establishment of any uniform, regular system of national education...

It must be allowed that these remarks may, in some measure, apply to any plan of public education that can possibly be formed. It is not, perhaps, possible to establish any system that can render education equally convenient and equally attainable by every individual of a nation in all their various situations and circumstances.

This observation must be particularly applicable to the condition of the *United States* of America and the widely dispersed situations of their citizens. In undertakings, however, of the first national importance, difficulties ought not to discourage. It does not appear more impracticable to establish a uniform system of national education, than a system of legislation or civil government; provided such a system could be digested as might justly merit, and meet with general approbation.

The good effects of such a system are almost self-evident...

Section Fourth

The Extent of a Plan of National Education considered

In a course or system of national education, there ought to be two, and I think, but two great leading objects to which it should be adapted, *the improvement of the mind, and the attainment of those arts on which the welfare, prosperity and happiness of society depend.*

Education ought to comprehend every science or branch of knowledge that is indispensibly necessary to these important objects. To confine it to a system that comprizes only the knowledge of mechanical, commercial, or lucrative arts, or even a knowledge of the world, as far as it can be attained by literary accomplishments, would be to view its advantages in a very narrow and illiberal light...

...Were the human soul taught to cultivate only the sordid dictates of avarice, or the knowledge of lucrative speculations, soon must that community lose a taste for whatever is most excellent in science, or best calculated to refine & improve the faculties of the mind. Where such a taste hath become prevalent in any state, it... may tend to enervate the patriotism, corrupt the virtue, or contaminate the morals of the community.

The course of education, instituted in the public seminaries, should be adapted to youth in general, whether they be intended for civil or commercial life, or for the learned professions, that of theology alone excepted.

Under this view it would comprehend a classical knowledge of the English, French, Latin and Greek languages, Greek and Roman antiquities, ancient and modern Geography, universal Grammar, Belles Letters, Rhetoric and Composition, Chronology and History; the principles of Ethics, Law and Government; the various branches of the Mathematics and Sciences founded on them; Astronomy; natural and experimental Philosophy in all their various departments. To which course also, at proper stages, ought to be added the ornamental accomplishments Drawing, Painting, Fencing and Musick.

It is a happy circumstance peculiarly favorable to an uniform plan of public education, that this country hath excluded ecclesiastical from civil policy, and emancipated the human mind from the tyranny of church authority; and church establishments. It is in consequence of this principle of our happy civil constitution, that Theology, as far as the study of it is connected with particular forms of faith, ought to be excluded from a liberal system of national instruction, especially where there exist so many various denominations among the professors of the christian religion. The establishment of education on some national or public plan would not prevent the several religious denominations from instituting, under proper instructors, Theological schools for such as were intended for the ministry, after their academical course has been compleated at the public seminaries. One institution of this kind, in each state, for each particular denomination... might be sufficient.

Section Fifth

On the Establishment of the Various Schools Necessary to Compleat A System of National Education

Provisionary laws being obtained for establishing an uniform system of literary instruction, under the proper sanction and authority of the nation, the first important object would appear to be the organization of proper schools and seminaries.

These should be arranged and situated in such a manner as most impartially to diffuse their advantages to the greatest possible extent, and also to afford the means of enabling all the attending youth to rise gradually from the first rudiments to the highest departments of knowledge and science.

In a liberal course of public education, no one stage ought to be better provided for than another, in whatever may best contribute to its success. From the elementary or grammar school up to the university... it should be considered, supported, and encouraged as constituting one entire system...

For the first stage... let parish schools, in each county of every state, be established at a suitable distance from each other and endowed with a few acres of land and a proper house...

Secondly, let the next stage consist of county schools or academies endowed also, and furnished as the parish schools, but on a much more extensive plan, hereafter explained.

Thirdly, let this stage of instruction consist of state colleges as already instituted and endowed in the several states of the union, but so regulated and organized as to fall in with the general uniform system.

Lastly, let the literary establishments be compleated by the institution of a national university...

... The greatest difficulty in a country so thinly inhabited in many places as this, would be dividing the counties in each state into parishes or townships, so as to render the situation of the schools convenient to all the inhabitants. Each state in the union being already laid out into counties, less difficulty would arise concerning the county academies. And with regard to the state colleges and university, it is a favourable circumstance towards carrying this plan into effect, that many of the former have already been founded, and that the idea of the latter also seems to meet with public approbation.

Hitherto, however, this country, one or two states excepted, seems to have fallen in with the error of many even of the most enlightened countries of the world; and that is, in providing or endowing most liberally a few seminaries for the completion of education; while the elementary, which most required the fostering hand of public bounty, has been left to support itself as chance or circumstances, sometimes the most adverse, might dictate.

In order to found... the several seminaries, let *a board of education* be incorporated, under the sanction of the united authority of the states. These gentlemen should be nominated and appointed in every state, either by the united government, or by the respective state assemblies: one or two in each state might be sufficient.... They might very properly be styled "Presidents of literary instruction and Members of the board of national education."

The attention, however, of one president would be inadequate to the superintendence of all the seminaries in one state.... There ought to be a rector appointed for each county in the state. The duty of those rectors should be, to assist in procuring proper tutors; visit every school in the respective counties, and, at least twice a year, to make a just report of their state and proficiency, and number of the students or scholars... The county rector should also attend quarterly the public examination of the primary schools, or at least twice a year, with such other local trustees or visitors as might be thought necessary. On those occasions there ought to be a catalogue of the youth produced by the master of each school, specifying their time of entrance and proficiency, leaving a vacant column to mark their progress between each successive examination...

The board of education, and consequently the whole community, by the assistance of such rectors, would be thus enabled to see the true state of literary instruction in every part of the union, at least every six months, and whether there existed any obstruction to its prosperity, either through a deficiency of proper teachers or any other cause, they would have the advantage of knowing where the defect lay.

The greatest apparent obstruction to the establishment of a uniform plan of national instruction consists in the difficulty of procuring proper tutors, well qualified and disposed to carry into effect the system laid down to them by the board. As much as possible, the salaries of the various teachers ought to be liberal, and fully equal to what men of their qualifications could make in any other department of business suited to their circumstances. The commodiousness and comfortable state of the houses built for both the primary schools and the county academies, endowed also with a suitable tract of land, would be a very great inducement, and the price of tuition for each scholar, or the fixed salary, whichever of these modes of payment the board might approve, would thus be rendered more moderate, at least to posterity.

SECTION SIXTH

On the Advantage of Introducing the Same uniform system of School-Books into a Plan of Public Education

One great inconvenience attending even the present mode of education consists in the scanty supply of the best editions of school-books, that is to be met in many parts of the United States. The great diversity, also, especially of the elementary books in education, serves much to distract and retard its success. Every teacher has his favorite system, and consequently the books best adapted to it are only those which he recommends. But in the present state of literary instruction, as there are few tutors who compleat the scholar even on their own system,[3] he is often not only under the disagreeable and injurious necessity of studying over again what he has learned, but also perplexed with the diversified editions or translations of the same author.

...There ought to be a Printer in each State, for the express purpose of supplying the various seminaries, in their respective states, with school-books and other literary publications, as should be recommended or directed by the Board of education.

It might not, probably, be found necessary to extend these regulations to the National University, at least, in their strictest terms.

Section Seventh

On the Establishment and Conduct of the Parish or Primary Schools.

In order to conduct Education on the best plan, it is necessary that the community be so convinced of its importance, as cheerfully to furnish every accommodation....The houses for the parish schools in each county should be sufficiently spacious for the use of the teacher's family and also to accommodate one hundred scholars....The best method for seating a room for this purpose is, to have it laid out into small single pews, somewhat similar to those common in churches; one rising a little higher than another...so as that the pupils would all sit with their faces to the teacher, having before them a desk suited either for the purpose of reading on, or writing. One of these pews might accommodate a different class, and being numbered, each class would, without confusion, regularly place themselves in their own pew.

Every such Primary school should be supplied with a teacher for every thirty, or at most, thirty-five pupils; and if it were be found necessary that they should consist of both sexes, the pews would be found useful in helping to preserve that delicacy and reserve which they should be early taught to preserve towards each another. Where, however, it can be done, it will constantly be found eligible to have girls educated separately under a mistress.

... It would constitute a very essential improvement if the teacher's wife could assist in the charge and education of such girls as attended, and particular encouragement ought to be held out to such teachers of the Primary schools as could be so qualified. Indeed it should be almost indispensible that the head-master of every school be a married man.

In the primary schools the course of instruction should be confined to a proper knowledge of the English language; writing, arithmetick and practical mathematics, compleated by some approved compend [sic] of history and geography.

From these seminaries should be excluded not only Latin, but also the French language, excepting for those whose education was not be extended to a higher stage of the course...namely the County Academies...

With regard to impressing youth early with the principles of religion and morality: However important this may be, yet, on account of preserving that liberty of conscience in religious matters which various denominations of christians in these states justly claim, due regard ought to be paid to this in a course of publick instruction.

It would, however, appear to be no infringement of this liberty in its widest extent for the publick teacher to begin and end the business of the day with a short and suitable prayer and address to the great source of all knowledge and instruction.

It might also be highly advantageous to youth, and in no respect interfere with the different religious sentiments of the community, to make use of a well-digested, concise moral catechism.

In each of these schools, at least three promising boys, whose parents could not afford to educate them, should be admitted at the expense of the parish or township to which the school belonged. The condition on which these boys should be received ought to be, that their parents should agree to have them be educated for the purpose of becoming teachers...A few of them who most distinguished themselves on publick examination, should be admitted to the county academies, and afterwards to the state colleges and university. This, in the course of a few years, would train up a proper supply of tutors, both masters and assistants for the different seminaries, and at the same time extend the blessings of literary instruction to hundreds who would otherwise be deprived of it.

SECTION EIGHTH. ON THE COUNTY ACADEMIES

The [Academy] houses...should be capacious, well designed and accommodated to the purpose. Besides the apartments necessary for at least two masters and their families, there ought to be, at least, two Halls for teaching, two Dining-rooms and two Dormitories, with an assistant's lodging-room to open into each, one for the Juniors and another for the Seniors.

Without entering more minutely into the plan of a suitable academy-house, it may only be observed farther, in general terms, that it should be sufficiently capacious to contain all the youth in the county, whose parents or guardians inclined to give them a classical and thorough mathematical education. They should be built...to contain at least two hundred, or two hundred and fifty students.

In this country, owing to chiefly to the precarious supply of schools and the scattered situations of the inhabitants, the childhood of life is too often passed ere the parents think seriously of the education of their children...The time allotted to the primary schools should elapse at the twelfth year of age; at least of all such as were intended for being admissible into the county academies; such as were not, should be continued till the age of fourteen. At the age of eight, even in rural or scattered situations, it would be sufficiently late to enter the primary school, and the space of four years would be a competent term to compleat the course...

The proficiency of the students who had compleated their three years' course at the Academy as here laid down, should consist, in addition to what they had acquired at the primary school, in a tolerable knowledge of the Latin and Greek languages, so as to translate with propriety and ease wither prose or verse, to be able to write Latin, if not classically, at least grammatically; a like knowledge of the French language; a tolerable acquaintance with ancient and modern history, geography, with such a knowledge prosody, Greek and Roman antiquities, rhetoric, criticism and composition, as it necessary to read the classicks with propriety and taste.

In addition to the rudiments of Mathematics previously acquired, they should by this time have also attained a thorough knowledge of Euclid's elements, at least of the first[,] six and the eleventh and twelth [*sic*] books; Conic sections, Algebra with its application to Geometry, and plain and spheric Trigonometry. Such students as were to be prepared for immediate business, and, as already suggested, not intended for the State college, might receive a less scientific course of mathematics, so that they could devote more of their studies to the useful or practical branches. It might be necessary that such continue a year longer at the County Academy.

Of the three boys admitted into each of the primary schools, at the expense of the publick, on compleating their course, each County Academy should receive at least five of such as discovered the best genius for literary instruction, on the conditions formerly specified. But it would be best to have it entirely unknown to the students in general, or even to these youths themselves, at least in this stage of their progress, what were the terms of their admittance...Five of such pupils, admitted into each County Academy in the state, and selected from those who discovered the best abilities and most amiable dispositions throughout the different parish schools, would, as has been already hinted, train up an adequate number of teachers to supply every vacancy in the whole system....By admitting such as discovered the brightest genius into the State College and National University, an ample field would be offered even the poorest in society, for exertion in literary improvement and the attainment of whatever can tend to call forth the most distinguished merit, equally conducive to their own happiness and that of the community.

Section Ninth

On Exercises of Amusement during the terms of Relaxation from Study.

Previous to entering on the subject of the State Colleges, it may be proper to make a few observations on the manner in which the youth should conduct themselves in the hours of relaxation.

During these hours they are indeed seldom at a loss for subjects or exercises of entertainment. Some of these, however, are certainly more eligible than others, and have a greater or less tendency to give the mind a frivolous or effeminate bias on the one hand, or if well chosen, a manly and vigorous resolution on the other. All playful exercises of the latter cast, if moderately indulged, are salutary to youth. Swimming is an almost indispensible qualification...On every species of gambling they should be taught to look with not only contempt, but abhorrence, and to view all exercises perverted by that spirit as the seminaries of corruption...

Section Tenth

On the State Colleges.

As has been elsewhere observed, it is a favorable circumstance for the establishment of an uniform plan of National Education, that in almost every State of the Union, a college has been instituted on a liberal scale.

It does not appear that it could operate contrary to the interests of those colleges to adopt an uniform plan of Education under the direction of a Literary Board...The privilege however of attending any State College the parents might prefer, could not, consistently with the claims of natural liberty, be denied...and also the terms of admittance, both with regard to the proficiency of the pupils and the prices of boarding and tuition, should be perfectly the same throughout the different Colleges.

... [Students] from the County Academies...ought to be admitted only on the following considerations:—

First, That they should have previously gone through the course of education prescribed by the Primary school and County academy; or if instructed by private tuition, that their progress should be equal to, and on the same plan with, such as were taught at those seminaries.

Secondly, That none, educated either publickly or privately, should be admitted but such as on public examination, give satisfaction both in their classical and mathematical proficiency.

Thirdly, That all students in the State Colleges should at least be intended for a triennial course which, as nearly as possible, ought to be from the close of the fifteenth till the expiration of the eighteenth year of their age.

This course of literary instruction should be suitably and progressively adapted to the time or number of years. During the first year's session the studies of each day should be divided between the Greek, Latin and French languages, and mathematics.... The elementary parts of mathematicks being acquired at the Academy, during this session the students should be introduced to the most useful practical branches, comprehending mensuration of various kinds, surveying and navigation, gunnery and fortification.

In order that the students in the State Colleges should have time to mix a little in society, see their friends and know something of the world as well as books, the vacation between each session should be extended to a longer duration than in the primary school, or county academy...

In the second session of this course, the students in their morning house should compleat their course of classical reading and criticism during the first half of the session, and in the other half be introduced to a concise view of rhetoric, logic and moral philosophy, during the forenoon studies; and continue through the whole of their course in the evening hours the compleat attainment of mathematicks, and particularly in this session geography by the use of the globes; the laws of motion, the mechanical powers, and the principles of astronomy...

On the opening of the third and last session...the students would be prepared for turning the chief part of their attention to Natural Philosophy.

A concise system of it, in all its parts, should be taught experimentally during this session, at least for two hours each day, and a suitable apparatus should be provided for this purpose. Each State College should also have an observatory and a proper apparatus for making astronomical observations.

Occasionally during this session the proper professors should continue lectures on the various branches formerly acquired; and each student designed for the National University should be prepared for taking a Bachelor of Arts' degree...

... In order to promote the interests of, and give greater dignity to, the National University, no degree higher than that of Bachelor of Arts should be conferred at any of the State Colleges...

SECTION ELEVENTH

On the National University.

There appears to be no subject on which a great, extensive, and enlightened, Commonwealth could with more propriety and justice exhibit, even to some degree of excess, its munificence, than in founding, endowing and supporting a suitable seat of national improvement in literature and erudition.

... A National university, placed at the head of the foregoing plan, and connected with every branch or seminary of the general system, would tend, not only to finish or consummate the whole literary course, but also confer upon it that national dignity and importance, which such a combination of public patronage and interest would justly expect and merit. It would thus constitute the fountain head of science, that center to which all literary genius of the commonwealth would tend; and from which, when matured by its instructive influence, would diffuse rays of knowledge and science to the remotest situations of the United government.

The local situation of the National University ought to be centrical, and well chosen with regard to healthiness and convenience. It might be of advantage in some respects to it, to be contiguous to the seat of government, in order that the youth, having an opportunity of occasionally seeing the Grand Council of the nation, should be animated by that patriotism, which they in turn might on a future day be called upon to exercise for their country.

Their contiguity also to the collected wisdom and respectability of the legislative body might, when considering themselves as almost situated under their inspection, be the means of enciting them to that laudable emulation which is so conducive to literary improvement.

But tho' it might be most eligible that the situation of such a seminary be contiguous to the seat of government, it does not appear that it ought to be within the confines of a great or populous city. In these in general, there abound too many scenes of seduction, too many examples of profligacy, and too many opportunities of vicious corruption. A few miles from such a city and also from the seat of government might occasionally afford all the advantages of both...

The university buildings, in magnitude and style of architecture, ought to be suitable in every respect to the important purposes for which they were designed, and also to the character and dignity of the nation.

The buildings should also comprehend a house for a Publick Library, a Museum, and also proper apartments for those who taught the ornamental arts, especially a Hall for Painting, another for Musick, and a third for Statuary....A Printer of the very first abilities and reputation...should be furnished with proper accommodations for carrying on that business, and...should keep a book-shop well supplied with such books and stationary as would be necessary for the students attending the University.

... On the most central part of the buildings a magnificent steeple should be erected with a proper bell. On the top should be a cupola or dome fit for an Observatory, and sufficiently large to admit of an Astronomical apparatus in the first style of improvement.

... Here also should be a Botanical garden, containing a house for the gardener, and a summerhouse hall for the purpose of lecturing upon that science. A building for a chemical laboratory and lecturing hall should be also erected in this enclosure, as being better secured against accidents than if connected with the University buildings.

The faculty of the National University should be an incorporated body, invested with proper authority to make laws and regulations respecting the government of the University and for preserving peace and order through all its departments. There ought to be a Professor of classical learning or belles letters and composition; a professor of Latin and Roman antiquities; a professor of Greek and Greek antiquities; a professor of Hebrew and Oriental languages; a professor of rhetoric, logic, and moral philosophy; a professor of natural philosophy; a professor of mathematicks; a professor of astronomy; a professor of history and chronology; a professor of law and the principles of government, and a professor of elocution and oratory. Besides these, the various professors in the medical department, and also the various ornamental arts, would compose that respectable faculty to whom the important charge of this seminary should be entrusted under the direction of the Literary Board.

It would appear most eligible that none of the faculty of the National University, whether principals or professors, should be clergymen of any denomination; or if they were, that they should suspend every clerical function during their being members of that body and devote themselves solely to their office.

The whole faculty should, with the utmost solemnity, attend on divine service, in a body, and an elevated and respectable pew should be provided for this, as on other publick occasions.

Agreeably to the uniform plan here laid down, students entering the University at the expiration of the eighteenth year of their age, would have finished their course at the end of the twenty first; and thus at the age of maturity would be prepared for acting their part on the theatre of the world.

CONCLUSION

In every country possessed of genuine freedom and impressed with a just sense of its value, nothing can be more worthy of public attention than an improvement in the means of publick instruction.— Wherever scientific knowledge is generally cultivated, there must the dignity and rights of man be best known and, consequently, not only the most highly valued, but also the best secured from corruption, and most ably maintained and vindicated from encroachment and usurpation.

But in order to [do] this it is necessary that the system of education should be generally suited to the citizens; that it should comprehend every description of situation and circumstance, uncircumscribed by partial endowments, local prejudices, or personal attachments.

NOTES

1. Ashley Foster, "Samuel Knox, Maryland Educator," *Maryland Historical Magazine* 50:3 (September 1955): 173–194; Wilson Smith, "Knox, Samuel": http://www.anb.org/articles/09/09–00417.html; American National Biography Online, February 2000 (accessed on September 18, 2012).
2. That is, family-based, or private.
3. In other words, due to high teacher turnover, rarely does one tutor provide a student with his complete education.

Review of Essay No. 3, "A Letter to the American Philosophical Society in Answer to their First Prize Question."

Though we will never know for certain, the author of essay No. 3 was probably William Smith (1727–1803).[1] Smith was born near Aberdeen, in the Eastern Highlands of Scotland, to Scottish Episcopal parents. A precocious boy, Smith attended parish and charity schools before attending the University at Aberdeen. He did not complete his degree at that time, but moved to London to work for charity organizations and publish essays, including at least two on education. In 1751 Smith emigrated to America, where his writings caught the attention of Benjamin Franklin, who recruited him to work at his Academy of Philadelphia. Together with Franklin, Smith transformed the Academy into the College and later University of Pennsylvania, serving as provost from 1756 to 1779, and again from 1789 to 1791. (In the decade in between, he served as the first president of Washington College in Maryland, which he hoped would function as the nation's leading university.) As an educational leader, Smith was a brilliant thinker who encouraged religious toleration and nondenominational ethics. Yet personally he could be quarrelsome and was allegedly overfond of his drink. Politically, his attachment to the Penn family before the revolution, and Loyalist leanings during it, made him many enemies. When the University of Pennsylvania consolidated in 1791, Smith was purposefully excluded.

The peer-review for essay No. 3 was a disaster. Initially, William Smith was assigned to the review committee. With no dignified way out (Smith was not known for his social skills anyway), he delayed his committee indefinitely until, finally, they were forced to replace him. At some point Smith's authorship seems to have become an open secret. A year later, when the APS convened a special committee to consider the propriety of a second essay contest, the group proposed new, unusually specific set of rules: that one single committee be elected to review all essay entries, "that no Member who intends to write upon the judgment, as a candidate for the premium, accept ... a seat in the Committee," and that "any member of the Committee who wishes to decline serving, must resign within two months after the election."[2] When essay No. 3 did not win, it was delivered in care of tavern keeper Alex Moore, as its author had instructed. It has never resurfaced. What follows is the peer review of essay No. 3.

↝   ↝   ↝

REPORT OF THE COMMITTEE APPOINTED TO MAKE AN ANALYSIS OF THE THIRD PIECE ON EDUCATION, SUBMITTED FOR THE PREMIUM.1797, JULY 23

The Committee appointed to examine the Communication No. 3 relative to the best System of liberal Education etc. respectfully present the following analysis of that Performance.—

The author introduces the Subject with this Remark.—That "if on the national Character of a People always depends their prosperity or decline, the great and first object of their Legislature should be to establish a Character on a the permanent basis of public Virtue and Industry." —Hence he proceeds to contemplate (as the principle objects of public Instruction), Morality, and the Arts and Sciences.—

"Hitherto," he says, "Morality was ever considered as inseparable from the principles of Religion" — "and because the Religion of the sacred Legislator seemed to comprehend the most pure and sublime moral truths, we scarcely attempted to impress the minds of our Children with any moral notions distinct from those of Christianity." —He acknowledges however that "If Christianity were uniform, it would be difficult to adopt in Politics a better code of morality than that of an universal Christian Religion." But, he affirms, "that the perpetual practice in all Sects to teach no other morals to their youth than those of their own creed, introduces dangerous effects, foments divisions amongst mankind, and subjects liberal and solid sentiments to religious prejudices." He concludes therefore that "if the Legislature wish to establish a perfect plan of moral instruction, they should propose a code that will no longer keep alive those religious prejudices among the different Sects."—

"After morality, the objects to which public Education should be chiefly directed are those of the Arts and Sciences which contribute to the progress of national Industry; the preservation of life, the internal order of Society, and the individual happiness of every citizen." —

"National Instruction should then embrace all the Arts and Sciences which are immediately useful to the Wants and Conditions of Life." The author then proceeds "to establish certain principles which would insure the Success of national improvement

1st. The ascertainment of the advantage of Education to every citizen from the most obscure to the most opulent.

2ndly. The choice of those arts and sciences which have a direct influence on the welfare of Society.

3rdly. Conferring Honors and Rewards due to mental abilities.

4thly. The uniformity of public Instruction.

"The first object would be attainable if the Children of the poor were educated in central and primary free Schools. In these Schools should be taught the elements of national Language, Arithmetic, morality, and a general description of the terrestrial Globe. The degrees of instruction acquired in the primary schools might accomplish the task of Education imposed on the laboring class of our fellow citizens." —

"The number of our Pupils will be naturally diminished in the second class of public Schools, which become central. They equally admit scholars who pursue a course of literature and eloquence, and others devoted to the Sciences that belong to commerce, navigation, the liberal and mechanical Arts. The learning of the central Schools should comprize the ancient and modern Languages, the belles Letters, Eloquence and a course of Philosophy."— "Philosophy is and should be considered as a rational Science, it embraces all nature, its Phenomena and Laws." "We should not enter on the Science of Nature without first paying due homage to the Supreme Creator who established its Laws."—["]As the first part of Philosophy should comprehend a religious Treatise on the Principles of Nature, Let us begin by fixing the attention of our Pupils on the majesty of the Supreme Being, and impress their minds with all that proclaims his existence.

"The History of Superstition (continues the author) inspires horror and disgust of error: We shall respect all modes of faith, but we hope by shedding the general influence of instruction on the mind, that the gloom of error will soon disperse among those who are guided by reason and a Love of Truth. – On such solid Foundations we shall establish with Security the principles of eternal and universal morality, which should be the private rule of the actions of men, as Justice, which determines the Rights of Nations, is the basis of their Laws, their Dignity and their prosperity. Such is the Path we should follow in Philosophy; all its other branches become general, and furnish those Subjects which relate to the different professions of Life."

["]A great national university in the Capital of the Union should complete the national Instruction."

"This Plan of national instruction would realize our Ideas of Success if it combined the rewards of merit with the honors thereof."

"The last object to be proposed in the System of national Education to insure the Success thereof would be to render it so uniform, that even all those States which are independent of one another, would form one extensive and combined family."—

"This principle (of Union) involves the fate of Nations, but this union can only result from a proper System of uniform education." —

After this Introduction to his Plan, which is amplified, in an animated Style, to the extent of 29 Pages, the Author proceeds to particularize the different Seminarys[:] their Constitutions, and Rules. In this he inverts the order of his Introduction, and begins with a Federal Institution.

Article 1. a Corporation of Learned Individuals, at least

2. 30 years of age, and to be chosen as Members of Congress are chosen.

3. Each State to send in Reproportions of 1 to every 4 Members of Congress.

4. The Delagates to meet yearly at the Seat of Government, in October and November. —

5. The Delagates shall meet during the interval for concerting such measures as may be for the advantage of Education.

6. The Federal Institution shall Superintend all the Primary Schools in the United States. — They may institute exercises and adjudge honorary Titles and Diplomas to the Learned of all nations.

7. They shall elect in each State a public Director or Provost.

8. —Relates to the internal arrangement of the Federal Institution

9. Their Resolutions shall be called Acts and have the Force of Law in the Union after being approved by the President and Senate U. S.

10. They shall regulate expenses, Salaries to Professors etc., also realize all acquisitions of Property.

11. They shall provide Library, Collections of natural Curiosities, Botanic Gardens etc. etc. etc.

12. The members may be elected twice in 6 years.

13. They shall make a Catechism or Treatise on universal morality adapted to the use of the national Schools; and shall regulate the Objects and Degrees of Study etc—

NATIONAL UNIVERSITY

Art. 1. In the Seat of Federal Government for the purpose of teaching the Arts and Sciences and conferring Degrees.

2. The President and Professors to be chosen by the Federal Institution and supported at the expence of the United States.

3. Discribes the Schools and Courses of Education.

4. The President and Professors may consult on internal Regulations, but otherwise they shall conform to the Acts of the Federal Institution. —

5. The Professors shall grant Certificates of literary attainments to the President who shall after examinations require Degrees or Diplomas from the Committee of the Institution.

6. The Schools of the University shall be open to all Citizens of the Union for an annual Sum not exceeding 20 Dollars.

7. This Course of Studies and Schools shall be free to any individual who shall obtain a priviledge gratis from the Provost of his State.

CENTRAL SCHOOLS.—

Art. 1. To be established by the State Government and within their own Circuit, and shall comprehend classical Learning and the education of Children.

2. They shall comprise the second period of national Instruction.

3. Their Principal objects are[:] One or two ancient, and several modern Languages, Eloquence or Retoreck. Penmanship, the Sciences adapted

to Navigation and Commerce, Geography, Astronomy History and Philosophy.—Then Branches to be divided into 2 Classes, the one limited, the other extended.—

4. The Professors and Teachers shall be chosen and Supported by their respective State Governments.—

5. There should be provision for a public and annual Course of natural Philosophy, and experimental Chemistry in each capital City.

6. In the Central Schools there may be Refectories or Academies for the accommodation of the Students.—

PRIMARY SCHOOLS.

Art. 1. Shall be established in all parts of the Union under the immediate authority of Corporations or Justices of the Peace and shall comprehend the first part of the education of young people and Children of all Sects may be received in them.

2. The primary Schools shall be inspected by the Provost delegated by the Federal Institution

3. No master nor mistress shall keep a primary School until they shall have sworn to observe the Rules enjoined by the Federal Institution.

4. The Language of the Country, Reading, writing Arithmetic and the Elements of universal morality, shall be the objects of Instruction.

4. The Provosts shall annually distribute premiums and annually render and account of the State and progress of improvement to the Federal Institution.[3]

ADDITIONAL ARTICLES.—

1. The universities now established may be the Central Schools

2. The Federal Institution shall give a Preference to the Professors actually employed in the State universitys.

3. The Mistresses shall rank with the Professors of the Central Schools. —

4. Learned Bodies, such as the Philosophical Societys, Colleges of Physicians etc may send one or more Deputies to the Federal Institution.—

Having gone through the detail of the Plan in all its parts, the Author returns to the Federal Institution which he considers as "the Centre of that enlightening wisdom which must at all times regulate the Labour of Education." —And he expresses his "utmost wish, and ardent hope that his part of the System may not appear objectionable."—He concludes by reminding the Society that " the great Washington himself" in his Speech to Congress introduces public Education, and recommends a National University to the Representatives of the People.

The foregoing is the Substance of a Work containing 47 Pages, and in order to enable the Society to judge of the fidelity of this analysis, References are made to the Several Pages from which Extracts have been taken. —In performing the Task assigned them, Your Committee have thought it their

Duty to exhibit the Principles and Plan of the Author, as nearly as possible, in his own language; and that these may appear in the finest point of view, they withhold every sentiment of applause or censure.

Committee Moreau De St. Mery
James Abercrombie
Jon Williams
Philadelphia, July 23 1797.
Read Nov. 17, 1797

NOTES

1. See chapters 2 and 3 in this volume.
2. APS, Report of the Committee appointed to consider the propriety of offering a premium for the best essay on the subject of education, February 15, 1799.
3. The original document contains two number fours in the list.

On Education and Public Schools

Hiram

Hiram was Francis Hoskins, which we know beyond a doubt from handwriting comparison. Hoskins was working as a clerk at the Philadelphia Rolls Office (which recorded deeds) in 1797, but by 1802 was listed in the city directory as an accountant. A prolific and eclectic writer whose ambitions outweighed his abilities, Hoskins entered and lost APS contests twice: in 1797 for education (which was ridiculed by the review committee), and in 1800 for navigation. In 1801 Hoskins mailed President Thomas Jefferson a handwritten table that calculated the value of the planet earth if it were made of solid gold, including a separate table that calculated the compound interest on one dollar at 5 percent per annum from 10 to 1,325 years. He did not get a reply.[1] Hoskins published at least two books: an undated math textbook he refers to in his essay, entitled *An Introduction to Merchandise. Arithmetick. In whole and broken numbers, designed for the use of Academies...*, and *The Beauties and Super-excellency of Freemasonry Attempted (1801)*. The latter book reflected the probable origins of his pseudonym: Hiram Abiff was a key figure in Masonic Lore.

To the Worthy and learned, the President, Vice President and Members of the Philosophical Society at Philadelphia

The Author has the presumption to lay the Inclosed before your Respectable Society, hope it may meet your favour and Esteem. Any Gratuity ordered for the present and future Work, if required will be thankfully Received by Gentlemen. Your very humble servant.   —Hiram—
January 2, 1797. —

Dedicated to the President, Vice President, and Members of the American Philosophical Society at Philadelphia. —

The Manuscript will be sent in Numbers, to that learned body of Men, for their Approbation and Support. The whole will be compleated as soon as possible.

A Plan,
for the Establishing Schools etc.
Advantageous to Masters and Scholars

1st. To provide each Master with a commodious lightsome school-house, with lodging rooms, or apartments, in or convenient to said house, a garden and some land to graze cattle on. If a single man, he can let his land. If he has a family, the land will be of great benefit to him. In either case he can instruct his pupils, at one third or one fourth less than the usual charge or else to instruct or teach, one third of his Scholars gratis, (or a certain specified number of orphans, and the children of the poorest inhabitants) by the recommendation of the principal inhabitants assembled for that purpose.

2nd. A Master can teach 30 or 40 Scholars, if he has more he cannot do them all Justice, and should provide an Usher. I know a Master, when his Scholars increased to more in number, than he could instruct, and not being able to hire an Usher, chose two of his best Scholars to assist him, who spent half their school hours, instructing the younger Scholars under his view, whereby they gave great assistance to their Master and the young Scholars learned as well as from their Master, who at certain times examined and taught them also. The two youths, improved by instructing others, and the time they had left for study, they improved with Care and diligence. And the master gave them every proper indulgence, the use of his books and instructions after school hours. Whereby in a short time by Application and Study became better Scholars, than their Master, which he to his credit acknowledged.

3rd. A Master should cause a list of his Scholars, to be called over every morning to mark the absent, and see those who come are clean, and in proper order. To those who learn most and best, some small premiums ought to be given. At other times half an hour's indulgence, to amuse themselves at some innocent recreation, same time to have a Watchful Eye over them.

4th. No Vacation, but in Winter, when the days are short, and weather severe.

5th. To encourage improvements, any Master who should make any useful improvement on his land, at his promotion, or Death, he or his Heirs shall be intitled, to one half of the money so expended, from his successor, within the space of one year.

6th. A few copper plate copy books would be very useful, and as all the scholars cannot have such books, as are requisite, and Useful, the Master ought to have some to teach by and lend to them in Want.— Spelling books are very useful—for if a Youth cannot spell well, he cannot read or write well. (To such as can afford it) Sheridan's Dictionary for pronunciation, is recommended. The new Dictionary, which is to be printed in this city, in weekly numbers, called the Encyclopedia (the Circle of Sciences and the Round of learning) Also the American Library being a Compendium of Knowledge— instruction and entertainment And also a new System of Arithmetick, for the Use of Schools adapted to the trade of the United States, in particular, and the World in General, by Hiram

(whose Name, and place of Residence will be given with the last number of the Work)—or sooner if required—

Another Plan for Establishing Schools in the United States.

In every Country Town to provide the Schoolmaster with an house and land value 25£ currency per year, for which he should instruct 10 or 12 children gratis every year, about one fourth of his Scholars, that if he received 75£ annually for the rest of his Scholars he would be well paid (about 100£ a year). To encourage improvements of every kind, if any Master should build or make an addition to his house, plant an orchard or improve his land, the expense not exceeding 100£, as he is only a tenant during life or pleasure, his successor in office should pay him or his Heirs, half his disbursements not exceeding 50£ within the space of one year. Or if the Country paid the money for him he should teach 4 or 5 children in addition to the former. Hiram

Philadelphia, Dec. 30, 1796

Note

1. The Thomas Jefferson Papers Series 1. General Correspondence. 1651–1827. Francis Hoskins to Thomas Jefferson, June 29, 1801. Tables on Globe Statistics: http://memory.loc.gov/cgi-bin/ampage?collId=mtj1&fileName =mtj1page024.db&recNum=53.

A Plan for the Education of Youth

Academicus

Academicus was a popular pseudonym in eighteenth-century English and American periodicals, used in connection with educational issues. In this case, Academicus was probably John Hobson, a Unitarian minister from Birmingham, England. Hobson fled Birmingham after the anti-Priestley riots of 1791, in which a mob burned down his church and home. Afterward Priestley and Hobson both left England for America, although it is clear from his absence in Priestley's correspondence that they were not close, and it is unlikely that they traveled together. In fact, Hobson's fondness for publishing inflammatory letters may have fanned the flames that drove them both to America. Priestly complained to a friend in 1788, "It often happens that friends give us more concern than enemies. I now fulfil my promise in sending you Mr Hobson's letter and my answer. He is a man similar to Mr Palmer but without his learning."[1]

In Philadelphia, Hobson apparently struggled to start a school, working as a tutor and, according to city directories, a grocer. In addition to writing inflammatory essays on political and religious toleration, Hobson wrote two essays on education before the APS contest. His "Academicus" entry in in 1797, which he admits is written in haste, seems to have been an intellectual exercise. Two years later, he donated a more polished, published education essay to the APS, entitled *"Prospectus of a Plan of Instruction, for the Young of Both Sexes, Including a Course of Liberal Instruction for Each."* He never completed the second part, for girls.

January 13, 1797

Sir,

It gave the subscriber a very particular satisfaction to see a Notification of May last, by order of the Philosophical Society of Philadelphia, proposing a premium for the best production of a system of liberal education etc. Your learned body having viewed it, as an object worthy your attention & recommendation, it is hoped, will prove the means of producing some plan worthy of the public approbation and patronage. The design of collecting and communicating a few thoughts for that purpose, was formed, on reading your publication; but hurry of business, arising from daily occupation, prevented its execution, untill the time limited for receiving communications was elapsed. The hope of reward was no motive with the writer, but merely the desire of offering a mite to the advancement of so important a cause; and if the enclosed hints, may in any measure prove useful to that end, his highest wishes will be fully gratified.

He is sorry to communicate them in so crude a state, but through want of time to transcribe and correct, they are submitted, such as they are, to the candid inspection of the worthy and learned Society by their very humble servant

Academicus

P.S. As there is no view to a compensation for the premium, there is no need of explaining the signature—

January 7, 13, 1797

Plan for the Education of Youth
A Few Outlines of a Plan for the Education of Youth Submitted to the Candid Inspection of The Philosophical Society of Philadelphia by Academicus

Read March 10, 1797

The object of a liberal education is the improvement of the human mind, so as to render it a source of happiness to itself, and of usefulness to others. A competent knowledge of its own nature and powers; the rank it possesses in the scale of being; and the various relations and obligations thence arising is necessary to this end.— The general circle of arts and sciences embraces these objects, and directs our purposes to their attainment.

But, in order to attain the knowledge of any art, or science, we might begin with its first rudiments, or most plain and easy principles. Language may be said to be the <u>First principle</u> of all knowledge.— We receive and communicate our ideas by it, and cloath them in it. An accurate knowledge of language, therefore, is necessary, as a first principle of education—

Words are the first elements of language; and syllables and letters, of words.— These are taught and learned, merely mechanically, by the impulse, or motion of the organs of speech. Their combination in sentences, so as to express thoughts, or convey sentiments by them with propriety, requires a further knowledge of their grammatical disposition, agreeably to the idiom of the language we use. In the common use of a vernacular tongue, we pay little attention, for the most part, to the rules of grammar, in arranging our words.— We learn by custom, the common mode of expression, and structure sentences, so far as to communicate our ideas intelligibly, and understand others by them, and this is all which by most people, is thought necessary. But whoever would acquire an accurate knowledge of any language, must pay a particular attention to its idiom, and what is called its <u>Minutia</u>.

The idiom of a language is that specific difference whereby it is distinguished from all others, and constitutes its proper standard.— In the phraseology of the english, we find such a coincidence with so many others, that it can scarcely be said to have any certain idiom, or fixed standard. It certainly has none in itself. The same thing may be said with respect to every other living language; especially amongst a people progressing in arts and knowledge. It is ever fluctuating; old phrases becoming obsolete; and new ones, either coined, or bouroughed from other languages, taking their places. Hence we see the best english writers, Milton, Pope, Young, Addison, Temple etc. arraigned daily, and condemned at the bar of modern grammarians. And almost every year, for ten or twelve years past, we have seen a new grammar ushered forth, to establish some new difference. This shews, that, a specific difference of the english tongue can not be fully ascertained in its present state; and that, to obtain a proper standard, we must apply to some fixed or dead language.

The Latin, of all others now extant, is the most easily attainable, and most accommodated to the english idiom. English grammars have, therefore, maintained their credit and reputation, amongst, the best judges in proportion to their conformity to this, as a standard— The same may be said with respect to the french, and, I believe with respect to all other living languages.— I know the studying of a dead language is much declamed against, and unmercifully condemned, as an unnecessary waste of time.— It must be granted, that it requires time to acquire a sufficient knowledge of the latin, so as to profit by it.— But while the pupil is doing this, he is at the same time acquiring also habits of industry and appreciation, which may be of the greatest use to him through life; bringing forth and strengthening his mental faculties, by exercises best suited to their capacities; furnishing his mind with a stock of the most delicate, elegant, nervous, and even of the most sublime sentiments, on the various occurrences in life; and above all, enlarging his capacity, and laying a foundation for his further advances in useful and ornamental improvements. He ought, also, to go through this study, at a period of life, before the faculties of his mind have acquired sufficient strength for more weighty studies.

From two to four years, between the ages of ten, and seventeen, is a sufficient length of time, for any boy of moderate genious, to acquire a competent knowledge of the latin. And it may justly be disputed whether any other study can be undertaken, within this period, equally advantageous in confirming habits of application and attention, and enlarging the capacity for further proficiency in useful knowledge.

But what renders the study of latin indispensibly necessary, to one who would acquire an accurate knowledge of the english, is this: that he has no proper standard without it.—The english has none; neither has any other

living language, while in a fluctuating state. This was once the case with
the latin, as it is now with the english. Whoever will peruse Horace's art of
poetry, or Cicero's epistles may find sufficient proof of this observation. But
so evident is this deficiency in every attempt to accommodate a grammar, to
the different idiom of the english tongue, that I'm confident of being supported by the suffrages of all who have minimally attended to the structure
of the language.

Besides professionalists of every nation, in explaining the several arts and
sciences, make use of terms boroughed from the learned languages, and a
greater proportion of those from the greek and latin— It is answered that
these are sufficiently explained. It may be justly replied, that no dictionary has
ever yet appeared, which gives all the different senses, in which words may be
understood, accordingly to their various combinations in sentences, and uses
to which they may be applied. Almost every different art and profession, claims
the privilege of using the same terms in different senses, suited to and understood by itself. — Thus the word Manus, in common conversation, signifies a
hand; but in a military treatise, it often signifies a band, or company of men.

And the word jus in law, or a tract of juris prudens, signifies a Right;
but in cooking it signifies Broth, or Gravy. And often, a little alteration of
the tone, or small inflection of the voice, in pronouncing the same word,
gives it a very different signification. These are things, some of which can
not be noted by dictionaries; and can be fully understood only by a knowledge of the language, which uses them. So that however well terms may be
explained, yet it does not afford such a satisfactory knowledge as we derive
from an acquaintance with the origins whence they are boroughed.—

Having premised these few observations, I shall now offer the following
outlines of a general plan of education.

And first, english schools, as they are accommodated to the larger bulk
of the people, claim a primary attention. It is a pity, they have been so much
neglected, and nothing has yet been done, to set them on a better establishment, and render them more productive of useful improvement. They are
often erected, and as often destroyed again, by the capricious humours of a
few individuals, which renders their permanency unstable & precarious.—
Reading, writing, and arithmetic are the branches of learning usually taught
in them; and these often in so ineffectual a manner, as to be of little use to
the learners; and at so expensive a rate, as to put it out of the power of the
poorer class of citizens, to gain an advantage from them.

To prevent these evils, the following hints are suggested—

Let a fund be provided, by a tax equitably levied on all taxable property
throughout the state, not exceeding eighteen pence, nor less than one shil-
ling in the hundred pounds and treasured in some productive stock, liable
to drafts in favour of trustees, herein after mentioned, agreeably to a law
provided for the purpose.

Let three, six, or nine trustees, as circumstances may require, be appointed
in each township, or district, either by the judges of the county courts, or
by vote of the citizens of each district, by order of court, duely notified as

least ten days before the holding such election which trustees so chosen or appointed, shall have the direction and superintendence of the schools in their respective districts.— It shall be their duty to fix on the proper seats of, and erect school houses; to employ teachers, and pay their salaries[;] to determine the number of scholars to be admitted; to visit the schools, at least once a quarter; to inspect their internal government and discipline; to take care that the principles of morality be promoted, not only by the[ir] example, but inculcated by the precepts of their teachers; and to take notice of, and encourage the progressive advances of the scholars.

It shall further be their duty to distinguish who are proper objects of charity and to see that the poor, in their respective districts, be taught. And at the expiration of every term, to certify to the nearest justice of the peace, the number of the poor taught, during the preceding term, whose attestation shall be their warrant to draw from the public treasury, the amount of the tuition money and other necessary expenses of such poor scholars, equally proportioned to the number of scholars taught in, and the salaries paid to the teachers of such school.—

They shall also have authority to levy by an equal tax, proportioned by the last preceding county vote, the remainder of salaries, and other expenses due in their respective districts, on the estates of all both poor, and rich, in proportion to the number of scholars they send.—

It shall also be their duty to transmit to the public treasury once a year, a just & full account, attested by some neighbouring justice of the peace, of the number of poor scholars taught, in their several districts, and the sums of money, expended by them, for that purpose.

These trustees, it is presumed, will give their service gratis. The office ought therefore to be circular. Let one third of their number resign every year, and their places be supplied by others, either by new appointment or election.—

I must here take the liberty of making a short remark, on the common mode of instruction, practiced in the most of our English schools, and offering what, to me, appears to be a useful and necessary improvement.

It has been observed, that the naming of letters, sounding of syllables, and pronouncing of words is taught, and learned meerly mechanically.— It is the fatal error of most of our schools to continue the same mechanic mode of teaching, thro' the whole little circle of education taught in them.

Children are tought to read sentences in the same manner they were tought to name letters, by the sound of the ear, and the mere help of memory; without affixing any ideas to what they read, or knowing that words are signs, or names of things. Their progress in this way, as it is uninstructive, can afford no pleasure; consequently, must be tyrsome and slow, and unproductive of that expansion of mind necessary to larger, and useful improvement.

This error suggests its own remedy.— Let the pupil, as soon as he is capable of giving the proper sounds of syllables, and joining them together in words, be taught at the same time, that they are names, or signs of things.

And let him pass over no word, without knowing its meaning. Inform him that the Letters Dog, Cat, etc. s[t]and for, or are the names of those little domestic animals he is so well acquainted with, and you will both surprize and please him. His curiosity will be thereby excited to know what every letter and word in his little book stands for.— As he progresses, let the same methods be continued. When he comes to read words connected in sentences, let him be asked the sense they contain, and let the ideas they convey be clearly represented to his understanding.— Thus, in a short time, instead of reading mechanically, by the mere sound of syllables, he soon begins to take the ideas. And, as the miscalling of a word, interrupts and destroys the sense, he is obliged, by a retrospect, to connect his own mistakes: And in this way, with any proper helps, he soon acquires accuracy and facility in reading; improvement and pleasure form it; and a taste for it. Whereas the boy, who had trudged on in the dull manner before described, for three, five, or perhaps seven years, as soon as he has gotten from under the discipline of the schools, hates ever after to touch, and even to see a book.

A similar remark may be made, with respect to the method of teaching arithmetic.— We frequently see boys, who, at the expense of much time and labor have gone thro' the Common rules, very ready in the use of numbers, and answering a question, agreeably to the rules laid down in their books, while they have them before them; but thro' wont of a sufficient knowledge of the reasons of these rules, as incapable of applying them, almost, as if they has never known figures.—

It will require much time, and very particular attention of teachers to prevent, or remedy these evils. Consequently the number of scholars must be less, and their lessons must be few and short in the day; but it is presumed, that their proficiency in the end, will more than compensate for their expense of time in the beginning.—

I shall now offer, briefly, a plan for the higher branches of literature, viz. The learned languages, logic, retoric, geography, Mathematics, nature and moral philosophy.

These several branches comprehend what is generally signified by the terms A Liberal Education; for the attainment of which, institutions should be established on such permanent foundations, as not to be affected by the fluctuating state of the number of students reporting to them; and so few in number as not to interfere with each others interests. To render them precarious in their continuance, or to increase their number to an undue proportion, equally destroys their utility.

Let the state therefore, be divided into convenient districts, containing not more than sixteen, nor less than eight thousand freeholders; And as soon as such free districts can produce twelve or more students of ability, and desirous to prosecute a liberal education, let an academy be established, and competent professors, in the seven branches of literature, be appointed, on sufficient salaries to engage men of abilities and liberal sentiments, to devote their time & service to them. Let a tax be levied on all taxable property, not exceeding nine pence, nor less than six pence to [each] hundred pounds, and treasured in some productive stock, with the additional tax of one dollar per pole, on all single free white male inhabitants above the age of twenty five years, with one third of a dollar for every year between twenty five and thirty five in the age of such inhabitant to be a fund for discharging the necessary expenses of such Academies.— Let them be placed under the direction of trustees, not exceeding sixteen, nor less than twelve in number, chosen annually by the legal electors, in each district whose business it shall be, to fix on the seats of such academics, and erect them in their respective districts;— to appoint Rectors, and necessary professors in them; to prescribe and pay their salaries; to dismiss on sufficient grounds;— to establish rules for the internal government and discipline of the same; to appoint public examinations and exhibitions of the students; and to certify their proficiency in the several branches of their improvement respectively.

Let them also be vested with funds sufficient, not only for defraying the necessary expenses of such academies, but also for the support of such poor youth, as by their prompt genious, bid fair for usefulness in any of the learned professions.—

The english district schools may be combined with such academies, as often as circumstances will admitt.

It is a matter of the highest importance, to a republican government, to disseminate knowledge, and to keep the avenues of access to it, open to all, and especially to the middle, or even lower class of people. This is the class, to which we are to look for improvement in arts and knowledge; and which cultivates learning to its own emolument and the advantage of others. And, as the wealth of a republic, may be said to consist in the quantity of wisdom, and information its citizens are possessed of, it ought therefore to be always kept with in their reach. Whenever it becomes a Monopoly in the hands of the rich, the liberties of the state become a boon to the highest bidder.

On a plan of this kind, a number of the most influential characters, in every township, county, and district in the state, would be engaged in the interest of learning, and officially called upon to patronize and encourage it. And it is unknown to all but those, who have had the opportunity of observing, what effect the public patronage, and even the misjudging opinion of the vulgar has, on the ingenious minds of youth, in prompting them, to a generous emulation, and laudable ambition to excel.

NOTE

1. See R. B. Rose, "The Priestley Riots of 1791," *Past and Present* 18 (November 1960): 68–88; Letter to Rev. Theophilius Lindsey, on October 20, 1788, in John Towill Rutt, *Life and Correspondence of Joseph Priestley* vol. II p. 13. For the case supporting Hobson's authorship, see chapters 1 and 3 in this volume.

Concerning Education in Public Schools

Hand

The author of "Hand" remains anonymous. The word "hand" was not used alone as a pseudonym during the period, but the *New Work Magazine* reprinted an article in 1795 entitled "A Petition to those who have the Superintendency of Education," by "The Left Hand," ascribed posthumously to Benjamin Franklin. While the original handwritten essay by Hand survives, the original image of a hand probably does not. The title on an accompanying cover sheet (figure 11.1) is in the handwriting of APS secretary Jon Williams, who presumably redrew the image of the hand himself. What the hand signified is a matter of conjecture, beyond its possible reference to the Franklin essay. It seems more than coincidence that John Archer, a student of Dr. Benjamin Rush during 1796 and early 1797, repeatedly drew a hand that he incorporated into a signature-like device while taking notes during Rush's lectures (see figure 11.2). Unfortunately, John Archer's handwriting does not match that of "Hand." Nevertheless his obsession with developing a hand signature at exactly the same time that the Hand essay was submitted to the APS does suggest that, perhaps, he and/or another medical student of Rush's may have been the author—as do the disputatious tone and unpolished writing style.

In order to a degree of accuracy in replying to the first question of the American Philosophical Society—pending the present year—or, that, for the best system of particular finished education, on the one hand, and of public schools at large, on the other; it seems proper, and is perhaps necessary to distinguish between its preceding clauses and its last—as about objects differing from each other, in degree at least—the former, requiring that only which is most perfect or complete (practically alone it is to be presumed however;) while the other asks only for what will be most extensively useful to mankind in the gross?—and that of the first, we see to, our taking up in the same sense the leading term therein; as, what constitutes "liberal education"?— and whether any particular mode of "literary instruction" (some degree of

Figure 11.1 Cover sheet in the handwriting of Jon Williams. The original drawing of a hand does not survive. Courtesy of the American Philosophical Society.

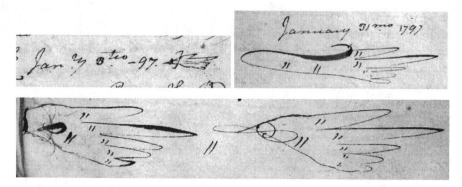

Figure 11.2 Drawings of a hand signature from "Notes on Dr. Rush's lectures" by John Archer (1796–97). Courtesy of the Historical Medical Library of the College of Physicians of Philadelphia.

it being, in common general understanding, essential to anything which merits the name) be required as indispensibly connected with it?—how they and our common school tuition are to be peculiarly suited to our species of governments—and, in what manner adaptable thereto for the greatest good of all under them?

Much about the importance of private virtues to such as are of a public nature in motives or tendency; and of knowlege in youth early and generally disseminated toward the perfection of either—and of their almost universally beneficial effects—both on the individual citizen and the public of every government, in the least republican—and about the preferability in other views than the last between public and private modes of education will here be passed over; from the principles of all the former being well established in the general sentiment, however deficiently so, by our practice, and the last, as being in a great measure excluded from our consideration by the very terms of the first clause in the question: for "liberal education," whether found, or, not found in every of our present colleges and college universities (the number of which, especially the latter; as most of the literary institutions in the different states are or claim to be—and want of respectability in many, form no small objection to them and fall little short of making them a burlesque on it) is, from the usual import of the words to be sought for in them alone.

"Literary instruction" too, tho', unlike the former not confined, in its acceptation, to any, precise formulary; either academic—or, of mere private institution, is to be presumed better in the first—independently on the manner of impressing the head and heart there—by emulation, the strongest of all incitements—by frequent public exhibitions, of unavoidable obligation—and, the daily opportunity of being the principal actors in mimic or represented scenes of all the most important concerns and exercises of after public or professional life and competitions; without the thought-dissipating, mind-distracting, interest-deluding and often in turn too deluded-cares, clashings, necessities and vices of the world even in its miniature of a small discontented and divided family—Considerations that would induce us to look for the greatest perfection of literary culture in the former, apart from the correlative "liberal" confining our view of the contemplated instruction to public collegiate courses alone. And persuaded I am that we can never approach too near to the Spartan model of making education, which means, or should mean, every proper useful preparative for future life; wholly a public concern even to the exclusion of the parent from interference therewith, beyond contributing toward it—to be done either by each individually for his own; or jointly and rateably by all for all as the children to this purpose of the State; so that the after occupation of each son—be at its selection, through the proper officers, his past instructors—those officers (of whom the one professing the branch most likely to be elected, if any such; if not, of the one nearest like it, in some public recognized seminary always to be one approving the choice) to discuss and determine openly among themselves at a Board for that purpose, the kind of genius and turn of mind of the youth and select employment for him accordingly. The eligibility of which plan before any yet practiced I freely hazard, notwithstanding the opinion of the late Doctor Johnston, of so justly distinguished memory in England, that this choice was well or best vested in the parent: but this was so pronounced by him only as between the probable caution and real earnestness on the one hand, of the father in the welfare, worldly success and reputation of his off-spring—and the wild self conceit of wilful obstinacy of the child himself on the other not for an adequate judgment or skilful (because a moderate and modest) application of their judgments by either—clearly, if practisable with due liberty, it was a less exceptionable rule in Egypt of old; which obliged children to continue in their father's calling—and evidently had the advantage over our present alternative, in certainty and uniformity of object and in far and long preserved and transmitted experience; and probably too in a willing acquiescence by every new practiser beyond any hopes from arbitrary caprice in our one case or from extravagance and vain conceit (forever disdaining improvement) in the other of the as yet with us equivocal dilemma.

Nor would I have this regulation confined to preparation for the learned professions only—or other education justly to be called liberal in reference to the destined ornamental use to be made of it by its followers—from all which together the Community may perhaps have the highest expectations—as likely to furnish, in time however, its representatives and rulers; but would also have it applied to the other or remaining ingredients of a perfect whole—in the mass of its common citizens; not only the most numerous description of any in society; but from the universality of the character and because it will ever decide eventually that of its representation and government, the most important of all to be rightly impressed and formed. How this is to be effected for the solitary good of the individual in his best cultivation has already been suggested—by not only seeking genius wherever to be found; but by improving the sort of each in its proper sphere—or, to qualify any mere selfish being for its own few, small, sordid purposes, might even as to the great body of every community, be left to its present broad channel of family or self will and its appendages, of themselves paying and employing their own teaches; but, as subserving other interest of relations to the utmost flow and extent of a public and a world, in all their aspects; the requisite improvements of even that very limited education itself demand at the least a change of most common school masters and of the source of their appointment making that competent only to the authority of the higher seminaries of learning and making each of these accountable as visitors for the qualifications of all the publicly employed teachers within their respective limits to be assigned them; not only that the common kind of neighborhood school learning shall be well taught in each; but that none of those Schools shall be suffered to go without plain, easy, familiar discourses regularly delivered several times a year by fit persons sent round to perform circuits for the purpose—on the subject of science and morals as indispensibly requisite to every free or good government—the further and other benefits of them in all countries—of laws and their faithful observance more especially of such as are fundamental viz. relate to the election, qualification and conduct of rulers—to be raised to the office if possible, only by a free unbiased vote as one of the highest duties—next those immediately personal from ourselves to our Creator, that we owe to conscience, our neighbor, our country and our God—To this effect one out of many sentences from "Paley's moral and political philosophy" (which may serve as a model both in matter and in manner, for such lectures) is worth codes of prohibitory statues and prosecutions on them for undue influence of elections. With the virtue of independence as with chastity, none but that of the <u>soul</u> can be guarded against seduction or if it could is worth the expence of the required centinels = If afterwards the pupils were called upon to give an account of what had been inculcated etc. it would be a still farther improvement evidencing how far the address to them had been understood and evidently was or was not attended to by any of them. All other peaceable persons should be allowed the privilege of attending at least the lecture part, as to these studies, in general so little regarded—probably because so seldom brought to mind and thus unriveted upon us either by reflexion or by habit; of which last we are so much the creatures, as often scarcely to own reason for a guide.

While this degree of political knowlege, to be made attainable, nay the hearing of it, a matter of course at all common English schools; Should after a while be indispensible in every free citizen—at least with every elector— much more may be required of those to be elected;—and most all from those to receive important general offices of the public by appointment of administration—not perhaps from being in general more arduous and critical than elective ones but as in this restriction of the number to receive them interfering less with a due portion of free-agency in the citizen?

For the qualities and criterions of merit for selecting persons to fill these important stations of either kind, exhibitable therefore in education as points to be aimed at I shall content me with a reference to 1st Blackstone's commentaries p. 9 and again to pages 27 and 33 of the same book where will be found his opinion supported by that of Cicero and Aristotle among the ancients—for the propriety of making legislation, laws in general of politics, the kinds of science most connected with those higher departments in relation to the present question, not only subjects of instruction, but, from the absurdity in supposing men to be born legislators,—of such as shall be strictly and regularly academic—and in p 131 of Delolme, of how few comparatively are fit for the offices of legislation. Indeed rejecting the terms of the question and authorities; nothing can be more demonstrable than the superiority of an <u>education</u> of the <u>public</u> kind for <u>public life</u>; nor than the goodness of literary outline at least of discipline most generally pursued in our more public seminaries: and it is to me not a little extraordinary that in a <u>republic</u> especially the idea should not have occurred more generally of making the nature and reciprocal rights obligations of government as between rulers and the ruled—together with those between both conjointly and other nations, by the laws of nature and nations—an academic study—and that under an administration, so justly claiming to have been independent and for its conduct in most things so truly and highly to be respected; no greater progress should have been made in forming to and for ourselves; by signal literary and liberal new establishments in language, in science and in manners—a distinguishing characteristic standard of our own (as the best remedy against inconveniences and confusion from introducing among us those of other countries) to be derived from one general national university, serving at once as a centre of assimilation and of union in our tastes, our dialects, our habits and our ideas—unfortunately of themselves too much at variance, and, intensed, by a chimerical fondness for foreign ties ever hostile to each other. In short nothing being so well calculated to remove prejudices unfounded, which most prejudices, from their very constitution, are, as mutual intercourse, in early life especially, it can never be too much cherished between different parts and parties before they come to the capital purposely to combat each on the great political Theatre of interests—partial, selfish and local.

Nor is this acquiring of liberality, the only advantage to be had from early good impressions. The virtuous Addison has told us in one of his spectators, that you have no greater security for right intentions than that first ideas be formed from books—before any be taken upon trust from the world; because, whether the authors of those books were virtuous in their own lives or not—(men's different actions taken together having sometimes to say for them with the poet so well translated

>"we see the right and we approve it too;
>"The wrong condemn, and still the wrong pursue.")

their writings reach us, as inciters to virtue along—no others of any authority having yet been generally enough countenanced to come down to us fitter for any other purpose—with which sentiment, his brother statesman and acute fellow philosopher Lord Bolingbroke fully concurs in his letters on history p. 36–37—that in written Treatises in general, unlike what happens in our converse with the world, we do not find Virtue and Vice confounded; or, both of them often transposed for a while from their own to the opposite side—and the latter from being thus successful inducing mere men of the world, for want of further observation, to deem it the better policy; instead of; as books would caution them; looking to the end, which often turns to a sad reverse—Not only individuals therefore but republics at large, whose sole safety or probable prosperity lies in the knowlege, private virtue & unconstrained public good morals of their citizens—especially of the ruling part of them from their conspicuous high example—should endeavor so to dispose of youth, on which the whole man ever after very greatly depends—as that first impressions will tend right, apart from the slower aids of reflexion— and that those aids will strengthen the good and correct the bad Sensations already found there. The greater delicacy, nerve and discernment of each of which faculties when rightly trained in the emulating ardor of youth promises from them a usefulness to the public and a reputation of ultimate success to the individual—which, with all the eagerness worldly taught crooked paths are often pursued, no extent of native capacity alone, exerted only in middle or after life, will ever afford to either.

Religion or the doctrine of teaching us the result of this life's conduct, in one to succeed, has hitherto been kept [out] of the case; but if the beneficial effects of a good behavior here, anticipated as attending it in a world to come, be superadded to those derived from it in this, it will contribute not a little to a present just estimate—even with political bodies—now too often appearing to hold themselves no way accountable here or hereafter for things done in that capacity; or in other words, that it seems indifferent to them what means they employ to effect a present purpose so it be but efficacious; but surely while we are restrained by every consideration human and Divine from doing what will injure even one fellow creature—we ought to believe we were not left at liberty to wrong a greater number with impunity—and that sacrificing others at the shrine of our avarice, ambition or other inordinate appetites, while there is a just providence above, will not long continue our gratifications—and on any fair calculation for ourselves and posterity can never be our interest.

The right inducements of interest and duty are the more necessary to be instilled into the members of public bodies in a government, from their number, losing us the aid of the most powerful of all restraints, Shame, on them in that situation—or if not totally inapplicable, yet frittering it away by division, down to nothing: for never was there a truer saying—than that "many cannot blush"—do what they may and be they individually, or rather pretend they to be, ever so scrupulous.

To recapitulate by gradation.

Let the state pay and choose—at least choose or approve each common neighborhood school-master—and let their schools and every person who will attend them for the purpose be instructed in public duties by moral-politic missionaries from the colleges—Let these, as state institutions remain much on their present footing for usual collegiate studies—but add to them the province of solely qualifying (by adequate, matriculated attendance and exercises, or their diploma certifying equal qualification through any other source ascertained by their sufficient examination) for the learned professions and higher public offices—jointly with the national institution=and that one alone for the chief executive diplomatic and judiciary of the United States=or for as many of those or other of our general civil officers—as shall be found conveniently practicable to be thence only appointable on the use of which restriction, to secure at the least tolerable competency, we may yet be convinced, under a less prudent and judicious administration than we have hitherto been blessed with.

Concerning Education in Pennsylvania

Freedom

The author of Freedom leaves us few clues as to his identity. Surprisingly, the stand-alone pseudonym "Freedom" does not appear anywhere in the largest modern databases of Early Republican writing.[1] What we do know of Freedom is that his essay focuses primarily on higher learning, with an unusual emphasis on (and familiarity with) medical education. It is also reasonable to assume that Freedom lived in, or near, Pennsylvania, given that the essay chooses to focus on that state specifically. His knowledge of major authors on education, college curricula, and the writings of American polymath Hugh Williamson and Scottish physician John Gregory places him within the circle of Philadelphia intellectuals who orbited the American Philosophical Society and the College of Physicians of Philadelphia. Despite searches for Freedom's spidery handwriting among APS regulars and the correspondents of Thomas Jefferson, his identity eludes us. The peer review of Freedom's essay does not survive.

⌐ ⌐ ⌐

THE BEST PLAN FOR CONDUCTING A LIBERAL EDUCATION, SUITED TO THE GOVERNMENT OF THE UNITED STATES; OR TO A REPUBLICAN CONSTITUTION IN GENERAL, AND THE BEST METHOD OF ESTABLISHING COUNTRY SCHOOLS IN PENNSYLVANIA:

In considering this proposition, it may be viewed in two respects: First, as it may be applied to those studies, and modes of instruction which exist at present; with respect to the facilitating their acquisition, and in pointing out, the means of carrying these methods to a greater degree of perfection than they have hitherto acquired.

And secondly we are to consider whether the present objects of study are all really necessary, and which of them should be curtailed, or totally dropt, and which should be extended and taught more fully. And we are likewise to consider, whether other objects of pursuit, as necessary…[document damaged], than any in use, have not been totally neglected or considered in a manner superficial, and general when it deserved to have been considered more particularly in all its parts, and relations.

These are undoubtedly circumstances which, in the highest degree, merit our attention in a liberal republican education; we all know that there are many of the circumstances of the times we live in, which differ widely from those of former times, as well as our local situation does, in both these respects we stand upon very different ground, both with respect to our sources of information in many useful arts, and sciences, and our courses of education should therefore necessarily be different in many respects, as observation, experience, and reason may enlighten us, from time to time, as we cannot yet reasonably suppose ourselves arrived at the acme of human wisdom. As there is no mention made of the learned professions, I presume the Society only means in the first place the general education of a citizen, or a gentleman, which should necessarily precede, or accompany that of a professional man; and all of these I believe might be conducted in different, and, I believe in better modes, than they have hitherto been pursued, in most institutions; and although improvements in them have hitherto been but very rarely, and seldom adopted, yet it should form a fundamental clause of every literary Institution, or society, whether School, College, University, or Academy etc. that the modes and subjects of study should be reviewed and amended from time to time.

When we consider the means by which useful knowledge is attained, by the human mind, we shall find that the Senses are the avenues by which all is conveyed to the intellect, our primary object therefore is, to put them in the most direct way, for acquiring useful knowledge, as well as wisdom, etc.; and to quicken their perceptions by explanations, and demonstrations, but principally to discriminate, and to point out the really useful parts of knowledge, from what is otherwise, especially with relation to the objects of the student's pursuit etc.

The teaching, and learning to fix the attention, and applying with steadiness, and resolution, to the pursuit of the proper objects of study, and the tracing abstruse subjects through their mazes, our languages, are far more deficient than our senses, for it is but a few of our Ideas of sense, that we are able to express with clearness, and perspicuity, so as to convey them fully and without diminution to others. In this respect some languages are more full, or more deficient in particular parts. This may be easily proved by considering our principal organs of sense, and their sensations, as in sight we can perceive instantaneously, at the first sight, the different variations in the countenances of thousands of our acquaintances, whereas we could never convey all these by language to another, here we can go little farther comparison, the ear can distinguish, innumerable varieties of musical sounds, and notes, and can even distinguish the different voices of thousands of those whom we have often heard before, without being able to give a full account of them in words. And likewise in taste, and Smell we have an uncountable number of sensations, which we cannot convey fully in words, when we consider these subjects, we shall be enabled to perceive the absolute necessity of practice, as well as instruction, in order to acquire perfection in any art, or Science. For by practice, we acquire something like a second instinct; or an inexpressible facility in distinguishing, and choosing, or selecting, by the exercising of our senses. For these reasons a person can never arive at any tolerable degree of perfection, in any thing without practice, and use; but with acute senses, and a capacious mind, enlarged by information, and diligent application, we may a[r]rive at proficiency, in any pursuit, attainable by the human capacity. It is upon this account that example is better than precept, in any pursuit, and likewise this is the reason why theory without practice, is of very little consequence in any Art; and yet true theory is of the greatest advantage next to experience, but we must not mistake hypothesis for theory, and by that means substitute a counterfeit for a precious coin, or antique.—

With respect to the elements of literature, I have known it to be a custom in London to learn children to write their letters, in order to impress them the better upon their memories, when learning them, as well as to use them betimes to handle their pens. And this mode I believe may have its advantages, and the experiment is very easily tried. But those who learn them these rudiments, and the particular sounds, or syllables, and words, which the different combinations of letters are shown to denote, should be careful that they do not acquire any improper accents, or tones, as they are very difficult to get rid of when once acquired; when Children have learned to read; Gramar, and particularly orthography should be attended to critically, and the different parts of speech, as verbs and nouns, and their variations, or conjugations, and declensions, as these are subjects which their minds are early capable of comprehending, though it has commonly been too much neglected, at this early period. The rules of Syntax may be deferred to a later period, when they can read classical, or approved authors, in order to prepare them for composition, and at the same time that they are learning these things, it would be very proper that they should be employed one part of every day, in learning to write, as it does not depend upon the memory, but is a manual, or mechanical art, which is only to be acquired by exercise. In learning the grammatical rules of our vernacular language, it should be in as plain, and concise a manner as possible, to make it intelligible to the tender capacities of children, and afterwards when they have obtained a general knowledge of it, the particulars may be descended to more fully, but Rhetoric, which teaches the ornaments of language, and Logic, or the methods of arranging our Ideas, and forming a discourse should as Francis Bacon says, be refered to a later period when their minds may be better stored with Ideas and things. For without these as this accurate observer says, these sciences are as difficult to be learned properly, as it would be to paint the wind.

Natural history may be ventured upon, in the next place, as it is a study of which children are particularly fond of, especially that of animals, and vegetables, and the principles of mineralogy. Short and easy epitomies of these sciences only should be ventured on at first, and afterwards they may be followed to greater perfection. Those who are intended for the learned Professions, and for whom alone, the dead languages, particularly latin, is necessary, should in the first place be tolerable proficients in their own language, that is they should be able to read, speak, and write it, with gramatical propriety, and thus by understanding the gramar of their own language, which they may learn much easier, than that of an unknown language, this last will be much easier to them.

French is a useful, as well as fashionable, and polite language, and it is very probable that it will become more useful, and more general every year. One or other of these languages are the general mediums, of communication over all Europe at present, but the latin is used still less and less, and the French becoming more general. It is probable it may at no distant period answer all the purposes of the latin, as all that is wanted among the well informed is one general language to answer as a medium of correspondence from one, to another, and as the french is the easiest acquired, it may answer that purpose better than any other, especially as there is no magical influence in latin nor even in Greek; this last language has long since ceased to be wrote, unless in school exercises. Neither is there much probability that it will be ever revived, again. But as it was the original language of science, and many of our technical terms are derived from it, those who have leisure and opportunity may find it of some use, or at least amusing, as we are not to expect any fund of information from it, in the present age, all its treasures having been long ago exhausted, by repeated reiteration, etc. Hebrew is only of use, to the Clerical orders, and as they have only the bible in it, unless they could procure the talmud and other books of the caballa from the jews, it cannot [be] of an extensive use.

Whether the learning of the languages should precede Arithmetic, or the science of numbers, and Geometry, or science of magnitude, and other branches of mathematical learning may altogether depend upon circumstances as the inclination, or opportunity, may answer; however as they are totally independent of one another, either may be followed without the other, but as languages depend almost totally on the memory, they suit children in their younger years, better than the mathematical studies, where reason is required; as this is the product of a more mature judgement. French may be of use to a Merchant, or trader, but latin will certainly be ten times more trouble for them to learn, than any use it ever can be of, especially in this country, therefore I would recommend the study of things rather than words to them.

Arithmetic is very necessary for all classes of men, or at least the principal rules of it, but the complicated method of Italian bookkeeping can only be of use in the mercantile line, but those who are intended for the practical branches of the mathematicks, should first learn Geometry, and trigonometry, and then they may proceed to the practical branches [such] as Mensuration, Guaging or Surveying, or Navigation. But in order to understand this last branch, they must understand the principles at least of Geography, and Astronomy, the two sciences, I would particularly recommend to all who have a capacity for them, especially professional men, as the one makes us acquaint with the globe we live on, and the other with those which surround us, and they serve to enlarge the mind very materially and to infuse liberal, and extended Ideas of things in general, and on this account they are very useful for all men of information, and may be taught the principles of them at schools or academies or Colleges, before entering fully into them [in] a general course of philosophy, as we shall show hereafter.

In a republican government, it is very necessary that a knowledge of oratory and Criticism should be pretty generally understood, or Dialecticks in general, for this Purpose they should learn Rhetoric, and Logic, as rhetoric only teaches ornaments and beauty of a language, it is not so essentially necessary, only that a knowledge enables a person the better to detect its fallacies, and errors, when ornamented with its graces, and it has on this account been proscribed by some rigid people. Logic is of more real use, as it teaches the manner of arranging our Ideas, and expressing ourselves with perspicuity, and precision, but before it can be learned to advantage, the mind should be tolerably stored with the knowledge of things, particularly Geometry, as it in some degree explains the principles of it to the eye, and to the intellect, and even the higher branches of mathematicks may be of use upon some occasions, as Algebra, Fluxions, these studies teach the necessity of fixing the attention, and study in order to understand a subject in a proper manner, and on that account very necessarily precedes Logic, especially with the volatile and unthinking. Logic as well as every other science should be as much as possible divested of the technical jargon of the Scholasticks, and its principle made as plain, and easy as possible at first, but may afterwards be followed to more perfection, as may also Gramar and the science of Dialecticks in general; by understanding Logic, one can the better detect Sophistry, in any shape, whether in speech, or writing, as in this science, the construction of sophisms are commonly explained, but I would by no means advise the following of this subject farther, as a great deal of time may be lost in this way to very little or no purpose, as in arguing for, and against a question, which in the days of Scholastic pedantry, was very much in fashion.

Those intended to study military tacticks besides Arithmetic, Geometry, etc. must proceed to the higher branches of mathematicks, as Conic sections, and the doctrine of Parabolic curves, Projectiles, etc., as the method of forming fortifications, depends on Geometry, as well as the drawing up an army and their different evolutions, and Gunnery is explained by projectiles and Parabolic curves, and a small knowledge of Chymistry explains the composition and force of Gunpowder etc.

For Francis Bacon says in his advancement of Learning, that we cannot well extend, or improve, any Science by keeping close to the rules of that Science alone, but by going to higher branches of learning, and to collateral Sciences: we may extend any Science and render it more generally useful. He also says that besides taking a general, and distant view of any subject of study we are to come nearer to it, and view all its parts particularly. And Condorcet in his view of the human mind say[s] that in order to extend the

Sciences, those which are at a distance from one another must be brought nearer and into contact with one another; for this purpose their connections should be preserved as far as possible, and their similarities should be pointed out, in order that they may illustrate each other, and they should be taught together, or a general view of them should be given as far as they have any relation to one another, and afterwards every one particularly by itself.

In the early periods of Grecian Philosophy all the then known parts of human wisdom were taught in one course of instruction, as the doctrine of mind and Spirits, along with the doctrine of the properties of matter or bodies, and medicine was considered as a part of this great, and comprehensive course; but this plan, I believe most people will agree with me was too large. As Physicks, or the doctrine of matter, may be very properly separated from that of mind and metaphysicks although the mind, and the body, act, and react upon one another, as every person may perceive in himself, and others, without much deep study, or penetration. Nevertheless I believe we may carry our divisions and subdivisions too far, at least at the outset, and thereby cause confusion, and perplexity, the very things which we should be most upon our guard against; I mean that the branches of the tree may by strikeing off too soon from the main Trunk, both deform and weaken it, and cause confusion, and perplexity to the learners especially.

Natural Philosophy may be taught in one compleat general course, comprehending, The Mechanical and Mathematical, the Chymical, and Organic, and their applications in explaining the phenomena of Nature and the doctrine of Magnetism, Electricity, etc., as Miscellaneous parts of the course. By the Organic philosophy I mean the doctrine of Animal, and Vegetable life as explained by Anatomy, and Physiology, Zoology etc.. And this course may be again very properly divided into three, the Mechanical and Mathematical comprehending the Philosophy of the mechanic arts and Trades, may form one compleat course as proposed by Dr. Williamson; the other two subjects have long been the subjects of particular courses in the Schools of medicine at least.

The general Doctrine of the mind may be taught in another compleat course comprehending Morals, or Ethicks, Politicks in general, and political economy, the laws of nature, and of nations, Jurisprudence, and Metaphysicks and natural Theology and the doctrine of [opposites] etc., and these may again be prosecuted separately, as convenience or inclination may answer.

But it would be useless, to attend lectures etc. upon each of these subjects separately, as it would be, in general, and particular history; the principal thing wanted in this respect is that the Students should be directed in their choice of books of the best authors in each of these subjects, for these studies where there are no experience to be acquired by the eye and the other senses, but where all depends upon the intellect may be prosecuted much better in retirement than in seminaries of Learning, but where complicated machinery etc. is to be exhibited, or experiments to be made, and shewn the pupils in order to convince their sense of sight etc. especially if they are of a dangerous nature, as they often are in Chymistry, and in the healing Art, then it is safest and best to first see them performed by an experienced practitioner[.] In distant parts of the country where teachers cannot well be supported, young men, and youths may very advantageously form themselves into Societies, to meet weekly or oftener, and by this means follow their Studies; by this means they will stimulate one another to improvement, and if they can have a teacher to come periodically or other men of information to give them instruction in the best modes of following their respective pursuits so much the better, as they may consult people by letter with respect to the mode of following their studies and pursuits or any other difficulty which may occur to them[.] It would not appear more difficult for one teacher in different branches of Learning to attend ten or twelve of these small associations in rotation, than it is for a Clergyman to attend two, or more, different congregations, and preach to them in the same day, a thing not uncommon; it is true it would require some prudence in the students; their behavior may be regulated by their own private agreement, in their association[.] By this means almost any, the most open and thinly inhabited country might be supplied with forms, and means of instruction[.] This mode of association is the manner by which the Chineese children and young men pursue their studies and improve one another in the language and laws and customs etc. of their country, as soon as they have learned to read, and write to a certain degree of perfection[.] They never attend Colleges or Universities unless when they come there for examination, which is carried on with the greatest strictness, and impartiality, the poorest child in the empire having it in his power with sufficient Talents to become the next in power to the emperor.

The methods and modes of study we have here recommended, are the best methods for diffusing the sciences and the arts, and making them more generally understood[.] But for improving, and extending them by practice and cultivation, another mode of pursuit must be followed, for here we must descend to particulars, and discriminate, and examine, all their peculiarities, and variations, but at the same time preserve in our minds the general connection of the whole. To be successful in pursuits of this sort the enquirer should be well acquaint[ed] with both the theory and the practice of his Art or Profession, or otherwise, he may wander long in the dark, and immagine he is making new discoveries, or improvements, when he is only doing what has been done long before[.] On this account the history of the rise, progress, and present state of every art or Science should be carefully studied, by the help of best authors upon the subject.

It would be of the greatest consequence, to the improvements of the Arts and Sciences that they should be more generally, and particularly understood and cultivated by more hands, and heads, than they are at present[.] Then besides that improvements would be more frequent, merit in the different Professors, and Practitioners would be more generally known, and understood; and insinuating and superficial characters could not then so readily supplant modest merit, nor could quackery in any Profession so readily palm itself upon mankind, by apeing true Science, and empirical practices: This would promote a spirit of emulation for excellence, and detect the low and mean arts which the narrow minded, and most ordinary characters are always the most compleat masters of; Then real worth and excellence in any profession or employment, could scarcely be concealed long together.

Besides it is very necessary in a republican government, that the people should be very intelligent and well informed in every thing wherein their welfare or interest is concerned; In a Monarchy, or Aristocracy, only a few of the people are permitted to think, or judge for themselves, and the great body of the people must follow the priviledged order in every [way.] In such a state the mental faculties must lie dormant, and this in a great measure is the case in all absolute Monarchies, and it is not much different in Aristocracies.

Besides we should examine the bad effects of Ignorance in a republic. The bad effects of it becoming too general would be very great, as the most ignorant are always the most tenacious of what little Ideas, or notions, true or false, they have imbibed, and it is scarce possible by any reasoning or even by experiments exhibited to them to alter their oppinions, although many of their Ideas are no more than the effects of impressions, which they take for realities, or hearsay reports etc. It is very evident that a more general diffusion of useful knowledge, and wisdom, is the most effectual way to banish this disagreeable, and untractable disposition, for if information, and mental abilities, were more upon a level, people would not differ so much as they do in sentiment.

In a republic, there should be every means used, in order to diffuse information, so that every Citizen, even those of the poorest parents, and smallest connections, should have it in their power, in case they have ability, and are industrious to arrive at the summit of information, in any pursuit, whether of the Sciences, Professions, Offices or employments, in the republic to which they belong; because every Citizen must be eligible to any of those appointments, or employments; even the making information more general, will facilitate the acquisition of it very materially, but hitherto only a small number of those, who were capable of receiving useful learning, have had it in their powers to pursue it, by reason of the manner in which it was taught, and learned[.]

In teaching the learned Professions, as well as the Sciences, often the principal outlines of the whole are laid down, and their connections with other arts and sciences pointed out, and their origin, progress, and present state handed down, and all that belongs the subject in general explained, and illustrated, then the Subordinate branches should be struck off, and each pursued separately, in order, by those who mean to go to the particulars, and of course to be fully informed in the pursuit.

The advantages of conducting a liberal Education in this form are so great, and as it appears to me so obvious at first sight, that I cannot but wonder that it has not been more prevalent before our days; it has, we are aware been followed in some particulars, but not to the extent which it merits being followed to, and even where it has been followed, it would in some instances appear to be more through chance than design, the whole of its utility not having been understood. By getting a general view, of the whole of any

Science, upon a small scale, the connection of all its parts are more easily understood, and their different relations to each other are better comprehended and easier retained in the memory, than when each branch is pursued by itself or disjointed in an insulated manner[.] Besides when a student has got an Idea of the outlines of his pursuit, formerly in his mind, he [can] far more readily take in, and understand, and digest the particulars, and will be able without confusion to trace each to its proper place, and its relative situation; neither will repetitions of other subjects be more frequent, nor near so frequent as they are in the common method, where different pursuits often interfere, and intrude upon each other. This is evident enough in Medical Science, where the different courses frequently interfere with each other. There are few subjects which would serve to illustrate this subject better; than by applying it to the study of Geography: for we begin this study with a Globe, which is a very small emblem of the world, and first explain the general doctrines, as its axis, poles, equator, parallels of lattitude and Meridans, ecliptic etc. and the Zones, diurnal, and annual rotation, and afterwards we come to its particular larger divisions and proceed from them to the smaller, each separately by itself, one by one etc. etc.

General, and particular History may be studied in retirement, to as great advantage at seminaries of Learning, provided the students are supplied with the best authors and are directed in their choice of them[.] This is all the help they are apt to stand in need of, for this purpose, especially if they understand chronology and geography[.] If we take a view of most institutions at present in existence, we shall find: that unless proper care be taken, in the appointment of teachers, and professors, and electing them only for a certain time and to be rechosen, or displaced, according as they have fulfilled their offices with propriety or otherwise, that the best of rules may otherwise be rendered abortive, in the making of appointments of professors or teachers[.] Men of the greatest abilities in the different departments of Science, and literature should be invited by advertisements in the public papers, and otherwise, and the choice should be made by the most competent judges, upon Oath, as is now done in the medical department of the University of Dublin and likewise in Paris, and every true lover of the Sciences would wish it to be more general, through every department of Literature.

In the rules and regulations for conferring Academic honours, merit should be the only circumstance considered, and no specific time of attendance should be required[.] The strictness of the examinations alone should keep ignorance at a distance, as well as reward diligence, and merit; and in whatever manner, or place, the student may have studied he should be equally admissible to all the highest honours of his pursuit, upon undergoing a candid but critical and severe examination; by means such as these, the honour, and reputation, of any Scientific institution, may be established[,] raised and supported; which cannot be done when time is more looked to, than proficiency in studying. For the purpose of conferring the highest honours in the learned professions, we may expect prominent practitioners to be at least more disinterested and candid judges than the teachers; and an equal

number at least of these should be associated with the others for this purpose so as to form a board of examiners, which should be liberally rewarded
for their trouble by the funds arising from the fees and perquisites paid by
the young candidates[.] When this business of finishing an education is left
totally to teachers we cannot expect that their credentials should do much
honour to the young candidates, for in case they have attended the usual
time there is scarce such a thing as ever refusing them when they go through
the forms for obtaining them[.] And at all times we may expect some thing
like that partiality between a father and son, and the certificate of a master
is not of a very different nature, and by this means Diplomas etc. have fallen
into disrepute with men of the best information, and if we will but consider
the old gothic rules for granting them in many seminaries, we shall find that
popular superstition, and ignorance, are all they have to depend upon.

A more useful manner for young students, and practitioners to pass the
first years of their studies, after they have gone through some or all the most
necessary forms of instruction in the Schools, and attended to the practice
of some of the most eminent of the profession would be, to practice at first
only the most easy and most plain, and obvious parts of the profession, in the
art of healing, Surgery, and pharmacy are of this description. As the effects
of Surgery are the most obvious to the senses, and would be a very proper
introduction to the treatment of internal diseases, the treatment of which
is more obscure, and in law there is the Attorney part of it, which would
answer very well as an introduction to the profession of an advocate which
requires more study and greater abilities, but in the clerical profession there
is no subordinate branch, unless it be that of a teacher or curate, therefore
study, and the example, and advice, of eminent men in the profession, are the
principal rules for them to form themselves by.

The necessity of practice, as an exercise for the senses, which was before
taken notice of applies to the practice of the healing in all its force, as that
sagacity in distinguishing the different disorders of the human body[,] is not
to be attained in any other manner, and eve[n] [a] sensible and experienced
Physician knows that there are many things to be observed and learned, in
diseases, by the accurate exercise of the senses, of sight, smell, touch, etc.,
which cannot be fully communicated from one to another, in any words,
no more than we could communicate, the variety of ways by which we can
distinguish our numerous acquaintances by their countenances, or the different sounds of their voices[.] And the niceties of every other sense are
as inexpressibly numerous, and accurate, as those here mentioned, and this
shews the uses of practice in its full light[.] I am however nothing the less
in favour of verbal instruction, that is a very necessary, and instructive, part
of a finished education, and is indispensably necessary, as the best talents
without instruction must proceed like one groping in the dark as the ancient
inhabitants of the world were obliged to do[.] And there is no profession in
which extensive information, and practice is more necessary than in that of
medicine, the objects of it, so often evade the strictest scrutiny of the human
senses.

Therefore besides the general studies of the profession, every distinct and separate part of it should be studied by itself particularly, in order to form an accomplished practition[er.] Besides[,] genius is more indispensably necessary in this, than in any other of the learned professions, or indeed than in any other employment except perhaps the General of an Army, or the Statesman, or financiers[.] In the other professions a good memory and extensive information are the principal requisites.

In order to render the Science, and the practice of the healing art, more extensively usefull, and more universally understood, it would be a very desirable object to diffuse it more generally among men of education, in a rational and liberal manner[:] not by recipes and quackish books, but rationally and philosophically. For this purpose, a course of lectures upon the healing art in general should be given, at every eminent seminary of learning, exhibiting a general chart of all the branches of this usefull Science; this is a plan which I have often wished to see come into fashion[.] It would be both one of the pleasantest, as well as the most usefull, parts of polite and accomplished education; neither is the subject so impracticable, as one would at the first be apt to suppose, especially after such a course of Physicks and experimental philosophy as we have proposed[.] It will not be attended with any superior difficulty, as Anatomy, Physiology, and Chymistry should form a part of a general course of Physicks[.] I do not mean that one intended to live by the practice of Physic should stop here, but that other gentlemen may[.] This plan would be so far from encouraging quackery, that in according to the oppinions of many of the wisest men, it would be the most certain way to cut it up by the roots; and finally to banish it[.] For by diffusing a rational knowledge of medicine, the vain pretensions Nostrum-mongers, and the workers of miracles, would be seen thro' and despised, and themselves meet with merited contempt, and they may be employed in a manner more usefull to society in other trades [–thus showing] the value of extensive information, and experience, and a particular acquaintance with every part of the profession[,] its true principles, and practice[.] In the country, this part of information would be of the greatest advantage, and especially to the southward, where it is common for every planter, to keep a medicine chest upon his plantation, and either himself, or his Overseer, prescribes in cases of necessity, which frequently happens with those far from medical assistance[.] Besides[,] a general, and rational knowledge of the art, will enable people the better to choose, where a choice is in their power[.]

A plan of this sort may be disliked by some old fashioned characters, but the liberal and well informed, will I hope entertain very different sentiments. This general course I would recommend to medical students, as their first after Philosophy, and before they go to the different branches particularly, as in this many of the general doctrines of the profession may be taught which [do] not so properly come under any other branch of instruction[–]all of which they should attend to, in order to prepare them for practice. A cours of this sort if properly conducted would soon become one of the most usefull in a medical education. By this means improvements in the healing art would become more common, by the numbe[r] of Gentlemen of liberal minds, and improved understandings cultivating it in some particular parts, though they do not live by it as a profession. This was the oppinion [of] candid and liberal Dr. Gregory, and of many other Physicians, and Philosophers of eminence at all times: but the mysterious and illiberal character of some members of the profession in former times, and in some places hitherto, would wish to cover it with a veil of obscurity, by clothing it in dead, and in foreign Languages[.] And this very circumstance has been the reason why it has been taken for an imposition upon the ignorant, and little better than Magic or Astrology, or tricks of incantation. The connection of the healing art with Natural as well as with moral Philosophy, and metaphysicks, the origin progress and present state of the Art, the best means for preserving health etc. the best methods of studying and observing the modus operandi of medicines, the deviations from health and their remedies.

NOTE

1. Including Early American Imprints, Eighteenth Century Collections Online, and Proquest's American Periodicals.

CONTRIBUTORS

Nancy Beadie is Professor of Education and History at the University of Washington, Seattle. She is the author of *Education and the Creation of Capital in the Early American Republic* (2010) which won the History of Education Society Outstanding Book Award, and a coeditor, with Kim Tolley, of *Chartered Schools: Two Hundred Years of Independent Academies, 1727–1925* (2002). She has twice received the History of Education Society's prize for best article published in a refereed journal, and her articles have appeared in numerous journals, including *Social Science History*, *History of Education Quarterly*, *History of Education*, and *Pedagogica Historica*. She is a past president of the History of Education Society and a past vice president of the American Educational Research Association for the History and Historiography Division.

Lisa Green recently received her doctorate from the Graduate School of Education at the University of California, Riverside, where she studied the history of science curriculum. She is a former chemist having held positions in hospitals, industry and academia. Her dissertation work centers on the influence of the modern synthesis of evolution on the textbooks of the Biological Sciences Curriculum Study in the early 1960s. Through the research mentoring session she has also developed an interest in the work of the American Philosophical Society (APS) and science education in the early republic. She has presented papers at the History of Education Society and American Educational Research Association annual meetings. She was a library fellow at the APS for the 2010–11 academic year.

Benjamin Justice, editor, is Associate Professor of Education and History at Rutgers University. He is the author of *The War That Wasn't: Religious Conflict and Compromise in the Common Schools of New York State* (2005), which was a finalist for the Outstanding Book Award by the History of Education Society and winner of the Researcher of the Year award by the New York State Archives. He has written numerous articles and book chapters on the history of education in America, and his work has appeared in *History of Education Quarterly*, *Teachers College Record*, *Social Education*, *American Journal of Education*, the *American Historical Review*, and *New York History*. He has served on the editorial board of *Educational Researcher*, and has been given the Outstanding Reviewer Award by the American Educational Research Association.

Carl F. Kaestle is University Professor and Professor of Education, History, and Public Policy at Brown University. His scholarly record on issues from literacy development in the United States, to the evolution of urban school systems, to the federal role in school reform place him among the top education historians in the nation today. He is the author of numerous books and articles, including *Pillars of the Republic: Common Schools and American Society, 1780–1860* and *Education and Social Change in Nineteenth-Century Massachusetts.* His affiliations include the National Academy of Education, and the National Research Council.

Hilary Moss is Associate Professor of History and Black Studies at Amherst College. She is the author of *Schooling Citizens: The African American Struggle for Education in Antebellum America* (2009), which won the Outstanding Book Award from the History of Education Society. Her research on the relationships among race, education, and civic identity has appeared in *New England Quarterly* and *History of Education Quarterly.* She currently serves on the editorial board of *History of Education Quarterly.*

Margaret Nash is Associate Professor of Education at the University of California, Riverside. She is the author of *Women's Education in the United States, 1780–1840* (2005). Her research focuses on the role education plays in the historical construction of identity, including the social contexts for and meanings of education, the question of who gets educated and why, and the relationships between education and citizenship and between education and policy. Her work has appeared in numerous anthologies and journals including *History of Education Quarterly, Teachers College Record*, and *Educational Studies.* She is a past Program Chair for the History and Historiography Division of the American Educational Research Association.

Adam R. Nelson is Professor of Educational Policy Studies and History, University of Wisconsin-Madison. He is the author of *The Elusive Ideal: Equal Educational Opportunity and the Federal Role in Boston's Public Schools, 1950–1985* (2005) and *Education and Democracy: The Meaning of Alexander Meiklejohn, 1872–1964* (2001). His work has appeared in numerous anthologies and journals, including *New England Quarterly, History of Education Quarterly*, and *Peking University Educational Review.* He is currently working on a history of nationalism and internationalism in the American research university.

Campbell Scribner is an assistant professor of education at Ohio Wesleyan University. He participated in the American Philosophical Society research project while a graduate student at the University of Wisconsin, where he completed a doctorate in history and educational policy studies. His work has also appeared in *The Wisconsin Magazine of History* and *History of Education Quarterly.*

Eric Strome is a graduate student at Teachers College, Columbia University, pursuing a PhD in history and education. His dissertation aims to unearth the pedagogies employed by American higher education reformers during the Age of the University in an attempt to reassess the influence of the German University on American institutions.

Kim Tolley is a professor in the School of Education at Notre Dame de Namur University. Her publications have appeared in such journals as the *History of Education Quarterly, Teachers College Record, Social Science History, The North Carolina Historical Review,* and the *Journal of Curriculum Studies.* She has received the History of Education Society's prize for best article published in a refereed journal. Her book, *The Science Education of American Girls: A Historical Perspective* (2003), received the Outstanding Academic Title Award from the Association of College and Research Libraries, Honorable Mention for Best Book by a New Scholar (Division F, AERA), and Honorable Mention for the Outstanding Book Award from the History of Education Society. She is coeditor of *Chartered Schools: Two Hundred Years of Independent Academies in the United States, 1727–1925* (2002) and editor of *Transformations in Schooling: Comparative and Historical Perspectives* (2007). Tolley has served on the editorial board of the *History of Education Quarterly* and on the board of the *History of Education Society.*

INDEX

Printed in the United States of America